D0931749

TAKING SIDES

Clashing Views on
Controversial Issues in Human Sexuality

Edited, Selected and with Introductions by

ROBERT T. FRANCOEUR, Fairleigh Dickinson University

The Dushkin Publishing Group, Inc.
Guilford, Connecticut 06437

Library of Congress Catalogue Card Number: 86-48002

Manufactured in the United States of America

First Edition, First Printing

ISBN: 0-87967-661-2

TAKING SIDES

Clashing Views on
Controversial Issues in Human Sexuality

*Where there is much desire to learn, there of necessity will
be much arguing . . .*

—John Milton

STAFF

Jeremy Brenner	Program Manager
Brenda Filley	Production Manager
Lynn Shannon	Designer
Libra Ann Cusack	Typesetting Coordinator
Diane Barker	Copy Editor

PREFACE

In no area of American society today are clashing views more evident than in the sides we are taking on human sexual behavior. Almost daily, in the news media, in congressional hearings, and on the streets, we hear about Americans of all ages taking completely opposite positions on abortion, pornography, contraception, homosexuality, the AIDS epidemic, the skyrocketing incidence of teenage pregnancy, gay and single parent families, and the rights of the state to regulate sexual behavior.

Some claim pornography is destroying the moral fabric of our society while others, with equal energy, defend their right under the First Amendment to purchase and view pornographic or erotically explicit videotapes and men's magazines like *Playboy, Penthouse,* and *Hustler* at newsstands and stores.

Some defend women's right to control their own bodies and the Supreme Court's decision legalizing abortion, while others work to make abortion illegal again. Some antichoice advocates are so convinced of their position they have even bombed abortion clinics.

Parents picket to keep children with AIDS out of schools, even as medical experts maintain there is no danger of other children being infected by non-sexual contact. A young man, arrested for sodomy in his own home in Georgia, challenges his arrest, only to have the United States Supreme Court rule that states can prohibit and punish sodomy (anal intercourse), even for heterosexual married couples. One wonders how the police can enforce such a law.

Required sex education in public schools, the distribution of free contraceptives in high schools, premarital sex and extramarital sex, the ordination of gay and lesbian ministers, antidiscrimination civil rights legislation to protect homosexually-oriented persons, the morality of contraceptives, childrearing in keeping with the dictates of the Bible and traditional sex roles for boys and girls are all some of the controversial issues about human sexual behavior that are being discussed today.

Equally as evident as the controversial issues are the people and groups that have lined up on either side of the battle lines. On one side, fundamentalist Christians, conservative Catholics, Vatican officials, Orthodox Jews, fundamentalist Muslims, members of the Moral Majority, and others defend "traditional values" in marriage and family life, sex roles, and the procreative purpose of human sexuality. Orthodox rabbis and Conservative Jews join Catholic bishops to fight the addition of two words, "sexual orientation," to civil rights legislation, thus protecting gay persons in Chicago, New York and other cities from discrimination in employment and housing.

On the other side of the battlefield are leaders in mainstream Protestant churches who ordain acknowledged homosexuals to the ministry, and oppose censorship and laws regulating private consenting adult sexual behavior. Quietly or publicly in full-page advertisements in the *New York Times,* Catholic nuns, priests, and laypersons dispute and reject the Vatican blanket condemnation of abortion. Along the way, many of these Catholics also question the official condemnation of "unnatural" contraception, masturbation, premarital sex, divorce, and homosexuality.

For this edition of *Taking Sides: Clashing Views on Controversial Issues in Human Sexuality,* I have gathered lively and thoughtful statements by articulate advocates on opposite sides of a variety of sexual questions. Whatever personal positions you hold on these questions, it is vital for the strength of our democratic society that you understand and appreciate the different positions people take on these issues along with the philosophical biases and religious beliefs behind your own position and theirs. Democracies are strongest when they respect the rights and privileges of all citizens, be they conservative, liberal, or middle-of-the-road, religious or humanist, advocates of minority and unpopular views, as well as those who constitute the majority view. Although you may disagree with one or the other answers offered for each issue, it is important that you read both statements carefully and critically. Reject a position if you will, but only after you have read both views carefully and listened with an open, inquiring mind to how the position you disagree with is defended. In disagreeing intelligently, your own position may be strengthened. However, in some questions, you may find yourself changing your position somewhat. If that happens, you will know *why* you changed your position. In any event, you will have learned firsthand what it means to live in a democracy built on pluralism and tolerance of others.

Benjamin Franklin once remarked that democracies are built on compromises. But you cannot have healthy compromises unless people talk with each other and try to understand, appreciate, and respect their different ways of reasoning, their values, and their goals. Open and frank discussion of controversial issues is what this book is all about. Without healthy controversy and open exchange of different views, intolerance and bigotry could easily increase to the point where our democratic system could no longer function. Democracy thrives on controversy.

ACKNOWLEDGEMENTS

Facing the task of tracking down the best essays for inclusion in this collection was not an easy one. In several cases, I was greatly helped by friends and colleagues who agreed to write original essays for inclusion. I am particularly grateful to the following for this major assistance: Vern Bullough, Peter Gardella, Father Depaul Genska, Sister Jeannine Gramick, Richard Kenney, Father Robert Nugent, Lawrence and Ellen Shornack, Rabbi Rami Shapiro, and William Stackhouse.

I must also acknowledge the advice, help and important leads supplied by Leigh Hallingby, manager of the Information Service and Library at SIECUS (Sex Information and Education Council of the United States) in New York City, my good friend and colleague Linda Hendrixson, Fran Avallone, director of the Right to Choose Education Foundation (NJ), and Ted Fitch, Pepper Pathe, and Ulla Volk in the reference library at Fairleigh Dickinson University. Finally, I am also grateful to Herb Samuels for adding his insights on the black perspective.

Robert T. Francoeur
Madison, New Jersey
1987

CONTENTS

Betty Winston Baye believes that the main problem in male/female
relationships today is that many men say they want an educated,
independent woman with her own career, but when it comes to living in such a relationship, too many of them can't handle this type
of woman. Donald Singletary believes women want to be liberated,
but at the same time aren't willing to bear the cost. Women just
haven't faced up to what they really want and expect from men, so
they send out too many confusing signals.

George Gilder, author of *Sexual Suicide* and an editor of the *New
Leader,* argues that the differences between men and women constitute the most important fact of human society and that the drive
to deny these differences, in the name of women's liberation, marital openness, sexual equality, erotic consumption, and homosexual
romanticism, is suicidal. Sandra Lipsitz Bem, a developmental psychologist, claims her research and that of others indicates that
men and women can function much better in complex societies
such as ours if they are allowed some flexibility in their sex roles
instead of being squeezed into rigid polarized gender roles.

Lisa Davis (pseudonym for a well-known Hollywood screenwriter)
tried a variety of lifestyles and finds monogamy the most satisfying
because it provides a sense of continuity, saves energy, promotes
personal growth and ultimately makes true intimacy possible.
Novelist and journalist Phyllis Raphael believes that the American
style of exclusive monogamy is an unnatural and unattainable ideal
that cripples personal development. She believes that monogamy
with multiple relationships on the European style is more realistic
for our times.

Lonny Myers, a physician and sexologist, proposes a variation on
"open marriage" in which the husband and wife respect each
other's right to privacy. Robert H. Rimmer, author of *The Harrad
Experiment* and other underground classics of the sexual revolution, takes the unusual tack that our cultural emphasis on sexual
and emotional exclusivity and on jealousy as the sign of true love
makes "open marriage" impossible for most couples.

Jeannine Gramick, a Catholic nun working with gay and lesbian
persons, argues that the main reasons many people reject
homosexuality and bisexualty as unnatural is that the dominant
heterosexual majority believes its lifestyle is the only acceptable
orientation. Robert Gordis, biblical professor at the Jewish Theological Seminary, claims that homosexuality is "an abnormality, an illness." He argues for rejecting both the traditional religious reaction
to homosexuality as an abomination and the fashionable doctrine
that homosexuality is alternate lifestyle of equal value and legitimacy with heterosexuality.

Rabbi Rami Shapiro and Robert T. Francoeur, a Catholic priest, propose that the time has come for our society and religious institutions to acknowledge the growing pluralism in adult relationships and family structure. William Stackhouse, a consultant for the Human Sexuality Program of the United Church (Congregationalists) Board for Homeland Ministries foresees some real obstacles with this proposal. In this view, the closer an alternative lifestyle is to the traditional model, the easier it will be for the religious and civil authorities to accept it.

PART II: EDUCATION ISSUES

Lawrence Shornack, a sociologist, and Ellen Shornack, a child and family therapist, argue that the new sex education attempts to institutionalize the sexual revolution by indoctrinating students in the ideology of sexual permissiveness. Peter Scales, Director of Education for the Planned Parenthood Federation of America, rejects the Shornacks' arguments, pointing out that it contains serious misrepresentations, myths, inaccuracies, distortions and innuendos used to buttress a shaky thesis.

Richard Kenney, director of ambulatory pediatrics and adolescent medicine at Charlotte Memorial Hospital in North Carolina, argues from the experiences of such clinics that they appear able to address a number of problems of adolescents in a cost-effective and medically efficacious manner. In preventing pregnancy, they save $25 for every one dollar spent. Phyllis Schlafly, founder of the Eagle Forum, claims that sex education and the associated health clinics have been promoted by some educators and social workers to provide themselves with jobs. Rather than encouraging teenage abstinence, this education has legitimized teenage promiscuity and caused the rise in teenage pregnancies since the 1950s.

PART III: PRENATAL ISSUES

Senator Orrin G. Hatch argues that abortion is a worldwide calamity. He supports a constitutional amendment that will overturn the US Supreme Court decisions legalizing abortion and halt the carnage of abortion by restoring respect for all human life as a right protected under our Constitution. Despite claims of the anti-choice advocates that they are pro-life, James W. Prescott, a developmental neuropsychologist and cross-cultural psychologist, argues that their real motivation comes from an authoritarianism that consistently supports human violence, is indifferent to pain and suffering, and denies the personal right of self-determination, especially in sexual issues.

Women's health counselor Susan Ince recounts her personal experience of being interviewed for surrogate motherhood. She believes surrogate motherhood for pay should be banned because it exploits women and is a form of reproductive prostitution. Lori B. Andrews, a research attorney at the American Bar Foundation, argues that despite the many legal conflicts and complications of surrogate motherhood, society must consider the right to privacy and self-determination of a childless couple.

Gena Corea, founder of the Feminist International Network on the New Reproductive Technologies, argues that the immediate and most socially devastating outcome of the new techniques for predetermining or selecting the sex of fetuses is gynicide. Peter Singer, Director of the Centre for Human Bioethics at Monash University in Australia, and Deane Wells, a member of the Australian Parliament, emphasize that the benefits these techniques would have in promoting population control outweigh alarmist claims about unbalanced sex ratios.

PART IV: SOCIAL ISSUES

Justice White, arguing the majority opinion, claims that, unlike heterosexuals, homosexuals do not have a constitutional right to privacy when it comes to engaging in oral or anal sex even in the privacy of their homes because of the traditional social and legal condemnation of sodomy. Justice Blackmun, dissenting from the majority opinion, argues that since the right to be left alone is the most comprehensive of human rights and the most valued by civilized men, the state has no right or reason to prohibit any sexual acts engaged in privately by consenting adults.

Robert Nugent, a Catholic priest who has worked with homosexual men and women since 1971, sees no valid basis for opposition to civil rights for homosexuals based on concerns about homosexuals in sensitive positions being blackmailed, the role models that would be provided by homosexual teachers, or the influence of homosexuals who would be allowed to adopt children or retain custody of children after a divorce. Terry Teachout, a student of psychology at the University of Illinois, warns advocates of gay rights legislation that the conservative majority in this country has no philosophical objection to certain kinds of intolerance, and that this majority has a right to preserve its integrity, which it will do if pushed far enough.

Hilary Johnson says lawyers and feminist organizations are beginning to compile evidence that they believe link pornography and male violence irrefutably. Carole S. Vance, an anthropologist, argues that large-scale studies have failed to demonstrate a clear relationship between pornography and violence against women.

Commissioner Bruce Ritter, founder of Covenant House for runaway teenagers, describes the Meese Commission Report on Pornography as a cautious, reasoned and balanced documentation of the national problem of pornography and a needed remedy to the invalid conclusions of the 1970 commission. The Shadow Commissioners argue that the Meese commission was totally biased from the start, carefully selected its witnesses, and ignored or distorted the testimony of witnesses who did not confirm their previous conclusions.

Charles Winick, coauthor of *The Lively Commerce: Prostitution in the United States*, argues that it would be "extremely foolhardy to base public policy on the temporary or neurotic needs of a very small element of the population." Whether prostitution is legal or illegal, it is always surrounded by an array of socially undesirable third parties, such as pimps, as well as violence, blackmail and drugs. Depaul Genska, a Franciscan priest, disagrees with Winick and is firmly convinced that the present criminalization of prostitution is immoral, ineffective, and carries an excessive financial price. Decriminalization of prostitution, Genska argues, is the least immoral and most acceptable alternative.

Historian Vern Bullough believes that most of the antisexual attitudes in Western culture can be traced to Christianity's traditional discomfort with sexuality and sexual pleasure, particularly because of its acceptance of a dualistic view of our world. Peter Gardella, professor of religion, argues that, while sexual pleasure was often condemned as sinful by Christian writers in the past, our recent sexual revolution grew in part from the surprising interaction of Protestants and Roman Catholics within American culture.

John Leo, a social critic and a senior writer for *Time* magazine, brings together statements from a wide variety of family life specialists, sociologists and sex counselors to defend his claim that the sexual revolution is over because it was a failed experiment in sexual freedom that was rejected, beginning around 1975. Lester A. Kirkendall, professor emeritus of family life at Oregon State University, argues that the real sexual revolution is just beginning. The changes which will produce the revolution include the separation of sexual relations from reproduction, the minimizing of male/female differences, a breakdown in the rigidities which have walled off certain sexual expressions as unacceptable, and a shift in the sources we accept for our appraisal and decisions about moral/ethical issues in sexuality.

INTRODUCTION: SEXUAL ATTITUDES IN HISTORICAL AND RELIGIOUS PERSPECTIVE

In his 1963 best-seller, *The Presidential Papers,* Norman Mailer wrote that "It's better to commit rape than to masturbate. . . . The ultimate direction of masturbation always has to be insanity." In stating his views so bluntly, Mailer inadvertently provides us with an insight that can guide us through this collection of clashing views on a variety of sexual issues. Mailer's preference of rape over masturbation echoes less blatant views of masturbation expressed in a paragraph on "sex fluid conservation" in the 1934 edition of *The Boy Scout Handbook* which implies that any "habit" that causes a boy to lose "vital fluid" tends to weaken him and makes him less a man, and less resistant to disease.

HISTORICAL MODELS

In the Middle Ages, theologians divided sexual behaviors into those which were "natural" and those which were "unnatural." Since they believed that the natural function and goal of all sexual behavior and relations was reproduction, masturbation was unnatural because it frustrated the natural goal of conception and continuation of the species. Rape certainly was considered illicit because it was not within the marital bond, but at least it was procreative, and thus a "natural" use of sex. The same distinction was applied to other sexual relations and behaviors. Premarital sex, adultery, and incest were natural uses of our sexuality while oral sex, anal sex, and contraception were unnatural even when engaged in by a married couple with 10 children. Heterosexual vaginal intercourse was natural, though it might be illicit if it were fornication or adultery, but a married couple having intercourse with a condom or while using the pill were engaging in "unnatural" sex. Homosexual relations, of course, were both illicit and unnatural. In this value system, which Mailer echoes, indeed "It's better to commit rape than to masturbate."

Many people today, probably a strong majority, totally disagree with Mailer's view. Ultimately, it is because they do not accept the premises of medieval Christian philosophy which form the basis for Mailer's conclusion. For many, perhaps most Americans, sex and sexual intercourse do not have to occur within marriage. Nor must they be always directed toward reproduction. Nor, for many people today, does the sexual play and interactions of two persons always have to culminate in vaginal intercourse.

In recent years, several analysts of our clashing values systems have suggested models or paradigms which, when placed side by side, highlight the two bases people usually choose from when they take sides on a controversial issue.[1] Despite the varied issues we face in sexuality, people usually are fairly consistent in the positions they take. They may not be fully aware of why they take the stands they do, but when pressed to explain their premises, their choice of one or the other of the two philosophical bases usually becomes clear.

This split in world views became very evident to Americans with recent developments in the Middle East, in the politics of Iran, Egypt, and other Muslim countries. On one side of the spectrum are the Muslims who see the world as a process, an ever-changing scene in which they must struggle to reinterpret and apply the basic principles of the Koran to new situations. On the opposing side of the spectrum are the Muslims, led by the Ayatollah Khomeini, who overthrew the Shah and are now trying to return Iran and the Muslim world to the authentic faith of Mohammed and the Koran. This means purging Iran's Islamic society of all the western and modern customs the Shah encouraged. Anwar Sadat, the late President of Egypt, was assassinated by Muslim fundamentalists who opposed his tolerance of Muslim women being employed outside the home and wearing western dress instead of the traditional black, neck-to-ankle chador. These fundamentalists also were repulsed by the suggestion of Sadat's wife that Muslim women should have the right to seek divorce and alimony.

MODERN PARALLELS

There are interesting parallels to this split between the two different world views, the fixed and the process views, in American culture today. Religious fundamentalists, New Right politicians, and the varied members of what is loosely termed the Moral Majority believe that we need to return to traditional values. These varied groups often share a conviction that the sexual revolution, new attitudes toward masturbation and homosexuality, a tolerance of premarital and extramarital sex, sex education in the schools instead of in the homes, and the legalization of abortion are compelling evidence of a dying culture that must be rejected. In their view, sexual promiscuity and the social tolerance of homosexuality, typical examples of the "unnatural uses of sex," have led to the epidemics of herpes and AIDS.

At the same time, other Americans argue for legalized abortion, civil rights for homosexuals, decriminalization of prostitution, androgynous sex roles in child rearing, and the abolition of all laws restricting the right to privacy for sexually active, consenting adults.

Recent efforts to analyze the doctrinal systems behind these two value systems have revealed two distinct world views or philosophies tenuously coexisting for centuries within the Judaic, Christian, and Islamic traditions. When Ernst Mayr, a biologist at Harvard University, traced the history of biological theories, he concluded that no greater revolution has occurred in the history of human thought than the radical shift from a fixed world view rooted in unchanging archetypes to a dynamic, evolving world view based on populations and individuals. While the process or evolutionary world view may be gaining dominance in western cultures and religious traditions, the Moral Majority and religious New Right in the United States, the rise of Islamic fundamentalism in Iran and the Near East, and the growing vitality of Orthodox Judaism provide ample evidence that the fixed world view still has clear influence in moderating human behavior.

One fascinating characteristic of these two world views is that they permeate and color the way we look at and see everything in our lives. One or the other view colors the way in which each of us approaches a particular political, economic, or moral issue, as well as the way we reach decisions about sexual issues and relationships. However, one must keep in mind, as we pursue this analysis of world views, that no one is ever fully and always on one or the other end of the spectrum. The spectrum of beliefs, attitudes and values proposed here is an intellectual abstraction. Real life is not that simple. It is a useful model that can help us understand each other's positions on controversial issues, but it is only a model. The fixed and process world views are at the two ends of a continuum that includes a wide range of approaches to moral and sexual issues. While individuals often take a fixed position on one issue and a process position on a second issue, these general categories are instructive when examining the impact of religious doctrines on childhood sexuality, because individuals generally tend to adopt one or the other approach and maintain a fairly consistent set of intertwined religious values and attitudes.

RELIGIOUS DOCTRINES

Religious doctrines, and their adherents, can be divided by the opposing world view which underlies their religious beliefs and doctrines. Either the world is a completely finished universe in which human nature was created by some supreme being, perfect, complete and unchanging in essence from the beginning, or the world is a universe characterized by continual change with human nature constantly evolving as it struggles to reach its fuller potential or what it is called to become by the deity. Either one believes that the first human beings were created by God as unchanging archetypes, thus determining standards of human behavior for all time, including our fixed roles as males and females, or one believes that human nature, behavior and moral standards have been evolving since the beginning of the human race. In the former view, a supreme being created human nature. In the latter view, the deity is creating human nature with human collaboration.

Coming out of these two views of the world and human nature, one finds two distinct views of the origins of evil and sexuality. If one believes that human nature, the purposes of sexuality, and the nature of sexual relations were establishedd in the beginning, then one also finds it congenial to believe that evil results from some original sin, a primeval fall of the first humans from a state of perfection and grace. If, on the other hand, one believes in an evolving human nature, then physical and moral evils are viewed as an inevitable, natural growth pains that come as humans struggle toward the fullness of their creation.

Table 1 outlines the doctrinal positions, moral approaches, and sexual prescriptions that flow logically from these two world views within the Christian tradition. With appropriate modifications, this dichotomous table can be adapted to a similar divergence of world views and sexual value systems in the Judaic and Islamic religious traditions. However, as you will find in reading the essays on controversial issues in this collection, values and attitudes do vary within particular religious traditions. For instance, the Vatican's position on homosexuality fits nicely within the authoritarian Type A religious tradition while Jeannine Gramick, a Catholic nun, and Robert Nugent, a Catholic priest, adopt the opposite position working from Type B religious perspective in Issues 5 and 13. In debating with Sister Jeannine Gramick whether homosexuality and bisexuality are as natural and normal as heterosexuality, Robert Gordis works out of a Protestant Type A religious value system. At the same time, because of the very high value placed on children and family, even quite orthodox Jews are willing to accept the use of artificial insemination and surrogate mothers, Issues 10 and 11, which tradition-oriented Vatican statements roundly condemn. This is in spite of the fact

3

TABLE 1

Continuum of Sexual Values Derived from Two Distinct World Views Within the Christian Tradition

	Christian Religions Type A	Christian Religions Type B
Basic Vision	COSMOS—A finished universe.	COSMOGENESIS—An evolving universe.
Typology	Like the universe, humankind is created perfect and complete in the beginning. Theological understanding of humans emphasizes *Adam.*	Like the universe, humankind is incomplete and not yet fully formed. Theological emphasis has shifted to *The Adam, Christ,* at the end of time.
Origin of Evil	Evil results from primeval "fall" of a perfect couple who introduce moral and physical evil into a paradisical world.	Evil is a natural part of a finite creation, growth, and the birth pains involved in our groping as imperfect humans struggling for the fullness of creation.
Solution to the Problem of Evil	Redemption by identification with the crucified Savior. Asceticism, mortification.	Identification with *The* Adam, the resurrected but still fully human transfigured Christ. *Re-creation,* growth.
Authority System	Patriarchal and sexist. Male dominated and ruled. Autocratic hierarchy controls power and all decisions; clergy vs. laity.	Egalitarian—"In his kingdom there is neither male nor female, freeman or slave, Jew or Roman."
Concept of Truth	Emphasis on one true Church as sole possessor of all truth.	Recognition that other churches and religions possess different perspectives of truth, with some elements of revelation clearer in them than in the one true Church.
Biblical Orientation	Fundamentalist, evangelical, word-for-word, black-and-white clarity. Revelation has ended.	Emphasizes ongoing revelation and reincarnation of perennial truths and values as humans participate in the creation process.
Liturgical Focus	Redemption and Good Friday, Purgatory, Supernatural.	Easter and the creation challenge of incarnation. Epiphany of numinous cosmos.
Social Structure	Gender roles clearly assigned with high definition of proper roles for men and women.	There being neither male nor female in Christ, gender roles are flexible, including women priests and ministers.

Ecological Morality	Humans are stewards of the earth, given dominion by God over all creation.	Emphasis on personal responsibility in an ongoing creation/incarnation.
Self-Image	Carefully limited; isolationist, exclusive, Isaias' "remanent." Sects.	Inclusive, ecumenical, catalytic leader among equals.
Goal	Supernatural transcendence of nature.	Unveiling. Revelation of divine in all.
Human Morality	Emphasis on laws and conformity of actions to these laws.	Emphasis on persons and their interrelationships. We create the human of the future and the future of humanity.
Sexual Morality	The "monster in the groins" that must be restrained.	A positive, natural, creative energy in our being as sexual (embodied) persons. "Knowing," Communion.
	Justified in marriage for procreation.	An essential element in our personality, in all relationships.
	Genital reductionism.	Diffused, degenitalized sensual embodiment.
	Heterosexual/monogamous.	"Polymorphic perversity."
	Noncoital sex is unnatural, disordered.	Noncoital sex can express the incarnation of Christian love.
	Contraceptive love is unnatural and disordered.	Contraception can be just as creative and life-serving as reproductive love.
	Monolithic-celibate or reproductive-marital sexuality.	Pluralistic-sexual persons must learn to incarnate chesed/agape in all their relationships, primary and secondary, genital and non-genital, intimate and passing.
Energy Conception	*Competitive.* Consumerist. Technology-obsessed.	*Synergistic.* Conservationist. Concerned with appropriate technologies.

Type A Christian traditions are derived from a fixed world view in which creation was essentially finished with Adam and Eve. Type B Christian traditions are based on a belief that creation is an ongoing process in which humans participate.

TABLE 2

A Dichotomous Paradigm Based on Western Sexual Values and Behaviors

Hot Sex	Cool Sex
Definitions	
High definition of sex.	Low definition of sex and sex roles.
Reduction to genital sex.	Sexuality coextensive with personality.
Genitally focused feelings.	Diffused sensuality/sexuality.
Time and place arrangements.	Spontaneous.
Highly structured games.	Lightly structured with few games.
Clear sex role stereotypes.	Little if any role stereotyping.
Many strong imperatives from socially imposed roles.	Few imperatives, self-actualizing encouraged.
Value Systems	
Patriarchal.	Egalitarian.
Male domination by aggression.	Equal partnership as friends.
Female passivity.	
Double moral standard.	Single moral standard.
Behavioral Structures	
Property oriented.	Person oriented.
Closed possessiveness.	Open inclusiveness.
Casual, impersonal.	Involved, intimate.
Physical sex segregated from life, emotions and responsibility.	Sex integrated in whole framework of life.
Nonhomogeneous, grossly selective of playmate.	Homogeneous, finely selective in all relationships.
Screwing sex objects for conquest.	"Knowing" sexual persons.
Genital hedonism.	Sex as communication.
Concerns	
Orgasm obsessed.	Engaging, pleasuring communications.
Performance pressures, sex obligatory when possible.	Sexual relations truly optional.
Fidelity = sexual exclusivity.	Fidelity = commitment and mutual responsibility.
Extramarital relations as escape.	Comarital relations a growth reinforcement of primary bond.
Fear of emotions and senses.	Embracing of emotions and senses.
Nudity a taboo, prelude to sex.	Nudity unrelated to sex.
Sexuality feared, tenuously situated.	Sexuality accepted, securely situated.
Entopic relations, viewed as "property" that can be lost or used up.	Synergistic relations, mutually reinforcing.
Frequent alcohol and drug use.	
Territory and personal distance.	Few drug-altered states.
	"Grokking."

SOURCE: Adapted from Francoeur and Francoeur (1974).

In 1967, Marshal McLuhan and George B. Leonard suggested a dichotomous model of sexual values, based on McLuhan's conception of "hot" media with high definition (photographs and print) and "cool" media with low definition and high participant involvement (cartoons and television). In 1974, Francoeur and Francoeur expanded this basic insight, as shown here.

that orthodox Judaism and the Vatican both fit on the Type A side and share a common agreement on many other sexual issues.

This general split in world views comes through with a powerful consistency in an analysis of traditional and contemporary western sexual values. Table 2 gives an updated summary of my analysis of the split between traditional "hot" and contemporary "cool" sexual attitudes, expectations and values.

Another paradigm is worth mentioning here to emphasize the importance of the two ways people view the world and the attitudes, beliefs and values they draw from that philosophical base. This model resulted from years of analyzing cross-cultural data, surveys of college students' attitudes, and voting patterns in our state and federal governments. James W. Prescott began by examining the effects of the lack of nurturance and somatosensory stimulation of infant monkeys raised by Harry and Margaret Harlow and the adult behavior of these same monkeys. In the Harlow studies, some monkeys were taken from their mothers right after birth and raised with only a wire mesh figure and nursing bottle serving as a surrogate mother. Only monkeys were raised with a fur-covered surrogate mother and nursing bottle. Control infants remained with their natural mothers. Without the normal touching and cuddling of a parent, the test infants quickly became antisocial, withdrawn, and often autistic in their behavior. They were terrified at the approach of another monkey and at the possibility of being touched. Infant monkeys nurtured and cuddled by a natural mother were peaceful and socially well adjusted when they grew up. Prescott then began to wonder whether these effects would carry over in human childrearing.[2]

From these varied biological, developmental, and cross-cultural studies, Prescott derived a behavioral/attitudinal paradigm which links somatosensory affectional deprivation or positive nurturance in infancy and childhood with adult behaviors and attitudes (Table 3). His statistical analysis reveals a causal connection between parental attitudes, child rearing values, and the subsequent social adaptation, or lack of it, in the children when they grow up. In societies or families which encourage body pleasuring and somatosensory nurturance, parents commonly share a wide variety of non-violent values, attitudes, and behavioral patterns for which their children are neurologically scripted by a high level of nurturing touch and somatosensory input during infancy, childhood and adolescence. The attitudes, behavioral patterns and values listed for Low Nurturance Cultures in Table 3 show considerable overlap and correlation with the religious values of a fixed world view, Type A religious views, and traditional hot sexual values. Similarly, the attitudes, values and behaviors found in High Nurturance Cultures closely parallel those of religious systems with a process world view, Type B religious perspective, and cool sexual values.

In subsequent statistical analyses using both contemporary American, Canadian and European data, Prescott correlated the lack of childhood nurturance with negative attitudes toward gun control laws, abortion, nudity, sexual pleasure, masturbation, premarital and extramarital sex, breastfeeding, and women. Other values consistently associated with this perspective include a glorification of war and the frequent use of alcohol and drugs.

TABLE 3

A Cross-Cultural Behavioral/Value Paradigm
Based on Somatosensory Affectional Deprivation

Low Nurturance Cultures	High Nurturance Cultures
(1) Patrilineal.	(1) Matrilineal
(2) Polygyny has high incidence.	(2) Polygyny has low incidence.
(3) Women's status inferior.	(3) Women's status not inferior.
(4) High avoidance of in-laws.	(4) Low avoidance of in-laws.
(5) High incidence of mother/child households.	(5) Low incidence of mother/child households.
(6) High community size.	(6) Small community size.
(7) High societal complexity.	(7) Low societal complexity.
(8) Small extended family.	(8) Large extended family.
(9) Wives are purchased.	(9) Wives are not purchased.
(10) Slavery present.	(10) Slavery absent.
(11) Grandparental authority over parents is present.	(11) Grandparental authority over parents is absent.
(12) Subsistance is primarily by food production.	(12) Subsistence is primarily by food gathering.
(13) High class stratification.	(13) Low class stratification.
(14) Low infant physical affection.	(14) High infant physical affection.
(15) High infant physical pain.	(15) Low infant physical pain.
(16) Low infant indulgence.	(16) High infant indulgence.
(17) Low reduction of infant needs.	(17) High reduction of infant needs.
(18) Delayed reduction of infant needs.	(18) Immediate reduction of infant needs.
(19) High infant/child crying.	(19) Low infant/child crying.
(20) Breast-feeding less than 2½ years.	(20) Prolonged breast-feeding over 2½ years.
(21) High child anxiety over performance of responsible behavior.	(21) Low child anxiety over performance of responsible behavior.
(22) High child anxiety over performance of obedient behavior.	(22) Low child anxiety over performance of obedient behavior.
(23) Low smiling, laughter, humor.	(23) High smiling, laughter, humor.
(24) High anxiety over transition: infancy/childhood.	(24) Low anxiety over transition: infancy/childhood.
(25) Low or no food taboos during pregnancy.	(25) High number of food taboos during pregnancy.
(26) Abortion highly punished.	(26) Abortion permitted.
(27) Strength of desire for children is high.	(27) Strength of desire for children is low.
(28) Postpartum sex taboo greater than one month.	(28) Postpartum sex taboo less than one month.
(29) Premarital coitus punished.	(29) Premarital coitus permitted.
(30) Extramarital coitus punished.	(30) Extramarital coitus permitted.
(31) Female initiation rites present.	(31) Low or absent female initiation rites.

(32) Sex disability present.
(33) Castration anxiety is high.
(34) High sex anxiety.
(35) Narcissism is high.
(36) High exhibitionist dancing.
(37) High display of wealth.
(38) Contracted debts are high.
(39) High adult physical violence.
(40) Bellicosity is extreme.
(41) High killing, torture, mutilation.

(42) High personal crime.
(43) Incidence of theft is high.
(44) High warfare.
(45) Military glory emphasized.
(46) Superordinate justice present.
(47) Supernaturals are aggressive.
(48) Fear of supernatural rather than fear of humans.
(49) High God is present.
(50) High religious activity.
(51) Belief in reincarnation present.
(52) High asceticism in mourning.
(53) Witchcraft highly present.
(54) Religious specialists are full time.
(55) Political integration at state level.

(56) Metal working is present.

(32) Sex disability absent.
(33) Castration anxiety is low.
(34) Low sex anxiety.
(35) Narcissism is low.
(36) Low exhibitionistic dancing.
(37) Low display of wealth.
(38) Contracted debts are low.
(39) Low adult physical violence.
(40) Bellicosity is low.
(41) Low or absent killing, torture, mutilation.

(42) Low personal crime.
(43) Incidence of theft is low.
(44) Low or no warfare.
(45) Low military glory.
(46) Superordinate justice absent.
(47) Supernaturals are benevolent.
(48) Fear of humans rather than fear of supernatural.
(49) High God is mainly absent.
(50) Low or no religious activity.
(51) Belief in reincarnation absent.
(52) Low asceticism in mourning.
(53) Witchcraft low or absent.
(54) Religious specialists are part-time.
(55) Political integration at community and family level.

(56) Metal working is absent.

SOURCE: Adapted from Prescott (1975).

Laboratory experiments pioneered by Harry and Margaret Harlow expanded with cross-cultural analyses by James W. Prescott indicate a clear causal relationship between the lack of somatosensory pleasuring during infancy, childhood and adolescence and a high level of adult violence. In societies that encourage body pleasuring and somatosensory nurturance for their youth, one finds a very peaceful adult society. A wide variety of values, attitudes, and behavioral patterns show a definite correlation with the absence or presence of nurturance and body pleasuring in any given culture. The dichotomous summary shown here is based on extensive statistical studies of correlations by neurophysiologist James W. Prescott. The data presented here are a more recent unpublished update of that published by Prescott in 1975.

Societal factors which were correlated with high infant nurturance include a lack of strong social stratification, prolonged breast-feeding, a high sense of humor, an acceptance of abortion, premarital and extramarital sex, low anxiety about sex, little sexual dysfunction, a negative view of war, and a peer relationship between men and women.

APPLICATIONS TO TODAY'S WORLD

If all this sounds a bit too theoretical for our purposes here, consider the correlations Prescott found when he surveyed college students. The survey results, Tables 4 and 5, reveal that college students who have relatively negative attitudes toward sexual pleasure tend to view sexual pleasuring in any form as dangerous or unacceptable. In Table 4, the percentage figures on the left indicate the strength with which each variable or statement contributes to an overall personality description shared by persons who approve violence, condemn physical pleasure, rate the use of alcohol and drugs higher than sex, and see themselves as politically conservative. Table 5 shows how student attitudes on premarital and extramarital sex correlated with their attitudes about alcohol and drugs. An r figure of 1.0 would indicate that a person accepting a particular statement on the left would always find premarital, or extramarital sex, as the case might be, unacceptable. Correlation coefficients, r, between .70 and .50 are highly significant. This means that a strong majority of the college students surveyed who found premarital sex unacceptable also get hostile and aggressive when they drink alcohol (r = .68), find drinking more satisfying than sex (r = .70), and find drugs more satisfying than sex (r = .73).

Religious beliefs undoubtedly affect the child-rearing practices of our parents, which in turn color the way each of us views our sexuality and our attitudes toward different sexual behaviors and relationships. But other factors also affect the way we view our sexuality.

ETHNIC VALUES

Dating from the aftermath of the Civil War, the American black experience has been characterized by conflicting forces. According to historian Jacqueline Jones, black wives and mothers were expected to continue working outside the home, particularly by members of the white power structure, both northern and southern, who were attempting to rebuild the war-torn South. But the labor of black women, which helped transform and improve postbellum southern society and economy, was not a form of personal self-fulfillment. Instead, it was essential to family survival. In the same period, the black male faced contradictory tasks. He was expected to provide for his family even though the doors of economic opportunity were closed to him. At the same time, if he were able to provide for his family while his wife maintained the household, he was seen as being dominated and emasculated by a wife who did not want to work! What was considered "normal" for middle-class white males and females, was an aberration for black males and females. This tension between ideal roles and the realities of the marketplace has continued to be a source of contention for blacks. It has also profoundly affected the black view of sexuality. In Issue 15, for instance, Robert Staples points out that among American blacks, pornography is "a

I am especially grateful to Herb Samuels, a consulting sexologist and active member of the Society for the Scientific Study of Sex, who is responsible for the careful comments on the experience of black Americans which give an important balance to this too brief introduction.

TABLE 4

Attitudes Toward Violence Correlated
with Attitudes Toward Sexual Pleasure

Violence Approved
.85 Hard physical punishment is good for children who disobey a lot.
.81 Physical punishment and pain help build a strong moral character.
.76 Capital punishment should be permitted by society.
.75 Violence is necessary to really solve our problems.
.74 Physical punishment should be allowed in the schools.
.69 I enjoy sadistic pornography.
.54 I often feel like hitting someone.
.43 I can tolerate pain very well.

Physical Pleasure Condemned
.84 Prostitution should be punished by society.
.80 Abortion should be punished by society.
.80 Responsible premarital sex is not agreeable to me.
.78 Nudity within the family has a harmful influence upon children.
.73 Sexual pleasures help build a weak moral character.
.72 Society should interfere with private sexual behavior between adults.
.69 Responsible extramarital sex is not agreeable to me.
.61 Natural fresh body odors are often offensive.
.47 I do not enjoy affectional pornography.

Alcohol and Drugs Rated Higher Than Sex
.70 Alcohol is more satisfying than sex.
.65 Drugs are more satisfying than sex.
.60 I get hostile and aggressive when I drink alcohol.
.49 I would rather drink alcohol than smoke marijuana.
.45 I drink alcohol more often than I experience orgasm.

Political Conservatism
.82 I tend to be conservative in my political points of view.
.77 Age (Older).
.51 I often dream of either floating, flying, falling, or climbing.
.45 My mother is often indifferent toward me.
.42 I often get "uptight" about being touched.
.40 I remember when my father physically punished me a lot.

In his study of college student attitudes on sexuality, violence, drugs and alcohol, Prescott found significant correlations. In his early work on neuroanatomy, Prescott had found adjacent neural centers in the brain, one center processing pleasurable sensations of touch and the other responding to painful sensations and responsible for violent behavior. Following through from this finding and his cross-cultural studies, Prescott hypothesizes that lack of nurturance and body pleasure in infancy and childhood fails to stimulate the pleasure center, thereby letting the pain/violence center develop uninhibited and leading to a violence-prone adult. If pain and violence are frequent experiences in childhood and adolescence, then the pain/violence center is stimulated and the pleasure center inhibited. The two centers appear to operate in reverse tandem: if one is stimulated, the other is inhibited.

This hypothesis puts into perspective the attitudes of college students shown in this Table and in Table 5. Notice how various experiences and positive attitudes toward violence, alcohol and drugs are correlated with negative views of sexuality and sexual pleasure.

TABLE 5

Attitudes Toward Drugs and Alcohol Correlated
with Attitudes Toward Premarital Sex

Drug Relationships	Mean	Premarital Sex Not Agreeable (5.3) r	Extramarital Sex Not Agreeable (3.5) r
I use and experiment with drugs quite often.	4.8	.52	.18
I smoke marijuana quite often.	4.0	.27	.05
I drink alcoholic beverages quite often.	3.8	.32	.11
I get hostile and aggressive when I drink alcohol.	5.1	.68	.30
I would rather drink alcohol than smoke marijuana.	3.4	.35	.32
Alcohol is more satisfying than sex.	5.3	.70	.34
Drugs are more satisfying than sex.	5.4	.73	.34
I take drugs more often than I experience orgasm.	4.8	.47	.13
I drink alcohol more often than I experience orgasm.	4.8	.44	.17

SOURCE: Reprinted from James W. Prescott. 1975. Body pleasure and the origins of violence. *The Futurist*. Vol. 9, No. 2, April, p. 71.

In a second part of his study of college student attitudes, Prescott found some other interesting correlations between negative attitudes toward premarital sex and violence, drugs and alcohol.

trivial issue." "Blacks," Staples writes, "have traditionally had a more naturalistic attitude toward human sexuality, seeing it as the normal expression of sexual attraction between men and women. . . . Rather than seeing the depiction of heterosexual intercourse or nudity as an inherent debasement of women, as a fringe group of [white] feminists claims, the black community would see women as having equal rights to the enjoyment of sexual stimuli. . . . Since the double [moral] standard has never attracted many American blacks, the claim that women are exploited by exhibiting their nude bodies or engaging in heterosexual intercourse lacks credibility." While middle-class whites may be very concerned about pornography promoting sexual promiscuity, most black Americans are much more concerned about problems of poverty, employment opportunities, and teenage pregnancy. Similarly, attitudes toward homosexuality vary between white, black, and Hispanic cultures. In the macho tradition of Latin America, homosexual behavior is a sign that one cannot find a woman and make it as a true man. In lower socioeconomic black cultures, this same judgment may prevail, but it is not reinforced by the Latin macho tradition.

In any discussion of contrasting views on sexual issues, one should be sensitive to the extent to which contrasting ethnic attitudes may more or less color one's position. There are definite contrasts between the ways Italians and Irish view sexuality and sexual issues, or the ways in which French and Polish ethnic values differ. Even more critical is the contrasting positions of western European and North American values with Eastern values. Hindus in India accept sexuality and sexual behavior as a natural part of everyday life in a way that westerners find very disconcerting. Westerners today would be as horrified or surprised as Abbe Dubois was 150 years ago when he reported on a religious festival: "The goddess, placed in a beautifully ornamented palanquin, is carried in a procession through the streets. In front of her there is another divinity, a male. These two idols, which are entirely nude, are placed in immodest postures, and by help of a piece of mechanism, a disgusting movement is imparted to them as long as the procession continues. This spectacle excites transports of mirth, manifested by shouts and bursts of laughter." Cultural and ethnic variations are important factors in the positions we tend to take on controversial issues of human sexuality.

SOCIOECONOMIC STATUS

Socioeconomic status is a third factor that greatly influences the ways in which we view sexuality and sexual issues. A typical example, often encountered by sex therapists and marriage counselors, is the blue collar, working-class couple where the husband is pressuring his wife to engage in oral sex because of what the has read in some men's magazine. She might allow her husband to perform cunnilingus on her because she is ultimately passive in this situation. But if she takes the active role and performs fellatio on her husband, he is likely to react, despite his pressuring her, by putting her in the same negative category as the free and easy women he knows at the local bar. If the wife gives into the pressure, she loses status, but if she refuses, her husband reacts by calling her "frigid" and "uptight." Generally speaking, men and women in the lower socioeconomic segments of our population are much more conservative and less venturesome in sexual matters than are the middle and upper economic groups. Cultural values sometimes put us in no-win situations.

These insights into religious perspectives, racial and ethnic influences, and socioeconomic factors may help by giving us an overview as we examine the controversial issues in this book. Think of how religious, racial, ethnic, and socioeconomic factors in your own background may affect the positions you take on specific issues. Try to appreciate these same factors as you listen to others explain their views which may clash with yours.

NOTES

1. Details of the perspectives offered in this introductory essay can be found in the author's chapter on "Religious Reactions to Alternative Lifestyles" in E.D. Macklin and R.H. Rubin, eds., *Contemporary Families and Alternative Lifestyles: A Handbook on Research and Theory* (Sage Publishers, 1983). In that chapter, I summarize and give a complete comparison on seven models developed by researchers working independently in quite distinct disciplines. Included are: a behavioral model based on a comparison of chimpanzee, baboon and human social behavior by the British primatologist Michael Chance; a cultural/moral model based on an analysis of British and French arts, fashions, politics, lifestyles and social structures proposed by British science writer and philosopher Gordon Rattray Taylor; a cross-cultural comparison based on child-rearing nurturance patterns and adult lifestyles by neuropsychologist James W. Prescott; a model relating lifestyles and values with technological and economic structures by economist/engineer Mario Kamenetzky; a model of open and closed marriages created by George and Nena O'Neill, authors of the 1970s best-seller *Open Marriage;* and my own model of "Hot and Cool Sexual Values," which I adapted from an insight by Marshall McLuhan and George B. Leonard.

2. J.W. Prescott. (1975). Body pleasure and the origins of violence. *The Futurist.* 9(2), 64-74.

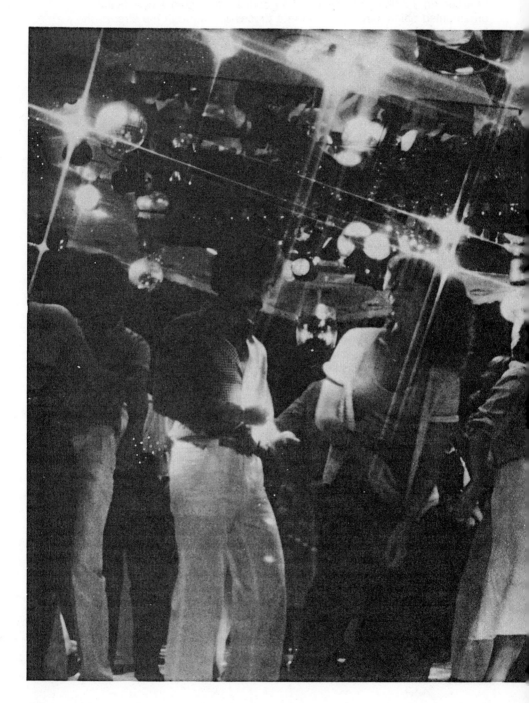

Courtesy Bermuda News Bureau

PART 1
RELATIONSHIP ISSUES

In Victorian America, men and women had very few options. Their roles in society were clearly spelled out with a double moral standard. As the breadwinners, men were allowed considerable social and sexual freedom. Women, on the other hand, were expected to be innocent, submissive, domestic and lacking in any interest in sex. Women had to marry, because without a husband there were very few socially acceptable ways for a grown woman to support herself.

This environment changed radically with the growing affluence of the middle class and effective contraceptives and antibiotics for sexually transmitted diseases. The economic and psychological liberation of women, liberal divorce laws, a skyrocketing proportion of single adults, gay liberation and a growing shortage of available men for women over 30 seeking husbands all contributed to the radical changes in the nature of relationships between men and women.

In the 1980s, men and women of all ages can choose from a variety of lifestyle options. Among these choices are: single, cohabitating or married, celibate or sexually active, sexually exclusive or not, as a parent or not, and in heterosexual, homosexual or bisexual relationships. This new social environment poses new questions for all of us.

Is the "New Woman" the Main Cause of Turmoil and Tension in Male/Female Relations Today?

Are Traditional Sex Roles Preferable to Androgynous Roles?

Is Monogamy the Best Form of Marriage?

Is Open Marriage a Viable Lifestyle for Today?

Are Homosexual and Bisexual Relations Natural and Normal?

Should Our Society Legally Recognize a Variety of Adult Lifestyles?

ISSUE I

IS THE "NEW WOMAN" THE MAIN CAUSE OF TURMOIL AND TENSION IN MALE/FEMALE RELATIONS TODAY?

YES: Donald Singletary, from "You New Women Want It Both Ways," *Essence* Magazine, July 1985

NO: Betty Winston Baye, from "You Men Want It All," *Essence* Magazine, July 1985

ISSUE SUMMARY

YES: Donald Singletary believes women want to be liberated, but at the same time aren't willing to bear the cost. Women just haven't faced up to what they really want and expect from men, so they send out too many confusing signals.
NO: Betty Winston Baye believes that the main problem in male/female relationships today is that many men say they want an educated, independent woman with her own career, but when it comes to living in such a relationship, too many of them can't handle this type of woman.

   A hundred years ago, Victorian middle class marriage automatically defined a person. It gave white men and women a definite status and a clear set of social obligations, rights and social and sex roles.* In this culture, American women had but one role, that of domestic wife and mother. A woman was expected to spend her life preparing for, and then devoting her full time and energy to, her family.
   Middle class Victorian men, for their part, were strong, unemotional, noble protectors of children and women. Biology was destiny for both men and women. In view of woman's obvious physical and mental inferiority, woman's inferior social and legal status was unquestioned.

*The experience of blacks in America has been very different. See the introductory essay, page 10, for this perspective.

There were rumblings of a revolution stirring in male/female relations as far back as the mid-1800s. Among middle class whites, the movement for women's right to vote began in 1848 in Seneca Falls, New York, when the first women's rights convention declared "We hold these truths to be self-evident, that all men and women are created equal." In the aftermath of the Civil War, white women gained some degree of economic flexibility with careers in nursing and as business secretaries. Though it was small in numbers and quickly disassociated from the suffrage movement, the "free love" movement raised anarchistic questions about the social and legal rights of women, the need for marriage, the right of women to divorce their husbands, sexual freedom for women, the positive social aspects of sex apart from reproduction, and the intellectual equality of men and women.

Between 1865 and World War I, major questions were raised about women's right to love and sex apart from marriage, the role of women in society, and how easy or difficult divorce should be. World War I opened the doors of factories and business to women and the "Roaring Twenties" gave our society its first taste of women's liberation. The Great Depression of the 1930s and World War II, however, marked a temporary hiatus during which revolutionary pressures built silently as men and women struggled to survive as individuals and as a nation.

By 1940, the educated but functionless middle-class American wife had degenerated into a malevolent caricature of "Mom." In his novel *Generation of Vipers,* Philip Wylie described "Mom" as:

> a middle-aged puffin with an eye like a hawk . . . about twenty-five pounds overweight, with no spirit, but sharp heels and a hard backhand . . . In a thousand of her there is not sex appeal enough to budge a hermit. . . . She nonetheless spends several hundred dollars a year on permanents and transformation, pomades, cleansers, rouges, lipsticks, and the like—and fools nobody except herself. . . .

In the 1950s, a revolution began to reach the surface among "the lost sex." It was the era of Alfred Kinsey's studies of the sexual habits of American men and women, of rock 'n' roll and Elvis Presley, of the birth control pill and *Playboy* magazine. In 1963, Betty Friedan finally identified "the unnamed disease" that was destroying American women. *The Feminine Mystique* captured the suppressed and frustrated rage of many women. It also catalyzed many of them to action. After simmering for over a century, the women's liberation movement was finally and effectively launched. Changes were set in motion that continue to have repercussions as the following essays demonstrate.

YES

YOU NEW WOMEN WANT IT ALL!

1A: Why is it always sex, sex, sex? Can't a man talk to me as a professional?
1B: All men want to do is talk business; there's no romance.
2A: These guys are together all day at work; now they come in the club and they're still over there in a group talking to each other.
2B: Damn, I can't even come in here to have a quiet drink with my girl-friend without men coming around to hit on us.
3A: I feel that as a woman today I can have just as much freedom as a man. That means a casual affair is okay.
3B: I don't understand men. They want to jump into bed as fast as they can. They don't want any commitment.

In each of the above, statements A and B were made by the same woman at different times. In the second example they were made in the same evening.

Imagine eating in an expensive restaurant. You pick up the shaker and it reads: "salt or sugar." Or picture the announcer's voice at the beginning of a boxing match: "In this corner we have the liberated woman. And in the same corner we have the woman who wants to be 'kept.' " Let's place the man in the role of referee: How does he judge this fight? Yes, it is confusing, isn't it? Not to mention annoying. It is very annoying. What we have there are examples of mixed messages, conflicting signals. And to put it bluntly, it is the women who are sending the confusing signals and the men who are getting confused. Not to mention angry.

In the last few years—since women began their quest for greater personal independence, better jobs and pay comparable to men's and the right to make decisions about what they do with their bodies—men have struggled to understand this "new woman." The signals that we are getting are that women want to take charge of their own destinies. They want to compete alongside men for the fruits of success in society. They no longer wish to rely on men for the things that they want out of life. Instead they have opted to get it themselves. Although these changes do in fact create some anxiety among men, many feel that they will ultimately free men from some of the traditional male responsibilities society has imposed upon them. Ideally, this should mean men no longer have to carry the full burden of financial support, decision making and being the aggressor in romantic pursuits. Right?

Wrong! That's one message women send. But there is another message that says, "I'll have my cake and eat yours too."

A perplexed former coworker of mine once said, "You would hope that a woman making, say, $35,000 a year could go out with whoever she wants—even the guy in the mail room. But no, she wants somebody who makes $45,000 a year! Why? Because she's still looking to be taken care of."

For this man and for many others, the assumption is that once a woman has the necessary financial security, the need to form relationships on the basis of what a man earns is gone.

Not so.

It's what some of us call the "my money, our money" syndrome. Here's a typical example: A man and woman meet through a mutual friend. Both single, they begin chatting about themselves. They are both professionals, make approximately the same money, and each has attended a good college.

SHE: You're very nice to talk to. It's so refreshing. A lot of men these days can't deal with an independent woman. They seem to always want the upper hand, and if you are making the same bread, they become insecure. I think they still expect women to be impressed with what they do.

HE: That's true. I even see it in some of my own friends. But I like a professional woman, not one who's dependent on a man.

SHE: That's me. Hey, why don't we have dinner sometime? I know a great little place.

They go out to dinner at an expensive restaurant that she choses. At last, he thinks, a woman who doesn't wait for the man to take the initiative, an independent woman! Wow, I never thought I'd be taken any place like this by a woman.

The check comes, and she waits patiently for him to pick it up. Thank goodness our hero has his American Express card up to date. I know guys who've had to excuse themselves from the table and dash out into the streets in search of a bank cash machine. In fact, I've been one of those guys. It's tough. You have to run out in the bitter cold (it's *always* cold) without your coat because you don't want the waiter to think you've left without paying. As one of my cronies put it, "Women want it all today, from soup to nuts— and the man has to pay for the meal."

No one is suggesting, least of all me, that women *have* to pay or date "dutch." But when one professes her liberation, as did this woman, the man has the right to expect her to follow through. The emerging new woman has not only created confusion for men; she has created some problems for women as well. At least one of them, as you might expect, is a paradoxical one. Now that women have more money and more mobility, there don't seem to be any men around. Not *any* men, mind you, but those with the "right stuff." In conversations between women and men, women and women, coast to coast, the question "Where are all the men?" always rears its head.

I defy you to find one man, one *real* man, who actually believes there is a shortage of men. Yes, I know what the statistics say. But what I and other men see is quite different. We see women who walk around as if they couldn't care less about a man. Women don't have time.

One of my own former girlfriends once told me that she was having a difficult time deciding on what to do with her new status. She had recently passed the New York bar and had gotten a new job. "I don't know what I should be: a socialite, a hard-boiled attorney, or sort of work out a blend of my professional and social life," she mused. Curiously, none of the choices included me, so I asked, "Where do I fit in?" She stared blankly for a moment, as if she'd come home and discovered she'd forgotten to buy catsup. Then she said, "You know, Donald, sometimes I think you really have a place in my life, and sometimes I think if you walked out the door and never came back, it wouldn't faze me at all."

I had to ask.

Had it not been about nine below zero (it's *always* cold) that February night, I would have left right then. (I have since garnered lots more pride.)

Women sit at tables in fours and fives wondering where all the men are, while the men sit a few feet away at the bar. The women almost never initiate anything. Believe me, if there were only ten eligible women in New York, I'd have two of them. If I didn't, it wouldn't be because I didn't try.

It is baffling to men why women are not more aggressive. One has to assume that they are simply not interested. Here are some examples of what "eligible" men are saying.

Women don't have time for you these days. I swear, making a date is like making a business appointment. Everybody's got calendars and datebooks.

While women are in their twenties, they party like crazy and tell you not to pressure them into relationships. Then all of *a sudden they hit 30 and uh-oh! Everybody races the clock to get married and make that baby. What are we, sperm factories? I'm supposed to get married so you can have cut crystal?*

It's quality I'm looking for, not quantity. I don't care how many women there are out there, it's quality I want. By the time you weed out the workaholics, the ones so bitter about their past lovers that they hate every man, the ones that want you only for your money/prestige, the druggies (yes, women do that too) and star seekers (noncelebrities need not apply) and ones who want fathers for their children, the margin really narrows.

I'll believe women are liberated when one walks up to me, says, 'Hey, good-lookin', ' buys me dinner, pats me on the cakes and suggests we go to her place for a nightcap.

It's ironic. Women are always telling me that men are intimidated by independent, assertive women. Where are they? On a recent *Donahue* show dedicated to single men, one man posed this question: "How many women out there would drive two hours to pick me up, take me out and spend $100, bring me back home and leave?" Yes, I'm certain some have done it. Just as I know there are some readers who have figured out the number of angels on the head of a pin. However, although the number of miles and dollar amount might seem exaggerated, the routine is one that is typical and expected of men.

I remember once being headed out the door at about 9:30 on a Saturday night when the phone rang. It was a woman I dated once in a while, and she invited me out that night. Already headed elsewhere, I respectfully declined. "Well, excuse me," she said, obviously miffed. "I guess I have to book ahead."

I remember that I really had something to do that night, I think it was open-heart surgery or something, so I explained that to her. She wouldn't have cared if it really had been open-heart surgery; she felt rejected, humiliated.

I hate to tell you this, but whenever you ask someone out, there is a possibility they will say no. Men know it, they live with it. I'll never like it, but I have gotten used to it.

Oh, you thought we had it easy, huh?

Women, I honestly think, believe it is easy for men to approach them. If that were true, I would be dating Jayne Kennedy *and* Diahann Carroll. Talking to a woman for the first time, especially without an introduction, is always a crap shoot. For me, it is worse. It is tantamount to walking down a dark alley knowing a psychopath with a big baseball bat and little mercy is in there. Approaching someone means you have to bare yourself and lay some of your cards on the table. That's not easy—particularly with the "new woman" who waltzes into a room like it's the set of *Dynasty*. Thumbs up if she likes you; to the lions if not.

I'm certain that it's easier for many men. And I'm equally certain that I've fooled lots of women with my cool, sophisticated facade. It comes with years of practice and experience.

What men are seeing and hearing from women, either directly or indirectly, is that there is a very bad problem with self-image. I'm not quite sure why. It seems contradictory. There are more women than ever before who are well educated, have lucrative careers and are well dressed and good-looking.

Therein may lie the problem. Women are insecure not only about the shortage of men but also about the increasing number of what they see as competition—other women.

I've said it myself. A woman walks into the room and I'm introduced to her and I think, *Okay, you went to a good school, you've got a good job and you look good. So what? So do most of the women in this room. In fact, so do most of the ones I meet.* Increasingly, there is nothing exceptional about being young, gifted and cute. It has, in many circles, become a given. Male friends of mine often say, "Why do women place so much emphasis on what they do professionally?" That automatically sets up a false criterion that men fall prey to. It creates a value system that emphasizes material things. Women, of course, are not solely responsible for that. Throughout history men have shown off their uniforms, three-piece suits and jobs since shepherding paid top dollar. However, at the same time, our criteria for women were based largely on hair, ankles, calves—you get the picture.

Nowadays we find ourselves asking more questions about education, career goals and so on. These are valid questions for anyone to ask, mind you, but they are not by any means the sole criterion for what makes a good human being, let alone a good relationship. It does, on the other hand, keep the mind beyond the ankles, which is a step in the right direction.

Years ago men chose women who could cook, take care of a house and raise children. Women chose men who would make good providers. Today more and more men do their own cooking and cleaning, are becoming closer to their children. Women, on the other hand, are becoming more self-supporting. This sounds to me like a marvelous opportunity for people to find some other reasons for relationships and shed some old ones. However, that does not seem to be happening.

1. IS THE "NEW WOMAN" THE CAUSE OF TURMOIL?

It becomes extremely difficult to decipher the signals. One says, "I want a man who's sensitive, caring, spiritual and warm." The other says, "I have this list of things that I feel I should have. I want a man who can help me achieve them and move up in society."

There is a curious other side to the pursuit of Mr. Right Stuff. When women settle for less, it is *far* less. I'm talkin' triflin' here. But for some reason, Brother Rat seems to capture their attention. The story has become a tired soap opera.

I knew a woman, a professional, good school, good job, condo, the whole ball of wax. She could never find a guy good enough. She always broke off the relationships, saying that the men would feel bad because she made more money; their fragile egos would be crushed. She went out with a good guy. A professional, a nice person. They were to be married. At the last minute she shifted gears and decided she wanted more time as a career woman. She left him. She spent her days bemoaning the fact that she had nobody. Then she met a rogue. Not the charming, sophisticated, Billy Dee Williams type, but a sleazy, coke-dealing, never-had-an-honest-job type. She let him move into her apartment; he spent her money and left her in debt and with a great loss of self-esteem. Yet at a given opportunity, whenever he came through town, she would take him in for a few days and, yes, lend him money.

Figure it out.

I have spent nearly all my adult life in the communications business as a writer, journalist and media specialist, and ten years in corporate public relations. None of these things, however, prepared me for the biggest communications gap of all— that between men and women.

It happened so suddenly. Things hadn't changed very much for decades. Then came the middle sixties, while the Black movement was in full fury, and eventually people began questioning, challenging, their sexual roles. Age-old ideas about love, marriage, sex, family and children began to change for women—and for men as well.

When women were fragile little princesses (they never really were, but they played the part), it was a lot more palatable for men to play the role of Prince Charming. There is, at least among college-educated, professional women, little impetus for a man to feel he has to sweep you off your feet as you stand together, pinstripe to pinstripe, Gucci to Gucci, M.B.A. to M.B.A. But there you stand, waiting for him to open the door and take you to dinner. During the day he holds the door at work and she's furious. At night she stands in place until he opens it.

What's a guy to do?

How does one approach the new woman? Should he be forward? more aggressive and to the point? Or should he be more subtle? Should he try to appeal to her intellect through conversation? Or should he be more romantic? Can he assume she is more sexually liberated or that she is seeking only a "meaningful relationship?" How do you separate platonic friendships from romantic inclinations? Who pays the bill? Does the fact that she's "career oriented" mean that she doesn't want or have time for a relationship?

Women are facing a backlash from men that will rival the white backlash of the seventies and eighties. And, like the white liberals in the sixties, the disenchanted men are the "nice guys"—the guys who feel they have been gentlemanly, supportive, considerate. All of a sudden the message they are getting is one of distrust, as they're portrayed as abusers, ne'er-do-wells, drug abusers and cheats. And after struggling to survive the street, college and/or military service and the day-to-day strife of the work world, they are being sent messages that say women's struggles make theirs pale by comparison. Not only that—they are the ones responsible for it!

Liberation. Independence. They're words that imply hard-won, newfound freedom. Freedom from the shackles of the past. That should include the freedom to look at relationships in a new light. Taking one or two bad experiences into each relationship thereafter is not being liberated. It is being shackled, weighed down, by your past. Understanding that the changes that took place for women also changed the perspective of many men is important. It means that realignments in relationships are necessary.

I once had the experience of working with a group of five women. All of them had previously worked together and had been friends for some time. Their business-like demeanor made me want to straighten my tie, let alone my files and desk. We would have group meetings prior to every division meeting. They would stress how we would go in as a group, pose a common front. But once inside the meeting, something interesting happened. They broke ranks, and each tried to impress the boss. How? By fluttering eyelashes, flashing toothy smiles and laughing at all his dumb jokes.

It caused one of my male coworkers to remark, "You know who the new woman is? She's the old woman, only she can't cook"—a sexist response evoked by a group of women who lapsed into a stereotypical role.

As bleak as some of this may seem, things are actually getting better. Change did move in very swiftly, and we are all, men and women alike, getting used to it. Certainly most of us over 30 grew up in an America where girls played nurse and boys played soldier. So it will take a while. But regardless of the changes, and the time it takes, there will always be a misread signal somewhere.

And it will *always* be on a cold night.

NO

Betty Winston Baye

MEN WANT IT BOTH WAYS!

I thought the 1980's would be different, especially after the revolutionary sixties, when it was common to hear some Black men hollering about how Black women should walk ten paces behind their "kings" and have babies for the revolution. I thought that in the eighties, Black men and women had declared a truce in the war between the sexes and that we had reached, or were striving to reach, a level where we could enjoy each other's company as equals.

I know now, however, that I hoped for much too much. Though I don't presume to paint all Black men with one broad brush stroke, it seems to me that there are men—too many—who, for reasons that only they and God understand, find it necessary to lie and pretend that they just love independent women. That's what they say at first, but as their relationships develop, it becomes painfully obvious that what they really want are women who work to help bring home the bacon but also cook, clean and take care of them and their babies on demand. These new men want women who are articulate and forceful when they're taking care of business—but who, behind closed doors, becoming simpering sycophants who heed their every wish.

I am an independent woman, and I'll tell anybody that what my mother and many of the women of her generation did to keep home and family together I won't do, not for love or money! Whenever I meet a man who says he's interested in me, I tell him up front that I don't do no windows. I don't love housework. I don't love to cook, and I certainly don't reach climax thinking about having to clean up behind a bunch of kids and some mother's son. If a man wants somebody to make him home bread and fresh collard greens every night, then I'm definitely not the girl of his dreams.

Now, I realize that I'm not every man's cup of tea. But take it or leave it, that's where I'm coming from. I'll gladly work every day to help bring home the money so that my man and I can pool our resources to go out to dinner every once in a while, take a few trips during the year and to pay somebody willing (or needing) to cook, clean and do laundry.

Surprisingly, my attitudes don't turn too many men off—in fact, brothers seem turned on by my honesty and independence. My ex-husband is one case in point. At the dawn of our relationship, he swore to me that I was just what the doctor had ordered. Said he'd never met a woman like me—intelligent, witty, educated, self-sufficient and not all that hard on the eyes. He went on about how he was just so thrilled that I had "chosen" him.

At first, everything was wonderful. But soon after I acquired a sweet contract to write my first book, the shit was on. It occurred to me that my beloved husband was just a bit jealous of my success. Before I knew it, I realized that he got some kind of perverse pleasure out of trying to insult me and make me look small in the eyes of my friends and professional colleagues. I remember how one time, for no special reason, he got up and announced in front of my childhood friend, her husband and their children that I was "a stupid bitch." Now, he had already published a novel, and to me he was a fine writer who could handle the English language as smoothly as butter sliding down a hot roll. But my book, and the money I got, just seemed to set him off. Not surprisingly, the marriage was finished before the book hit the shelves.

Had what happened in my marriage been an isolated case, I might have concluded that it was just "my problem"—something we women tend to do a lot. But it wasn't isolated. All around me, women friends of mine were and still are bailing out of relationships with men who say one thing, then do another.

A friend of mine got married a few years ago to a man she'd been dating for more than a year. This was a marriage made in heaven, or so she and we thought. Both she and her husband were talented go-getters who seemed to want the same things out of life. When they first met, she says, he told her he didn't dig her just for her body but also for her sharp mind. Before long, however, it became clear that the only thing he wanted to do with her mind was to cause her to lose it. She says he wanted her to be dynamic by day and servile by night. Finally, after much verbal and physical abuse, she split. Thankfully, her memorable excursion into his insanity didn't last for long. Now she's recovering quite nicely.

Strong, dynamic, intelligent, independent women are what men of the eighties say they want. They claim they want their women to go that extra mile, but what they really mean is that we should work twice as hard but not forget our responsibilities at home. When a woman spends time with *their* children, cleans the house or cooks for *their* family, it often goes unnoticed. No matter how tired she is after a demanding day at work, the expectation is that these are *her* responsibilities. But when a man spends time with *their* children, cooks food for *their* family or cleans *their* house once a month, he acts like he deserves an Academy Award.

Money is another area that has the brothers confused. For example, there are the men who say that if we women want to be truly liberated we should be willing, on occasion, to pick up the tab for dinner or for a night on the town. The fact that many of these same men often get their jaws wired when women, in the presence of a waiter or others at the table, reach for their wallet and pull out the cash or credit card says they're not ready for liberation. They don't mind women paying but would much prefer that they slip them the money under the table, the way women used to do.

And there are also the double-talking men who claim they can handle a woman who makes more money that they do. At first, everything is all right, but in order to assuage their egos, some men start thinking that "just because" they are men, they must exert control over their women's money and become personal financial managers of sorts. She's smart enough to make the money, he knows, but he believes she doesn't have enough sense to know how to spend it, invest it or manage

1. IS THE "NEW WOMAN" THE CAUSE OF TURMOIL?

it. "Are you sure you can afford this?" is a common question, but one rarely asked out of concern for a woman's finances. He knows she can afford it; he'd prefer to think she can't.

Many of the same men rattle on about how if we women want equality, we should buy gifts for them, as they allegedly have always done for us. Gift giving is nice, but for women, it can be a double-edged sword. One well-known singer tells the story of how she bought gifts for her man, which he gratefully accepted. But she says that after a time, the man got real nasty and told her that he couldn't be bought—he wasn't for sale.

And, of course, there are the men who seem to think that success drops out of the sky—that it doesn't require had work and long hours. I've seen men hotly pursue women whom they know are busy and then get bent out of shape if the sister pulls out her datebook to see when she's free. These women say they are tired of feeling guilty and trying to explain to some yo-yo that they can't just saunter off to dinner on the spur of the moment when they've got a report to finish or a meeting to attend.

Brothers are all for liberation when it works to their advantage. Yet, what we have found out is that when men don't want a serious commitment, they encourage us to be independent—to be open-minded enough to accept the terms of an "open relationship." But try that same rap on them, and we're in for trouble. Try saying, "Okay, baby, I don't want a commitment either"; or better yet, beat them to the punch. All of a sudden they've decided that they're in love and want to settle down. They get jealous and accuse us of "using" them.

And what about men who claim they want total honesty with their women? For many men, total honesty means that they want the freedom to talk openly about their prior involvements, including relating to their women intimate details about how many other women they've slept with or how many have aborted their babies. In return, a man like this often demands that his woman tell all her business to keep things in balance. Unfortunately, what many sisters have found—often after they are laid out on a stretcher or when they've had their past sexual exploits thrown in their faces in the heat of an argument—is that many men can't handle total honesty, especially if it's sexual honesty. Many men still seem to buy into the Madonna/whore syndrome. They still believe that their peccadillos are understandable because everyone knows that "boys will be boys." Women, however, especially *their* women, are supposed to be innocents who somehow, perhaps through osmosis, instinctively know how to turn them on in bed.

There are dozens of other ways that men send out mixed signals to the women in their lives and show, through their words and deeds, that they really want it both ways. They want us to drive the car—but from the backseat. Mostly what they want is for things to be the way they used to be. That, however, is a pipe dream. Black women, like their counterparts of other races, are liberating their minds and their bodies from the shackles of the past. Increasingly, women are refusing to waste their lives trying to decode men's mixed messages and buying into some man's macho fantasies. Instead, many women who are or want to be high achievers are accepting the fact that the price of success may be temporary loneliness. And even that loneliness is relative, since many of us have learned that having a man isn't all there is to life.

POSTSCRIPT

IS THE "NEW WOMAN" THE MAIN CAUSE OF TURMOIL AND TENSION IN MALE/FEMALE RELATIONS TODAY?

Listening to Baye and Singletary offer their analyses of the main problem in male/female relationships today suggests an interesting shift of perspective. Our great-grandparents, grandparents, and even some of our parents never asked this question because they had very clear roles and a strong sense of moral obligation that left them with an unquestioned duty. Today's men and women have new expectations. They look for love, for happiness, and for emotional support in a relationship whose main purpose only a few generations ago was to provide status and economic support for all members.

But reading Baye's viewpoint as a woman also might lead the reader to wonder what the message would be if the gender nouns and pronouns she uses and the female/male stereotypic roles she refers to were reversed. Could Baye's article have been written, with minor changes, by a male? Could Singletary's male discourse be just as easily reversed and written by a woman with the appropriate changes in gender nouns, pronouns and roles?

One wonders, too, how a gay or lesbian couple might respond to this dialogue between a heterosexual man and woman. Do gay and lesbian couples encounter similar tensions, or different ones in their intimacy?

A volume or two could easily be gathered, exploring not just the male/female tensions of blacks and whites, but also the experiences of Hispanic, Cuban, Latin American, Mexican, and Philippine men and women. First and second generation Arab-Americans, and recent immigrants from Southeast Asia face their own tensions.

But a concluding remark might apply to the two views presented here, and to any others the reader might encounter elsewhere. There is a commonly experienced human failing that leads us to blame someone else when something, including an intimate relationship, doesn't work. But blaming the other gender doesn't solve the problem of intimate relationships today. How much are Baye and Singletary diverted from the real problem in intimate relationships by the temptation to blame the other sex? "You men want it both ways!" "You women want it all!" Do these charges promote or hinder real communications in the very confusing situation of human relationships today? If Baye and Singletary, or any other male and female, sat down to discuss the main problem in intimate relationships today, how much honesty, objectivity, and listening would there be? To what extent is this the real problem? See the bibliography for further readings on this subject.

ISSUE 2

ARE TRADITIONAL SEX ROLES PREFERABLE TO ANDROGENOUS SEX ROLES?

YES: George Gilder, from *Sexual Suicide* (Quadrangle/The New York Times Book Co., 1973)

NO: Sandra Lipsitz Bem, from "Androgeny vs. the Tight Little Lives of Fluffy Women and Chesty Men," *Psychology Today,* September 1975

ISSUE SUMMARY

YES: George Gilder, author of *Sexual Suicide* and an editor of the *New Leader,* argues that the differences between men and women constitute the most important fact of human society and that the drive to deny these differences, in the name of women's liberation, marital openness, sexual equality, erotic consumption, and homosexual romanticism, is suicidal.

NO: Sandra Lipsitz Bem, a developmental psychologist, claims her research and that of others clearly indicates that men and women can function much better in complex societies such as ours if they are allowed some flexibility in their sex roles instead of being squeezed into rigid polarized gender roles.

Two major roots of our psychosexual development are closely interwoven. During pregnancy the biological framework is established for our future lives as sexual persons. The brain develops under the direction of genes and hormones in a silent uncharted process at the same time our sexual anatomy is differentiated in very obvious ways. After birth, socialization and enculturation take the lead, building on this biological substrate and interacting with it in subtle ways that we are barely beginning to understand or appreciate.

So many factors come together in forming our gender role identity that psychologists and sociologists have created a plethora of theories, each emphasizing a different aspect or factor. Determining the relative importance of these factors is impossible. Parents, schools, peers, and other symbolic agents of socialization like television, toys, magazines, books, and movies, are all involved in our socialization as boys and girls, men and women.

Always, the demands of our socialization are limited by different biological roots of behavior in males and females. Behind our behavior always is a physiological substrate. Even so, the power of socialization and enculturation to determine sex roles is immense.

In discussing sex roles, anthropologist Margaret Mead wrote that:

> Sometimes one quality has been assigned to one sex, sometimes to the other. Now it is the boys who are thought of as infinitely vulnerable and in need of special cherishing care, now it is the girls. In some societies it is girls for whom the parents must collect a dowry or make husband-catching magic, in others the parental worry is over the difficulty of marrying off the boys. Some peoples think of women as too weak to work out of doors, others regard women as the appropriate bearers of heavy burdens, "because their heads are stronger than men's." The periodicities of female reproductive functions have appealed to some people as making women the natural sources of magical or religious powers. . . . In some cultures women are regarded as sieves through whom the best-guarded secrets will sift, in others it's the men who are the gossips. Whether we deal with small matters or with large, with the frivolties of ornament and cosmetics or the sanctities of man's place in the universe, we find this great variety of ways, often flatly contradictory [in different societies], in which the roles of the two sexes have been patterned. But we always find the patterning.

Sex roles and conformity to those roles are essential if an individual is to relate to and be accepted as a part of the whole society. Sex roles allow us to maintain a stable society.

In most cases, sex roles remain fairly constant, changing only slowly over centuries. However, in the rapidly changing dynamics of an industrial and post-industrial culture such as we find in Europe and North America, revolutions in sex roles can come in a matter of a few decades. The result is incredible tension and stress for all concerned, as the two essays on the opposite sides of this issue illustrate.

YES   George Gilder

SEXUAL SUICIDE

There's an extraordinary chorus in the land these days—all bouncing between water beds and typewriters and talk shows—making sexual liberation ring on the cash registers of revolution. They haven't much in common— these happy hookers, Dr. Feelgoods, answer men, evangelical lesbians, sensuous psychiatrists, pornographers, dolphins, swinging priests, polymorphous perverts, and playboy philosophers—but they are all at one in proclaiming the advent of a new age of freedom between the sexes.

Nothing is free, however, least of all sex, which is bound to our deepest sources of energy, identity, and emotion. Sex can be cheapened, of course, but then it becomes extremely costly to the society as a whole. For sex is the life force and cohesive impulse of a people, and their very character will be deeply affected by how sexuality is sublimated and expressed, denied or attained. When sex is devalued and deformed, as at present, the quality of our lives declines and the social fabric unravels.

Even our attitude toward the concept "sex" and "sexuality" illustrates the problem. The words no longer evoke a broad pageant of relations and differences between men and women, embracing every aspect of their lives. Instead, "sex" and "sexuality" are assumed to refer chiefly to copulation, as if our sexual lives were restricted to the male limits, as if the experiences of motherhood were not paramount sexual events. In fact, sexual energy animates most of our activities and connects every individual to a family and a community, and through these to a past and future. Sexuality is best examined not as sexology, physiology, or psychology, but as a study encompassing all the deepest purposes of a society.

The differences between the sexes are perhaps the most important condition of our lives. With the people we know best, in the moments most crucial in our lives together, sexual differences become all-absorbing. Intercourse, marriage, conception of a child, childbearing, breast-feeding are all events when our emotions are most intense, our lives most thoroughly changed, and society perpetuated in our own image. And they are all transactions of sexual differences reaching in symbol or consequence into the future.

These differences are embodied in a number of roles. The central ones are mother-father, husband-wife. They form neat and apparently balanced pairs. But in the most elemental sexual terms, there is little balance at all. In most of the key sexual events of our lives, the male role is trivial, easily dispensable. Although the man is needed in intercourse, artificial insemination can make his participation rudimentary indeed. Otherwise the man is completely unnecessary. It is the woman who conceives, bears, and suckles the child. Males are the sexual outsiders and inferiors. A far smaller portion of their bodies is directly erogenous. A far smaller portion of their lives is devoted to specifically sexual activity. Their own distinctively sexual experience is limited to erection and ejaculation; their primary sexual drive leads only toward copulation. Beside the socially indispensable and psychologically crucial experiences of motherhood, men are irredeemably subordinate.

The nominally equivalent role of father is in fact a product of marriage and other cultural contrivances. There is no biological need for the father to be around when the baby is born and nurtured, and in many societies the father has no special responsibility to support the children he sires; in some, paternity isn't even acknowledged. Without long-term commitments to and from women—without the institution of marriage—men are exiles from the procreative chain of nature.

One of the best ways to enrage a young feminist today is to accuse her of having a maternal instinct. In a claim contrary to the evidence of all human history and anthropology—and to an increasing body of hormonal research[1]—most of these women assert that females have no more innate disposition to nurture children than do men. The usual refrain is, "I know lots of men with far more interest in babies than I have." But whether instinctual or not, the maternal role originates in the fact that only the woman is necessarily present at birth and has an easily identifiable connection to the child—a tie on which society can depend. This maternal feeling is the root of human sexuality. If it is not deeply cultivated among the women, it does not emerge among the men. The idea that the father is inherently equal to the mother within the family, or that he will necessarily be inclined to remain with it, is nonsense. The man must be made equal by the culture; he must be given a way to make himself equal.

A man's predicament begins in his earliest years. A male child is born, grows, and finds his being in relation to his own body and to the bodies of his parents, chiefly his mother. In trusting her he learns to trust himself, and trusting himself he learns to bear the slow dissolution of the primary tie. He moves away into a new world, into a sometimes frightening psychic space between his parents; and he must then attach his evolving identity to a man, his father. From almost the start, the boy's sexual identity is dependent on acts of exploration and initiative. Before he can return to a woman, he must assert his manhood in action. The Zulu warrior had to kill a man, the Irish peasant had to build a house, the American man must find a job. This is the classic myth and the mundane reality of masculinity, the low comedy and high tragedy of mankind.

Female histories are different. A girl's sexuality normally unfolds in an unbroken line, from a stage of utter dependency and identification with her mother through stages of gradual autonomy. Always, however, the focus of female identification is clear and stable. In a woman, moreover, sexual expression is not limited to a series of brief performances: her gender is affirmed and demonstrated monthly in menstruation, her breasts and womb further represent an extended sexual role. Even if a woman does not in fact bear a child, she is continually reminded that she can, that she is capable of performing the crucial act in the perpetuation of her family and the species. She alone can give sex an unquestionable meaning, an incarnate result.[2]

Regardless, then, of any other anxieties she may have in relation to her sexual role and how to perform it, she at least knows that she has a role. Her knowledge, indeed, is ontological: it is stamped in her very being—with the result that women rarely appreciate the significance of the absence of an extended sexual identity in men. Women take their sexuality for granted, when they are aware of it at all, and assume that were it not for some cultural peculiarity, some unfortunate wrinkle in the social fabric, men too might enjoy such deep-seated sexual authenticity.

Throughout the literature of feminism, in fact, there runs a puzzled complaint, "Why can't men *be* men, and just relax?" The reason is that, unlike femininity, relaxed masculinity is at bottom empty, a limp nullity. While the female body is full of internal potentiality, the male is internally barren (from the Old French *bar,* meaning man). Manhood at the most basic level can be validated and expressed only in action. For a man's body is full only of undefined energies. And all these energies need the guidance of culture. He is therefore deeply dependent on the structure of the society to define his role in it.

Of all society's institutions that work this civilizing effect, marriage is perhaps the most important. All the companionship, love, and inspiration that have come to be associated with marriage are secondary to its crucial social role. Marriage attaches men to families, the source of continuity, individuality, and order. As we should have long ago discovered from the frequent ineffectiveness of schools, prisons, mental hospitals, and psychiatric offices, the family is the only agency that can be depended upon to induce enduring changes in its members' character and commitment. It is, most importantly, the only uncoercive way to transform individuals, loose in social time and space, into voluntary participants in the social order.

Of course, families can exist without marriage. Almost always, they consist of women and children. The problem is this leaves the men awash in what one set of marriage counselors approvingly terms the "nowness of self." And the problem with *that* is the willingness with which men grasp their "nowness." Throughout history, societies have recognized the great price to be paid in securing family commitments from men. The alternative male pattern of brief sexual exploits and predatory economics accords very nicely indeed with the many millions of years of male evolution as a hunter. Women have had to use all their ingenuity, all their powers of sexual attraction and discrimination to induce men to create and support families. And the culture has had to invest marriage with all the ceremonial sanctity of religion and law. This did not happen as a way to promote intimacy and companionship. It evolved and survived in the course of sustaining civilized societies, where love, intimacy, and companionship might flourish.

MEN AND WORK

Every society has a sexual constitution

that undergirds its economy, politics, and culture. Although its central concerns are marriages and families, nearly every contact among human beings contains a sexual charge. How all these charges are organized—the nature of the sexual constitution—will deeply influence the productivity and order of the community. It will determine whether social energies are short-circuited and dissipated, or whether they are accumulated and applied to useful pursuits. It will determine whether the society is a fabric of fully integrated citizens or whether it is an atomized flux, with disconnected individuals pursuing sex and sustenance on the most limited and anti-social scale.

At every job site, in every classroom, in every store, office, and factory, this system comes into play. To anyone else, a man at work is performing an economic task, subject to legal and political regulation. But to the man himself, this formal role probably seems incidental. To him the job is chiefly important because of the connections it affords with his co-workers and with the existing or prospective women and children in his life.

A job is thus a central part of the sexual constitution. It can affirm the masculine identity of its holder; it can make it possible for him to court women in a spirit of commitment; it can make it possible for him to be married and thereby integrated into a continuing community.

Crucial to the sexual constitution of employment is that, in one way or another, it assures that over the whole society, class by class, most men will make more money than most women. Above an absolute minimum that varies from country to country, pay and poverty are relative. And for most men, most importantly, that means relative to women. A man who does not make as much money as the sig-

nificant women in his life—his girlfriend, wife, and closest coworkers—will often abandon his job and will pursue women in the plundering masculine spirit that the women's movement so woefully condemns.

The feminist contention that women do not generally receive equal pay for equal work, correct in statistical terms, may reflect a preference for male need and aggressiveness over female credentials. In any case, this tendency should be considered in light of the greater cost to the society of male unemployment. The unemployed male can contribute little to the society and will often disrupt it, while the unemployed woman may perform valuable work in creating and maintaining families. In effect, the system of discrimination, which the movement is perfectly right in finding nearly ubiquitous, tells women that if they enter the marketplace they will probably receive less pay than men, not because they could do the job less well but because they have an alternative role of incomparable value to the society as a whole. The man, on the other hand, is paid more, not because of special virtue, but because of the key importance of taming his naturally disruptive energies. The male job advantage, therefore, is based on the real costs of female careerism to raising children and socializing men. The society will have to pay these costs one way or another.

It is vital here to understand the sexual role of money. Particularly in relatively poor communities, a woman with more money than the men around her tends to demoralize them. Undermining their usefulness as providers, she weakens their connections with the community and promotes a reliance upon other, anti-social ways of confirming their masculinity: the priapic modes of hunting and fighting. A society of relatively wealthy and independent women will be a society of sexually and economically predatory males, or a society of narcotized drones who have abandoned sexuality entirely.

A male's money, on the other hand, is socially affirmative. If the man is unmarried, a much higher proportion of his money than a woman's will be spent on the opposite sex. His money gives him the wherewithal to undertake long-term sexual initiatives. It gives him an incentive to submit to female sexual patterns, for he knows he will retain the important role of provider. His sexual impulses can assume a civilizing, not a subversive, form.

The women's movement argues that most women work because they *need* the money. That is precisely the point, and these women must be permitted to earn it. (They will not be helped, incidentally, by the competition of increasing numbers of non-poor women for jobs.) Those who support children should receive child allowances. But men also need the money—and need an increment above the woman's pay—for unfortunately non-rational uses: for the "luxury" spending on women that is necessary if men are to establish and support families. The more men who are induced to serve as providers, the fewer women who will be left to support children alone.

Nothing is so important to the sexual constitution as the creation and maintenance of families. And since the role of the male as principal provider is a crucial prop for the family, the society must support it one way or the other. Today, however, the burdens of childbearing no longer prevent women from performing the provider role; and if day care becomes widely available, it will be possible for a matriarchal social pattern to emerge. Under such conditions, however, the men will inevitably bolt. And this development, an

entirely feasible one, would probably require the simultaneous emergence of a police state to supervise the undisciplined men and a child care state to manage the children. Thus will the costs of sexual job equality be passed on to the public in vastly increased taxes. The present sexual constitution is cheaper.

Of course, the male responsibility can be enforced in many other ways, coercively or through religious and social pressures. It is perfectly possible to maintain male providers without taking social costs into account in determining wages and salaries. In modern American society, however, the "social pressures" on women for marriage and family are giving way to pressures for career advancement, while the social pressures on men are thrusting them toward sexual hedonism. The society no longer recognizes, let alone communicates forcefully, the extraordinary social costs incurred when women neglect their role in male socialization. In fact, it has begun to actively promote the delights of easy sex, while indulging a pervasive cynicism toward married love.

At this point, therefore, any serious governmental campaign for equal pay for equal work would be destructive. It would endorse the false feminist assumption that a greatly expanded female commitment to careers would be economical—using "human resources" that are now "wasted." The fact is that the triumph of a careerist ideology among American women would impose ultimate costs to the society far greater than the net contribution of the additional women in the work force. Already, save for the exceptional minority, female careerism is imposing heavy psychological penalties on women themselves, since most of them will not be able to fulfill themselves in careers. The feminists would establish an ideal chiefly practicable for themselves. The rest of womankind would be told, preposterously, that they are inferior to men unless they make comparable salaries. . . .

THE EFFEMINATE STUD

In all these economic questions the feminists are right in virtually every superficial way. Men *do* get paid more than women; women *are* persistently discouraged from competing with men; the minority of women who are sufficiently motivated *can* perform almost every important job in society as well as men; job assignments by sex *are* arbitrary and illogical; most women *do* work because they have to; the lack of public child care facilities *does* prevent women from achieving real financial equality or opportunity.

But at a deeper level feminist women are terribly wrong. For they fail to understand their own sexual power; and they fail to perceive the sexual constitution of our society, or if they see it, they underestimate its importance to civilization and to their own interests. In general, the whole range of the society, marriage, and careers—and thus social order—will be best served if most men have a position of economic superiority over the relevant women in the community, and if in most jobs the sexes tend to be segregated by either level or function.

These practices are seen as oppressive by some; but they make possible a society in which women can love and respect men and sustain durable families. They make possible a society in which men can love and respect women and treat them humanely.

What is happening in the United States today is a steady undermining of the key conditions of male socialization. From the hospital, where the baby is abruptly taken from its mother; to early childhood, when he may be consigned to public care; to the home, where the father is frequently absent or ineffectual; to the school, where the boy is managed by female teachers and is often excelled by girls; possibly to a college, where once again his training is scarcely differentiated by sex; to a job, which, particularly at vital entry levels, is often sexually indistinct and which may not even be better paid than comparable female employment—through all these stages of development the boy's innately amorphous and insecure sexuality may be further subverted and confused.

In the end his opportunity to qualify for a family—to validate in society his love and sex through becoming a husband and provider—may be jeopardized. The man discovers that manhood affords few wholly distinctive roles except in the military, which is less inviting than ever. The society prohibits, constricts, or feminizes his purely male activities. Most jobs reward obedience, regularity, and carefulness more than physical strength; and the amount of individual initiative and assertiveness that can be accommodated by the average enterprise is very small indeed. Thus the man will find few compensatory affirmations of masculinity to make possible his expected submission to female sexual and social rhythms; and without a confident manhood he feels a compulsive need to prove it sexually, which he will do in ways that feminists, like the respectable women they are, fear and despise.

The American woman, meanwhile, becomes increasingly self-sufficient. While men are almost completely dependent upon women for a civilized role in the society and for biological and sexual meaning, women are capable of living decent—though often discontented—lives without men. The culture no longer much disapproves of unmarried mothers. The state affords them welfare and, increasingly, day care and maternity leave. In any case, birth control and legalized abortion give women complete control of procreation; and sexual liberation—not to mention masturbation and lesbianism—opens sexual enjoyment to them with only the most tenuous commitment to males. In fact, women are more than ever willing to adopt as their own an impulsive male sexuality, and although men may consequently find sexual partners more readily than before the meaning of their sexuality is diminished and they can derive less assurance from it. How could it be otherwise when more and more men and women now confront each other, *Joy of Sex* manuals in had, joined in a grim competition of orgasmic performance. The barely discriminate ruttings of the liberated woman find a nice complement in the stud vanity of the swinging male.

The stud, like his chief activity, is without significance except in dramatizing the largely spurious glamour of primitive masculinity: the love- 'em-and-leave- 'em style of most of our male heroes in novels and films. But the ordinary man may also come to feel his sexual role devalued in a context of overt sexual liberation. And he too will turn away from the family. He watches televised football and other sports for hours on end and argues about them incessantly. He becomes easy prey to jingoism and the crudest appeals for law and order. And he is obsessed with women. He tries as much as possible to reduce them to their sexual parts, and to reduce their sexuality to his own limited terms: to meaningless but insistent copulation. Exiled from the world of women, he tries to destroy consciousness of its superiority by reducing it to his own level. He insists—against all his unconscious and ulterior

knowledge—that women are as sexually contemptible as his society tells him he is

He turns to pornography, with fantasies of sex and violence. His magazines—*Male* and *Crime* and *Saga* and *True Detective* even respectably prurient publications like *Playboy* and its refined imitators—are preoccupied with barren copulation, or with war, perversion, and crime. He is an exile, an outlaw under the sexual constitution. Often he becomes a literal outlaw as well.

What he is *not* is a powerful oppressor, with hypertrophied masculinity. Such men lead impotent lives, and, as Rollo May asserts, violence is the product of impotence grown unbearable. Their problem is a society inadequately affirmative of masculinity: a society seduced by an obsessive rationalism and functionalism—a cult of efficiency, and a fetish of statistical equality—to eliminate many of the male affirmations which all human societies have created throughout history to compensate for male sexual insecurity and female sexual superiority. The women's movement seems determined to create more and more such exiled "chauvinist" males, all the while citing their pathetic offenses as a rationale for feminism.

Thus the society both provides for its own disruption and leaches itself of positive male energies. Engels said that marriage is the handmaiden of capitalism; one could say, however, that it is the handmaiden of any productive society. For male insecurity is also the "divine unease" that in socialized males, strong enough to submit to women, produces the driving force behind a society's achievements in industry, art, and science. It is wrong to suggest that either women's liberation or male irresponsibility is chiefly to blame for our current predicament. Both phenomena are reflections of larger trends in the society hostile to enduring love. . . .

The beginning of a man's love in a civilized society lies in his desire, whether conscious or not, to have and keep his progeny. For this he must choose a particular woman. His love defines his choice. His need to choose evokes his love. His sexual drive lends energy to his love, and his love gives shape, meaning, and continuity to his sexuality. When he selects a specific woman, he in essence defines himself both to himself and to society. Afterwards, every sex act celebrates that definition and social engagement.

The sex act then becomes a human affirmation, involving a man's entire personality and committing it, either in fact or in symbol, to a long-term engagement in a meaningful future. In fact, one can say that the conscious or unconscious desire to have children with a specific partner is a workable definition of sexual love. It is not, in bold specific terms, the only definition. But across the range of sexual experience in a civilized society, this motive seems to run strongest in the phenomenon of love.

This concept of sexual love, originating in the desire for children and symbolized in genital intercourse, again emphasizes the differences between the sexes. A man's love is focused on the symbols and associations of a woman's procreative powers—embodied in her womb and her breasts and elaborated in her nurturant sentiments, her tenderness, and her sense of futurity. The woman loves the man for his strength and protectiveness, for temperamental qualities that provide an ability to support and protect here while she bears their children—or while she surrenders to orgasm. She loves him for his ability to control her in sexual intercourse and for his submission to the extended demands of her sexuality.

Beyond these primal attractions, of course, both the man and woman will seek a companionable and compatible partner. Both, that is, will seek someone whom they can imagine enjoying over time and who respects the values they want to transmit to their children. Such a relationship, it should go without saying, will accommodate a wide range of sexual activity, from deliberate attempts to conceive children to casual sex play. . . .

The differences between the sexes are the single most important fact of human society. The drive to deny them—in the name of women's liberation, marital openness, sexual equality, erotic consumption, homosexual romanticism—must be one of the most quixotic crusades in the history of the species. Yet in a way it is typical of crusades. For it is a crusade against a particular incarnate humanity—men and women and children—on behalf of a metaphysical "humanism." It seems unlikely, however, that the particular men and women one meets in the real world will ever voluntarily settle for long in an open house of barren abstractions.

NOTES

1. The increasingly conclusive evidence that the two sex roles originate in profound biological differences is summarized and appraised in a brilliant new scholarly study by Steven Goldberg, *The Inevitability of Patriarchy* (Morrow).

2. Doris Lessing, a writer frequently praised and published in *Ms.*, states the case with her usual vehemence. Speaking of feminist characters in her own work, she said in a recent interview, "We're very biological animals. We always tend to think that if one is in a violent state of emotional need, it is our unique emotional need or state, when in matter of fact it's probably just the emotions of a young woman whose body is demanding that she have children. . . . Anna and Molly [in *The Golden Notebook*] are women who are conditioned to be one way and are trying to be another. I Know a lot of girls who don't want to get married or have children. And very vocal they are about it. Well, they're trying to cheat on their biology. . . . It will be interesting to see how they're thinking at thirty."

NO

Sandra Lipsitz Bem

THE TIGHT LITTLE LIVES OF FLUFFY WOMEN AND CHESTY MEN

In American society, men are supposed to be masculine, women are supposed to be feminine, and neither sex is supposed to be much like the other. If men are independent, tough and assertive, women should be dependent, sweet and retiring. A womanly woman may be tender and nurturant, but no manly man may be so.

For years we have taken these polar opposites as evidence of psychological health. Even our psychological tests of masculinity and femininity reflect this bias: a person scores as *either* masculine *or* feminine, but the tests do not allow a person to say that he or she is both.

I have come to believe that we need a new standard of psychological health for the sexes, one that removes the burden of stereotype and allows people to feel free to express the best traits of men and women. As many feminists have argued, freeing people from rigid sex roles and allowing them to be *androgynous* (from "andro," male, and "gyne," female),] should make them more flexible in meeting new situations, and less restricted in what they can do and how they can express themselves.

In fact, there is already considerable evidence that traditional sex typing is unhealthy. For example, high femininity in females consistently correlates with high anxiety, low self-esteem, and low self-acceptance. And although high masculinity in males has been related to better psychological adjustment during adolescence, it is often accompanied during adulthood by high anxiety, high neuroticism, and low self-acceptance. Further, greater intellectual development has quite consistently correlated with cross-sex typing (masculinity in girls, femininity in boys). Boys who are strongly masculine and girls who are strongly feminine tend to have lower overall intelligence, lower spatial ability, and show lower creativity.

In addition, it seems to me that traditional sex typing necessarily restricts behavior. Because people learn, during their formative years, to suppress any behavior that might be considered undesirable or inappropriate for their sex, men are afraid to do "women's work," and women are afraid to enter "man's world." Men are reluctant to be gentle, and women to be assertive. In contrast, androgynous people are not limited by labels. They are able to do whatever they want, both in their behavior and their feelings.

A MEASURE OF ANDROGYNY

I decided to study this question, to see whether sex-typed people really were more restricted and androgynous people more adaptable. Because I needed a way to measure how masculine, feminine, or androgynous a person was, I developed the Bem Sex Role Inventory (BSRI), which consists of a list of 60 personality characteristics: 20 traditionally masculine (ambitious, self-reliant, independent, assertive); 20 traditionally feminine (affectionate, gentle, understanding, sensitive to the needs of others); and 20 neutral (truthful, friendly, likable). I gave a list of 400 such traits to a group of undergraduates, who rated the desirability of each characteristic either "for a man" or "for a woman." I drew the final list for the BSRI from those characteristics that both males and females rated as being significantly more desirable for one sex than for the other.

The masculine, feminine and neutral characteristics appear in random order on the test, and a person indicates on a scale of one ("never or almost never true") to seven ("always or almost always true") how accurate each word is as a self-description. The difference between the total points assigned to masculine and feminine adjectives indicates the degree of a person's sex typing. If masculinity and femininity scores are approximately equal, the individual has an androgynous sex role.

My colleagues and I have given the BSRI to more than 1,500 undergraduates at Stanford University. Semester after semester, we find that about 50 percent of the students adhere to "appropriate" sex roles, about 15 percent are cross sex typed, and about 35 percent are androgynous.

With the BSRI in had, we were in a position to find out whether sex-typed people really were restricted and androgynous people really more adaptable. Our strategy was to measure a number of behaviors that were stereotypically either masculine or feminine. We selected these particular actions to represent the very best of what masculinity and femininity have come to stand for, and we felt that any healthy adult should be capable of them. We predicted that sex-typed people would do well only when the behavior was traditionally considered appropriate for his or her sex, whereas those who were androgynous would do well regardless of the sex-role stereotype attached to the particular action.

The masculine behaviors that we selected were independence and assertiveness. The study of independence brought students to the lab for what they thought was an experiment on humor. In fact, they were there to test conformity versus independence of judgment. Karen Rook and Robyn Stickney placed each person in a booth equipped with microphones and earphones, and showed him or her a series of cartoons that had been rated earlier for humorous quality. As a new cartoon appeared on the screen, the students heard the experimenter call on each person in turn for his or her rating. Although they believed that they were hearing each other's voices, they were in fact listening to a preprogrammed tape. To provoke the students into conformity, the tape included 36 trials during which the taped voices answered the experimenter falsely, agreeing that a particular cartoon was funny when it wasn't, or vice versa.

THE LIMITATIONS OF FEMININITY

We predicted that feminine women would be less independent that anyone else, and we were right. They were far more likely to conform to the incorrect taped judgments than masculine men or androgynous students of either sex. Only 33 percent of the feminine women were very independent (more independent than the average of all students), compared to 70 percent of the masculine and androgynous students.

Jeffrey Wildfogel carried out a similar study to measure assertiveness. He called students on the telephone with an unreasonable request: when would they be willing to spend over two hours, without pay, to fill out a questionnaire about their reactions to various insurance policies for students? At no time did he actually ask *whether* the people he called would be willing to participate. He simply assumed that they would, and asked them to indicate when they would be available.

In this situation, agreeing would cost a person time, effort and inconvenience, but refusing required the student to assert his or her preferences over those of the caller. The preliminary results confirmed our expectation that feminine women would find it harder to be assertive than anyone else. When Wildfogel asked the students later how difficult it was to turn the caller down, 67 percent of the feminine women said that they found it very difficult, compared to only 28 percent of the masculine men and androgynous students.

The feminine behaviors that we selected all measured the extent to which a person was willing to be responsible for or helpful toward another living creature. We

expected that this time the masculine men would be at a disadvantage.

In the first study, Jenny Jacobs measured how responsive people were toward a six-week-old-kitten. When students came to the lab, Jacobs explained that she wanted to see how different activities would affect their moods. Actually, we wanted only to determine their reaction to the kitten. For one of the activities, therefore, we put a kitten into the room and asked the student to respond to it in any way he or she wished. We simply recorded how often the student touched or petted the kitten. Later on in the experiment, we gave each person the opportunity to do anything in the lab room that he or she wanted: play with the kitten, read magazines, work puzzles, play with a three-dimensional tilting maze, or whatever. This time we measured how much the students played with the kitten when they didn't have to.

As expected, the masculine men were less playful than anyone else. Only nine percent of them showed a high level of playfulness with the kitten, compared to 52 percent of all the other students. But there was an unexpected result: the androgynous women played with the kitten more often than feminine women, who are presumably so fond of small, cuddly things, 64 percent to 36 percent.

MACHO MALES
AND CUDDLY BABIES

We conducted two further tests—this time with human beings instead of kittens. Carol Watson and Bart Astor measured how responsive people would be toward a six-month-old baby. The student thought the study was about babies' reactions to strangers, but actually we observed the students' reactions to the baby. We left each person alone with the infant for 10 minutes while the experimenter and one of the baby's parents watched from a one-way mirror. We recorded what each person did, such as how often he or she talked to the baby, smiled at it, or picked it up. Once again, the masculine men were the least likely to play much with the baby. Only 21 percent of them were highly responsive, compared to half of all the other students. And this time the feminine women did respond warmly, but no more than the androgynous women.

The last experiment, conducted by Wendy Martyna and Dorothy Ginsbert, explored people's reactions to a person with emotional problems. The students came to the lab in pairs for what they thought was a study of acquaintance, and they drew lots so that one would be a "talker" and the other a "listener." In fact, the talker was our confederate who delivered a memorized script of personal problems. The listener was allowed to ask questions or to make comments, but never to shift the focus of the conversation away from the talker. We recorded the listener's reactions, such as how often he or she nodded and made sympathetic comments, and later we asked each listener how concerned he or she felt about the talker's problems.

Again, the masculine men were the least responsive; only 14 percent of them were above average in reacting sympathetically or in showing concern, compared to 60 percent of the other students. And the feminine women reacted most strongly to the talker, showing more concern than even the androgynous women.

The pattern of results for these five experiments suggests that rigid sex roles can seriously restrict behavior. This is especially the case for men. The masculine men did masculine things very well, but they did not do feminine things. They were independent and assertive when they needed to be, but they weren't responsive to the kitten, or the baby, or to a person in need. In other words, they lacked the ability to express warmth, playfulness and concern, important human—if traditionally feminine—traits.

Similarly, the feminine women were restricted in their ability to express masculine characteristics. They did feminine things—played with the baby, responded with concern and support for the troubled talker—but they weren't independent in judgment or assertive of their own preferences. And for some reason, they didn't respond to the kitten; perhaps feminine women also are afraid of animals.

In contrast, the androgynous men and women did just about everything. They could be independent and assertive when they needed to be, and warm and responsive in appropriate situations. It didn't matter, in other words, whether a behavior was stereotypically masculine or feminine; they did equally well on both.

THE RIGID BARS OF SEX ROLES

In order to find out whether sex-typed people actually avoid opposite-sex behavior, Ellen Lenney and I designed a study in which people could choose an action to perform for pay. We said that we were going to photograph them for a later study, and that we didn't care at all how well they did each activity. In fact, we gave them only one minute for each performance, long enough for a convincing photo, but not long enough for them to complete the task.

Then we gave the students 30 pairs of activities, and asked them to select one from each pair to act out for pay. Some of these pitted masculine activities against feminine ones (oiling a hinge versus preparing a baby bottle); some pitted feminine against neutral (winding yarn into a ball versus sorting newspapers by geographical area); and some pitted masculine against neutral (nailing boards together versus peeling an orange).

We predicted that masculine men and feminine women would consistently avoid the activity that was inappropriate for their sex, *even though it always paid more*. We were right. Such individuals were actually ready to lose money to avoid acting in trivial ways that are characteristic of the opposite sex. That was particularly true when the person running the experiment was a member of the opposite sex. In that case, fully 71 percent of the sex-typed students chose highly stereotyped activities compared to only 42 percent of the androgynous students.

We went one step further, because we wondered how sex-typed people would feel about themselves if they *had* to carry out an opposite-sex activity. We asked all the students to perform three masculine, three feminine, and three neutral activities while we photographed them, and then they indicated on a series of scales how each activity made them feel about themselves. Masculine men and feminine women felt much worse than androgynous people about doing a cross-sex task. Traditional men felt less masculine if they had to, say, prepare a baby bottle, and traditional women felt less feminine if they had to nail boards together. When the experimenter was a member of the opposite sex, sex-typed students were especially upset about acting out of role. They felt less attractive and likeable, more nervous and peculiar, less masculine or feminine, and didn't particularly enjoy the experience.

ANDROGYNY IS DESTINY

This research persuades me that traditional concepts of masculinity and femininity do restrict a person's behavior in important ways. In a modern complex society like ours, an adult has to be assertive, independent and self-reliant, but traditional femininity makes many women unable to behave in these ways. On the other hand, an adult must also be able to relate to other people, to be sensitive to their needs and concerned about their welfare, as well as to be able to depend on them for emotional support. But traditional masculinity keeps men from responding in such supposedly feminine ways.

Androgyny, in contrast, allows an individual to be both independent and tender, assertive and yielding, masculine and feminine. Thus androgyny greatly expands the range of behavior open to everyone, permitting people to cope more effectively with diverse situations. As such, I hope that androgyny will some day come to define a new and more human standard of psychological health.

POSTSCRIPT

ARE TRADITIONAL SEX ROLES PREFERABLE TO ANDROGENOUS SEX ROLES?

One of the more interesting, and in a way amusing, consequences of the tension over changing sex roles has been the quest of American men, and some Europeans and Australians, who obviously share George Gilder's total devotion to traditional sex roles. Frustrated and repelled by the products of the women's liberation movement, a growing number of such men are turning to international marriage brokers, the mail-order matchmakers.* Filipino brides are most popular because they often speak English and have been socialized to follow the traditional role of a domestic and submissive wife and mother, although other Asian brides are also sought out by men looking for a traditional wife.

Even in this country, the tensions over sex roles has led to a quiet revitalization of traditional roles. In the 1970s, in the midst of the sexual revolution and best sellers like *The Joy of Sex* and *More Joy of Sex,* two books appeared among the top best sellers of the decade. They were seldom noticed by book reviewers, and when reviewed, ridiculed for their "simplicity" and "exploitative view of women." Yet, *Fascinating Womanhood* by Helen Andelin and *Total Woman* by Marabel Morgan sold millions of copies. Inspired by a series of booklets popular in the 1920s and the Victorian view of women as having four virtues—piety, purity, domesticity and obedience—these two books caught the attention of many women and men confused and disturbed by the turmoil of the sex revolution and the new emphasis on androgyny. Workshops promoted the traditional values in posh suburbs, large cities, and small towns. While many smiled at this attempt to return to traditional values, others found the message refreshing.

The question not addressed by the phenomenon of oriental mail-order brides, the Total Fascinating Woman, and George Gilder's detailed argument is whether the once functional traditional sex roles which supported Victorian society are viable in today's world. The question not addressed by advocates of more flexible, androgynous sex roles is how to soothe the tensions created by such rapid change in a basic component of our society and how to allay the real fear that adopting the new sex roles is social suicide. See the bibliography for further readings on this subject.

*See: L. Belkin. "The Mail-order Marriage Business," *New York Times Magazine Section,* May 11, 1986, pp. 28ff.

ISSUE 3

IS MONOGAMY THE BEST FORM OF MARRIAGE?

YES: Lisa Davis, from "Vive Monogamy," *Forum* magazine, November 1979

NO: Phyllis Raphael, from "Sexual Exclusivity is Unworkable," *Forum* magazine, June 1977

ISSUE SUMMARY

YES: Lisa Davis (pseudonym for a well-known Hollywood screenwriter) tried a variety of lifestyles and finds monogamy the most satisfying because it provides a sense of continuity, saves energy, promotes personal growth and ultimately makes true intimacy possible.

NO: Novelist and journalist Phyllis Raphael believes that the American style of exclusive monogamy is an unnatural and unattainable ideal that cripples personal development. She believes that monogamy with multiple relationships on the European style is more realistic for our times.

Instinctively, when marriage is mentioned, most of us think of two commitments, "Until death do us part" and "Forsaking all others." Romance coupled with sexual and emotional exclusivity is the ideal of married life. Yet the American reality belies this myth. The average American marriage lasts seven years. Well over half of all marriages end in divorce. Serial polygamy, by way of divorce and remarriage, is a common lifestyle, as is the single parent family. Extramarital sex is common.

The American ideal of marriage is only the most recent in the evolution of human relations. For centuries, marriage was a dynastic affair, arranged by parents and families whose main motives were economics, social status, and extension of family alliances. Christianity supposedly brought the reality of love into marriage, but with the dire warnings of religious leaders about the dangers of sexual passion, that love was supposed to be asexual, passion-less, and intellectual.

In the Middle Ages, the troubadours sang of courtly love, a passionate love for an unattainable woman, usually the wife of a noble lord. Lancelot loved Guinevere "in desperate silence," but the consummation of their love destroyed it when King Arthur discovered the infidelity of his wife and best friend.

Four hundred years ago, the Protestant Reformation triggered the evolution of two major new patterns.

In Spain, Italy and much of France, the traditional family-arranged economic-based marriage blended with the courtly love code. The exuberance of sexual passion burst forth in extramarital affairs. For the middle and upper class, lifelong marriage could exist alongside a socially accepted mistress or lover.

In northern Europe, the middle class was uneasy with courtly love and the southern acceptance of adultery as a reward for love. The solution, in this second model, was to shift the object of romance from the wife of someone else to the single woman, and then to one's own wife. In this puritan-bourgeois tradition, love and marriage were wedded to create the most meaningful and intimate of all human relationships. In the past century, as divorce became more common, extramarital sex became the mortal enemy of marriage and society because it led to divorce.

It was this northern European tradition that became dominant in the United States, with well over half of all marriages ending in divorce. In less than a century, Americans had in practice openly abandoned "Until death do us part." At the same time, with considerable hypocrisy, we had also abandoned "Forsaking all others." That aspect of modern marriage is taken up in issue 4.

YES

Lisa Davis

VIVE MONOGAMY!
IT'S STILL THE BEST!

There was a time when friends asked me whether I could ever be happy with one man.

"Absolutely not," I used to tell them.

I believed I needed at least three or four men to satisfy a variety of needs—lover, companion, skier, tennis player, scuba diver, shoulder to cry on and chess player on rainy nights. I felt that one man could not possibly meet all my needs. And I believed that monogamy was equivalent to mediocrity.

My feelings have since changed. I have discovered that monogamy has many advantages: It provides a sense of continuity, saves energy, promotes personal growth and a sense of identity. Ultimately, it makes possible a complete sharing of inner emotions. I have found that being monogamous, I no longer need to compromise. Having only one lover, I now enjoy a freedom of emotional expression that enriches rather than detracts from my personal growth. I still play tennis and have lunch with other men, but emotionally and sexually I now am committed to Stephen.

I met Stephen at a time when my life was filled with a variety of men—a doctor, a millionaire real estate contractor, a lawyer, a truck driver, a dentist and a successful businessman. I enjoyed the variety. They were all nice men and independent people like myself. In the spirit of the "me decade," I cherished self-reliance. I didn't even notice that we were all so damn independent that we never connected. Perhaps some of the men felt (as I did) an inner sense of isolation—a gnawing hunger for true intimacy.

The restlessness that once was so mysterious suddenly became obvious. After two disappointing marriages, I was afraid of *never* finding intimacy. I dared not even acknowledge its absence in my life. But Stephen was more capable of intimacy than any man I had met since a college sweetheart more than a decade ago. Stephen reawakened my need to be physically close to a man and my capacity to reveal my most personal feelings, hopes, desires, triumphs and tribulations.

The night we met he approached me in such an empathetic, non-judgmental manner that I astonished myself by answering his extremely personal questions—questions that I ordinarily would have rebuffed. I shared with him a wish I had long ago forgotten: "I'd like a man I could go to church with."

Our conversation turned to the subject of intimacy and the difficulties people have in finding it. He said he was writing a book on the subject. He asked me if I had an intimate relationship, and I asked him if he had an intimate marriage. The expression on his face became solemn, "Not as intimate as I'd like to be." I later learned that Stephen could not finish his book on intimacy because working on it was a painful reminder of the intimacy he had failed to achieve in his twelve-year marriage to someone who was sadly unresponsive to him.

Although we had traveled different paths during our lives, we discovered that we had started out looking for the same total human commitment—and once believed that we could find it in marriage. But we had both given up this hope.

Immediately after the initiation of our sexual relationship, Stephen left his wife and told me that he wanted to marry me. Although he did not ask me to commit myself totally to him, I took my first step toward monogamy: I told all the men I had been dating that I had fallen in love.

During the first week or two, being monogamous was fairly easy. Because I did not care whether or not I dated most

men, being in love was a good excuse for saying "No." I felt some regret turning down one invitation to a celebrity ball and another for a weekend sail on an eighty-foot yacht, but for the first few weeks nothing could seduce me from the passion I had found in my new love.

And then one day I was tempted. Stephen, a friend of his and I were eating brunch in a restaurant on the beach. While Stephen and Sam were engrossed in shop talk, I noticed a handsome young man staring at me. He looked away whenever our eyes met, but he continued to make intense eye contact from time to time.

He began to seem vaguely familiar, and then I realized that he was a well-known British actor. After I recognized him, I was too embarrassed to look at him again, but as he left, some friends of mine who had been eating a few tables away were also leaving. As I called goodbye to them, the actor turned expectantly as if he thought I was addressing him. It was obvious that he was interested in me and I was flattered. I thought of calling a press agent friend to find out how to contact my admirer and suggest that we get together.

When Stephen and I were alone later, he teased me, "I bet you'd like to go to bed with him." I told him my fantasy of contacting him, hastily adding that I wouldn't do it. Stephen admitted to feeling jealous but said that would be *his* problem. He said, "Do what you have to do, but if you make it with him, it will change the character of our relationship. What you do affects the nature of your being. But do whatever you do out of your own conviction, not because of what I say." He assured me that he would continue to love me no matter what I did. The ball was in my court.

Looking back over my marriages as well as other exclusive relationships in my past,

I could see that breaking the exclusivity did indeed change the character of the relationships. Now that I had found the man I had been looking for all my life I didn't want to mess it up. That night I made a conscious decision to exclude all other sexual relationships from my life. I prayed that God would give me the strength to keep this commitment.

Because of my past propensity for sampling sex the way a gourmand samples food, Stephen was skeptical when I told him of my decision. He didn't give me any accolades, but the decision itself gave me a feeling of goodness. I had made a conscious choice that was to dramatically change my life.

These alterations I attribute directly to the rewards of practicing monogamy. The most obvious advantage is that monogamy is an energy saver. I no longer pore over the singles' activities announced in the newspaper, wondering if I should go to something on Friday or Sunday if nobody calls for a date. I no longer spend time on an agonizing search for the right man to share my theater subscription. I no longer sit by my phone wondering if someone will call. I no longer have to clean my apartment and put away my papers before every date.

On an emotional level I save energy by not having to play different roles. If I'm sad or grumpy, I can say so. If I feel like skipping down the street and yelling with joy, Stephen rejoices in this behavior. I don't have to stop and ask myself whether my actions are going to embarrass someone. By being with a man who understands and loves me, I feel unrestrained. Less of my energy is tied up in pleasing a variety of people. There is a stability in my life that allows me to focus my energy in one direction.

Underlying the energy-saving qualities of monogamy, there is now a sense of continuity in my life. I can plan what I am going to be doing next month, and for the years to come. Together we are able to share and build a wealth of experiences. I no longer find myself discussing a movie with someone only to realize that I saw it several months ago with someone else.

Although it was exciting to go sailing with one person for a weekend and to Palm Springs with someone else the next weekend, now I am content to spend nearly every Sunday with Stephen. We go to church early in the morning, sample a different restaurant for brunch, and then come home and spend the afternoon making sweet love.

Because of stability and continuity in our relationship our lovemaking has brought us so close together that we sometimes cry in ecstatic moments of sheer joy. I now feel that I have more sexual variety in one person that I had before in several. I have discovered that sexuality in a continuing relationship is richer in its nuances. In comparison, sex with multiple partners is—paradoxically—less rather than more varied in that the actual physical orgasm is much the same, even when the partner is different. In a monogamous relationship, the emotional component constantly generates new heights of both physical and psychic ecstasy.

Another rewarding change that I attribute to monogamy is greater personal growth. Contrary to what the human potential movement has led many of us to believe, commitment to another person does *not* limit one's vistas for self-expansion. In fact, for me, a continuing relationship provides a warm accepting environment that promotes the fulfillment of my potential. For example, I have found great joy and truth in the concept that it is better to give than to receive. In giving to Stephen, especially when he had just left his wife, I discovered in myself an untapped reserve of empathy and ability to give emotional support. In giving, I found a new sense of self-esteem. In return, Stephen responded by loving and caring for me. Basking in his love and appreciation, I felt freer to be me. I am now more spontaneous and more loving toward others than ever before.

With the new sense of self-confidence that monogamy has given me, I am also more adventurous. Even though I had already ventured a jump out of a plane to write an article on skydiving, there were still things I was timid about. One of those was singing. Since childhood, I was told that I could not sing, so I didn't . . . at least not unless I was drunk or I thought nobody could hear. Stephen also said he couldn't sing. But that didn't stop him. He sang anyway. One evening we were so enraptured about being together that we skipped home from a restaurant singing our song, "Lotta Love," at the top of our lungs, from deep in our hearts.

Many people who shun monogamy say, "I'm not ready for an involvement at this stage of my life; I really don't know who I am yet." Although there may be those who are truly lost and not fit for a committed relationship, for many of us monogamy provides the continuity that is a key ingredient of identity. In *Identity and Intimacy*, William Kilpatrick writes that identity is "a conviction of self-sameness—a bridge over the discontinuities which invariably creep or crash into our lives." People who suffer from amnesia or who have been interred in concentration camps and have lost touch with their past are robbed of their identities. Victor Frankl, an Austrian psychiatrist, was one concentration camp inmate who helped others remain in touch with their identities. He gathered around him other prisoners who were also enthusiastic rock-climbers; they met regularly to talk about their past adventures and future expeditions. The prisoners were able to hold on to their identities through continuity—by sharing both common past experiences and planning for the future.

In twentieth-century America, we live in a society where friendship is elusive at best. Though we are not cut off from friends by prison bars, there are other distancing factors such as divorce, job changes and social mobility. In such a tumultuous, chaotic and fragmented society, monogamy offers the continuity that enhances identity. Monogamy is a lifeline that can give us a feeling of stability as well as the courage to attack the future with greater confidence.

Perhaps the greatest reward of monogamy is the quality of intimacy that is made possible. Monogamy does not guarantee intimacy—as Stephen found in his first marriage—but it provides a framework within which a couple *can* relate intimately. Because intimacy requires that you open yourself and become vulnerable, it is difficult, if not impossible, and perhaps not even desirable, to become intimate with people whom we may not be seeing next month, next week, or even the next day: If you bare your soul to someone who doesn't call again or is busy every time you call, you end up feeling exposed and rejected, perhaps even humiliated. If you engage in multiple relationships and accumulate too many rejections, you may become permanently handicapped in your ability to relate intimately.

Stephen and I started off relating intimately. But with our commitment to monogamy, the depth of our intimacy has increased, almost daily. With every argument we have, we are forced to examine our fears and resentments toward one another. While people who do not relate intimately attempt to bury anger and resentments, we believe that such negative feelings will only bottle up their positive feelings. Therefore, through the trust and confidence we have built within a continuous monogamous relationship, we are able to risk revealing every anger and frustration. By clearing the air, we are able to achieve heights of ecstasy—sexually, intellectually, spiritually and emotionally.

I have truly met a man suited for all my moods and desires. My fondest hope is that I, too, suit all of his moods and desires.

NO

Phillis Raphael

SEXUALLY EXCLUSIVE MONOGAMY IS UNWORKABLE!

Five years ago I had an awful quarrel with another woman. She was a friend of mine and she did something vile to me, something personally and professionally devastating, and I was very angry with her.

I'm not going to go into what our quarrel was about because that's not important, but what is important is that she was wrong, absolutely, totally wrong, and I was right, completely right. I wasn't the only one who thought so. Everyone did.

My quarrel with this woman went on for five years. Every time I saw her at a party or at a professional gathering, I took pains to ignore her. Every time I could I made it a point to say something rotten about her to anyone who cared to listen.

I was very bitter, and my bitterness continued until the day I decided to give up. My decision had nothing to do with her; she was still wrong and I was still right. But I was tired of carrying my anger around with me. It was a burden, like dragging a heavy suitcase around all the time. That night I walked up to her at a party. It was just before Christmas. I put my hands on her shoulders and turned her lightly toward me. "I hope you have a good holiday and a happy New Year," I said—and I meant it.

She looked puzzled, walked away for a few moments, and then came back. "Let's not fight anymore," she said. "Let's be friends." We embraced and talked for a while, and it was over. Five years of anger had come to an end. I felt very good and I know she did, too.

I've told you this story because it has to do with "giving up." It wasn't disgraceful or uncomfortable to give up my anger. Instead, it actually made my life easier and better.

Who was right and who was wrong had nothing to do with it. My giving up didn't make her action any more correct than it had ever been. It's just that giving up was a sane, practical, and positive thing to do. Finally, I looked at things as they really were, accepted them, and chose to live with them in the best way I could.

3. IS MONOGAMY THE BEST FORM OF MARRIAGE?

That incident made me think about all the other areas of my life in which I had not given up, in which I had stubbornly clung to outmoded ways of thinking and feeling. I had learned most of this behavior in my childhood and I clung to it because I thought it was "right."

Of course, monogamous behavior was one of things that I had always expected of myself as well as of those I loved. There was no question about my belief in monogamy. It was bred into my bones by everything my parents ever taught me, by every movie I ever saw, and by every fairy tale or story I ever loved as a child.

But, as the case of my anger toward my friend showed me, who or what is right simply can't always be the bottom line if you want to live happily in this world.

Let's look at the facts about monogamy. In his book, *Sexual Behavior in the Seventies,* Morton Hunt puts the statistics for infidelity in marriage at 50 percent and rising all the time. The divorce count in this country is now up to one out of every three marriages, and most of those divorces are directly attributable to infidelity.

That men and women are not by nature monogamous is a fact of life. It has nothing to do with right or wrong or what we might wish. It just is.

Despite those facts, most of us still yearn to experience a monogamous relationship; we still want a love that lasts a lifetime. The most touching expression of that wish is something I read recently in the preface of a book written by Linda Wolfe, a friend and contemporary.

In her book *Playing Around,* a report on adultery among women, Linda quotes a remark made by her new husband shortly after her second marriage (infidelity ended her first one). "What I want from a relationship," said her husband, "is the feeling that I will never want to wander. You give me that. I want you always to give me that."

I loved what he said. I think it expresses something practically all of us feel. I hope he gets it, but I think it would be naive of him to count on it—or for them to end their marriage if he doesn't get it.

Nearly every one of us has had experiences with infidelity, either overt or covert. The experiences have been painful and have bred mistrust, anger, and alienation.

My lover, a divorced man, has told me that he often dreams that I have been unfaithful to him, although I have not. I am aware of his occasional infidelities, and I know about the other woman in his life, a woman with whom he has been involved on and off for many years. I find the situation difficult and I sway back and forth between staying with him and leaving.

I often wonder what I would do if someone else were to come along who would demand or expect fidelity from me. The romantic in me, the child who watched old movies and loved fairy tales, yearns to believe I could comply, but the pragmatic adult questions whether this is possible.

Knowing what I do about myself and the world, could I promise a lifetime of fidelity? Could I, like Linda Wolfe's husband, expect someone else to give me the feeling of "never wanting to wander"? I think not.

Shortly after I had ended my five-year quarrel, I went to London to visit some old friends. I spent Christmas day with them, a married couple who have two grown sons.

My friends are expatriate Americans who have always been rather offbeat, and since they have been living in Europe they have picked up some rather permissive European attitudes toward sex. Both the husband's lover and the wife's lover had

Christmas dinner with us. They were a young German woman and a man from Australia. There was no sweat or strain. Everyone had a marvelous time.

The German woman gave the husband a manicure and helped the wife in the kitchen. The Australian man traded quips with the husband. A mild, joking kind of flirtation took place between me and the couple's eldest son. The wife remarked that she couldn't think of anyone else she would rather have her son "have it off with."

Although I am too American and uptight and puritanical to be like they are, I loved their relaxed attitude. They had truly given up. They had replaced romantic illusion with reality, accepted themselves and each other as they really were, and were having a great time. Instead of dissolving in anger, pain, or divorce they had survived as a happy family (albeit an unconventional one) sharing Christmas dinner together.

Another incident brought home the difference between American and European attitudes even more sharply. While I was in London I called a man with whom I had once had an affair. He had since gotten married. I suggested that we have lunch together, but he wanted me to come to his home for dinner.

"Are you sure your wife wants to view the remains?" I joked. "Absolutely," he replied. "She knows all about you. She'd love to meet you." I couldn't believe it, but it was true. I went to their house for dinner, and we talked openly about our affair. I liked his wife and she liked me.

How different from my present love affair, where I am kept secret from the other woman my lover is involved with! How different from the pain I experience in that situation! How much easier life is when people are willing to give up.

I am not certain that such openness is possible in America today, although I know that life would be a lot more comfortable if it were. But I do believe that at some point a kind of private reconciliation is possible for each of us, and that by giving up our dreams we will suffer less and live better.

While we can't all bring our lovers and ex-lovers home for dinner, we can accept that we and those we love may sometimes want to wander. It is the nature of the beast, as they say, and it is unlikely that we will tame the beast in any of us.

An acceptance of the fact that none of us is truly monogamous isn't really so terrible. Instead it may be a truly adult way of loving oneself and another person; that is, loving them as they really are and not as our illusions would like them to be.

Initially, when I accepted this assignment and discussed it with the Forum editor, it wasn't supposed to turn out this way at all. In our discussion we both agreed that what the article would say is that since men and women are not monogamous, it might be a good idea for all of us to accept this fact and stop torturing each other by revealing our extramarital affairs.

It seems to me that women have always been better at keeping quiet about that than men. I'm not sure why. I think it might be because they are more in touch with their feelings, or because they simply aren't as possessive as men.

I still believe that women are generally more matter-of-fact than men about the facts of life. They don't find it necessary to run home and report every amorous adventure, nor do they break up their marriages because of them.

Men, or at least the ones I know, take these matters more seriously, perhaps too seriously. Maybe it's because they cling more steadfastly to illusion than women

53

and, like Linda Wolfe's husband, are romantic enough to wish more devoutly "never to want to wander."

However, I'm not sure that people *should* keep their love affairs secret, nor is that the point. The point is not that we should stop torturing each other, but that we should stop torturing ourselves.

Had I not given up my anger toward the woman with whom I had quarreled, I might not have known that. Much of our agony is self-induced and springs from self-delusion. Only when we come to terms with how much holding on to the illusion of monogamy makes us suffer personally can we decide how open we will choose to be. I think it's a valuable thing to know.

POSTSCRIPT

IS MONOGAMY THE BEST FORM
OF MARRIAGE?

Each reader will react differently to the preceeding essays, accepting this point or rejecting that one, based on their own life experience and observations. The challenge is to listen carefully to what each of the observers reports, to weigh their various points against each other, and then interpret everything in terms of one's own values and expectations. This, of course, means we have to be open always to new insight, new experiences, and new interpretations.

Often, when we ask some couple whose relationship has flourished over many years what were the factors that made their relationship so rewarding, their autobiographical analysis ends up with the conclusion that it was a process continually requiring lots of time, energy and communication. The process is what counts. We learn from others, but then we must apply what we learn to individual demands as our own changing personality interacts with that of another changing person. See the bibliography for further readings on this subject.

ISSUE 4

IS OPEN MARRIAGE A VIABLE LIFESTYLE FOR TODAY?

YES: Lonny Meyers, from *Adultery and other Private Matters: Your Right to Personal Freedom in Marriage* (Chicago, Nelson-Hall publishers)

NO: Robert H. Rimmer, from "Why Open Marriage Won't Work," *Forum* magazine, February 1978

ISSUE SUMMARY

YES: Lonny Meyers, a physician and sexologist, proposes a variation on "open marriage" in which the husband and wife respect each other's right to privacy.

NO: Robert H. Rimmer, author of *The Harrad Experiment* and other underground classics of the sexual revolution, contends that our cultural emphasis on sexual and emotional exclusivity and on jealousy as the sign of true love makes "open marriage" impossible for most couples.

In their classic survey of *Patterns in Sexual Behavior,* Ford and Beech found that only 29 of the 185 contemporary cultures studied, less than 16 percent, restrict men and women to a single partner. Moreover, less than a third of the 29 monogamous cultures completely disapprove of both premarital and extramarital relations. In regard to these findings they said:

> "Sociologists have sometimes asserted that monogamous mateship represents a peak of societal evolution and that our own ideal form of marriage is a criterion of advanced civilization. Insistence upon monogamous unions is unquestionably a product of societal evolution, but it is not also correlated with other criteria of advanced cultural status. Some of the most 'primitive' peoples are strictly monogamous in their ideals." (Harper & Row, 1951, p. 108)

Today, indications are that between a third and two-thirds of all married couples in America have at least one extramarital relationship. This situation has led some people to ask a new question. Which commitment is more important, a life-long relationship or exclusivity? Is it possible that the two European models of marriage discussed in the introduction to Issue 3 can be blended into a new style of marriage, better suited than either to today's social context?

The drive for sexual equality and the sexual revolution of the 1960s and 1970s brought this question to the fore. In 1968, in their book *Honest Sex: A Revolutionary Sex Ethic By and For Concerned Christians*, Rustum and Della Roy placed the emphasis on long-term commitment and suggested that we redefine fidelity. They coined the term "comarital relations," suggesting the possibility that monogamy could exist as a primary relationship between husband and wife and be reinforced by committed secondary or comarital relations which might or might not include sexual expression.

Although the O'Neill's 1972 best-seller *Open Marriage* dealt only briefly with the possibility of comarital relations, the term "open marriage" quickly became part of our language and thinking on the subject of marriage. Ramey's "intimate friendship" and the Francoeurs' "satellite relations" enriched the conceptualization of a new form of non-exclusive monogramy.

But then came the 1980s, with a conservative revival, herpes, and AIDS. Is open marriage a viable option today? The following essays face that question.

YES   Lonny Myers

FREEDOM IN MARRIAGE: IT WORKS!

What happens to our freedom as individuals when we get married? How much personal independence can be maintained? Quite a bit, if we desire it, but many of us trade in our autonomy for the sort of "oneness" we have been told marriage should be.

Years, months, or sometimes only weeks after the wedding, when the joys of togetherness begin to wear thin, we often feel uneasy and disillusioned. This is because we have been raised to believe that we are incomplete without a spouse, and the compulsive togetherness that usually characterizes the early years of marriage reflects our view of ourselves as incomplete individuals.

I believe it's time we began to regard marriage as the union of two *whole* persons. It is possible to love another person deeply and not feel the need to spend all available free time with him or her. When both partners feel this way, they can budget the time they will spend on their own, accountable to no one for their actions. This approach makes marriage a *want,* not a *need.*

As I see it, there are four basic ways in which people achieve independence within marriage. Let's take a look at how they work.

FREEDOM WITH SECRECY

In this arrangement, one spouse (or both) has secrets he/she does not share. People involved in this sort of relationship are simply putting respect for their own personal needs above respect for the views of their partner, and they do not wish to confront their partners with their needs.

The play *Same Time, Next Year* beautifully illustrates freedom with secrecy. A man and a woman, each married to someone else, meet for one weekend every year for twenty-five years. These encounters enrich both their lives with no demonstrable harm, for they keep their annual rendezvous strictly secret.

The woman's husband never learns of her unusual affair; the man's wife accidentally discovers his involvement several years before her death, but never reveals her knowledge to her husband.

Adapted from, *Adultery and Other Private Matters,* by Lonny Meyers and Hunter Leggett. Reprinted by permission from *Forum* magazine, October 1977. Copyright © Forum International Ltd.

In real life, of course, there is always the possibility of a showdown should a spouse discover the unapproved activity.

At that time the wayward partner had better be prepared for honesty. He or she should display no guilt or shame, but rather should express the feeling that whatever was done was done out of need, and that it was better to be responsible and not to wave a red flag in the spouse's face.

The wayward partner should also acknowledge that it was easier to let his/her spouse live with an illusion than to force a showdown, but that now they have to discuss their life together in a new light.

At this point, the partner who has been caught may give up the secret activity to please the spouse, or he or she may issue an ultimatum, not out of choice, but because circumstances have made it impossible to do anything else. As often as not, however, this sort of showdown never takes place. Millions of people live and die harboring unshaken illusions about their mates.

FREEDOM WITH RESTRICTIONS

Some married people simply do not *want* to do anything that would be upsetting to their spouses. At any time they want to feel comfortable about having their activities known to their partner.

They may have many independent pursuits, including travel, meeting friends, hobbies, community work, etc. But visiting a nudist camp, smoking pot, using a faith healer, or having an affair may be excluded only because they do not appear on their spouse's "approved list."

However, this kind of autonomy suggests that, even when apart, each partner is incomplete and feels the need for permission to indulge in certain activities. It is as though their judgments are inadequate and they must take a set of rules with them, a list of do's and don'ts. Often, even though the roles may periodically reverse, such people relate in a parent-child fashion.

Of course, many couples do not parent each other, but decide together what they want for their limitations. This may work out fine, providing present needs are being met and one partner is not rigidly adhering to an old contract which the other wants to renegotiate.

Some people never get a chance to defend their views when they propose an activity which is unacceptable to their partners. For example:

• Sally throws a fit whenever Sam suggests they try pot.

• George shouts and stamps when Gladys says she would like to spend a weekend at a nudist camp.

• Ida becomes depressed when Ira suggests going on a skiing weekend with his college pals.

• Henry cannot understand why Helen wants to try group sex, and he calls her a whore whenever she mentions it.

• Francine thinks religious cults are for suckers, and puts Frank down whenever he indicates his desire to explore one.

Why can't Sam smoke pot, Gladys go to a nudist camp, Ira have his skiing weekend, Helen try group sex, and Frank explore a religious cult? Aren't these people adults who are capable of making their own decisions?

Yet, according to the concept of complete honesty and total sharing which has become a part of modern marriage, they must confront their spouses with their frustrations (if they stick to the approved list) or their transgressions (if they decide to indulge in the unapproved activity).

When a couple have been married for several decades, it often turns out that one partner has grown more psychologically and become more imaginative than the other. The less imaginative partner has a vested interest in maintaining the status quo, but the more imaginative partner feels somewhat stifled and may secretly indulge in an occasional act not on the approved list. Then freedom with restrictions becomes freedom with secrecy for that partner.

FREEDOM WITH AN ULTIMATUM

When the ultimatum technique is used, one partner states a condition that is non-negotiable and the other partner must take it or leave it. Most people are less assertive (or arrogant, depending on your point of view) and tend to express their needs in a more general way, remaining open for reasonable compromises. However, I know two people who did present their spouses with ultimatums and let the chips fall where they may.

One was Kay L., who began to feel smothered by her marriage after only a few months of total sharing. She announced that she was going to take one night a week off, free of any restrictions except those of her own conscience. Everything else was negotiable. She preferred Friday nights, but would settle for another night. She would be home by one a.m., or an hour earlier if her husband insisted.

However, she would answer no questions about where she had been or what she had done. Her only commitment was to act responsibly and meet her obligations the following morning.

She urged her husband to join her and enjoy his own night off, preferably the same night. But whatever his reaction, she was going ahead with her plans. As of this writing they are both taking Friday nights off and the system is working for them.

Another example of the ultimatum technique involved Allan H., a man who went through a radical psychological change and declared that he was going to revamp his life style. In effect, he said to his wife Betsy, "I love you very much, but lately I've been thinking that neither one of us is really free. I'm beginning to realize that I've got to start flying on my own if I want to be true to myself."

"And that means that I intend to have sexual relationships with other women. This may sound cold to you, but I know it's going to be the best thing for both of us. And don't forget that I want you to fly too."

Well, it took them four years and a lot of hard work to reach the open marriage they enjoy today. At first, Betsy just felt numb when she thought about Allan's ultimatum. She had always been a very dependent person and had always looked to her husband for support and approval. And now her husband was telling her that her wifely behavior wasn't what he wanted.

After many tearful nights, Betsy finally got up the courage to confide in an old friend of hers who had always seemed like a strong, independent woman. Gradually, Betsy realized that Allan's ultimatum might actually be a good thing for her, too, and she finally learned to look to herself for support and approval. Now Allan and Betsy respect each other and feel free to live their own lives without fear.

FREEDOM WITH
NO RESTRICTIONS

Finally we come to an arrangement that is workable only when husband and wife feel whole and complete within themselves and can negotiate the amount of private time each will have in light of other obligations such as job, home, community commitments, or children.

The time may amount to one hour a week or an entire summer. But the principle is always the same: during the budgeted time, Big Brother is not watching. Each partner is totally free, and the activities pursued are limited only by the conscience of the person involved. It is up to the partners to choose whether or not they want to tell each other what they do during their budgeted time.

Ted and Mary B. are a case in point. They have enjoyed private time for several years. They originally agreed to no-holds-barred activities, but decided not to tell each other what they were doing during this time. However, as time went on, their confidence in their own ability to cope with certain situations grew. Each became convinced that he/she could handle hearing about the other's extramarital affairs, but that the other could not.

They have discussed eliminating the secrecy and sharing their private activities. But Ted is afraid that Mary wouldn't be happy if she learned about his several one-night stands or his one summer-long love affair two years ago. And Mary is sure that Ted wouldn't be pleased about her participation in group sex, which she has done three times.

Thus, each one is happy when the other indicates a preference for privacy. They are truly seeking outside enrichment to their marriage without threatening that marriage, and for them, not telling is essential to achieving their goal.

This absence of *total* honesty in their relationship hardly makes them unique. How many couples do you know who share all their sexual fantasies, all their personal mail, all their dreams, frustrations, and occasional resentments?

Everyone has secrets, and being frank in every situation would be a surefire way to end most marriages. Budgeted time for private activities enables husbands and wives to retain their individuality and their personal freedom, while building a loyal, strong primary relationship.

Granted, there will always be spouses who demand the freedom to do whatever they please, *whenever* they please, and others who have no need for independent activities. The former flaunt their independence and the latter don't even desire it. Most of us are somewhere in between.

But change is occurring. The women's movement is helping women to view themselves as whole people, not just as appendages of their husbands, and the variety of life styles which are now available, from living-together arrangements to open marriage, are broadening the horizons of both women and men. Hopefully, more and more people will enter marriage because it is a life style they desire, not because they need to be made complete.

In a marriage of two whole people, the demand for freedom will inevitably arise. Total freedom within budgeted time can greatly enrich such a marriage.

NO

Robert H. Rimmer

SEXUALLY OPEN MARRIAGES RARELY SUCCEED

There is a great new American daydream—the sexually open marriage. If there are any readers who have made it work for more than two years, I'd like to hear from them. Over the past ten years I have received hundreds of letters from couples who have experimented with open marriage and have ended up divorced, or finally given up post-marital experimentation.

I am fascinated by alternative life styles, as readers of my novels know, and I believe we should be experimenting with them far more than we are. I'm not only convinced that we can both revitalize and create new marriage and family structures, but that we *must* lay the groundwork for new kinds of family interaction to replace the slowly vanishing nuclear family. Not only should we encourage and subsidize experiments with new family and marital styles, but we should gradually legalize some of the alternate methods on an *a priori* basis, and thus make them more socially acceptable.

However, I simply do not believe that the sexually open marriage is a workable, enjoyable alternative marital style. Unlike swinging, sexually open marriage is not a post-marital adventure which a couple share; it allows partners both mental and genital intimacy with another person independently from their marital relationship.

Most first-time marriage partners are probably embarrassed to admit to each other that they wish to have an open marriage agreement or understanding. Before they are married, they may discuss the possibility of having independent friendships with the other sex over the course of a long marriage, but the whens and the hows and any thoughts about whether these will involve sexual contact are usually vague and undefined.

Most men (and practically all women, because they are unsure of the extent of a particular male's possessive instincts) hesitate to admit—even to themselves and especially in the first bloom of love—that they might wish to experience sexual and mental intimacy with other persons during their married life.

The truth is that most of us don't know how to cope with the "infidelity" that we assume is implied by our desire for more than one intimate sexual friendship. In actuality, the concept of mental infidelity—sharing with another person aspects of one's personality that one doesn't reveal to a spouse—is even more frightening than sexual infidelity.

While some career-oriented men and women who have delayed marriage into their thirties or who have been through a divorce may be sophisticated enough to have informal agreements about their extramarital sex lives, in my opinion, they aren't typical. Most of these people are at relatively high income levels and their life style is based on sharing a good portion of their lives with casual friends.

If they are away overnight in pursuit of business, political, or career objectives, they are able to fit another sexual friendship into the pattern of their mobile lives without too much involvement. In many cases, they have learned how to compartmentalize secondary relationships so that they won't become unsettling to the mate. In fact, their extramarital relationships are often completely unknown to their partners. Obviously, these couples do not have marriages which could be considered sexually open.

There are other types of marriages in which a limited degree of sexual freedom may exist. A partner who is low-keyed sexually may give a spouse permission to have another sexual relationship. Interestingly, this sort of agreement is not always confined to unresponsive wives and their dissatisfied husbands. Many liberated women who discover that their husbands are inadequate to meet their sexual needs, and prefer a live penis to a vibrator or dildo, convince their husbands that they must have another sexual relationship. Women seem to be very open about their extramarital activities under these circumstances. Many even succeed in integrating the second relationship into a viable ménage-à-trois.

But once again, this is a special kind of marriage in which some sort of concession has been granted by one partner to the other. Despite tacit agreements between partners, outside relationships may pose a threat to such marriages. For example, a married man who becomes involved with a single woman often discovers that she wants to become his wife. The key to survival in these sexually permissive marriages, as distinguished from sexually open marriages, is to maintain a relatively casual involvement with the secondary partner and share little or no details of one's extramarital mental or sexual life with the mate. "If you do it, don't tell me about it" is the credo for many monogamous marriages of long duration.

Sexually open marriages, on the other hand, require honesty about the existence of outside relationships. Both partners agree that they are free to pursue extramarital relationships, and they may even discuss their other partners with each other. Why don't these marriages work? Quite simply, they are sabotaged by the pressure of a million mundane problems and demands that fill our waking hours—and by human nature.

Let's look at a sexually open marriage through the eyes of Dick and Jane, who have two children. Like millions of Americans, Dick and Jane would have found the idea of a sexually open marriage repulsive *before* they were married. But after six years of marriage, they are no longer locked into a belief in romantic matrimony or sexual fidelity for a lifetime. They've read so much about the potential of sexually open marriage for strengthening a relationship that they are curious. They wonder if they are still sexually attractive to anyone else. They might not reveal it when they sit down to talk about opening their marriage, but the chances are good that one of them is already meeting another special person.

They do discuss the fact that their children have peer group friends whose Daddies and Mommies probably behave quite monogamously. So they agree that because of the children, a secondary sexual relationship cannot be enjoyed within the confines of their home. They also agree that they will have to hire babysitters, because sitting while one's spouse is enjoying his/her sex life with another person is obviously not very conducive to marital happiness.

Dick, who hosts his own radio talk show, meets many women, but he keeps wondering what it would be like to go to bed with Jill, his program director. Jill's only twenty-sex (seven years younger than Jane) and is involved with him in his work in a way that Jane has never been.

Jane has been taking courses in writing at the university and Jack, her professor (who is married and in his late forties), believes that Jane has great talent, and, undoubtedly, with his guidance, will write a bestseller. Jack is sure that Jane appreciates his teaching abilities far more than his wife Alice, who tries to be a "total woman," but is pretty much involved with her suburban friends, and church and club projects. Besides, Jane is nearly ten years younger than Alice.

Dick never pays much attention to Jane's writing and long ago Jane stopped tuning in Dick's afternoon talk show to listen to the endless boring telephone calls he receives.

Dick tells Jane about Jill, and Jane tells Dick about Jack. They assure each other that their marriage and their children come first. The night that they give each other permission to go to bed with their newfound friends, Dick and Jane have the best sex they have ever had together. They feel they have achieved a new peak of mental as well as physical intimacy.

A few days later Jane confesses to Dick, "A fuck is a fuck, but Jack will never compare with you." And Dick tells Jane that Jill is nice, "a different body, but if it comes to a choice, you're still my only girl."

Jill, however, is single and has her own apartment, while Jack is married. Dick can meet Jill in privacy. Jack can't come to Jane's house because of her agreement with Dick, and motels are expensive. Still, Jack seems more "involved" with Jane than Jill is with Dick. Keeping his relationship with Jane a secret from his wife (he tells her he must attend late faculty meetings and help students), Jack takes Jane to plays and movies.

Jill dates other men besides Dick. But Jane is a little peeved that Dick and Jill have plenty of opportunity for sexual intimacy. Though she doesn't tell Dick she is feeling insecure, Jane is sure that Jill's vagina is tighter than hers and that she has no stretchmarks on her stomach since she has no children.

When Jane tells Dick that Jack has the loan of a friend's apartment Saturday night (Jack tells Alice that he's attending a writers' conference) and she'd like to stay overnight with Jack, Dick is a little shocked. He could have spent the night with Jill. He even considered it, but didn't dare put the idea to Jane. Now Jill had made a date with someone else for Saturday night, and even if she were free, at this late date Dick wouldn't be able to find a babysitter willing to sleep over.

To top it off, when Jane returns on Sunday, Dick discovers that she and Jack saw a movie that he had wanted to see with her. When he asks Jill to go to this movie, she tells him, "It was really terrible"—she saw it Saturday night with Tom.

You can multiply these interpersonal comedies geometrically. No matter what the state of a particular monogamous marriage, but especially when there are children, opening it and reverting to dating on a single basis is the first step toward even greater marital unhappiness than a couple may have started out with.

One couple I know, who had been married eighteen years, decided to give each other a sexually open marriage as a Christmas present. Actually, the proposal came, as it often does, from the husband, but the wife agreed to go along with it. The husband went to bed with visions of sugar-plums and the miles of vaginas he was going to explore in the coming year dancing in his head.

By the end of January, his wife had shyly announced to him that she had capitulated to a business associate who had often asked her to go to bed with him. Six months later, the now bewildered and more than a little jealous husband had managed a couple of brief sexual encounters—but by that time his wife was deeply involved with another man.

While marriage and sex counselors may disagree with me, I think the search for post-marital sexual options, including sexually open marriage, is simply a reflection of the driving human need to be confirmed by another person as a total human being. In many monogamous marriages one partner or the other, purposely, or often inadvertently, closes the door to full communication. It can happen very early in marriage, or gradually over a period of years. A lack of shared interests, hobbies, of life goals, or the growth of one spouse in different directions from the other,

creates an environment of limited mental communication, and this subtly affects the quality of sexual intimacy.

Great, joyous sexual surrender—extended lovemaking through a whole evening—is no longer possible with the original marriage partner. Without mutual mental surrender, sex becomes a chore. So a couple seek additional partners outside their relationship, partners who will accept them as they really believe they are, to whom they can open up completely. But complete mental surrender walks hand in hand with sexual surrender. Few people manage one without the other.

There are many reasons why a policy of sexual openness may gradually erode a marriage. Because sexually open marriages, by definition, permit relationships in which one spouse does not participate, they create insecurity for one spouse, or both. Even people whose career is the highest priority in their lives rarely have a strong enough sense of self to cope with the kind of subtle rejection that inevitably can occur in a free-flowing sexually open marriage.

What's more, because they are short-term relationships, outside liaisons can easily foster "the romantic illusion." In may ways it really is easier to be oneself with a relatively uninvolved stranger than with a long-time spouse. Because of that, it is easy to convince oneself that the quality of the more revealing, but less involved, mental and sexual relationship is better.

Needless to say, if a person develops deep interpersonal involvements with one or more outside partners, then the time available for the marriage will suffer. Loving, or simply liking, two people of the other sex, and keeping their needs and your needs in control so that one relationship or the other is not eroded, is a very difficult task.

4. IS OPEN MARRIAGE A VIABLE LIFESTYLE?

Are there other kinds of sexually open marriages that will work? I believe that there are. Some of these possibilities, like synergamy, corporate marriage, intimate friendships, triads, LovXchange, and Love Groups, I have explored within the context of my novels. They have one thing in common: additional intimate friendships and sexual relationships, instead of being pursued by each partner separately, are shared with another couple or possibly two other couples. Then, within the group of four or six people, the intimate sexual relationships, as well as some of the mental intimacies, are purposely kept dyadic (one-to-one), but overriding these individual relationships is a one-for-all feeling that gives the group a lovely shared ambiance.

One thing I am sure of: any one of these more structured experiments can offer a more significant personal growth experience than the more hedonistic and self-oriented approach of sexually open marriage, which encourages the individual partners to pursue their own particular satisfactions. The essence of love is sharing, and it is in the sharing of love among couples that the future of post-marital alternatives lies.

———

POSTSCRIPT

IS OPEN MARRIAGE A VIABLE LIFESTYLE FOR TODAY?

Two conclusions are unavoidable from the preceeding essays and those in Issue 3. First, there is no one ideal pattern of human relations. And secondly, whatever lifestyle you choose, it will bring its own unique, and often unpredictable, combination of benefits and risks.

Given these conclusions and the fact that each of the essayists are speaking from their own personal experience or from that of others who have confided in them, it is impossible to pick out weakness or flaws in their arguments. It is not easy to assess issues of this nature in the same objective and empirical terms that can be applied to other questions. One might, for example, compare divorce rates during periods of sexual openness with those during periods of sexual conservatism, but that would not give any meaningful insight into the successfulness of a particular style of marriage because of the tremendous numbers of other variables and the changing social attitudes toward divorce.

Each of us must bring to these questions his or her own set of values and inclinations and establish the kind of intimate relationships that will be most consistent with them. See the bibliography for further readings on this subject.

ISSUE 5

ARE HOMOSEXUAL AND BISEXUAL RELATIONS NATURAL AND NORMAL?

YES: Jeannine Gramick, from an essay written for this volume.

NO: Robert Gordis, from *Love and Sex* (Farrar, Straus and Giroux, 1978)

ISSUE SUMMARY

YES: Jeannine Gramick, a Catholic nun working with gay and lesbian persons, argues that the main reason many people reject homosexuality and bisexuality as unnatural is that the dominant heterosexual majority believes its lifestyle is the only acceptable orientation.

NO: Robert Gordis, biblical professor at the Jewish Theological Seminary, claims that homosexuality is "an abnormality, and illness." He argues for rejecting both the traditional religious reaction to homosexuality as an abomination and the fashionable doctrine that homosexuality is an alternate lifestyle of equal value and legitimacy with heterosexuality.

Erwin Haeberle, a historian and philosopher of sexology, has pointed out that the concept of sexual orientation and the words homosexual and homosexuality did not exist until they were created by the Hungarian physician Benkert in 1869.* Throughout the ancient and medieval worlds, there were many terms for sexual relations between two persons of the same sex and for persons who might, at one time or another, engage in same-sex behavior, but there was no term to label a person by his or her sexual orientation. Benkert, like many of his medical colleagues, believed that an erotic attraction to a person of the same sex was a mysterious condition characteristic of a very small group of people. This condition, he believed, set this minority apart from others.

Today, we know that Benkert was wrong on two grounds. Sexual orientations are a matter of degree rather than an either-or condition. Sexual orientation is not an exclusive label as the experience of bisexual persons proves. Life is too varied to support simplistic divisions like homosexual versus heterosexual. Unfortunately, we live in a culture that continues to label people.

In June, 1969, the New York police raided the Stonewall Inn in Greenwich Village in one of their routine harassments, only to be confronted by unexpected resistance. The gay liberation movement was born, and American society began to face the reality of millions of Americans who are homosexual and bisexual in their orientation.

Since the Stonewall Inn Riot of 1969, homosexually-oriented men and women have increasingly and openly demanded their civil rights. They have worked for legal protection against discrimination and struggled to be recognized by the churches on an equal footing with heterosexually-oriented persons. These efforts have created major and fundamental debates.

Many claim that our society and the churches should not acknowledge or agree to demands for recognition because heterosexual relations and behavior are the only natural, normal and acceptable sexual orientation. Both the structure and the biological function of the sexual organs are obviously designed for heterosexual union. Sex was obviously created and is designed for reproduction. Both nature and God have decreed that homosexual behavior and relationships are unnatural, and therefore sinful. Moreover, the acceptance of homosexuality has been a major factor leading to the downfall of many great cultures, such as ancient Greece and Rome. Any acceptance of homosexuality and bisexuality would undermine the strength of the family, which is the whole basis of every society and culture.

On the other hand, gay men and lesbians claim their orientation is not a choice. They are born, like heterosexuals, with a particular sexual orientation. Since they did not freely choose their orientation, discriminating against them is totally unjust and immoral. They cite anthropological and sociological evidence that homosexual and bisexual behavior and relations are an open part of everyday life in many cultures, present and past. They also cite research indicating that the sexual orientation of every human starts with a combination of unknown biological factors including variations in hormone balances and developmental patterns in the brain which encode a range of neurological pathways establishing certain tendencies before we are born.

Although the mental health professions no longer consider homosexual and bisexual orientations pathological in themselves, this has not ended the debate over how our society should respond to sexual orientations and behaviors other than those which are strictly heterosexual. Beyond the social issues lies the issue of morality and the religious concept of certain behaviors being regarded as sinful.

*For a discussion of terms related to sexual orientations, their history and usages, see: E. Haeberle (1978) *The Sex Atlas,* New York: Seabury Press, pp. 446-453, and J. Boswell (1980) *Christians, Social Tolerance and Christianity,* Chicago: University of Chicago Press, pp. 42-45.

YES Sr. Jeannine Gramick

HOMOSEXUALITY AND BISEXUALITY ARE JUST AS NATURAL AND NORMAL AS HETEROSEXUAL BEHAVIOR AND RELATIONS

For the last 15 years I have worked in church ministry for lesbian and gay Catholics. Much of the time has been devoted to providing educational opportunities for heterosexual people to discuss the sensitive topic of homosexuality in a calm, reasoned and impassioned way. When I have met resistance from well-meaning heterosexual people to accepting homosexual individuals as persons, the bottom line has usually been, "But homosexuality is just unnatural." I try to pursue the conversation in a reasoned manner by asking them to explain their statement and to define, as best they can, what they mean by the words "unnatural" and "natural."

Over the years, their explanations and definitions have been varied. I am convinced that people have unconsciously absorbed from the dominant culture a deep-seated feeling of antipathy toward homosexuality for which they have tried, usually unsuccessfully, to provide a semblance of rational argument. For a good part of my adult life, I also unquestioningly assumed that homosexuality was unnatural. But from meeting thousands of lesbian and gay people over the years, from reading reliable research in the field, and from reflecting on what it means to be natural, I am now convinced that homosexual and bisexual feelings and behaviors are just as natural as heterosexual ones.

In the pages which follow, I shall present some of the reasons or arguments I have heard on both sides of the question. I shall examine what it means to be "natural" and, in so doing, shall draw upon historical, anthropological, psychological, and biological evidence. That the main stumbling block to my argument comes from theological and philosophical discourse demonstrates to me that these disciplines either have failed to deep abreast of scientific developments or have willfully ignored current findings in order to legitimate a preconceived notion of divine intent for the human order.

How can I say that bisexual and homosexual feelings are as natural as heterosexual ones? What does it mean to be "natural"? Let us consider the definition of the word from various disciplines.

HISTORY

Goethe once wrote that homosexuality and bisexuality can be considered natural because they are as old as the human race itself. Some people, such as Goethe, would say that something is natural if it has existed and continues to exist over time and place. This is a definition of "natural" which I have heard among a number of professors in academic circles.

Historical knowledge would certainly affirm Goethe's belief. It is fairly well-known that particular societies at different historical times socially approved of homosexual and bisexual liaisons. Between the eighth and second centuries before the Christian era, Greek art and literature assumed that virtually everyone responded at different times both to homosexual and to heterosexual stimuli. Such an attitude was implicit in the nonphilosophical writings as well as in the philosophy of the time. In Plato's *Symposium,* the guests at a dinner party take turns delivering speeches in praise of Eros, the god of love. Most of the examples used by the speakers are homosexual. In expounding his own view of eros in the work, Plato describes a male responding to the beauty of another male, and not to a female, as the starting point of his philosophical understanding of ideal beauty. Probably because homosexual relations were so commonly accepted, Plutarch, another Greek writer, in his *Dialogue on Love,* had to argue passionately in defense of the naturalness of heterosexual love.

The historian A.L. Rowse has documented numerous cases of homosexual persons throughout history. Let us consider only a relatively few of these. The famous twelfth century English king, Richard the Lionhearted, seems to have been bisexual, though obviously preferring the company of his male minstrel. The coronation festivities of the fourteenth century English king, Edward II, were almost halted by Edward's conspicuous attentions for Piers Gaveston, his constant male companion whom, historians say, "he adored." When the powerful barons murdered his beloved Gaveston, the king could only take the body to his own foundation, grieve intensely and pray for his loved one's soul. From his passionate love letters to a fellow monk and from his close male attachments, historians believe that the medieval scholar Erasmus was also homosexually oriented.

The Renaissance genius, Leonardo de Vinci, wrote that heterosexual intercourse was "so ugly that, if it were not for the beauty of faces and the liberation of the spirit, the species would lose its humanity," i.e., the human race would cease to propagate. At age 24, the reserved and aristocratic de Vinci was accused of having sex with a 17 year old male and imprisoned for two months. More withdrawn and mysterious than ever after his release, de Vinci engaged a "graceful and beautiful," irresistible youth as an apprentice and taught him to paint. Although the youth stole from his master as well as from his master's clients, de Vinci overlooked his faults because of his strong attachment to the youth. As with other tragic love stories, the man left de Vinci but the master painter was to find happiness in the devotion of another man who remained faithful to him until de Vinci's death.

Although he was de Vinci's contemporary, Michelangelo Buonarotti could not have been more unlike de Vinci in temperament and personality. While Leondardo was calm, courteous and an introvert, Michelangelo was abrupt, aggressive, impatient; the two men disliked each other.

Unmarried like de Vinci, Michelangelo was dominated by the nude male body in his sculptures, paintings, and drawings. His preference for males was well known during his lifetime although there is no documentation concerning his sexual practice. After his death his love poems to Cavalieri, who became the passion of his life, were altered so that they appeared to be addressed to a woman.

Although a host of eminent historical figures were homosexual, most of those known to us are male because most of our religious, literary and political information has been written by men about men and for other men to read. Only in more modern times have women produced historical records of themselves. Despite this significant handicap, historical data do indicate that lesbian women have existed, though certainly more hidden, throughout the ages. The word lesbian derives from the ancient Greek poetess Sappho who lived on the island of Lesbos with her community of female admirers. . . .

ANTHROPOLOGY

Not only have bisexual and homosexual individuals existed at all times throughout history, but they have also existed in almost all cultures which anthropologists have studied. In those cultures where homosexuality or bisexuality has not been observed, anthropologists point out that language and communication problems may have obscured evidence of them. Moreover, those societies in which no homosexual behavior is evident are very sparsely populated ones, such as the Alorese in the mountains of Timor. We would expect that in such close knit groupings it would be difficult for individuals to engage in relationships disapproved of by the group.

Not only were bisexual and homosexual practices condoned and even encouraged among the ancient Greeks and Romans, but also the ancient Celts, Scandinavians, Egyptians, Etruscans, Cretans, Carthagenians, and Sumerians accepted same-sex behavior. The greatest approval of homosexuality in ancient times came from the lands surrounding the Tigris-Euphrates and the Nile Rivers and the Mediterranean Sea. With the exception of the Hebrews and perhaps the Assyrians, the ancient cultures of the Mediterranean did not restrain the homosexual instincts of their people.

In the past, the Far East also tolerated homosexuality and bisexuality. From ancient to modern times same-sex behavior has been acceptable in China and Japan. In China, where male brothels were common, boys were trained for prostitution by their parents. In Japan during the feudal period, male homosexual love was considered more "manly" than heterosexual love. Male geishas in teahouses were prevalent until the middle of the nineteenth century and still existed until they were suppressed at the end of World War II by the American occupation forces. Today homosexuality and bisexuality in both Japan and China remain more hidden. . . .

In some cultures homosexuality is identified with sex-role stereotyping. Among the Koniag of Alaska, the Largo of East Africa, the Tanala of Madagascar, and the Chukchee of Siberia, some males are raised from early childhood to perform female tasks and to dress as females. Known as the "berdache," such a male often becomes the "wife" of an important man in the community and lives with him, but the berdache may have heterosexual affairs with a mistress and father children. The berdache often enjoys a considerable amount of social prestige and assumes a position of power in the community. He usually becomes a shaman, a kind of priest, medicine man or religious figure, who is believed to possess supernatural powers which may be transmitted by sexual relations.

An example of socially expected and approved bisexuality involving a large segment of the male population is found among the Siwans of Africa. Both married and unmarried men are expected to have bisexual affairs and those males who do not engage in same-sex behavior are considered odd. In a number of cultures, such as the Keraki of New Guinea and the Kiwai, homosexual behavior is sanctioned as part of male puberty rites. In a detailed study of cultural data from 76 societies, 64% of the cultures surveyed approved of some form of homosexual behavior and considered it normal and socially acceptable for at least some members of the community.

So it seems to be clear from historical and anthropological data that homosexuality is natural if "natural" is defined to be existence over time and place. But there are other ways to consider the meaning of the word "natural."

PSYCHOLOGY

A second approach involves what is psychologically instinctive. From a psychological perspective an action is considered natural if it originates from an impulse or drive; an involuntary want or need coming from within an organism is natural to that organism. If such an instinctive urge is not impeded, an individual will seek to satisfy the inclination.

A substantial minority of human beings have an instinctive tendency to fulfill same-sex desires. The sex drive itself is innate and instinctive. In most people, this sex drive is directed primarily toward the same gender; for still others, their sexual attractions are equally strong in intensity and frequency toward both genders. As a conservative estimate, approximately 7% of women and 15% of men are strictly bisexual or predominantly or exclusively homosexual in orientation and behavior.

Until the last decade or so, thousands of lesbian and gay persons sought out psychiatrists and other therapists to help them to change their same-sex feelings. Unfortunately, thousands of these individuals wasted their time and money as the experts now believe that a change in orientation, i.e., in desire and attraction, is not possible.

The helping professions have failed in their long attempt to reverse sexual behavior in homosexual people. For example, Masters and Johnson presented only one actual case of reversion or conversion to hetersexual functioning among 54 male subjects, and this individual was identified as bisexual at the outset. In another study of 106 homosexual men, only 29 became exclusively heterosexual in behavior and this change was not known to have lasted beyond two years. More than half of these men were initially bisexual and most of the subjects required 350 or more hours of therapy. Thus, even with a high degree of motivation, an expenditure of much time and money, and an existing predisposition to bisexuality, the possibility of actually altering behavior is extremely low, costly, time consuming and short lived.

These reports concern alteration of sexual behavior. There is not known documentation of permanent alteration of same-sex feelings, attractions and desires. If it is virtually impossible to modify a homosexual orientation, then these same-sex feelings must be very deeply ingrained in the person's psychological makeup.

73

5. ARE HOMOSEXUAL RELATIONS NORMAL AND NATURAL?

The psychologist Frank A. Beach once claimed, "Various social goals and ethical laws are violated by the homosexual individual [and, we may add, the bisexual one], but to describe [such] behavior as 'unnatural' is to depart from strict accuracy." While same-sex genital behavior may indeed be the natural psychological result of same-sex love and attractions, strong social sanctions imposed in many cultures have frequently inhibited such innate responses to same-sex stimuli and have conditioned people to respond to heterosexual stimuli. Despite strong social taboos, countless individuals persist in expressing these desires and feelings of love for their own gender. If, as some would claim, only heterosexuality is psychologically natural, i.e., instinctively imprinted within an individual's personality structure, how can heterosexuality be obliterated or obscured in millions and millions of people? If, then, "natural" is defined as that which is instinctive and freely acted on without restraint, same-sex feelings and attractions do indeed seem to be quite natural for a significant proportion of the human population.

BIOLOGY

A third definition of natural is illustrated in such phrases as "laws of nature," "naturalist," and "natural history." What is congruent or consistent with the "laws of nature" is deemed natural. This approach to nature involves a study of non-living phenomena, plants and animals. From this perspective, a given characteristic is "natural" for human beings if it is in accordance with their animal heritage.

What is needed is an application of animal data to human behavior. In research on the sexual behavior of species below the human, homosexual activity appears frequently in infrahuman primates, such as apes, monkeys and baboons especially as they approach adulthood, although this may not be exclusive in many cases. Only recently have scientific studies been conducted to observe same-sex behavior among sub-primate mammals. These studies indicate that homosexual behavior appears in lower mammals, frequently among domestic stock such as sheep, cattle, horses, pigs and rabbits.

There is some preliminary evidence that aquatic species many have a higher psychological status than such terrestrial animals as dogs, cats, cows, and horses, and that they may consequently form stronger relational attachments. One story is related about two male porpoises who formed a very close attachment with each other after several months. One of the porpoises was removed from the tank and then returned after a three week separation. Their reunion was described as follows:

"No doubt could exist that the two recognized each other, and for several hours they swam side by side rushing frenziedly through the water, and on several occasions they leaped completely out of the water. For several days, the two males were inseparable and neither paid any attention to the female."

Examples of homosexuality have been found even among the nonmammalian species. Any two male or female pigeons will engage in same-sex behavior when placed together. Phylogenetic data indicate that same-sex behavior becomes both more common and more complex as one ascends the evolutionary scale. Innate homosexual behavioral patterns are not exclusively human phenomena but are definitely consonant with the human's mammalian background. As such, they are natural in the biological sense.

THEOLOGY

A fourth meaning for the term "natural" will often be given by religious persons, but primarily in discussions about sexuality. Traditional religious arguments maintain that there are necessary links between marriage and sexual intercourse and between intercourse and biological generation. The classic explanation hinges on the Stoic exultation of natural law. Between the fifteenth and nineteenth centuries most theologians writing on sexuality divided sexual sins into two categories: those in accordance with nature (i.e., open to procreation) and those contrary to nature (i.e., inhibiting procreation). Thus anal and oral intercourse, masturbation, bestiality, coitus interruptus, and intercourse during pregnancy were considered unnatural; adultery, fornication, and rape were considered sinful but natural.

Religious adherents would refer to biology, often in contradictory ways to substantiate their arguments. At times the term natural was equated with animal behavior when, for example, Thomas Aquinas considered contraception "against nature, for even beasts look for offspring." Yet, at other times, nature was described as what was different from animals, when, for example, the position in human intercourse of the woman beneath the man was thought to be natural because any other position was comparable to "brute animals." Like the early Church Fathers, the scholastic theologians selectively chose their analogies of what was natural in order to reinforce views already held.

Frequently the theological argument is accompanied by explanations regarding the physiological purpose or function of bodily parts. A functional argument goes something like this: God intends that the necessary purpose of the sexual organs is reproduction. Since homosexual activity cannot result in procreation, such acts are contrary to God's intent and are thus unnatural.

The hidden assumption of human ability to know divine intent with certitude can certainly be challenged. How can humans know God's will with moral certainty and without reference to reason and logic? When appeals are made to divine revelation, who decides and interprets revelation?

An obvious function of the genital organs is reproduction. But to maintain that a particular bodily organ serves only one purpose or must serve a certain specified purpose seems provincial at best. In the human evolutionary development, hands serve as a means of grasping, not of walking. Yet who would object that hands be used in conveying greetings or other messages with emotional content because such actions are contrary to the nature of hands? Would anyone deny that the mouth, whose primary function is food ingestion, has another and socially more aesthetic function of verbal communication?

If other parts of the body may serve multiple purposes, why is it that the sexual parts may not? To claim, as some have, that the sexual parts are not morally equal to other parts of the body and are of special value because they involve the generation of life betrays a lack of appreciation for other bodily parts and systems, all of which likewise contribute to life. Placing a hierarchy of value on bodily parts leads to an idolatry or sacralization of some parts. Would proponents of a theology which maintains that there is a single or special purpose of sexual parts refuse to admit that another function of the penis is demonstrated in the biological process of elimination of urine?

Many sexual moralists today acknowl-

75

edge more than one purpose of human intercourse. They differentiate between the reproductive and unitive functions of sexual intercourse and maintain that the two functions need not be present simultaneously in every genital act in order to render the action ethically responsible. In fact, they point out that concern about the modern world's population explosion and about a reasonable care and stewardship of the earth's resources challenge traditional notions of the meaning of sexuality. They thus liberate God from being controlled by a rigid and predetermined view of reality.

A similar theological case is often made by appealing to the structure of the human body: God intends heterosexuality because the male and female sexual parts "fit." As the vagina is an obvious receptacle for the penis, any use of the male sexual organ other than for the deposit of semen in the vagina is believed to be unnatural. An examination of the male and female bodies in which the parts manifestly "fit" shows the truth to be self-evident. Although axioms require no demonstration, such reasoning illustrates an argument by limitation or restriction. The fact that one form of linkage is obvious and rather common does not render alternative ways "unnatural." Because human genitalia fit together in one way does not preclude other ways of sexual union.

Underlying these philosophical and theological approaches is a definition of nature as that which makes an object what it essentially or actually is or what God intends it to be. The key question, of course, is "What is the divine purpose?" Do such arguments merely interpret human preference and prejudice as God's will?

Along with divine intent, one must also examine human motives to determine whether insistence on the unnaturalness of homosexuality, or even other sexual acts, is merely a reflection of an unconscious desire to legitimate the existing social order. Unfortunately, the expression of same-sex feelings and desires is often perceived as some kind of threat to the heterosexual structure. Unexamined cultural assumptions influence human perceptions and judgments; what is conveniently regarded as natural is often an expression of a deep-seated cultural bias. Appeals to God's intent are at least questionable and can lead to such absurd deductions as "If God wanted human beings to fly, God would have given them wings. Therefore, the airplane is unnatural." While the faith of those who hold these positions cannot be questioned, their interpretation of human sexuality and divine intent regarding sexual expression certainly can and should be.

CONTEMPORARY VIEWS

A current understanding of nature is one which is dynamic and constantly in flux. Aristotle taught that fire by its nature moved away from the center of the universe. When science demonstrated the Copernican theory in which the earth was no longer viewed as the central planetary body, the Aristotelian concept of the nature of fire was revised. Similarly, the ancient Greeks believed that every earthly object was composed of earth, air, water, or fire. But a deeper understanding of physics and chemistry demanded a more sophisticated explanation of the nature of any object in the universe. As species of living objects themselves are gradually being transformed by evolution, the human perception of such objects' nature is constantly adapting and in need of revision. Even slight variations in successive generations of a species influence the constantly developing human understanding of nature.

Unless rigid or static, a construct of human nature which was popular 500 years before the Christian era or 1300 years after is not identical to a contemporary perception of human nature which can incorporate scientific advancement and current data from the behavioral sciences. Accurate knowledge regarding human reproduction was not discovered until after 1875. Basing their philosophical and theological arguments in the context of the biology of their day, religious leaders of the past cannot be faulted for an understandably limited analysis of human sexuality. But with the quantum leaps that have been achieved in biology, psychology and sociology, the twentieth century mind must subject traditional religious arguments about nature to more thorough and critical analyses. Today's personalist interpretation of human nature is not bound by a static view reminiscent of Freud's "biology is destiny" but rather is struggling to free itself from biological imperatives.

CONCLUSION

When all the rational debate is over concerning what is natural and what is unnatural about human sexuality, what many people, perhaps subconsciously, mean is that same-sex attraction is not experienced by the majority of people. This may indeed be the case since Kinsey's figures indicate that approximately 72% of females and 76% of males are exclusively heterosexual in feelings and behaviors; i.e., they experience not even minimal same-sex attractions or fantasies. These percentages may be somewhat higher than actual fact since they were computed almost 40 years ago when people were less willing to acknowledge their same-sex feelings.

If North American society tolerated a gay or lesbian lifestyle, I believe that it would be highly likely that the incidence of bisexuality and homosexuality would become more visible. This would not result from supposed mass conversions of confirmed heterosexual individuals to homosexuality; rather, people would feel freer to express the homosexual or bisexual feelings they already have. Since there is evidence that in societies that condone bisexual and homosexual behavior a heterosexual lifestyle is still predominant, one can reasonably conclude that not everyone would engage in predominantly homosexual behavior.

The majority can, and often does, reveal its prejudice and intolerance for diversity. Because the majority of individuals feel, react or believe one way, must all persons do so? As long as the minority group does not harm or infringe on the majority lifestyle, the two should be able to coexist peacefully. The sociologist Becker who has written considerably about the societal outsider states, "Social groups create deviance by making the rules whose infraction constitutes deviance, and by applying those rules to particular people and labelling them as outsiders."

I harbor a cherished hope that all peoples in the human family may live together as true brothers and sisters. Only when the dominant majority in each culture accords proper respect for the rights and dignity of the racial, ethnic, sexual, economic and religious minorities in its midst can we hope to have a truly free and just society. Only when our unspoken fears and insecurities are recognized and our unnamed ignorance and biases erased, can we work collaboratively in realizing the fullness of the exciting human project upon the earth.

NO   Robert Gordis

HOMOSEXUALITY IS NOT ON A PAR WITH HETEROSEXUAL RELATIONS

Nowhere else is the confrontation between the classical religious tradition and emerging contemporary attitudes sharper than with regard to homosexuality. Biblical law and biblical life are completely at one in condemning the practice. The sexual codes in the Torah describe male homosexuality as an "abomination" punishable with death like other major infractions of the moral code, such as incest and sexual contact with animals (Lev. 18:22; 20:13).

The practice is clearly regarded as worse than rape, as is evident from an incident narrated in Chapter 19 of Genesis. Two strangers, who are actually angels sent by the Lord to survey the sinful city of Sodom, are given hospitality by Lot, Abraham's nephew. When the townsmen hear of the strangers in their midst, they besiege Lot's house and demand that he turn the wayfarers over to them for homosexual abuse. Horrified at this breach of the ancient custom of hospitality, Lot offers instead to send out his two virgin daughters to the mob to do with as they wish. When the mob refuses the offer and tries to storm the door of Lot's house, it becomes clear that the city is beyond hope, and its destruction is decreed by God.

A similar tragic incident, going back to an early, lawless period shortly after the conquest of the land, is reported in Chapter 19 of the Book of Judges. A traveler passing through the town of Gibeah in Benjamin is denied hospitality by the townspeople. Only one old man gives lodging and food to the stranger, his concubine, and his animals. When the Benjaminites learn that the stranger is being housed among them, they gather and demand that he be handed over to them for sexual purposes. The host remonstrates with them in vain, offering to turn over his daughter and his guest's concubine to satisfy their lust. When the mob does not desist, the guest takes his concubine and pushes her out of doors. They rape her and abuse her all night and leave her lifeless body on the threshold. The book of Judges goes on to narrate the punishment visited upon the Benjaminites, leading to the virtual extinction of that tribe from the household of Israel.

There are many instances where rabbinic law has modified biblical attitudes in the direction of greater leniency, but this is not true of homosexuality. Here the attitude remains strongly negative, though the practice receives relatively little attention in the Talmud, probably because the rabbis believed that "Jews are not suspected of committing homosexuality and buggery."

This persistent feeling of revulsion toward homosexuality was nourished by a variety of historical causes. During the biblical period, the fertility cults that were widespread throughout the Middle East included intercourse with sacred male prostitutes at the pagan temples. From the Canaanites these practices, along with idolatry in general, penetrated into the religious practices of the Hebrews during the early days of the Davidic kingdom. These functionaries were finally banished from the precincts of the Temple, but only after repeated and determined efforts by several Judean kings, Asa, Jehoshaphat, and Josiah.

During the Greco-Roman era and beyond, the opposition to homosexuality by Jewish rabbinic leadership was a reaction to its widespread presence in the ancient world, where it was furthered and encouraged by pagan society and religion. Homosexual liaisons played a significant role in the social and cultural life of the ancient Greeks and Romans. Indirect evidence of the strong hold that homosexuality had on the Greco-Roman world is to be found in Paul's Epistle to the Romans. In the strongest of terms he castigates homosexuality as "dishonorable" and "unnatural." That he places homosexuality at the head of a list of offenses would suggest that the practice was widespread. It is also noteworthy that he first levels his attack against the women and only then turns to the men as "likewise" engaging in these "shameless acts." (1:26, 27)

This negative attitude toward homosexuality has been maintained by Jewish tradition to the present time. It regards homosexuals as flouting the will of the Creator, who fashioned men and women with different anatomical endowments and with correspondingly distinct roles to play in the sexual process.

All these objections to homosexuality in Judaism were intensified in Christianity because of several additional factors. Most of the converts to the early Christian Church were former pagans who had been exposed to the presence of homosexual practices in their previous environment. Paul, as well as the Church after him, therefore felt it incumbent to attack the practice with all the power at his command. Moreover, as we have seen, classical Christianity was basically unhappy with the sexual component of human nature in general. It had to concede that sexual contact was legitimate, first because the instinct cannot be successfully suppressed by most men and women and, second, because it is essential for procreation. Since this last factor is obviously lacking in homosexual activity, there is no justification for yielding to "unnatural lust."

In sum, both Judaism and Christianity, in spite of differences in their approach to sex, have regarded homosexuality as a violation of God's will and a perversion of nature.

The subsequent weakening of religion and the growth of secularism in the Western world did little to reduce the sense of hostility toward homosexuality. The new emphasis on the cultivation of the body and the development of athletics in the modern period underscored the goal that men should be men. Nowhere is masculinity revealed more unmistakably than in sexual potency. Psychoanalytic theory, particularly in its classical Freudian formulation, saw male and female sexuality as the fundamental element in the human personality, which, when diverted from "normal" channels, becomes the source of psychological and physical trauma. In this respect as well, homosexuality ran counter to the values of the age. As a result of all these factors, as well as vestiges of the religious approach, homosexuality continued to engender feelings of revulsion going beyond the bonds of rational response.

Perhaps the most sensational manifestation of this reaction came at the end of the nineteenth century. In 1895, the brilliant and gifted English dramatist and poet Oscar Wilde was prosecuted by the Crown for having homosexual relations with Lord Alfred Douglas. Wilde was convicted, imprisoned for two years, and emerged from this experience a man physically broken and creatively ruined.

Wilde is by no means the only example of talent or genius to be found among homosexuals. More or less plausibly, many distinguished figures of the past and the present have been described as homosexuals. It is likely that lesbianism is as common as male homosexuality, but it is felt to be less offensive because its manifestations seem less blatant.

The hostility of society to homosexuals is reflected in the statute books. Homosexual behavior is treated as a crime in China and the Soviet Union; in the United States, homosexual soliciting is a criminal act. To be sure, such laws have often not been enforced in this country, particularly in the recent past.

By and large, the penalties accorded to homosexuals have been social and economic rather than legal. Homosexuals have been driven underground and have had to suffer all the psychological traumas associated with a closet existence. They have been forced to deny their desires and to pretend to interests and feelings not their own. Always there is the human propensity to cruelty, of which the twentieth century has made us painfully aware. Add to it the negative attitude toward homosexuals in the religious tradition and in secular law and you have a moral base for flagrant discrimination and hostility toward homosexuals in housing and employment.

The alleged effeminacy in dress and demeanor of homosexuals has been the butt of ridicule and scorn in public and in private, on the printed page, the radio, television, the screen, and the stage. This in spite of the alleged high percentage of homosexuals in the artistic, literary, and entertainment worlds.

Only within the past two decades has the public attitude begun to change. The general weakening of traditional religion has diminished the influence of biblical and post-biblical teaching on the subject. In addition, sexual experience without regard to procreation has increasingly been accepted and glorified as a good in itself, if not as the *summum bonum* of existence. Hence, homosexuality has lost some of the horror it conjured up in earlier generations. Above all, in our age, the drive for new and exciting experiences, however untried and even dangerous they may be, has led to new patterns of sexual conduct, like sexual communes and wife-swapping, not to speak of various forms of perversion. Advocates of homosexuality have, therefore, felt free to argue that they are simply practicing an equally legitimate life style, a variant pattern to the dominant heterosexuality of our culture. Some have maintained that 10 percent of the population are homosexual, a figure that can neither be demonstrated nor disproved.

Substantial success has already crowned the efforts of the various organizations in the gay liberation movement to remove [discrimination] in employment and housing from homosexuals, in the United States. In France, Italy, Sweden, Denmark, Switzerland, Mexico, and Uruguay, the practice has long been decriminalized. Great Britain took the same step in 1967 and Canada in 1969.

What approach toward homosexuality should modern religion sanction and modern society adopt? No excuse can or should be offered for the cruelty that traditional attitudes toward the practice have engendered in the past. Nevertheless, the classical viewpoint of Judaism and Christianity, that homosexual conduct is "unnatural," cannot be dismissed out of hand.

Here a brief theological digression is called for. That the goal of the universe and, by that token, the purpose of existence are veiled from man has been the conviction of thinkers in every age. Koheleth in the Bible and the medieval philosopher Maimonides are at one with the Hasidic teacher Rabbi Bunam of Pshysha, who found his beloved disciple Enoch in tears. The rabbi asked him, "Why are you weeping?" and Enoch answered, "Am I not a creature of this world, and am I not made with eyes and heart and all limbs, and yet I do not know for what purpose I was created and what good I am in the world." "Fool!" said Rabbi Bunam. "I also go around thus."

Nevertheless, we may perhaps catch a slight glimpse of the purpose of the Creator, or, if secular terms be preferred, the direction and goal of the life process in the universe. The lowest creatures in the evolutionary ladder, the single-cell organisms, multiply by fission, the splitting of the cell into two equal parts. As a result, each of the two new beings possesses exactly the same attributes as the parent, no more, no less, no change. Only with the emergence of multicellular organisms does bisexuality appear on the evolutionary ladder. Fission is now replaced by bisexual reproduction, which becomes the universal pattern. This fundamental change seems to indicate that the Author of life has intended the life process to be not a perpetually static repetition of the old but a dynamic adventure, with new combinations of attributes constantly emerging through the interaction of a male and a female producing a new organism different from both its parents. It therefore follows that, in purely secular biological terms, homosexuality is an aberration from the norm, a violation of the law of nature.

It may be objected that since man is not merely a creature of nature and is free to modify his environment and perhaps even his heredity, what is natural is not the sole touchstone of what is right for man. There is, however, good reason for believing that homosexuality is a violation not only of nature but of human nature as well. No attribute is more characteristic of humanity than the gift of speech. Language is probably the greatest intellectual achievement of primitive man. Imbedded in the structure of all languages is gender, a recognition of bisexuality, which, by extension, is applied to every object in the real world. Gender remains basic to language and to thought for the most sophisticated of moderns.

For later stages of human development, it may be noted that no society has made homosexuality its basic or even its preferred pattern of sexual conduct. This is true even of predatory groups that could have replenished their ranks through captives taken in war.

Transposed into theological language, heterosexuality is the will of God. It therefore follows that homosexuality is a violation of His will, for which the traditional term is "sin." The concept of sin in general may seem outmoded to modern ears and, in any event, too harsh a term to apply to homosexuality. But the etymology of the Hebrew word *het,* like its Greek counterpart, *hamartia,* is derived from marksmanship and means "missing the mark," as has already been noted. Sin means a turning aside from the right path that can and should be followed. Consequently the Hebrew's *teshubbah,* generally translated as "repentance," means "returning" to the right road.

Judgments and attitudes aside, what are the facts about homosexuality? In spite of the vast interest in the phenomenon, very little is really known about its origin and nature or any possible treatment. Modern psychologists may be correct in believing that latent homosexual tendencies are to be found in most people. If this is true, it would seem that homosexual patterns of behavior become dominant for some men and women because they are stimulated by personal contact with homosexuals. If, therefore, homosexuality is culturally induced, it would be a flagrant example of a conscious and often conscienceless distortion of normal human nature.

On the other hand, homosexuality may be the product of a genetic disturbance. In this case, it must be regarded as a biological abnormality. Whether the practice is the result of heredity or of environment, or of both, intensive research is needed to discover the etiology of homosexuality and then to search for a remedy, or at least for methods of treatment.

For centuries, society, abetted by religion, has been guilty of condemning as a sin and punishing as a crime what should have been recognized as an illness. In fact, physical illness in general was regarded as a Divine visitation, a punishment for sins for which the sufferer himself was responsible. This attitude is not altogether dead today. Recently, the president of a mammoth bank in New York demonstrated that he is obviously afflicted with massive spiritual myopia. He declared that physical illness is a crime against society committed by those who are ill, and that therefore society has no obligation to provide medical care and other social services to the sick poor.

If homosexuality is an abnormality or an illness, as has been maintained, a parallel to our problem in several respects may be found in alcoholism. So long as the alcoholic was regarded as an incorrigible sinner, little progress was made in curing this major malady. It is only in our day, when alcoholism is being recognized as a disease, probably genetic in origin though socially stimulated, that genuine progress has begun to be made overcoming it.

The analogy is helpful in another respect as well. Experts are agreed that the will to recover, as expressed in total abstinence, which is encouraged by such programs as Alcoholics Anonymous, plays an indispensable role in the treatment of alcohol addiction. It is also known that only a fraction of all alcoholics, somewhere between one third and one half of all patients who undergo treatment, recover fully or substantially.

At the present level of our knowledge, the percentage of homosexuals who can be "rehabilitated" is almost surely lower than that of alcoholics. To a substantial degree, this is due to the varying attitudes of contemporary society toward two phenomena. While alcoholism is universally recognized as a liability, homosexuality is often defended as a normal life style, a legitimate alternate pattern to heterosexuality. The gay liberation movement has vigorously opposed the older traditional view of homosexuality as a sin. It is not more kindly disposed to the more modern concept of homosexuality as an illness. It uses every available means to propagate the idea that homosexuality is an entirely proper life style.

Nevertheless, if we are not to fall prey to the old prejudice or to succumb to the new fashion, we must insist that homosexuality is not normal. To the extent that men and women cannot control their homosexual desires, they are suffering from an illness like any other physical disability. To the degree that they can hold the impulse in rein and fail to do so, they are committing a sin, a violation of the will of God or, in secular terms, an aberration from the norm.

However, a basic caution is in order. Ignorant as we are of the etiology of the disorder, we are in no position to determine to which category a given act belongs. Hence, homosexual activity, when carried on by adults in private and violating no one's wishes and desires, should be decriminalized on the statute books. The practice belongs to the rabbinic category of an act that is "free from legal punishment (by human agency), but forbidden." The homosexual in contemporary society has a just claim to be free from legal penalties and social disabilities.

Yet there are some critical areas where blanket removal of all restrictions against homosexuals may be unwise. Such a decision should be reached without panic or prejudice, on the basis of a careful investigation of all the relevant factors. Sensing the widespread erosion of conventional moral standards everywhere, homosexual groups are pressing for much more than freedom from discrimination and harassment. They are demanding that homosexuality be recognized as a legitimate and normal alternative to heterosexuality.

Some Christian theologians, troubled by the tragic and undeniable fact that Western society has been grievously lacking in compassion for homosexuals, have attempted to give a Christian justification for homosexuality. One Catholic writer explains away the biblical condemnations of homosexual practices as "Old Testament legalism." A Protestant theologian takes his point of departure from the Christian doctrine that salvation is directed to all mankind, so that all human beings are equally sinful in the eyes of God. He, therefore, leaps to the non sequitur that "no human condition or life style is intrinsically *justified* or righteous—neither heterosexuality nor homosexuality, closed nor open marriage, celibacy nor profligacy." He proceeds to express doubts as to whether the family centerdness of contemporary Christianity can be justified theologically, since both Jesus and Paul were suspicious of family ties! He concludes that there are three life styles open to men and women intrinsically equal in moral validity: marriage, celibacy, and homosexuality.

The lengths to which sympathetic souls may be led are evident in the secular sphere as well. In fact, like the generous Irishman who was asked, "Isn't one man as good as another?" and answered, "Sure, and a whole lot better, too," some advocates have argued that homosexuality is not merely as good as heterosexuality but better, since it avoids the possibility of increasing the population! The same logic would lead to the conclusion that sterility is healthier and more beneficial than fecundity.

It is perhaps a sign of the times that a recent radio broadcast referred to a sadomasochist liberation movement, which calls itself the Til Eulenspiegel Society. This group, whose size was not indicated, demands "equal rights" for the practice of sexual perversion, including such forms as flagellation and sodomy, which, they insist, are also legitimate alternatives.

Having mastered the modern art of lobbying, homosexuals carried on a campaign among the members of the American Psychological Association and, in 1974, succeeded in having homosexuality removed from the list of abnormal patterns of behavior. An effort is being made in some quarters to reverse the ruling of the American Psychological Association. The argument advanced by gay liberation groups is that homosexuals are basically healthy, well-adjusted individuals who do not seek medical or psychiatric treatment because they do not need it. Spokesmen for homosexuality, aware of the widespread frustration and unhappiness with conventional marriages, have urged the claim. In a growing number of cases, homosexuals have asked the clergy to officiate at homosexual "marriages." No comparative study is available of either the permanence of homosexual unions or of the quality of life of homosexual couples.

On the other hand, testimony has been advanced to show that the self-acceptance and satisfaction with life expressed by many homosexuals is often only a facade for resignation and despair, all the more hopeless because it cannot find channels of expression. In their youth, it has been maintained, homosexuals have suffered from rejection and unhappiness, which are integral to their condition. In adult life, they continue to experience conflict, anguish, and pain which they deny even to themselves. It has also been argued that the growing militant assertion of "gay pride," coupled with the A.P.A. declaration that homosexuality is normal human behavior on the one hand and the generally negative attitude of society on the other, has intensified their unhappiness. That there is so much heat and so little light demonstrates only how slight is the authentic scientific knowledge available on this important issue. . . .

As is so frequently the case, truth and justice in this troubled area lie, not with the extremes, but with the center position. We can no longer accept the traditional religious reaction to homosexuality as a horror and an abomination. On the other hand, the fashionable doctrine being propagated in our time—that it is an alternate life style of equal value and legitimacy—must be decisively rejected. Homosexuality is an abnormality, an illness which, like any other, varies in intensity with different individuals. Until more efficacious means are discovered for dealing with their problem, homosexuals deserve the same inalienable rights as do all their fellow human beings—freedom from harassment and discrimination before the law and in society.

There can be no question that homosexuals are entitled to more than justice before the law. It is not enough merely to remove the various kinds of legal disability and overt hostility to which they have long been subjected. Whatever evaluation is placed upon their condition, be it moral, medical, or psychological, they are human beings, our brothers and sisters, who deserve compassion and love from their fellow men and, above all, from their brothers in kinship and in faith.

POSTSCRIPT

ARE HOMOSEXUAL AND BISEXUAL RELATIONS NATURAL AND NORMAL?

As debatable as this issue will continue to be in the foreseeable future, an interesting convergence of evidence is developing. Recent research is challenging long-held psychoanalytic beliefs that dominant, overprotecting mothers and ineffectual fathers are primary "causes" of male homosexuality. The new evidence rather strongly suggests that a substantial number of male homosexuals are born with an indifference to rough-and-tumble play and other typical boyhood interests. This indifference alienates and isolates them from their male peers and often from their fathers as well. Dr. Richard Green believes that this lack of acceptance and love from the father and male peers leads such boys to seek love from men later in life. Dr. Bell of the Kinsey Institute sees this early gender disconformity, the sense of being different from other boys, as the trigger that leads to romantic and erotic attraction to other males. But behind this socialization pattern appears to be the development of an inborn receptivity or tendency due to genetic, hormonal, or a combination of these two factors before birth. If research continues to confirm this explanation, what will its impact be on the argument?

To what extent are the contrasting views of Gramick and Gordis the outcome of two distinct world views? Gramick focuses on the phenomenon of human sexual orientations, on what has been and is in human experience. Gordis focuses on his interpretation of what the Jewish and Christian scriptures says should be, although this perspective leaves no room for the ongoing, developing human experiences of our sexual orientations and the ever-changing social and cultural environment in which we experience our sexuality. Is dialogue possible between these two perspectives? See the bibliography for further readings on this subject.

ISSUE 6

SHOULD OUR SOCIETY LEGALLY RECOGNIZE A VARIETY OF ADULT LIFESTYLES?

YES: Rabbi Rami Shapiro and Robert T. Francoeur, from the *Journal of Sex Education and Therapy,* 1(5): 17-20, with a 1987 update

NO: William Stackhouse, from an essay written for this volume.

ISSUE SUMMARY

YES: Rabbi Rami Shapiro and Robert T. Francoeur, a Catholic priest, propose that the time has come for our society and religious institutions to acknowledge the growing pluralism in adult relationships and family structure.
NO: William Stackhouse, a consultant for the Human Sexuality Program of the United Church [Congregationalists] Board for Homeland Ministries, foresees some real obstacles with this proposal. In his view, the closer an alternate lifestyle is to the traditional model, the easier it will be for the religious and civil authorities to accept it.

Despite claims that the sexual revolution of the 1960s and 1970s is behind us and that we are returning to the morality and traditional values and relationships of an earlier and more stable era, there is a disquieting issue that needs to be addressed. While there is renewed emphasis on commitment and responsibility in our intimate relations, repeated surveys of adult relationships suggest that we really are not returning to "the good old days."

We are, in fact, a very pluralistic society. We may prefer to ignore this reality, but figures from the US Census Bureau and Department of Labor confirm the growing pluralism of households and adult relationships in this country. The traditional nuclear family with a working father, domestic wife and two children probably accounts for around ten percent of American families. Incorporate in this ten percent the 40 to 60 percent figures for husbands and wives who have had extramarital sexual relations, and the mythical traditional American marriage is down to about five percent. The numbers of divorces and second marriages have been increasing for years, so that reconstituted families and serial polygamy are fast becoming the most common form of American marriage and family. More than one-fourth of American families with children—more than 60 percent of those that are black—are headed by a single parent. That is a rise from 12.9 percent in 1970 to 26.3 percent in 1985. The size of the average American household has dropped from 2.79 in 1980 to 2.67 in 1985. One quarter of all households are now single-person households. The median age for marriage is now 23.1 for women and 25.7 for men, higher than it has been in decades. The percentage of never-marrieds continues to rise while one-third of all unmarried women have lived with a man. Four percent of all couples, 2,220,000 Americans, share a household with an unrelated adult. This is four times the incidence in 1970. The annual increase in the 1980s may only be half the 11 percent annual increase of the 1970s, but it is still rising despite the decreasing number of young adults.

We have no statistics on gay and lesbian households or families, but their number is certainly rising and becoming more visible in the wake of the gay rights movement.

The obvious message of these data is a growing pluralism in the relationships and family styles of Americans. One basic questions prompted by this changing reality centers on whether our society should ignore this reality and continue to approve only traditional monogamy with divorce and remarriage allowed as a safety valve, or whether we should adapt, in a pragmatic way, and give some civil and religious recognition to alternate lifestyles.

YES

Rabbi Rami Shapiro
and Robert T. Francoeur

WE SHOULD RECOGNIZE
CURRENT ALTERNATIVES
TO TRADITIONAL MONOGAMY

A FORETHOUGHT . . . in three contrasts . . .

More and more marriage is looked upon as a COVENANT, less as a CONTRACT. A covenant is expansive, all embracing. A contract is restrictive, limiting.

P.F. Palmer writes: "Contracts deal with things, covenants with people. Contracts are best understood by lawyers, covenants are appreciated by poets."

"Contracts are made by children who know the value of a penny. Covenants can be made only by adults who are mentally, emotionally, spiritually MATURE." A.J. Nimeth in *Of Course, I Love You: On Marriage* (1973:11)

In response to radical socioeconomic changes in America, the once monolithic pattern of middle class marriage and family has painfully fragmented into a wide pluralism of values, expectations and relationships. Pressed by socioeconomic liberation of women, effective contraceptives, the recent leisure revolution, increasing lifespans and open discussion in the mass media, a majority of middle class Americans have rejected the rigid sex roles of patriarchal sexually exclusive lifelong monogamy to meet their intimacy needs in more functional patterns of neogamy, to use Paula Dressel's term for "new forms of intimate bonding."

Every society, whether sexually permissive or restrictive, finds it useful and even necessary to regulate and structure its social relationships, especially sexual relations, in some way for the common good.

No human society condones promiscuous or indiscriminate mating. Every culture contains regulations that direct and restrict the individual's selection of a sexual partner or partners. Every society has its own concepts as to the number and nature of permissible partnerships that may be formed (Ford and Beach, 1951:106).

Mateships, based on economic as well as sexual cooperation are commonly regularized by civil and/or religious rites. Liaisons, being more exclusively sexual in character and less stable, are not as commonly recognized with rituals.

From, "Recognition of Alternatives to Traditional Monogamy in New Religious and Civil Rituals," by Robert Francouer and Rami Shapiro, *Journal of Sex Education and Therapy*, 1(5):17-20 with a 1987 update. Copyright © 1979 the American Association of Sex Educators, Counselors and Therapists, Washington, DC. Reprinted by permission.

Our hypothesis here is that our society has reached a level of maturity in its transition where the need for civil and religious recognition of individuals in new relational and familial patterns is now being acknowledged both civilly and religiously.

Our purpose is to document and highlight a basic Judaeo-Christian tradition, the covenanting of relationships, as a vital modality in this recognition. Revitalizing the covenanting tradition in our relationships can provide us with cultural, religious, emotional and psychological support and continuity during this transition. Revitalizing the covenanting tradition can facilitate the evolution of new religious rites suited to the diversity of neogamy. It can encourage a similar civil recognition, reducing current discrimination in housing, employment and taxation for persons in innovative lifestyles.

BASIC COVENANTS IN THE JUDAEOCHRISTIAN TRADITION

Brueggemann claims that "covenanting is the primary human activity," the source of social and personal vitality. All communities, he claims, are rooted in "covenant-making, covenant-keeping, covenant-breaking and covenant-renewing" (1977: 19). This is most evident in Judaism, much less evident in Protestantism, and very subdued in Catholicism. At the same time, Christian theologians have explored much more than rabbis the covenant tradition as a valid framework within which new rituals can emerge to accommodate and structure the growing variety of today's lifestyles and relationships.

Brith, or covenant, is a basic value in all Jewish life and community, from the ongoing creation relationship of [G-d] and His people, to tribal, cross-generational, sibling, parent-child, husband-wife, and household relationships.

The marriage covenant and its legalization in the *ketubah* or Jewish wedding contract, is an important form of brith. The *ketubah* is a necessary prerequisite to a Jewish marriage. It stipulates the conditions of the marriage, even down to its possible dissolution. In the past it has focused primarily, even exclusively on monetary conditions because other questions and factors of lifestyle were too well established and uniform in the community to warrant repetition. Today, however, the roles of spouses are open to question, doubt, and experimentation. Tradition has it that nothing is too sacred or too profane to include in a *ketubah.*

The *ketubah* is a marital contract. Whether one defines marriage as two individuals, more than two, or even a merger of entire families into a single covenant, once entered into, the parties are legally and morally bound to uphold their end of the bargain. A covenant well thought out and carefully prepared in writing could provide the basis for a far more steady marriage than the vague feeling, unreal romanticism and unarticulated hopes and expectations which start off too many marriages today (Schneid, 1972:57-68).

Opening up the *ketubah* to encompass marriage forms not traditionally accepted by the Torah or Talmud is based on the urging of Mishnah Berachoth 9:5 that the *halacha,* expressed in the Torah and Talmud, should be in tune with the needs of the people and their times. When the Jewish community supported polygamy and concubinage, the *halacha* and *ketubah* supported polygamy and concubinage. When the Jewish community inclined toward monogamy, tradition supported monogamy. In the Jewish tradition, people should be free to write their own *ketubah* or marriage contracts in a way that structures and legitimizes variations and alternatives to traditional monogamy such as sexually open marriages, swinging, multilateral threesomes and foursomes, group marriages and even gay unions.

The comarital or statellite relationships involve and affect the couple in the open marriage and another couple or single person. Whether the comarital relationship is sexual or not, the intimacy of the relationship does impinge on the covenant between the couple. This intimacy may profit from being included in the covenant of the primary relationship in terms of integrity, honesty and communications. Mutual obligations and limitations can be written into renegotiated marriage covenant(s) by the concerned parties, as Robert Rimmer suggests in the synergamous marriage ceremony of *Thursday, My Love* (1972).

Multilateral marriage, specifically the right of a Jewish man to have more than one wife and several concubines, was practiced by Oriental, North African and Spanish (Sephardic) Jews, but not by the Ashkenazi (Schneid, 1973:91). Sexually open marriages are a less intimate and less intense form of multilateral or polygamous marriages without their patriarchal bias. Even so, the concept of an *expanded ketubah* has yet to be explored by the Jewish community.

In *The New Intimacy*, Ron Mazur takes the most positive approach of any Christian theologian to an extension of the covenant tradition to sexually open marriages:

> Persons participating in an open-ended marriage covenant not only with each other, but with the whole Family of Man . . . Within such marriages the possibility of adultery is totally absent because exclusion, possessiveness, and jealousy have no place in the relationship. "Adultery" is a theological judgment which can only apply to the restrictive type of covenant.

> When one partner breaks the vow of "to thee only do I promise to keep myself," a relationship of trust is broken and he or she is unfaithful. But it's also possible to create a model of marriage—a covenant—monogamous in the sense that it's based upon an intended lifetime commitment between two but which nevertheless is open-ended because it does not exclude the freedom to have any number of intimate relationships with others (1973:14).

In a similar very positive vein are Rustum and Della Roy, authors of *Honest Sex,* Robert and Anna Francoeur, authors of *Hot and Cool Sex,* and Lonny Myers and Ron Leggett, authors of *Adultery and Other Private Matters.* In a more cautious but still open position are Catholic theologians like John Giles Milhaven, C. Jaime Snoek, and Kosnik, Carroll, Cunningham, Modras and Schulte, coauthors of *Human Sexuality: New Directions in American Catholic Thought.* Among more cautious but open Protestant positions are those of the workstudy document of the United Presbyterian Church, Methodist E.C. Hobbs, *Towards a Quaker View of Sex,* D.W. Ferm, and the British Council of Churches.

COVENANTS FOR NON-MARITAL RELATIONSHIPS

Traditionally marriage has been viewed as a longterm, if not life-long commitment. Many intimate relationships today do not have this expectation: *e.g.,* the casual, often non-exclusive sexual relationships of single persons and more committed patterns of non-marital cohabitation.

Early kubbutzniks endorsed the idea of living together without *ketubah.* The couple simply announced to the community that they were now living together, setting up house as autonomous agents without any change in legal status. When and if a child was born to the couple, the relationship became one of marriage, involving *ketubah* and a change in legal status. To mark this change the couple often took a new name as a symbol of their new covenant.

The Jewish betrothal covenant, *erusin* (Schneid, 1973:10), on which kubbutz cohabitation was based, evolved into a strong Christian precedent for extending the covenant idea to premarital sex in a variety of religious rituals. Sociological literature contains many mentions of *fensternl,* "windowing" or "window-courting" in Catholic and Luterhan communities of Bavaria and rural France, the rural Scandanavian custom of "taking your night feet for a walk," and "bundling" in northeastern colonial America (Francoeur and Francoeur, 1972:68-70); Murstein, 1974:317-18). These ritualized forms of non-marital sex were socially and religiously accepted by the community because of the concern to prove the bride-to-be's fertility before the final marriage ceremony. Of course, they are scarcely, if ever mentioned in theological manuals and books on Christian marriage.

At age 85, Lord Fisher, archbishop of Canterbury and Episcopal Primate, urged his church to revive the Jewish espousal custom as a church ritual. One benefit he saw was the removal of moral guilt still associated with "fornication."

Ten years ago, Margaret Mead advocated this step, suggesting "a serious commitment entered into in public, validated and protected by law, and, for some, by religion, in which each partner would have a deep and continuing concern for the happiness and well-being of the other."

Catholic theologians who favor this development include Snoek, Valente, Milhaven, Kennedy, and the recent study sponsored by the Catholic Theological Society. Important Protestant statements include The British Council of Churches, *Towards a Quaker View of Sex,* a work-study document from the United Presbyterian Church, Hobbs, Robinson, Ferm, and Mazur.

With cohabitation of older persons where social security and retirement benefits are a prime concern, Kosnik *et al.* "conclude that such relationships, which can be truly creative and integrative for the individuals involved, can also be morally acceptable, at least until such time as the civil restrictions to legal marriage are removed" (1977:145).

TWO NEW COVENANT RITUALS

Mazur (1973:83-97) argues persuasively that establishment of a church rite for divorce would not only make the inevitable divorces of some couples more humane and constructive, but that the open existence of these rites would also be an effective deterrent for needless divorces. Couples could renegotiate their covenant without dissolving it.

From biblical times on, Jewish tradition has included the *get,* or divorce agreement. In Jewish law, the couple, not the courts or rabbi, determine the content of the *ketubah* and the grounds for the *get.* The rabbi and courts are only involved to facilitate the couple's mutual agreement and supervise its official documentation (Schneid, 1973:70). The *erusin, ketubah* and *get* are designed to discourage people from rushing rashly into or out of a relationship. But they are also important from a social and psychological view in that they reaffirm and define the covenanting couple's situation in the fabric of society and the religious community.

In January 1977, the United Methodist Church adopted a "Ritual in a New Day."

91

This divorce ritual and covenant is held for a separating couple, for one former spouse alone, or as part of a remarriage. It includes a promise to free the former spouse from "claims and responsibilities," and especially from the "burdens of guilt and sterile remorse" over their failure to have a lasting marriage. With both spouses vowing their "I do," wedding bands are switched from left to right hand.

A second religious ritual for alternate lifestyles has come from efforts of the gay community to socially structure and religiously recognize their intimate unions. "Gay unions" are gaining acceptance among both Catholic and Protestant pastors on a grassroots level.

Celibate gay Jesuit John McNeill, author of *The Church and the Homosexual,* argues that human relationships, gay, straight, or bisexual, are morally good and should be recognized by the church when they express "loving concern," *chesed* or *agape,* the basic value/virtue in the Judaeo-Christian covenant. Some gay couples may want to covenant a traditional exclusive monogamous relationship. Others may want a variation of sexually open marriage. Still others, pressured into a heterosexual marriage before coming out of the closet, may negotiate an expansion of the heterosexual covenant.

CIVIL TRENDS AND PRESSURES

In January 1977 the California Supreme Court set a national precedent in the Lee Marvin *vs* Michelle Marvin decision. After nine years of non-marital cohabitation without a written or verbal contract, the court ruled that an implied covenant was presumed to exist and gave both parties rights equal to those of civilly or religiously married couples. In the view of the *Sexual Law Reporter,* "The Marvin

decision effectively encourages contractual 'marriages' and heralds the acceptance of alternative life styles" (March/April 1977).

In 1966 the Swedish Parliament achieved the same effect by statute that the Marvin decision accomplished by tort. Within five years the Swedish marriage rate dropped by fifty percent as more and more couples wrote their own covenant/contracts.

CONCLUSION

Brueggeman adds an important dimension to our suggestion of an extension of the covenant tradition to alternate lifestyles in today's society when he points out that all important relationships in biblical times were covenantal, meaning

a. based on commitment or vows,
b. open to renegotiation,
c. concerned with mutual decisions,
d. affecting all parties involved,
e. addressing important issues, and
f. open to various internal and external sanctions (1977:18).

Relationships must be shaped given the peculiar fears and hopes, strengths and weaknesses of persons involved, which means different families and relationships will be concretely different.

President Carter echoed this new recognition of pluralism in a tentative way, limited to federal family policy, in 1976:

"Values, jobs, lifestyles and needs of families vary widely. To envision a single model or a single way [of life] . . . would do great damage to the pluralism and diversity that make our country strong . . ." (Quoted by Giordano and Levine, 1977:51:2).

In terms of the Judaeo-Christian tradition, covenanting of relationships offers an excellent means of legalizing a variety of marital and non-marital relationships. It can provide a bridge from the past to the future for religious-minded persons. It can ease the social turmoil inevitable with the

Marvin decision. It can provide psychological, emotional and social support for the majority of Americans today who are not in traditional monogamous sexually exclusive life-long relationships.

The shift from civil contracts to personal, mutual covenants will accomplish two important things. First, it will get the state out of an area of personal relationships where it has no "compelling interest" and allow it to focus on protection of children and equitable property rights, two areas where it does have legitimate "compelling interest." Second, it will allow individuals the freedom and flexibility to design and renegotiate their commitment and covenant to meet their ever changing needs.

CONTRACTS ARE FOR CHILDREN; COVENANTS ARE FOR ADULTS

A 1987 Postscript

The above paper, written in 1979, suggested the need for religious and civil institutions to recognize and provide some structure and social support for the increasing number of men and women who find themselves in relationships and family structures other than heterosexual exclusive monogamy. Since then, the need has become more apparent to us. The social realities cited in the introduction have reinforced that need, despite the reluctance of most to recognize the realities of pluralism that are already with us.

In this postscript, we would like to add a few comments about a point we touched on briefly in our 1979 paper and a major new development we did not anticipate at that time.

Firstly, we need to point out that the pressures from homosexuals for recognition of "gay unions" has increased considerably since 1979. Churches and synagogues have appeared across the country, ministering to the lesbians and gay men who have a need for a religious and spiritual side in their lives and relations. These include the Christian Metropolitan Community Church, the Church of the Beloved Disciple (Eucharistic Catholics), and the Gay Synagogue, mostly in the larger cities. In liberal Protestant, Catholic and Jewish circles, individual ministers, priests and rabbis have shown a willingness to witness the union of gay and lesbian couples despite the fact that officially and civilly these unions have no status. The variety of religious-oriented homosexual groups has grown, with Integrity for Episcopalians, Dignity for Roman Catholics, Lutherans Concerned, and [Quaker] Friends for Lesbian and Gay Concerns among them. In 1986, the American Civil Liberties Union announced its intention to work for civil recognition of gay unions so that gay and lesbian couples may enjoy the economic and tax benefits that heterosexual married and cohabitating couples currently enjoy.

Our second point in this postscript is one that no one was aware of in 1979, a significant imbalance in our sex ratio and a shortage of men available for the women seeking husbands.

From colonial days to the mid 40s America had a surplus of men. Since single men could always "go west" and conquer a new frontier, they actually helped us grow as a nation. In the 40s the ratio began to shift and we now have a shortage of available men. The basis for today's "marriage squeeze" begins with three factors. Men tend to marry at a later age than women. Men also tend to marry younger women, especially if they are in midlife crisis and look to a bride in her 20s to rejuvenate them. At the same time, our birth rates fluctuate from year to year.

Why [are] there not enough available men

today for women born in the 40s, 50s, and 60s? Part of the answer is shifting birth rates during the baby boom of the 40s. Roughly 1,417,000 girls were born in 1947 with Sally. The year before Sally was born there were only 1,217,000 boys born, a shortfall of 200,000. In the early 40s there were even fewer males born. While Sally and her friends are competing for husbands, the men they would normally marry, the men born in the early 40s, have a surplus of women to pick from. The older Sally gets, the less attractive she becomes for men her age who, if they are single and looking, will usually look for a younger woman than Sally.

This is why we have to look at who marries who in the different age groups and the ratios of available males to available females in these groups. This means we have to take out of the marriage pool the single men who will never marry, the gay men who are not interested in women and men who are already living with a woman without being married.

In late 1984, Charles Westoff, director of the Office of Population Research at Princeton University, included all these factors in his calculation of a "Marital Opportunity Ratio" or "Availability Index" for white women in 38 metropolitan areas of the U.S. The only good news was for white women 20 to 24 years old. Since men usually take younger wives, women under 25 have a large pool of available men. For every 100 white women ages 20 to 24 in San Diego there are 179 available males. Houston has 149 males, Baltimore 133, Chicago 129, with Pittsburgh, Buffalo and Miami tied with 117 males for every 100 women age 20 to 24. Once a woman passes her 25th birthday, it's all downhill in the Marital Opportunity Ratio. For every 100 single white women between ages 30 and 34, San Diego offers only 83

men. In Houston the ratio is 90 available males for 100 women and Baltimore 70 per 100. Chicago and Miami have 68 males to 100 females. Pittsburgh and Buffalo have a low of 54 to 100. Most urban areas have roughly three single women in their late 40s or early 50s competing for every one available male. And it obviously gets worse as white women reach their 60s and 70s.

Westoff could not calculate the extent of the male shortage for black women because no one is sure to what extent urban black males are undercounted in the census. Still, the situation for black women appears even worse than it is for white women. Until recently, the U.S. Census lumped Hispanics with blacks or "others," so calculating the marriage availability ratio for Hispanics is practically impossible.

Estimates put the overall sex ratio at between 80 and 63 black men to 100 women in most urban areas. Poor nutrition and the lack of prenatal care in lower economic groups result in 8 to 9 percent more male fetuses dying in the womb than in middle or upper class pregnancies. Black male fetuses are 3 to 4 percent more likely to miscarry than white fetuses. Single mothers are also more likely to miscarry a male than a female fetus. With a higher proportion of single mothers in the black population, this only adds to the overall shortage of black males. When this overall ratio is converted into a marriage availability ratio the news is devastating. The overall shortage of black males is aggravated for young black women seeking a husband by discrimination in our penal system which sends a disproportionate number of young black males to prison. Proportionately more black than white males serve overseas in our armed forces. Violence and drugs add to the shortage of young black males. While no one has yet come up with good estimates of the actual number of men in the marriage pools for black women at different ages, I expect that when it is done the ratios will be much worse than those Westoff came up with for whites.

In theory, we could try to ignore this unbalanced sex ratio, but individual men and women are more likely to deal with it in whatever pragmatic ways they find personally tolerable. It would be much easier and healthier for these men and women if society would recognize their adaptive lifestyles. If that recognition were given, they would then be able to draw more comfortably on both civil and religious support systems monogamous married couples have enjoyed even when they break up and remarry other partners.

Two adaptations come to mind, polygamy and man-sharing.

Legalizing polygamy could help ease the man shortage. In a similar situation, shortly after World War II, the British and Finns considered legalizing polygamy. A hundred years ago, there were a dozen American groups endorsing variations of polygamy. The Oneida Community denounced selfish monogamy in favor of group marriage and amative sexual intercourse open to all members of the community. Some fundamentalist Mormons have openly returned in recent years to their polygamous tradition. When Colorado City, Arizona, became a full-fledged city in September 1985, the *Wall Street Journal* noted that the Mormon mayor had five wives while the town's founder, 98-year-old Leroy Johnson, had 16 wives. In 1953, a judge blocked then-Governor Pyle's effort to jail the polygamous men of Colorado City. According to the *Wall Street Journal,* between 30,000 and 50,000 people are practicing plural marriage, mainly in Utah, Arizona and Cali-

fornia. In Bigwater and Hildale, Utah, polygamy is taken for granted. American Moslems could easily pick up on this precedent and reassert the right the Koran gives Moslem men to have four wives. Some Christians and Jews might then claim religious discrimination unless they also are allowed more than one spouse.

[The] possibility of Christian churches recognizing alternate lifestyles such as polygamy has recently surfaced in the Third World. Following the breakup of European colonial powers in Africa after World War II, the native clergies began to question the imposition of western values and lifestyles and to affirm the value and integrity of their traditional cultures. At a 1986 assembly of African Catholic bishops, a "firm stand against" polygamy was taken "because it is incompatible with the Gospel message." At the same time, the bishops recommended development of a religious teaching that would enable the integration of polygamous families into the life of the church. The conference also dealt with the practice of trial marriages which are traditionally used to determine whether a couple is able to have children, a major concern in African society.

We mentioned polygamy in our 1979 article, but we were not aware of a second alternative already emerging in the black community as we wrote.

Today, it is obvious that adapting to the surplus of women could also lead to an acceptance of man-sharing and networks of intimate friends and spouses. Sociologist Laurel Richardson has described an emerging prototype in her survey of 700 women whom she describes as "the new other woman." The majority of Richardson's subjects had been married once and were not interested in marriage or "husband-stealing." The strong guilt associated in the past with adultery has weakened considerably, though most of the women were not enthusiastic about being involved in a series of short-term relations with married men.

"Man-sharing" was first documented in 1980 among urban blacks by black sociologists Joseph Scott at Notre Dame University and Bamidele Ade Agbasegbe at Cornell. Both see man-sharing or extramarital polygamy as a functional adaptation to the shortage of young marriageable black men. By 1983, the *New York Times* reported the growing popularity of "man-sharing workshops" for white professional women in New York City and Washington, D.C. A recent novel by Maxine Paetro explores this alternative in her novel *Manshare,* updating some of the alternative relationships proposed by Robert H. Rimmer in his novels *Thursday My Love* and *The Rebellion of Yale Marratt.*

NO   William Stackhouse

BOTH RELIGIOUS AND CIVIL INSTITUTIONS WILL HAVE DIFFICULTY RECOGNIZING ALTERNATE LIFESTYLES

When it comes to the recognition of traditional relationships, civil and religious structures are allied in maintaining what has come to be called the "traditional family." Indeed, clergy are licensed by the state and when performing marriages function simultaneously as both religious leaders and representatives of their state. As noted by Shapiro and Franceour, gay/lesbian members of various faith communities have called for recognition and support for their relationships. Theirs is a striking dilemma which illustrates well the similarities and differences in the function of civil and religious structures in respect to alternative relationships.

The devastating and virulent way in which AIDS has been found to affect men who have sex with men in America has had a profound impact on the entire gay/lesbian community and especially on gay men. Open and self-accepting gays and lesbians have confronted this epidemic with courage, stamina, love, caring, and practicality. Educational programs to promote health, build self-esteem, and educate gay men about safer sex practices, provided largely by and for the gay community itself, have had an impact unprecedented in public health statistics, as illustrated by the precipitous drop in venereal disease among gay men in major U.S. cities. And what, you might ask, does this have to do with civil and religious support for alternative relationships?

In the midst of these profoundly tragic circumstances, gay and lesbian persons are reexamining their perspectives on relationships. And it appears that the "wider community" is beginning to understand the insidious, lethal (death-producing) effects of the long-standing lack of institutional social support systems for gay/lesbian relationships. Gay men, many of whom indulged in a free-wheeling sexual expression growing out of both the sexual revolution and gay liberation, prompted to change behavior initially for health's sake, are now coming to view some of their needs and desires for committed relationships as more primary in their hierarchy of needs. While rejoicing in the experience of sexual expression as a central aspect of self-acceptance remains a hallmark of the gay/lesbian liberationist perspective, a profound new factor has entered the equation. AIDS has lead to the search for ways to engage in sex that are fun and safe, and often loving. And because of the gravely existential nature of the precipitating factor here, AIDS, individuals have approached this new equation of sexuality in a serious, qualitative, and at times spiritual way.

Most people want to be in a relationship. And most people know that relationships are not easy to maintain. The AIDS crisis has brought gays and lesbians to focus attention on the quality of their relationships. Quality relationships are difficult to maintain. The "wider community" is beginning to realize that many gays and lesbians desire an alternative which is really rather traditional. In the past many civil and religious institutions have met requests for recognition of gay/lesbian "marriages" or holy unions with what I might characterize as disbelief; it was a non-issue. How could these relationships possibly be compared with marriage? They can, and the fact that a few holy unions have occurred in probably every major city across the land is a witness to a reality which may no longer be ignored. The religious community can perform an important function through supporting these relationships during the time before civil recognition of these relationships is established. It is important to keep in mind that a central part of any religious marriage or service of commitment involves the corporate expression of the intention and responsibility of the community to give support to individuals as they strive to live up to their commitment to each other. And that is a central point with respect to the recognition and support of any alternative relationship. Whatever the nature of the relationship, if it can be concretely defined it will be pos-

sible for faith communities to consider making a pledge of support. And the closer the alternative fits the basic structure and function of whatever the tradition has supported the more likely it is that the institutional faith community may lend its support.

This conclusion leads me to note another way in which the gay/lesbian "marriage" may be becoming similar to a traditional marriage. The desire to bear and raise children, or be a parent, is not exclusive to heterosexuals. Many gay/lesbian individuals and couples have achieved a level of self-acceptance which allows them to seriously consider becoming a parent. Birth following artificial insemination, adoption, and foster care by gays and lesbians was virtually impossible to comprehend until these began to actually occur in recent years. Many gay/lesbian couples want to experience parenting together. Gay/lesbian or bisexual persons who had children within a previous heterosexual relationship are now raising those children within their homosexual marriage. And some gay/lesbian couples have become parents through new creative and intentional approaches. In one lesbian couple I know the desire for a family was strong for both women. The older of the two decided to have their first child. And in order to further establish their family connection the birth mother was artificially inseminated with sperm from her partner's brother. Imagine, as was actually the case, a proud and supportive grandfather giving out cigars at work on the occasion of the birth of his daughter's partner's child. These families are in many ways very similar to traditional families.

Individuals in relationships of whatever sort are hungry for recognition and support for their relationships. The examples I have given of gay/lesbian relationships could be metaphors for other arrangements. How do these examples compare to multilateral intimate, sexual, perhaps even parenting/familial relationships? And what about the increasing phenomenon of intentional single parenting by women? This choice is clearly an option for women regardless of their sexual orientation. Does the single parent family constitute an alternative relationship? Certainly there is a relationship between mother and child. It is committed, emotional, and primary. The civil implications of such a relationship are simple and historically rooted in maternity. But in the religious recognition of such an alternative the element of intentionality, that the woman chose to become a single parent, clashes with most tradition. Can religious communities celebrate and pledge their communal support to such a relationship of choice?

My response so far has been primarily focused on the recognition and support of alternative relationships by religious communities. It is my contention that the recognition of alternatives will come first within those religious communities which have the most local autonomy, or to put it another way, which have the least complex institutional hierarchy. Change occurs slowly in large complex organizations which are generally actually organized to make change difficult. The complex worldwide institutional bureaucracy of the Roman Catholic church is hard for us to even imagine. This institution has been confronted in recent years with attempts to change [and] reform, its positions regarding various aspects of sexuality (contraception, divorce, homosexuality, priestly celibacy, women priests) and as is typical with any such large organization the response has been to "lay down the law." On the other hand many Protestant and Jewish congregations have virtually complete local autonomy to decide what they will do. It is possible that in many such congregations people in the most unusual sorts of alternative relationships have found that their community is willing to give its recognition and support. Such institutional freedom is a significant element of our pluralistic U.S. society.

When it comes to civil recognition and support for alternative relationships, the example of the complex and institutionally conserving (or conservative) functioning of the Roman Catholic church is probably an appropriate analogy. Law changes very slowly. And when there are economic implications to civil change it is probably even slower. We are reminded of the economic advantages of the traditional marriage at least once a year, at tax time. There are numerous ways that our system of law and the business sector bestows benefits upon traditional relationships. Some examples include employee benefits (shared health insurance, life insurance, pensions), inheritance without a will, recognition of the privileged status of relatives to visit the sick in hospitals.

These examples have become very real concerns for many gay/lesbian relationships. Without complex partnership contracts or an uncontestable will, if a member of a gay/lesbian relationship dies the blood relatives may claim an inheritance. When such a couple has intermingled their assets for many years this becomes a very complex circumstance. Unmarried heterosexual couples, on the other hand, may have an enforceable implied contract or common-law marriage. This may also be a complex issue when couples are simply splitting up, as with divorce. Add children to the equation and the dissolution of alternative or traditional relationships becomes very difficult.

6. SHOULD SOCIETY RECOGNIZE LIFESTYLES?

The city of San Francisco has developed a system for giving "spousal" benefits for alternative relationships which fulfill certain standards and are registered with the city. Again, as with my point on religious recognition of alternatives, the closer the relationship is to the traditional type relationship, the more likely it is to gain recognition. But it is hard to imagine other cities making the sort of accommodations to alternatives that San Francisco has made. Remember, very few cities and states have passed even gay/lesbian antidiscrimination legislation. And, as of the Supreme Court's recent decision on privacy/sodomy, in many states heterosexuals and homosexuals alike are engaging in illegal sexual activities. The process of civil change and recognition of alternatives is very, very, slow.

POSTSCRIPT

SHOULD OUR SOCIETY LEGALLY RECOGNIZE A VARIETY OF ADULT LIFESTYLES?

This issue attempts to focus on one of the main consequences of the preceeding issues in this section on relationships. However, since the issue is so new, the two sides of the debate are not yet clearly articulated. Despite this, the issue of how civil and religious communities might respond to the expanding debates about pluralism in our lifestyles and relationships is included here as an open-ended summary for Part I.

Even while this volume of *Taking Sides* was being set in type in early 1987, delegates of the Newark, New Jersey, diocese of the Episcopal Church voted overwhelmingly to circulate for study and debate a lay/clergy report that advocates blessing ceremonies for non-marital sexual unions between homosexuals and for alternatives to monogamy for young adults, the widowed and divorced. Bishop Edmond Lee, presiding bishop of the Episcopal Church, told reporters he believed it was time for the church to begin to debate the issues raised in this report. "This is not to say that I agree with or support every point in the report." Bishop Lee said he particularly favored openness about homosexuality. The report is supported by the Reverend John Spong, Bishop of the Newark Diocese. Bishop Spong expects the document to spark a national debate on sexual ethics and hopes it will prompt church leaders to amend doctrine to embrace all believers. He believes the church should recognize the realities of premarital sex and cohabitation in today's society and give these realities some recognition and responsible structure within the life of the church. In summing up their views, the panel responsible for the report said that unselfish sexual relationships should be recognized if they manifest "healing, reconciliation, concern for others."

A vote was to be be taken in January 1988 whether to accept all or part of the report's recommendations as policy.

Whatever the outcome of the Episcopalian report and its impact on other churches, it is obvious that the issues raised in that report and in the two views offered here focus on a crucial issue for the near future: how should civil and religious institutions respond to the growing variety of human relationships in the last decade of the twentieth century? See the bibliography for further readings on this subject.

PART 2
EDUCATION ISSUES

In the days of Romeo and Juliet, children were considered adults around age seven when they became apprentices to learn a trade. They married in their early or mid-teens. Yet records suggest that they did not reach sexual maturity until their late teens. Adult status and marriage then, preceded sexual maturity.

Today the reverse is true. Puberty comes at 11 or 12 years of age, and even earlier for many boys and girls. Partial emancipation comes with entrance to college and full independence with graduation and full-time employment, but marriage is now commonly postponed until the mid- or late twenties.

In the past hundred years, as we shifted away from a rural economy where children worked on the farm, urban industry could not absorb all the young people. This, and other factors, led to the development of the public school system where teenagers could safely and profitably spend their extended adolescence.

In recent years, the public education system has become the focus of controversy in the face of epidemics of sexually transmitted diseases and teenage pregnancies. Some states have mandated sex education in all schools. In inner-city Baltimore, Chicago, Milwaukee and elsewhere, school-based health clinics have been advocated and fought against with equal vigor.

Roughly half of all American teenagers are sexually active, with over one million teenage pregnancies every year. Thus a major question has emerged as to how we can and should deal with the newly emerging phenomenon of the sexually mature, often sexually active teenager.

Is Sex Education in Schools an Attempt to Institutionalize a Sexual Revolution?

Are School-Based Health Clinics an Effective Way of Reducing the Incidence of Teenage Pregnancies and STDs?

ISSUE 7

IS SEX EDUCATION IN SCHOOLS AN ATTEMPT TO INSTITUTIONALIZE A SEXUAL REVOLUTION?

YES: Lawrence L. Shornack and Ellen McRoberts Shornack, from the authors' condensation of "The New Sex Education and the Sexual Revolution: A Critical View," *Family Relations,* October 1982

NO: Peter Scales, from "Sense and Nonsense About Sexuality Education: A Rejoinder to the Shornacks' Critical View," *Family Relations,* April 1983

ISSUE SUMMARY

YES: Lawrence Shornack, a sociologist, and Ellen Shornack, a child and family therapist, argue that the new sex education attempts to institutionalize the sexual revolution by indoctrinating students in the ideology of sexual permissiveness.

NO: Peter Scales, Director of Education for the Planned Parenthood Federation of America, rejects the Shornacks' arguments, pointing out that it contains serious misrepresentations, myths, inaccuracies, distortions and innuendos used to buttress a shaky thesis.

Since earliest times, youngsters in so-called primitive cultures have grown up taking their sexuality and sexual relations very much as a natural part of everyday life. In tribal cultures, sex education is an integrated part of growing up. In some cultures, like the Mangaians of the Cook Islands in the South Pacific, an older woman teaches the teenage boy the art of sexual intercourse after his circumcision. East Bay Melanesian children are encouraged to masturbate and engage in sex play until age four, after which sexual play is forbidden until marriage. However, between ages 11 and 15, young boys live in the men's hut and are introduced to homosexual relations by a lad their own age and an older man. Almost every variation of sex education you can think of is practiced by some tribal culture somewhere on this earth today.

Insights into the sexual education of children during the seventeenth century can be gained from engravings of that era showing adults and children gathered at the public baths. Since individual houses did not have the luxury of baths or indoor toilets which we take for granted today, open air or enclosed public baths were popular places for adults and children alike to relax, bathe and socialize. Here young people could meet and enjoy each other's company, share a meal, take a communal bath in the nude, while older men played cards in the buff or got a shave, couples cuddled, and mothers nursed their infants. After the Renaissance, a growing sense of privacy gradually led to a decline of the public baths, although many non-European cultures, particularly the Japanese, continue to enjoy communal public baths.

In many respects, this relaxed, congenial approach to sex education continued in America through to the early twentieth century. On the American frontier, life was often a matter of day-to-day survival with minimal luxuries and little, if any privacy. Farm life made it impossible to shelter children from the realities of animals mating and giving birth. In such cramped quarters, children learned the human side of sexuality.

With the growing affluence of the late-nineteenth-century industrial society, urban life, and the new emerging values of the middle-class family, a new type of architecture evolved. The home was divided into two roles, social rooms for entertaining and private rooms for bathing, toilet and sleeping. The home became a sanctuary from the harsh world outside, and a place where innocent Victorian children could be sheltered from the realities of all sexuality. In the Victorian value system, having sex was something a good wife did in order to have children, something that happened in the dark while she was asleep when her husband could no longer control his animal instincts. In the privacy of their own bedrooms, the innocence of Victorian children was safe. Women were expected to learn about "the facts of life" from their husbands on the wedding night.

This evolution in the atmosphere in which children grew up occurred along with the inversion in ages at which young people matured sexually and married centuries ago and today, the shift from rural to urban life, an extended period of adolescence, and the emergence of public school education.

Today's controversies over sex education are the natural outcome of all these changes which have led to a shift away from the home and family as the source of sex education, the decrease in influence of the parents, and the simultaneous increase in the role of public education.

YES
Lawrence L. Shornack
and Ellen M. Shornack

THE SEX EDUCATION MOVEMENT ATTEMPTS TO IMPOSE A SEXUAL REVOLUTION ON SOCIETY

Most people would probably agree that because of teenage pregnancy and parental inability to teach young people about sexuality, the public schools should offer sex education programs. However, most people have not had the opportunity to look closely at what programs sex educators have in mind. Everyone has heard, for example, that teenagers should be taught accurate information, but not everyone has heard that the schools "must teach the equality of the sexes [and be] against sexism and the double standard," nor is everyone aware that the American School Health Association endorses the view that sex education is not sex information but is best seen as "attitude development and guidance related to associations between the sexes." Therefore, this paper undertakes a close and critical examination of "the new sex education."

Although most schools have some form of sex education, advocates of the new sex education estimate that not 10% of school children receive an *adequate* sex education. The effort to ensure that all schools have an "adequate" sex education program is the work of an incipient social movement spearheaded by educational bureaucrats, academics, and counselors. Every social movement believes that it has a monopoly on the truth, which explains why you will not find critical discussion of the new sex education in education, social science, or counseling journals. A movement avoids dialogue by stereotyping its opponents; thus, critics are said to consist of a right-wing vocal minority. Finally, a movement seeks to change the social order and not merely to adapt to change.

THE GROUP-CENTERED APPROACH

The movement insists that young people cannot learn about sexuality without a classroom peer group guided by a "facilitator" employing techniques known as "values clarification," "sensitivity training," "consciousness raising," and the like. "In this last half of the 20th century, adults cannot make decisions for

Adapted and condensed by the authors from, "The New Sex Education and the Sexual Revolution: A Critical View," *Family Relations* magazine, October 1982. Copyright © 1986 by Lawrence L. Shornack and Ellen McRoberts Shornack.

youth," but the schools can provide a setting for sharing feelings and experiences, and training in decision making. However, before sex educators can run a "human relations" group, they must themselves undergo a reorientation to sexuality comprising three stages: *Desensitization* exposes one to anxiety-inducing films, artifacts, and the like, until one becomes comfortable with such experience; then, *sensitization* means that one "participates in a more open and trusting manner"; finally, during *incorporation* one now integrates the previous experience with one's lifestyle. This process might be viewed simply as one more rite of passage staged by the human potential movement for consenting adults. However, the goal here is "character education," that is, a state-enjoined *resocialization* of, first, sex educators and, then, the entire school-age population.

The group classroom "exercises" aiming at desensitization show the substance of the indoctrination program. In one, students are asked to publicly affirm their response to this: "If I am feeling the need for release of sexual tension, I would rather: a. Masturbate. b. Screw. c. Engage in vigorous physical activity." In another exercise, students must rank themselves somewhere from "Virginal Virginia" to "Mattress Milly." Evidently new sex educators believe that they must introduce locker-room language into the classroom in order to promote the view that sexual intercourse is all right so long as a contraceptive is used. Thus, "family life education" subverts family life.

THE NEW SEX EDUCATION AND THE SOCIOLOGY OF THE SEXUAL REVOLUTION

According to the new sex education movement, our society has undergone advances in knowledge such as development of the pill; at the same time, a social vanguard, chiefly the young, liberated themselves sexually. Because these changes are irreversible, society must facilitate adaptation to them. However, "sexual hangovers" in the older generation prevent adults from accepting sexual freedom for adolescents, creating confusion and anxiety for both parents and children. This *cultural lag* explains the upsurge in out-of-wedlock teenage pregnancies, and the problem will persist until society provides massive sex education and contraceptive services.

On the other hand, as early as 1972 Kingsley Davis pointed out that the rise in adolescent illegitimacy took place during the same period when both knowledge about sexuality and contraceptives were becoming more available. Societies have always held couples responsible for the children they produce. But in post-World War II America, parents abdicated their authority over children, the family-planning movement shifted contraceptive responsibility from the male to the female, the courts no longer enforced paternity obligations, and welfare institutions ensured economic security for the out-of-wedlock mother. Consequently, this "liberation of males" has left young females in a weak bargaining position, because males have little to lose from a pregnancy and may, in fact, gain status with their peers from it. The "sexual revolution" has actually been a period of family disorganization. Thus, 80% of first coitus takes place in available homes; and the proportion of girls coitally experienced is lowest in families headed by the father or step-father, higher in families headed by the mother, and highest where the head is a woman other than the mother.

It is utopian to think that we can segregate teenagers from family and community in the classroom, provide them with human relations exercises, and expect that they can create *ex nihilo* an ethic adequate to family formation. It is totalitarian to try to substitute state indoctrination for the family. The "sexual revolution" has left American society in a state of *disequilibrium,* not of cultural lag. Our task, therefore, is not to adapt to the inevitable, but to reform conduct that has gotten out of hand.

ACCEPTANCE OF SEXUALITY AND USE OF CONTRACEPTION

One theory of out-of-wedlock pregnancy is that a girl drifts into intercourse without benefit of contraception because she cannot admit to herself or to others that she is ready for intercourse. Thus, a survey of experts shows that sex education must aim at "Acceptance of . . . one's sexual behavior, from abstinence to intercourse . . . [and] reduction of sexual guilt." This is the goal of classroom group exercises. Promoters of "family planning" for adolescents generally assume that the problem is one of means (decision-making skills and contraception) rather than motivation.

What do studies reveal about the conditions in which intercourse, and pregnancy, occur? First, adolescent girls report that they *intended* about one third of all premarital pregnancies, hoping to achieve marriage or independence from parental control. Conditions in which teens begin intercourse include social attitudes such as belief in the equality of the sexes; peer pressure, as when girls denigrate virgins as "abnormal," or when males gain status by "scoring"; and weak ego strength arising from broken homes or from discordant family relations. Personality traits associated with premarital pregnancy include de-

pendency, infantilism, or spitefulness toward parents, and the desire to present a parent with a child. Events occurring during the pre-pregnancy period include object loss, such as death of, or separation from, parent or boyfriend; conflict with parents; and family members or neighborhood girls getting attention for their pregnancies.

In short, sexual motivation is a far more complex matter than the movement image of an individualized adolescent needing only human relations exercises in the classroom and contraception outside of it. Our society now leaves decisions that could result in an illegitimate child entirely to a socially isolated dyad, one member of which is often an immature, vulnerable teenage girl. Belief that all that is needed is effective contraception is the same kind of thinking that led to the problem in the first place. Nevertheless, the editors of a recent collection of articles from *Family Planning Perspectives* pin their hopes on a ten-year program of research to develop a contraceptive suitable for teenagers, preferably postcoital! Indeed, a 1978 study showed that even if all sexually active teenagers used contraception consistently, 467,000 premarital pregnancies would occur each year anyway.

ACCEPTANCE OF ONE'S SEXUALITY AND THE THEORY OF ADOLESCENCE

Can the new sex education in good conscience leave unexamined the question of whether adolescents are *emotionally* ready for intercourse? A university sex educator and counselor presented the following case to a workshop for teachers and counselors. A 16-year-old girl came to a school counselor and said that she was having an affair with an unemployed man of 24. She lived at home and concealed the relationship from her parents. Although her parents were divorced, she often saw her father; she believed that he would be very upset if he knew of the affair, perhaps to the point of not letting her go to college. The counselor checked to see if the girl was using contraception but was otherwise nonjudgmental; she continued this supportive stance until losing touch with the case when the girl went away to college, the man following her.

The counselor assumed that the conflict that brought the girl to counseling was *external*—between her values and those of her parents. But the parents did not know of the affair, so the conflict was *internal*—that of an adolescent still emotionally and financially dependent on her parents. A course of therapy more appropriate for someone this young and inexperienced would have been to earn the girl's trust, to reflect what she said of her parents' disapproval back to her, and to confront her with her own feelings of doubt. This counselor lacks, we suggest, an adequate theory of adolescence.

The adolescent must undergo individuation. The onset of puberty brings sexual feelings and the social expectation that one should begin to become independent of one's parents. Yet the adolescent is still emotionally attached to her parents. In fact, she inevitably experiences regression—an emotional reliving of the first individuation process that occurred during the second or third year of life, when she first experienced herself as separate from her mother. There is thus a reawakening of incestuous feelings toward her father and devaluation of her mother, both of which threaten self-esteem. Detachment from her parents entails rejection of their support and a narcissistic preoccuation with self. Nevertheless, she still feels the

urge at times to remain childishly dependent. It is only through gradual resolution of infantile conflicts that one gains emotional maturity and independence. With regression, the magical thinking of childhood returns, and when a pregnant teenager says that she thought she couldn't conceive while doing it standing up, she is not uninformed but immature. And all of this takes place when a good part of an adolescent's energy must be devoted to completion of formal schooling.

For some girls, sexual intercourse during adolescent regression expresses emotional involvement with parents; hence sexual gratification is either absent or is a kind of pain reliever. Moreover, fixation—arrested emotional devleopment—is a danger here. For other girls, intercourse may be an inner expression of disengagement from the parents, or a socially induced rite of passage. In any case, premature intercourse often means substituting genital activity for needed resolution of inner conflict. At best, emotional development may proceed in spite of adolescent coitus. At worst, early coitus may "shatter" a girl's ego ideal—which rests on an idealized image of her mother—resulting in "anxity, lowered self-esteem, and feelings of vulnerability."

The new sex education favors a quite opposite view of adolescence. "Guilt feelings aroused by negative, repressive and inadequate education about sexuality interfere with school work, friendships and family life; worry and anxiety hamper learning and enjoyment of daily life." Therefore, the main task is to eliminate guilt over sexuality in young people. However, anxiety in the young girl may be a realistic ego response to social pressures toward premature coitus as much as apprehension originating in the superego. The second author of this paper, a clinical social worker, recently encountered three cases of acute psychotic states in adolescent girls following initiation of intercourse. As id impulses overwhelmed the ego, the girls sought protection in a breakdown that took the form of a paranoid projection—"I feel bad things about myself" became "They are saying bad things about me." Each girl had been spending much time alone at home and thus had had insufficient parental protection. Unfortunately, these cases are only part of a clinical trend in recent years; more and more young people lack impulse control instead of being inhibited as in the past. Ironically, the new sex education, fixing its sights on a sexual upbringing that is largely a thing of the past, proposes to eliminate guilt indiscriminately and massively just at a time when adolescents need help in controlling their impulses.

The foregoing analysis applies to classroom as well as counseling, because sex eduators design exercises to "evoke feelings and behaviors which may otherwise never surface." A "roleworking" exercise has one student simulate disclosing homosexual tendencies to another student. There is no hint that one might live to regret "publicly affirming" homosexuality. A curriculum resource guide for grades 10-12 suggests that students write a "Dear Abby" letter expressing one of their emotional problems. A distressed 15-year-old told her therapist about having refused to answer questions about frequency of intercourse, and the like, on a questionnaire for a 9th-grade sex education course; the teacher responded by telling her, in front of the class, that she had "problems." The therapist herself had had a similar experience in a workshop on adolescent sexuality for professionals.

Sex educators speak of the peer groups that they form in the classroom as "therapeutic," in the belief that "self disclosure" is a "skill," a technique that possesses intrinsic value. Technique uninformed by an adequate theory of adolescence fails to fathom psychosocial problems and merely reduces the problems to dimensions that a technician can fathom.

THEORY, RESEARCH, AND INTERPRETATION

The empirical basis for the new sex education may be illustrated by the often-cited survey which found that nonpregnant visitors to a contraceptive clinic checked off more favorable responses to intercourse and masturbation than did pregnant visitors; nonvisitors were not studied, nor do we know to what extent girls who sought contraception actually used it. The researchers decided that contraceptive seekers had "accepted their own sexuality." Thus was born the movement doctrine to resocialize the entire school-age population.

Study after study has led to the conclusion that, "one of the most striking characteristics of teenage illegitimacy is that many adolescents who have had the benefit of the best sex education and have contraceptive materials available do not use contraception." The researchers who make this statement go on to say, as always, that we must do better; they propose training in sexual decision-making, where others see the problem in terms of self-esteem, or use of the wrong kind of contraceptive. We suggest that there are *no* empirical findings that would persuade these authors to disown sex education and "family planning," because facts are accommodated to the ideology of a social movement, not the other way around.

On the basis of clinical studies, we have concluded that inhibition is both normal and desirable for adolescents. But what of the contention that adolescents cannot delay intercourse because of earlier menarche and later marriage today? In fact, median age at marriage was *lower* during the 1960s and 1970s than it was in 1890. Age at onset of menarche has declined for the past 150 years, but the upsurge in teenage intercourse and illegitimate births did not occur until the 1960s. Early intercourse is not biologically determined so much as socially induced.

The cultural lag interpretation of the "sexual revolution" holds that adults must reconcile themselves to the "sexual liberation" of the young; this implies that "recreational" sex will increase as the affect associated with sex declines. By contrast, we contend that so long as children are raised in families, the first love objects will be the parents, and sex will thus remain charged with affect. Adolescence is the "terminal stage of childhood," and girls require protection rather than liberation. Today's adolescent is psychosexually the same as her counterpart of 30 years ago; the best evidence for this is exactly that out-of-wedlock pregnancy continues to increase in response to greater permissiveness. The Western family norm has long been that children ought to be legitimate and supported by the conjugal unit; to shift economic responsibility to the state would truly be revolutionary. Our view is that the current cycle of permissiveness will give way to a more restrictive period. This view gains some credence from the fact that neither the Oneida community, the Soviet Revolution, nor the Israeli kibbutz succeeded in destroying the "bourgeois" family.

THE NEW SEX EDUCATION AND THE POLITICS OF THE SEXUAL REVOLUTION

In democratic politics, one is duty bound to state one's position clearly and then defend it against opposing points of view. Should the movement be drawn into dialogue, its position would be equivocal. It is said that teachers should merely "facilitate" the "sharing" of feelings and experiences among the young, who are "more open" than their parents about sex. Yet we also hear that teachers embarrass students, put them "on the spot," and keep them on the "hot seat." The teacher announces the exercise in which participants' bodies touch as a "contest"; "enforced closeness" and feeling "safer" about revealing attitudes to the group come about through the use of "the legitimating structure of the game." This procedure manipulates students by involving them in activities that their upbringing taught to be acceptable (games) in order to make them feel safe about doing what their upbringing taught them is wrong (e.g., promiscuous body contact).

It is said that exercises merely clarify values and do not impose them. Yet students are encouraged "to look at sex as a smorgasbord," and human sexuality experts refer to fear of pregnancy and venereal disease as "puritanical." For the new sex education movement, the ends—promoting sexual tolerance and (supposedly) reducing pregnancy—evidently justify the means—manipulating, perhaps coercing, self-disclosure and attitude change; using peer pressure, on teachers as well as students; invading privacy as entailed in sharing intimacies in public; "building a sense of community" among those who already belong to a community.

Since all of this amounts to a massive resocialization of the young, it is not surprising that the movement tries to keep its position equivocal and undebated. We doubt that the majority of Americans who support sex education in the schools are aware that what is planned is nothing less than the "emotional re-education" of America's younger population through the process of desensitization, sensitization, and incorporation. The sexual revolution has meant that individuals are now to determine their sexual conduct; in practice, peers sanction conduct instead of family or community. If the new sex education has its way, the state will now shape peer control to its own ends. This indoctrination will institutionalize the sexual revolution. The result, we believe, will be to perpetuate the atomizing process which gave rise to the problems (increased teenage out-of-wedlock pregnancy and venereal disease) that the movement promises to alleviate.

Indulging ourselves in schemes to have the schools and family-planning clinics rescue us from our difficulties only puts off the day when parents and community must reclaim their authority and their responsibility. Meanwhile, the schools could do their part by affording students a sex education consisting of timely and competent teaching of reproductive anatomy and physiology, and reading such works as *Anna Karenina* and *Tess of the D'Urbervilles;* nothing more, nothing less.

NO

Peter Scales

TODAY'S SEXUALITY EDUCATION REPRESENTS THE ESSENCE OF DEMOCRATIC SOCIETY

In the October 1982 issue of *Family Relations,* Shornack and Shornack offer a "critical view" of sexuality education that, in this author's opinion, is distinguished chiefly by serious misrepresentations of the field today, and by an abundance of inaccuracies, myths, distortions and innuendo to buttress a shaky thesis. Their thesis apparently is that sexuality education is a social movement imposed from above by the educational bureaucracy onto an unsuspecting and unwilling populace. According to the Shornacks, this movement attempts to "change the social order rather than merely to adjust to change," and it does so by "indiscriminate" use of the group-centered approach. It forces self-disclosure, focuses on contraception, and seeks to "ensconce the principle of sexual liberation" by promoting acceptance of sexuality and by fostering an "uncalled for" tolerance for varying sexual values and beliefs. If only parents knew that such "resocialization" was going on, say the Shornacks, there would be far less support for sexuality education shown in public opinion polls.

This article is a response to the major thesis they raise, including an examination of some of the key inaccuracies and distortions the Shornacks have used to build their critical view. The article ends with a treatment of the positive values that more accurately represent the field of sexuality education today.

IS THERE A UNIVERSAL CURRICULUM?

The Shornacks erroneously assume that sexuality educators wish to "universalize" exemplary programs. On the contrary, responsible sexuality educators help communities define their local needs, and then help them respond to those needs. There is no universal sexuality education curriculum any more than there is a universal history or English curriculum. Here, the Shornacks are knocking down a straw man that simply doesn't exist.

They compound this error by quoting only a few examples of actual curriculum resources. There are scores of curricula and hundreds of resources used across the country that, if mentioned, would have given a more balanced view. One of the most widely used curricula for junior high students, for example, developed by Planned Parenthood of Rochester and Monroe County (NY), states:

> Many teenagers . . . think that, 'everyone is having sexual relationships' . . . It's interesting to find out that probably less than half of any given high school class is sexually experienced. It's nice to find out that there are some people who don't use drugs. It's nicest to find out that people still value your friendship even when you don't look, talk and act just like they do.

Another widely used resource outlines a model K-12 curriculum that notes "our main values about sexuality come from family life." The Interfaith Statement on Sex Education, a 1968 cooperative effort among the U.S. Catholic Conference, National Council of Churches, and Synagogue Council of America, has been an influential source for many secular programs. Numerous other sexuality education programs use material developed by the PTA, the March of Dimes, various church groups, the American School Health Association, the Future Homemakers of America and many others. The Shornacks mentioned none of these.

SOCIAL CHANGE
AND POPULAR CONSENSUS

The Shornacks offer less than a complete view of the dynamics of social cause and effect. In their view, sex education "implies an effort to *change* the social order rather than merely to adjust to change." Another view, perhaps a more accurate

and responsible one, describes sexuality education as both reflecting *and* bringing about social change, although the changes are not the sinister kind perceived by the Shornacks. The Shornacks say, similarly, that sexuality education is a "movement from above," imposed by professional educators upon people who don't want it. Each of these views would appear to deserve a response.

Sexuality education is hardly new, and, if it is a movement, then it is a movement of the establishment. In the late 1800s and early 1900s, the YWCAs, YMCAs, Child Study Association, and National Congress of Parents and Teachers all were speaking out on the need for sexuality education, and in the early 1930s, the U.S. Public Health Service was surveying principals to determine the need for sexuality education in the public schools. When Gallup conducted his first national opinion poll on sexuality education in the schools, he found that nearly 7 in 10 adults approved of it in 1943—these respondents of 40 years ago include many of today's parents and grandparents! The sexuality education controversies of the late 1960s lowered public opinion to 65% approval in 1971. Several years later, in 1975, Hottois and Milner studied over 500 of the nation's largest school districts. A little over half the sample of superintendents said their districts offered sexuality education, but in 80% of the cases, it was initiated, not by "outsiders" to the community, but by either the superintendents or the local PTAs. In other words, sexuality education was most often a local response to a locally felt need. More recently, an in-depth study of 23 U.S. communities found 70% had community advisory committees, including clergy and parents, to help develop appropriate local programs. More important, the programs with the most *signifi-*

cant parent involvement were the most comprehensive in their content. Thus, it is clear that sexuality education programs are responding to local needs as perceived by superintendents, teachers and parents. To the extent that the perceptions of these perhaps more involved people deviate from the rest of the community's perceptions, the resulting programs could be described as imposed. The foregoing and the following evidence, however, indicate that these programs are not imposed but requested.

In 1978, a study in Cleveland, representative of parents of 3-to-11-year-olds showed that parents wanted the most community help with the subjects schools had been neglecting. They included: contraception, premarital sex, abortion, masturbation, homosexuality, and questions of values and emotions in sexuality.

To the Shornacks' charge that these figures of support are spuriously high, one need only look a bit further. Between 1970 and 1977, Gallup reported that support for including *contraceptive* information in public school sexuality education nearly *doubled* to 70% (Gallup Poll, 1978). Another national survey by the National Opinion Research Center showed that, in 1977, over 80% of the respondents believed birth control information should be made available, *regardless of age or grade*.

Rather than being up in arms over sexuality education, most parents firmly support sexuality education and believe it to be a helpful influence on their children. In the 1981 Associated Press/NBC Poll, parents with children 17 and under—those most directly affected by today's sexuality education—were the most supportive group of respondents. Over 70% thought sexuality education gives students a healthy view of sex, and a whopping 90% rejected the claim that sexuality education

somehow encourages sexual behavior (NBC, 1981). To put these figures in perspective, political elections won by 60% or more of the vote are usually considered landslide victories; 90% popular support would appear to be overwhelming. Sexuality education is sought by parents and supported by parents.

Perhaps one reason for all this support is that parents surveyed in national studies apparently do not share the Shornacks' view that sexuality educators are bent on resocializing youth and separating them from their parents' influence. In fact, one observed effect of sexuality education classes is that parents and children talk *more* with each other about sexuality, thereby *strengthening* family communication. Some of the most frequently attacked leaders of the sexuality education field, in fact, began and continue to sponsor National Family Sexuality Education Week, an annual October series of events that is just part of the massive volume of programs and resources these groups provide to support parents as the primary sexuality educators of their children.

As quoted earlier, the Shornacks are apparently comfortable only with education that helps us merely to adjust to change rather than education that brings about change. In fact parents may welcome what the sexuality education movement considers good education, because it does both: it helps children adjust to different realities than the parents grew up with; and it also helps youth to become more active influencers of their environment and their destiny. Ironically, if our education simply helped teenagers adjust to fate rather than to exert control over their decisions, a variety of maladies and problems such as teenage pregnancy would doubtlessly *increase*.

THE IMPORTANCE OF EXAMINING VALUES AND LEARNING SKILLS

Sexuality education programs do use group-centered techniques in the classroom. They do encourage role playing, sharing of attitudes and feelings, small group discussions, and other human relations techniques. But the Shornacks' charge that these are used *indiscriminately* is thoroughly unwarranted.

There has been an increasing tendency for sexuality education programs to include more opportunities to examine values and develop skills, and to rely less exclusively on factual information, for several reasons. Today we have a greater awareness of behavior motivation. In a variety of areas, including smoking, driving, drinking and even voting, professionals have learned that supplying facts alone is not likely to affect behaviors that have complex determinants. For example, Cvetkovich, Grote, Lieberman and Miller (1978) found that teenagers often have intercourse because they don't know how to say "no," think having sex is expected, or want to please their partners. These are interpersonal, normative, and communications-oriented issues that are not easily resolved by facts alone. Teaching decision-making and communication skills, however, does seem to help increase students' ability to say "no," to resist reasonable demands, and to decrease their likelihood of becoming pregnant.

A key distinction which has emerged in the field accounts for today's greater emphasis upon values examination and skills development as compared to mere imparting of information. The distinction is between sexual learning, and sexuality education. Sexuality education frequently used to focus on anatomy, on the physical acts of sexual functioning and on the dangers that can come when youth engage in genital sex. Contemporary sexuality education, on the other hand, focuses on sexuality as an integral part of personality and human relationships. It implicitly recognizes that people's thoughts, feelings, emotions and values as males and females, sons and daughters, husbands and wives, fathers and mothers, are inextricably bound to their behaviors. It also recognizes that, far more than formal learning through school courses, we build our sense of our sexual selves more from nonformal or even incidental sources of sexual learning: "When the school is compared with the family, the peer group, the mass media, and the subtle learning which is inherent in the social structure, one can begin to see that its role as an influencer of sexual learning is not as primary as we sometimes assume." Young people are faced with countless decisions that involve sexuality every day, not necessarily decisions about sexual behavior, but decisions about whom to be friends with, what to wear, where to go—decisons that affect how they feel as young men and women, and whether or not they feel good about themselves. The desire to help young people better sift through this daily reality and better handle the decisions they face every day has prompted a greater concern with helping them to *think about sexual issues* more clearly, a goal that requires considering values and teaching skills as well as facts.

The foregoing discussion indicates that sexuality education focuses on more than sex. Sexuality education is most effective when it promotes knowledge, attitudes, and skills that are also important in all aspects of life. Sexuality education ideally is education for living in a complex world. For instance, in teaching about different sexual values and the importance of tolerating and respecting these differences, students may also be helped to understand and respect cultural, racial, and religious differences. In learning how to talk about sexuality, youths also may learn transferable skills that help them talk about other emotionally laden subjects. In studying the influence of family life on development values, students can learn how they might influence their own children someday (if and when they become parents) and can acquire greater understanding about the role of the family and other social institutions. In increasing their sense of competence in dealing with sexuality, young people can also be provided with experiences that might increase their feeling of confidence in dealing with other significant issues.

Finally, facts alone are insufficient because they do not respond to young people's actual needs. It strains credulity that the Shornacks believe the adolescent of today is psychosexually the same as his or her counterpart of 30 years ago! One needs only to collect young people's questions about sexuality to comprehend the scope of their concerns and to appreciate what the real curriculum should be. Young people's questions reflect the broad framework described already; they are certainly not limited to anatomical, social, or psychological concerns, but include all these. In addition, education based on young people's actual questions is more likely to be congruent with young people's differing levels of cognitive and moral development. Jorgensen (1981) has noted that a disjunction between typical sex education courses and students' cognitive development level is a major barrier to program effectiveness. Too frequently sexuality education courses focus on the physiology of human reproduction, the dangers of venereal diseases and similarly noncon-troversial topics. In contrast, a report of a Royal Commission in Australia noted that young people, when properly taught, show that they can think about difficult moral issues and make rational decisions about them. A further indication of the real concerns of students are questions this author has collected in recent years, all written anonymously on index cards:

Fourth grade
Why do girls grow faster than boys?
How come you have wet dreams?
Why do we have sex?
Why are the breasts important?
Why does everyone laugh when we talk about sex?

Seventh and Eighth grades
How good a relationship should you have to have sex?
What if saying no doesn't work?
What should you feel while you're having sex?
When do most people first have sex?
Does God always forgive you?
What if you get pregnant and don't know how to tell your parents?
Does the relationship differ after a sex act?
How can you tell when you really love someone and are ready for sex?
Is there anything wrong with oral sex?
Why do guys drop girls who haven't for girls who have?

Ninth through Twelfth grades
What is the best contraceptive?
Do most people masturbate?
If your religion doesn't allow contraceptives, what options do you have?
If a girl refuses to have sex until she's married, is that stupid?
If a girl is raped and gets pregnant, what should she do?

117

If the boy wants sex and the girl doesn't, what will happen to the boy?

Can you get pregnant if the penis goes in, but not all the way?

How can I make my girlfriend forget her old boyfriend?

How and where do you go to get treated for VD?

How do you put a rubber on?

When are you ready for sex?

What is a fantasy?

Whose fault is it if the child is gay?

Do you think frenching is gross?

Instead of providing answers for questions like these, the Shornacks propose only that high schoolers study reproductive anatomy and read *Anna Karenina*. And what will we do with younger children? Wait until they have sex before we help them come to terms with their sexuality? Our children are obviously getting sexuality education from sources that have no quality control. Thornburg (1981) reported a study of 1152 high school students showing that peers and media were the primary first sources of information on a variety of sexuality topics. More important, students who learned primarily from peers had the least accurate understanding of these topics. Do we really prefer "street talk" to the "straight talk" that will help them make decisions? Moreover, is the teaching of reproductive anatomy and physiology adequate for a seventh grader who wants to know what to do when "saying no" doesn't work?

SEXUALITY EDUCATION AS RELATIONSHIP TRAINING

Effective sexuality education also helps participants enhance their relationships, in part by increasing their self-esteem. Self-esteem can be significantly fostered by promoting respect for each individual's values and by stressing the wide range of behaviors that are normal. In this context, sexuality education may well increase self-esteem and regard for others. Sexuality education should stress the importance of being aware, not only of one's own values, needs, and motives regarding sexual behavior, but also of the other person's values, needs, and motives. The other person may be a parent, a sibling, a religious leader, a boyfriend or a girlfriend.

Because of a preoccupation with the changes of adolescence and its accompanying challenges, many young people are far less likely than older adults to recognize the impact of their behavior on others. Good sexuality education helps young people consider the consequences of their behavior. In part, this is accomplished by helping young people learn to take the other person's perspective in a given situation. One technique for doing this is to have students role play or behaviorally rehearse a particular situation, such as how to say "no" to a partner who is aggressively forcing him- or herself sexually on the other. The Shornacks criticize the use of role playing and state that sexuality educators are "manipulating" and "perhaps coercing" students into participating in these exercises. Yet forced self-disclosure is an anathema to good sexuality education. Parents can excuse their children from sexuality education classes (only 1% ever do) and students should and do have the right not to participate in these or any other exercises.

The Shornacks describe a teacher who told a girl who refused to answer a sex-related question in class that she had problems, and they decried this behavior. Who would not? Untrained teachers are more likely to make such irresponsible statements; thus this is an argument in support of training. That an occasional exercise betrays questionable judgment and may be inappropriate, and that some educators need a great deal more training and supervision is undeniable. But those offering critical views have an equal challenge and responsibility to avoid portraying the exception as if it were the rule.

ANTI-DEMOCRATIC BIAS OF THE CRITICAL VIEW

To the Shornacks' charge that sexuality education represents an attempt to change the social order, this author must respond that, in addition to helping students adapt to changed realities and adjust to social change, responsible sexuality education also is trying to bring about social change. Sexuality educators should work without apology toward their vision of a just society.

As a sexuality educator, this author is trying to change conditions that create health problems and human suffering. He does want young people to have the information, values and skills that can help them make decisions their counterparts of 30 years ago rarely had to make at their ages. He is trying to change a social order in which only a small percentage of parents feel equipped to talk with their children about sexuality and other important life concerns. He is trying to promote more respect and equality between the sexes. Adolescents are often vitally preoccupied with the question of their normality, and too many have used sex behaviors as the means by which they grade their worth. This author believes that girls whose self-esteem is based on factors other than their popularity with boys can better say "no" to sex and other risk-taking behaviors. He believes too that boys who don't feel the need to brag to other boys about sexual exploits, real and imagined, are less likely to exploit or pressure girls.

The Shornacks criticize sexuality educators for promoting equality between the sexes, and the Shornacks' own opinions lean heavily on protecting girls and restraining boys. The Swedish guidelines for sexuality education hold a lesson for us here in urging societies to reject a double standard in which "moral sentence is passed upon women for actions that a man can commit with impunity." This author believes that responsible sexuality educators also embrace that view because inequality can only be based on disrespect, and can only lead to vulnerability, prejudice, and exploitation. Finally, this author is trying to exert social change to inculcate a greater value for the tolerance and appreciation for the diversity that is the great richness of our democratic society. The Shornacks' essentially anti-democratic bias is revealed in their abstract, where they state that the "spread of sexual tolerance is uncalled for." Would they in earlier years have said that the spread of religious, racial, or ethnic tolerance was uncalled for? What is uncalled for in our society is prejudice. Ultimately, the ethic the Shornacks propose leaves precious little room for variability, for diversity, for differences, for choice. Hence, it leaves little room for democracy, for democracy is impossible without tolerance.

A NOTE ON SOME FURTHER INACCURACIES AND MYTHS

There are many inaccuracies in the Shornacks' critical view of sexuality education. A few of the most blatant can be responded to in this space.

1. *Myth:* Study after study shows sex education does not increase use of contraception.

Fact: Few studies have actually been conducted that bear on this contention, but those that have all indicate the opposite conclusion: that sexuality education can increase use of contraception if contraception is not censored out of the course. A recent national study showed that those with sexuality education had lower pregnancy rates. Sexuality education is not a panacea for endemic phenomena such as unplanned teenage pregnancy, but it is clearly a helpful and ameliorative influence.

2. *Myth:* The first goal of sexuality education is to reduce pregnancy through use of contraception.

Fact: The primary myth in that statement is that it is *through* use of contraception—rather than encouraging an informed choice that might include abstinence—that sexuality educators wish to reduce unplanned teenage pregnancy. Reducing unplanned and ill-timed teenage pregnancy is indeed an important goal of today's sexuality education. But, a recent survey of 179 large U.S. school districts and a study of over 600 Indiana superintendents and school board members each indicate that other goals, such as improving students' ability to make decisions about sexual issues, are equally or more important. Thus, young people should be helped to make more effective decisions that 1) help them avoid unplanned and ill-timed consequences and 2) promote their physical and mental health within their value system. These decisions should be based on self-esteem, knowledge of their own values, appreciation of their family, cultural and religious heritage, and respect for democratic principles. Rather than relying solely on use of contraception, the appreciation of one's basic values, raising of self-esteem and training in assertiveness and communication skills to say "no" all encourage reduction of teen pregnancy by providing the teenager with knowledge and skills necessary to choose and act on abstinence. If a teenager chooses to engage in sexual activity, however, increased use of contraception is preferable, in this author's opinion, to children bearing children.

3. *Myth:* Sweden has had compulsory sex education since the late 1950s and illegitimacy has gone up since then.

Fact: Surveys in the late 1960s showed the majority of Swedish schools did *not* have sex education and that those having it offered courses at most of about 10 hours duration, hardly massive resocialization. Even until 1977, the guidelines for sex education were conservative, e.g., the purpose of intercourse is for procreation, and courses should support fidelity between husband and wife. In fact, the Swedish teen birth rate dropped 50% between 1956, when sex education was supposed to become universal, and 1980. Of course, Sweden is a different culture with different cultural traditions and direct comparisons with the United States are inappropriate—in Viking days, brides-to-be often had to demonstrate their fertility by becoming premaritally pregnant.

4. *Myth:* Professionals consider teaching and counseling interchangeable

Fact: The Shornacks must have limited personal contact with sexuality educators or counselors. This author knows of no responsible educator or counselor who equates the two. Professional materials, such as the code of ethics developed by the American Association of Sex Educators, Counselors and Therapists, consistently point out that a good educator is careful not to allow a class or workshop, whether for youth or adults, to cross over into counseling.

5. *Myth:* Sexual activity is somehow related to lowered SAT scores.
   Fact: Do the Shornacks really believe this? Perhaps if they do, they will be the first to credit sexual activity for the recently reported *rise* is SAT scores!

A more accurate view of the values that underlie contemporary sexuality education is found in the following list developed by this author:

Sexuality is more than sex.

Sexual learning is a lifelong education process.

It is important to become aware of and examine one's own and others' values about sexuality.

Knowledge and information about sexuality and family planning are essential.

Adequate self-esteem is the key to making healthy, ethical, and effective sexual and fertility-related decisions.

Each sexual decision has an effect or consequence.

Sexual decisions should support the dignity, equality, and worth of each individual and they should take into account medical, psychological and social ramifications of sexual activity.

It is wrong to force or exploit someone into an unwanted sexual experience, to knowingly spread disease, or to bring an unwanted child into the world.

Parenthood requires many responsibilities that adolescents are usually unable to assume and capabilities they usually do not have.

Given its medical, psychological and social ramifications, young teenagers are usually not ready for sexual intercourse.

Parents are the primary sexuality educators of their children, though not the sole educators nor always the best transmitters of information, and social institutions such as schools, churches, and family planning centers should supplement, not supplant, them in this role.

It is best if children can, of their own free will, discuss issues related to sexual and reproductive health with their parents and other valued adults.

Formal programs of sexuality education are just one, although an important, influence upon values and behavior.

Parents, as well as other people in the community, should be involved in planning formal sexuality education programs.

Participation in sexuality education programs should be voluntary.

Education staff should be highly trained, participate in regular continuing education programs, and abide by the highest standards of professional ethics.

In a pluralistic, democratic society, a wide range of values and beliefs about sexuality is to be expected.

CONCLUSION

In sum, the Shornacks' critical view of sexuality education is based upon many factual inaccuracies, false assumptions, and some misleading reporting about the values, methods and effects of contemporary sexuality education. In their reply to [a colleague's] rejoinder, the Shornacks

121

state that [he] did not demonstrate that his approach "does no harm." Can the statement be reversed, i.e., have the Shornacks demonstrated that their approach would do no harm? On the contrary, their approach would seem to already be rejected by American popular opinion precisely because, in its central thesis that ignorance is bliss and that diversity is threatening, the American people perceive an approach that would be harmful to children, to families and to the health of our democracy. It would seem that the Shornacks are not afraid of sexual activity so much as *mental* activity: curiosity, inquiry, skepticism, analysis, dissent, judgment, and choice.

A major battle is brewing, and it is not over sexuality education per se, nor ERA, nor family planning for young people, nor abortion rights. Rather, it is whether Americans shall preserve for the next generation the basic principles of our heritage. It is about curiosity versus obedience, choice versus dictate, tolerance versus prejudice. Our challenge is whether we will pass on to today's youth the "highest aspirations of our society."

Sexuality education programs try to help young people make the best decisions they can, the best choices possible, from the best options they can identify. Sexuality education as a field does need to continually re-examine its assumptions, goals and methods, and look rigorously at both its intended and unintended effects. The evidence thus far, however, shows that sexuality education is enthusiastically sought and supported by those it affects most, helps young people make responsible decisions, lessens their risk of unplanned pregnancy, lessens their prejudices, and increases their tolerance for others. In its basic goal of promoting the dignity, equality and worth of us all through responsible decision making, it represents the very essence of our democratic society.

———

POSTSCRIPT

IS SEX EDUCATION IN SCHOOLS AN ATTEMPT TO INSTITUTIONALIZE A SEXUAL REVOLUTION?

One of many vignettes might be cited here to illuminate the ongoing debate over the extent to which public school education should be providing sex education for our youth and what should be included in that education.

In New York City as of mid-1986, a few schools had limited sex education programs. Then, suddenly, the news media discovered that a couple of high schools had expanded the function of the school nurse to include a school-based health clinic designed to provide teenagers from poverty-level families with a semblance of full medical care. In the process, some of these clinics were providing contraceptive information and condoms, diaphragms, and the pill for sexually active teenagers. This policy was justified by an appeal to statistics, with over 1300 pregnant teenagers giving birth and dropping out of school every year, another 13,000 reported abortions, and probably an equal number of unreported pregnancies and abortions. The focus of debate shifted from whether the board of education should mandate sex education to whether school-based clinics should be handing out condoms to reduce teenage pregnancy and the risk of AIDS. When the new debate shifted to the city council, the board of education was able to mandate sex education in all schools from kindergarten to senior high school. As soon as this reality was reported, some religious leaders revived the sex education debate, arguing that if sex education were now a mandated reality, then it would be acceptable only if it was clearly taught that sexual relations are only acceptable for married couples.

The emotions, conflicting views, and politics of sex education today are presented by the Shornacks and Peter Scales. In forming your view, consider both perspectives. See the bibliography for further readings on this subject.

ISSUE 8

ARE SCHOOL-BASED HEALTH CLINICS AN EFFECTIVE AND SOCIALLY ACCEPTABLE WAY OF REDUCING THE INCIDENCE OF TEENAGE PREGNANCY AND STDs?

YES: Richard Kenney, M.D., from an essay written for this volume

NO: Phyllis Schlafly, from the *Phyllis Schlafly Report,* June 1986

ISSUE SUMMARY

YES: Richard Kenney, director of ambulatory pediatrics and adolescent medicine at Charlotte Memorial Hospital in North Carolina, argues from the experiences of such clinics that they appear able to address a number of problems of adolescents in a cost-effective and medically efficiacious manner. In preventing pregnancy, they save $25 for every one dollar spent.
NO: Phyllis Schlafly, founder of the Eagle Forum, claims that sex education and the associated health clinics have been promoted by some educators and social workers to provide themselves with jobs. Rather than encouraging teenage abstinence, this education has legitimized teenage promiscuity and caused the rise in teenage pregnancies since the 1950s.

In the past couple of years, a sharp controversy has erupted and spread to many of our larger cities. It revolves around a new approach to coping with the health problems and the skyrocketing dropout rate of teenagers in the inner city and low-income families. Advocates of the new approach talk about providing students with "comprehensive health services." Opponents talk about "sex clinics" and "promoting promiscuity."

Most schools have a school nurse available to handle the usual gym accidents, throat cultures, bloody noses, drug prevention education, and family life or sex education problems that are a daily part of school life. Inner-city schools and students from low-income families have many of the same needs as more affluent schools and students, but the volume is much higher. Instead of a couple of teenage pregnancies, a few cases of VD, some drug and alcohol abuse, and the few dropouts found in a suburban school, the inner-city school often has large numbers of students with pressing needs. Instead of a few students who cannot turn to their families for support, counsel and a sense of belonging, there may be dozens. As a result, the function of school nurses and counselors has begun to evolve. As Dr. James Comer, director of the School Development Program at the Yale University Child Study Center, sees it, poverty, large families, low education levels and unconcerned parents often force adolescents in low-income families out of the mainstream of society's values. Hence the need for a new approach in certain schools.

The crux of the controversy is the policy of dispensing contraceptives and providing abortion counseling and referrals. A few clinics make prescription and non-prescription contraceptives available to students. Other clinics do not give out contraceptives, but have physicians who write prescriptions for pills and diaphragms and send the students off campus where they can purchase them.

Strong objections to the clinics have come from some Reagan administration officials, the National Right to Life Committee, several Roman Catholic bishops, a variety of black and Hispanic community leaders, and Dr. Gwendolyne Baker, executive director of the national board of the YWCA, among others. In the view of William J. Bennett, US Secretary of Education, school-based clinics promote promiscuity and constitute an "abdication of moral responsibility" by adults. "This is not what school is for," he has said. "It offers a bureaucratic solution—a highly questionable, if not offensive one—in place of the exercise of individual responsibility, not just by the children, but by the adults around them."

By the end of 1986, approximately 120 national organizations, including the National Parent-Teacher Association, American Baptist Churches, Child Welfare League of America, Campfire Girls, Girl Scouts, National Education Association and the Association for School Nurses had endorsed school-based health clinics.

In defending the school-based clinics in New York City, Mayor Koch pointed out that the premise is to encourage abstinence but that "You would have to be an ostrich if you believe that if you simply advocated abstinence that every teenager is going to do that." With nearly 3000 American teenagers becoming pregnant every day, the developing role of school-based health clinics will continue to fuel an ongoing debate.

YES
Richard Kenney, M.D.

SCHOOL-BASED HEALTH CLINICS ARE AN EFFECTIVE WAY OF MEETING THE NEEDS OF TODAY'S ADOLESCENTS

Over the past three decades, the adolescent age group has been recognized to require medical care directed at their particular needs. In comparison with their younger siblings and their grandparents, they constitute a relatively healthy population. But they have a number of physical and psychosocial problems that are seen in all age groups, as well as problems related to their rapidly developing bodies and minds—for example, acne, menstrual disorders, aberrations in growth rate, problems related to their sexuality, or experimentation with chemical substances.

Addressing the medical and physiological needs of this age group has been a challenge to those delivering traditional health care. Teenagers as a rule tend not to use the physician who took care of them through childhood—the pediatrician or the family physician. They seek medical care only on an emergency basis, not making visits for preventing problems or promoting good health. Episodic, illness-oriented contacts are the only opportunity the doctor has to advise them about the risks of their life-style behavior—the lack of a *balanced diet, exercise;* the risks of *sexual activity,* of their poor *self-image,* of *substance abuse.* As a result, various alternatives to the doctor's office have developed. The school-located health facility is one such mode of delivering health care to adolescents.

THE EVOLUTION OF SCHOOL HEALTH

The school health movement has a long history in this country—from Bowditch's work in the 19th century studying growth in Boston students, to the examination of students for contagious disease by physicians in several urban school systems. School boards generally have set medical policy, limiting school health activity to prevention and diagnosis; for instance, doing hearing and vision testing, or screening for scoliosis. During the past twenty years, however, communities have become aware that a large number of young people are not receiving necessary care, either because it is unavailable or, if available, not being used. At the same time, school systems began to recognize the wisdom in the phrase "a sound mind in a strong body," recognizing that their students might never obtain a diploma because of health reasons alone. Along with these changes has evolved the family with two working parents, and an increase in single parent households. Lastly, communities have realized that the major intractable problems of adolescent health care—premature sexual activity, with its attendant increase in pregnancies and sexually transmitted diseases; abortions; widespread substance abuse at younger and younger ages; the increase in accidents, suicides, and homicides—were worsening in spite of all their efforts. From this historical foundation and recent demographic change in our nation evolved the school-based health clinics (SBHC). For the purpose of discussion in this paper, a SBHC is broadly defined as a health facility within or in close proximity to a school and providing a variety of services to its students.

THE SCHOOL-BASED CLINIC MOVEMENT

The SBHC concept was a grass-roots movement, originating in a Dallas high school in 1970. Three years later, a program began in St. Paul, Minnesota. The number of these facilities increased slowly through the next sixteen years, spreading to major coastal cities and rural areas. Funding for these clinics has been through a blend of local, state, and federal sources. Most communities and their school systems have supported them through donated equipment, space, and services. The clinics are administered by health departments, hospitals, free-standing community health centers, or corporations.

The success of SBHC seems due to the following factors:

1) They provide primary medical care near or at the school.

2) They are run by medical personnel, physicians, or trained nurse practitioners.

3) They provide services related to the prevention and diagnosis of pregnancy.

4) Medications are prescribed.

Students welcome these clinics because they are readily available—being in or quite nearby the school—the staff is known to them, and their visit is treated as confidentially as possible. The student may use the clinic for any number of reasons, from a checkup to a counseling session. The clinic and its staff are viewed as supportive and helping, well-trained in the paradoxical behaviors of adolescents.

Parents welcome these clinics because they seek parental consent for their teenager's care, they involve the parents as much as possible in any health problem, including their teen's decisions about his/her sexuality, and they provide a full range of primary medical care at low or no cost.

So for the teenagers and their parents these school-located health facilities are accessible, available, and acceptable. School administrators prefer these clinics because they help keep the students healthier and therefore in school until graduation.

INDICATORS OF EFFECTIVENESS

More and more evidence is being accumulated to indicate the effectiveness of the SBHC phenomenon. First, the burgeoning growth of these clinics points out the increasing acceptance and support of many communities. Over sixty SBHC in nearly twenty states have been established in medically unserved or underserved areas during the past fifteen years—most in the last three years.

Second, the clinics are well-used by students—usage rates as high as 70 percent of a Kansas City high school population, 75 percent in St. Paul, and 85 percent in West Dallas. Within two months of opening, a new clinic in South Chicago tallied 2,000 clinic visits. In Jackson, Mississippi, in one year, over 7,200 visits were registered in four high school clinics. As in other clinics across the nation, almost half of the visits were made by males, a group that traditional medical settings rarely see except for treatment of traumatic injuries. In Kansas City, 63 percent of the students using the clinics indicated that they would *not* have gone elsewhere for help with their problem.

Third, the clinics have had a measurable impact on reducing the high school dropout rate. The program in Jackson is able to demonstrate a decrease in the dropout rate from 50 percent to 10 percent. In St. Paul, 87 percent of the students who became pregnant while in high school graduated, while the national average for such students is 50 percent.

Fourth, strictly defined, all SBHC to be so designated must provide comprehensive services, from vision testing to rubella (German measles) screening, from Tb skin tests to Pap smears. In the process, a significant number of undiagnosed or untreated health problems are being discovered in clinic attendees. In the West Dallas Youth Clinic, for instance, 100 students were found to have heart murmurs that required further medical evaluation.

Fifth, though in most SBHC less than 20 percent of clinic visits are related to issues of human sexuality, these clinics are beginning to show a significant impact on the unbudging statistics of adolescent pregnancy. Baltimore city girls, connected with two clinics evaluated by Johns Hopkins over a twenty-eight-month period, had a 30 percent *decrease* in the pregnancy rate; while girls from two similar Baltimore schools, but without such a pregnancy prevention program, had a 57.6 percent *increase* in pregnancies. Girls in the program postponed their first sexual encounter by an average of seven months longer than girls not in the program. For this twenty-eight-month study period involving 3,400 students, a seven-month delay is a statistically significant finding. These participating teens, males as well as females, were more likely to seek advice on contraceptive methods before their first sexual encounter, which encounter alone leads to 20 percent of all teen pregnancies.

SBHC are having a striking impact on infant mortality through earlier referral of young mothers for prenatal care and more coordinated follow-up of their needs. In the Dallas clinic, infant mortality for clinic registrants has dropped 92 percent. In 1984, infants born to non-clinic mothers had a mortality rate of 18.9/1000 live births. The rate for clinic users was 1.6/1000 live births.

SBHC have had a dramatic effect on reducing repeat pregnancies among teens who use their service. Prior to the establishment of SBHC in Jackson, the repeat pregnancy rate was 50 percent. By 1986, this rate was lowered to 16 percent. Indeed, in a subset of 128 teen mothers clinic-connected for at least one year, the rate was 3 percent, while national data indicate a 20 percent rate for a second pregnancy within one year of the previous birth. In the St. Paul program, only 1.4 percent of adolescent mothers who remained in school had a repeat pregnancy within two years or until graduation.

Recently a critic of SBHC has been using mismatched data from St. Paul. In an effort to prove the St. Paul clinics ineffective in reducing teenage pregnancy, this critic mixed fertility rates (number of pregnancies per 1000 female students) with the total female enrollment over three school years, as though they were directly related. But the rate per 1000 is not contingent on nor related to this total number. They are separate pieces of data. Student enrollment can be up, down, or steady, and the rate can also be up, down, or steady—they are unrelated facts.

This same individual also stated that in St. Paul's SBHC birth rates increased, while those of Minnesota as a whole declined. But what he and the writers of the Minority Report of the House Select Committee on Children, Youth, and Families (his source) do not mention is that during that time the St. Paul program expanded from two to four high schools, and that St. Paul became a haven for 12,000 Southeast Asian immigrants, many of high school age.

The impressive improvements in reduction of adolescent pregnancies highlight the core ingredient of the SBHC: that is, once a young person uses the clinic for any reason, from dental care to counseling to family planning services, that person cannot fall through the cracks of the system. If an appointment is missed, the clinic staff will find the student at school or at home to secure the necessary follow-up. Young people who are using the contraceptive pill have a monthly contact from the clinic. If a student needs care that is not provided by the clinic, the staff will assure that the appropriate referral is made and will personally follow-up to verify whether that student was actually seen at the referral agency. This commitment to designing a health care delivery system based on the developmental nature of teenagers is what makes the SBHC attractive to its users,

their parents, teachers, school administrators, and the taxpaying community.

The costs of these clinics vary according to physical size, staffing, services offered, and incurred costs. Average cost is about $100,000/year, ranging from $25,000 to $250,000. Perhaps a more useful figure is $100 to $125 per student per year for their primary care, based on the number of students using the clinic for all services. Providing comprehensive primary health care to adolescents for $125/year is a bargain. Far greater than the cost of these clinics are the medical costs, welfare costs, and other costs to a community for emergency or inpatient care, unintended adolescent pregnancies, and low birth weight infants.

At one hospital in Charlotte, North Carolina, in 1985, seventy-six premature infants stayed in the Intensive Care Unit an average of a twenty-one days at the cost of $13,500 each. Total bill: one million dollars. The same year, seventy-three adolescent mothers delivered by Caesarean section at the same hospital at a cost near $250,000. Six years before, in this same community, the medical and welfare costs to raise the children born to adolescents during that year (1979) were estimated to be seventeen million dollars. Thus, these clinics have the potential to save large sums of money while providing needed medial care.

VOICED CONCERNS ABOUT SBHC

The spread of SBHC across the country, their success, and their courage in forthrightly addressing adolescent needs has engendered a number of detracting statements. The most vociferous opponents of SBHC generally do not have children in the school with a clinic, nor in most cases do they even live in the area. Among these unfounded remarks are (1) they deliver care without parental consent or knowledge, (2) they interfere with a student's academics, and with available medical resources, (3) they cause promiscuity, (4) they encourage abortions, and (5) they are not cost-effective.

Parental Involvement in SBHC

SBHC place strong emphasis on developing communication with parents. No clinic delivers services without parental knowledge and consent. At the beginning of each academic year, the clinics inform parents of their existence and services and obtain permission for their teenager's care. Parents give permission for full or selected service. Clinic after clinic report that few if any parents refuse consent for their child to use the clinic services.

In many cases, the clinic staff facilitates the family's securing necessary health care for their teenager. Including parents in their son's or daughter's health care in this way is a major benefit to the family unit. With parents on clinic advisory boards, participating in counseling with their teens, and attending teaching sessions for themselves, they are informed supporters of SBHC.

Academics and the SBHC

Clinics are open during and after school hours but do not interfere with students' academic pursuits. Clinic visits are allowed only during a free study period. There is strict adherence to coordinating appointments with a student's schedule so that he or she will not miss class time. No student can utilize the clinic without an appointment.

Traditional Medical Care Delivery and SBHC

The SBHC movement is rooted in providing health care to medically disadvantaged youths. The high rate of clinic usage by high schoolers in underserved communities points up the fact that this segment of the population had not been receiving care from available medical resources. In Kansas City, the majority of students using the SBHC had not seen a physician for over five years. SBHC attendees are not welcomed in private offices, in large part because of their inability to pay the necessary fees. Also, the community's primary care facilities are not accessible, nor are they appropriately structured, with an adolescent's behavioral development in mind. Nevertheless, to avoid duplication of services while still being able to meet young people's health needs, SBHC have actively sought consolidation of services with other community agencies.

Traditional medical caregivers are feeling uneasy as SBHC are having—or threaten to have—an impact on the medical economics of those communities with a less well-defined, medically underserved population. However, the opposite is occurring in the few communities where SBHC have interacted with the private medical establishment. A private practitioner in Columbia, South Carolina, whose office is across the street from a high school that recently established a SBHC, expressed his disapproval to the clinic director. Yet soon after agreeing to receive referrals from the clinic, he had more new adolescent patients than he could accommodate. A private physician in Dallas had the same experience. Furthermore, because the clinics assure third party payment for referred patients, the accepting doctors are guaranteed reimbursement. The number of undiagnosed or untreated medical problems found by the clinic staff make it unlikely that physicians who are willing to participate in the care of these adolescents will see a drop in their patient load.

An alternative for private physicians, other than accepting referrals, is to contract with SBHC for the position of clinic physician on a part- or full-time basis. Such contractual arrangements have been made in some SBHC, particularly with private radiology and pathology groups, but has not yet reached the full partnership in care that is possible.

Teenage Sexual Behavior and SBHC

Do SBHC promote promiscuity? There is no research that suggests that the family planning component of SBHC contributes to increased sexual activity.

SBHC put major emphasis on encouraging students to abstain from sexual activity. Educational efforts in the clinic and in the classrooms are directed at teaching students how to say "no" to premature sexual activity and all chemical substances. The students are supported in their desire to remain abstinent, and they are given "verbal combat" skills to use when confronted with situations which, unplanned for, could lead to these risk-taking behaviors. Role playing typical boy-girl, boy-boy, or girl-girl interactions provides them with the verbal ammunition to maintain or reestablish their virginity (the second virginity) and have a positive self-image.

Only about a third of the sixty established SBHC provide contraceptives to their clinic users. At the SBHC in Muskegon Heights, Michigan, all students (male and female) seeking family planning services must first attend an educational session in which they explore their values, life goals, postponing sexual involvement, and the pros and cons of birth control methods.

A large study completed in 1984, the Mathtech study, indicated that programs in sex education that are linked with a SBHC show a decrease in sexual activity. Preliminary data collected from several thousand students in two schools with a pregnancy prevention program, matched with two schools without such a program, revealed that in the clinic schools the rate of sexual activity among students was the same or lower. Another study in the Kansas City clinics showed that, between 1983 and 1985, sexual activity reported by the survey respondents was essentially unchanged.

Among Baltimore high school students not already sexually active, data showed that those exposed to a program to increase knowledge about sexuality and change behavior had postponed the initiation of sexual activity to a later age than those who were not exposed to such a program.

As with the undocumented remark that SBHC promote promiscuity, there is no evidence to indicate that SBHC promote abortions. Nationally, the abortion rate is about 45 percent for adolescents aged fifteen to nineteen.

No SBHC perform abortions; many do not make such a referral. SBHC abortion rates are extremely low. The abortion rate is about 5 percent at the Dallas SBHC. In the St. Paul program, which is relatively well funded and more aggressive in pursuing its family planning component, the majority of girls with positive pregnancy tests carried the pregnancy to term.

The Cost-Effectiveness of SBHC

There is no question that these SBHC are cost-effective. As noted above, even a small reduction in the rate of adolescent pregnancies would generate more than the total annual cost of a clinic. If such calculations are done for early detection of undiagnosed but correctable medical problems such as hypertension, renal or heart disease, or significant psychological disorders, the cost savings to an individual and the community would have a very high cost to benefit ratio.

The Dallas clinic recently evaluated the effectiveness of preventive or early intervention care in reducing the hospitalization rate of its users. Analysis of their data indicated that the hospitalization rate for clinic registrants was consistently much lower than for non-users. Several benefits can be concluded from this: direct patient benefit experienced through improved quality of life (absence of disease or control of a chronic health care problem); a decrease in time lost from school or work; and personal financial savings from avoiding hospitalization. The community benefits from a healthier, more productive population; cost savings accrue to the taxpayer who bears the burden of medical care cost for the economically deprived. With a hospitalization rate four times lower than clinic non-registrants, this clinic saves the Dallas community $650,000 per year.

To draw once more on the St. Paul clinic, which has the most longitudinal data, and focusing just on family planning services in 1983, the cost of providing an average of 2.6 visits per patient per year was $111. Family planning visits totaling 1,100 students that year cost $122,550. Based on conservative national figures, without such services 60 percent of these patients would have become pregnant, resulting in an annual cost to the community of about $3 million in medical and welfare payments. For every $1 spent on this one component of its program, St. Paul saved $25.

CONCLUSION

Comprehensive SBHC seem to represent another step in the evolution of school services. Unlike most traditional school health programs, these clinics actually provide primary care in the major health areas needed by adolescents; they prescribe and/or dispense medications and they provide some family planning services. The limited research currently existing suggests that this is a promising model for providing adolescent health care and addressing the problems of teenage substance abuse and pregnancy. Health facilities in or proximate to a school are an answer to some of the unmet needs of young people. These programs appear able to address a number of the intractable problems of the adolescent years in a cost-effective and medically efficacious manner.

NO

Phyllis Schlafly

SCHOOL-BASED SEX CLINICS PROMOTE PROMISCUITY AND LACK OF RESPECT FOR SEX

Suppose the public schools were to install a course in "Substances" which teaches students that taking drugs is risky because it might damage your health, make you a dangerous driver, and even send you to jail, but that, if you think you might take drugs anyway, please visit our "substance clinic" in Room 202 where our "specialists" will teach you how to avoid getting caught and provide you with the necessary drug paraphernalia.

The probable reaction would be that parents would protest, a principal would be fired, and new school board members would be elected. But this is exactly the kind of argument that is fueling a new phenomenon: the installation of "sex clinics" inside public schools to dispense contraceptives to unmarried teenagers.

This radical concept has been propelled by the argument that teenagers are promiscuous anyway (the euphemism is "sexually active"), and therefore the schools should teach them how to avoid having babies. These school-based sex clinics and courses teach a strange new definition of the word responsible: "responsible sexuality" means enjoying promiscuity without guilt and without having a baby.

The promoters of sex clinics for schoolchildren are imposing on a captive audience their peculiar concepts, namely, that promiscuity is good but pregnancy is bad. They are saying, Step right up, teenager, and get your contraceptives here; have fun with your sex partner; the only thing that's wrong is having a baby.

About 30 such sex clinics have been quietly (even surreptitiously) introduced into public high schools in recent years. By October 1985, the promoters of this new industry felt confident enough to stage a national conference in Chicago to train hundreds of health service professionals who want to co-opt the schools as rent-free offices for their expanding bureaucracy.

The forces advocating sex clinics have wide access to foundation money and favorable media. CBS's *60 Minutes* gave Planned Parenthood a full segment in April 1986 to propagandize for sex clinics, omitting the usual hostile interruptions. Sex clinics were endorsed on NBC's *Today* Show on May 15, with Bryant Gumbel falsely saying, "there is no opposition."

The plan to install school-based sex clinics was criticized by Education Secretary William J. Bennett on April 11 as an "abdication of moral authority." He said that these clinics "legitimate" sexual activity while encouraging teenagers

From, "School-Based Sex Clinics vs. Sex Respect," by Phyllis Schlafly, *The Phyllis Schlafly Report,* June 1986. Copyright © 1986. Reprinted by permission of *The Phyllis Schlafly Report.*

to have "sexual intimacy on their minds."

Planned Parenthood and the health service professionals, who have a vested interest in providing costly taxpayer-financed "services" to an ever-expanding constituency of "clients," have a typical knee-jerk response. David Andrews, executive vice president of the Planned Parenthood Federation, answers that we face the alternatives of "ignorance" or "pregnancies."

Those are NOT the alternatives. The correct alternative is for the schools to each teenagers NOT to engage in premarital sex. When we dare to say that, the liberals and sex-clinic promoters make predictable replies.

First, they say, "That's impossible because it won't work." To which we should answer, "You cannot know that because it hasn't been tried." Ever since sex education was introduced into public schools about 30 years ago, these courses have taught schoolchildren how to do it but have censored out all judgmental warnings against premarital sex.

Second, they say "That's impossible because teenagers are sexually active anyway." To which we should answer, "A minority of teenagers are, but the majority are not. If the school legitimizes the immoral behavior of the minority, the school will be validating promiscuity by the majority."

Third, they say, "You can't impose your moral values on schoolchildren by telling them that premarital sex is wrong because that would breach the wall of separation of church and state." To which, we should answer, "Nonsense. There isn't any constitutional difference between teaching teenagers that it's wrong to have a baby and teaching them that it's wrong to engage in premarital sex. There isn't any constitutional difference between teaching

teenagers that it's wrong to drive a car without a driver's license and teaching them that it's wrong to engage in sex without a marriage license."

SEX EDUCATION?

There are many true and powerful reasons to justify teaching abstinence to teenagers without ever mentioning religion or right-or-wrong morality. The schools can teach students that promiscuity is bad, risky, unhealthy, and stupid (especially for girls) because its consequences can be incurable VD, emotional trauma, and a forfeiture of opportunities for a lifetime marriage to a faithful spouse and for career and economic advancement.

This nation has accepted all sorts of government restraints on our personal behavior that are not nearly so dangerous as teenage promiscuity. The seat-belt law and the 55-mile speed limit law are two examples. Teenage promiscuity is more dangerous to more people, and more costly for all of us, than violations of either of those laws.

Yet the public schools are aiding and abetting promiscuity in most of their so-called "sex education" courses. Here is a typical example. The following quotations are from the textbook used since 1978 in the Seattle, Washington, public high schools in a mandatory "Health" course:

"Premarital sexual intercourse is acceptable for both men and women if they are involved in a stable loving relationship. It has been suggested by some marriage counseling authorities that all couples should live together before they are married."

"Often promiscuity is labeled as 'bad' by persons who do not accept this type of behavior. As with other patterns of sexual behavior, one should not pin a 'good' or 'bad' label on a practice."

"Morality is individual; it is what YOU think it is. Your conception of what is right or wrong (morality) is an individual decision."

Reading further in this textbook called *You and Your Health* by William Fassbender, we find that it includes pornographic pictures and also teaches

- that homosexuality is a normal lifestyle—and that "gay rights" legislation should be enacted to stop "discrimination" against homosexuals and lesbians;
- that prostitution should be legalized;
- that it is NOT deviant for teenagers to watch others performing sex acts through binoculars, windows, or holes in walls;
- that "alternatives to traditional marriage" include "open marriage where outside sexual relationships can exist and will not harm the marriage," *and* "group marriage" where three or more people live together and "have sexual relations with each other." The textbook asks the student: "Do you *feel* that you might be interested in becoming a part of such a group?"

When parents start objecting to such promotion of promiscuity, some schools respond that they mention "abstinence" as an "option" to contraceptives. Here is one example of how phony that claim is. A Florida public school textbook includes a "birth control chart" listing eleven methods, one of which is "abstinence." But the chart lists the "disadvantages" of abstinence as follows: "pleasure and closeness of sexual intercourse are not enjoyed."

The social service professionals have designed increasingly bizarre plans for public schools to deal with venereal diseases. The latest scheme of those who hide kooky curricula behind the term "sex edu-cation" is a plan to teach schoolchildren how to practice "safe homosexual sex."

The State of Illinois set up an AIDS Interdisciplinary Advisory Council to recommend legislation to deal with the social problems posed by AIDS (Acquired Immune Deficiency Syndrome). The majority report of this Council relies almost totally on education as a means of breaking the chain of transmission of AIDS.

The majority report calls for "frank and explicit" education materials—and does NOT limit the use of such materials to targeted high-risk groups. Instead, the majority report states: "A comprehensive program for AIDS education for grade school aged and older children in the Illinois public schools is essential to the education of the public."

The majority report, written by State Representative Sam Vinson, states: "It is extraordinarily unrealistic to believe that the General Assembly is going to fund 'frank and explicit' programs about safe homosexual sex in public grade schools." The kind of materials that are being distributed by those who advocate education in "safe homosexual sex" are far too explicit and disgusting to publish in this newsletter.

SEX RESPECT

Now there is a new course for junior high schoolers that teaches teenagers how and why to say "no" to sex before marriage. This *Sex Respect* curriculum is currently being piloted in Chicago and St. Louis schools.

With creative lesson plans, cartoons, and jargon that appeal to teenagers, *Sex Respect* gives teenagers the confidence and knowledge to practice sexual abstinence. From a basic health (physical and emotional) perspective, teenagers learn why chastity is the positive and healthy alternative to the "popular contraceptive mentality.". . .

Is it realistic to believe that teenagers can be taught to abstain from premarital sex? Of course it is; that was the pattern for most teenagers until the last 20 years when "sex education" invaded public schools and pornography invaded primetime television. Even the American Association of Sex Educators, Counselors and Therapists heard a speaker at its 1986 convention in Los Angeles say that, if AIDS spread from homosexuals to heterosexuals, this could "send the nation's sexual mores back to the 1950s, when young people went steady, got engaged and later maintained a monogamous marriage."

PILL GOES TO SCHOOL

"Pill Goes To School" was the way the *Chicago Sun-Times* broke the news to Chicago area residents that DuSable Public High School has been aiding and abetting promiscuity of schoolchildren by handing out free contraceptives. The news shocked citizens, parents, and teachers, and opposition to the sex clinic has been rising ever since.

The nationwide plan to put free contraceptives in all public schools as soon as financing can be arranged was unveiled at a national conference called "School-Based Health Clinics" in Chicago in October 1985. The several hundred conferees were taken to inspect the DuSable operation as a "model." The plan is to launch the sex clinics with money from big foundations, and then load the costs onto the backs of the taxpayers; the conferees were told that funds could come from 57 federal agencies. The plan is to use the poor (usually in ghetto neighborhoods) as guinea pigs for this social experiment and then impose it on all public schools.

As more and more information surfaces about the sex clinic controversy in Chicago, it has become apparent that there is a vast array of well-known social service organizations, using charitable contributions and foundation money, which has been "networking" in order to "sensitize" communities to the asserted "need" for school-based clinics. Even the American Red Cross, known to the public for its good works in blood banks and disaster relief, is deep into the promotion of school-based sex programs. The goal is to expand the social service bureaucracy and to turn the schools into sites to dispense socialized medicine from the cradle to the grave.

It has become apparent that the promoters of sex clinics to not want to teach abstinence. If most high school students are virgins, they are not customers for contraceptives or abortion clinics. They will not be clients for the ever-expanding bureaucracy of social service and health care "providers" and counselors.

So the people who stand to make money out of teenage promiscuity try to sell the slogan that "they" must be given new funding and more personnel to cope with the "problem" of teenage pregnancy. The fact is that teenage *promiscuity* is the problem, and pregnancy is only one of the consequences of that problem. The problem cannot be solved by encouraging and legitimizing more promiscuity.

Yet, these contraceptive clinics in public schools promote the promiscuity of minors by giving them the devices to facilitate engaging in illicit acts with "sex partners." These sex clinics accept teenage promiscuity as "normal" and provide the paraphernalia for practicing it: the pill, the IUD, and condoms. These sex clinics also engage in all sorts of privacy-invading techniques and interrogations.

Here are some questions given to teenagers in the "psychosocial evaluation" used at the DuSable sex clinic: "If you could change your life, what would you do? What are your thoughts and feelings about birth control? Have you started having sex? If yes, are you using contraceptives? What type? Have you ever been pregnant? With whom do you live? Do you get along with your parents? Do you have any sisters or brothers? If so, do you get along with them? What is your relationship like with your boyfriend? What do you worry about most of the time? Do you sleep well at night?"

Here are questions from the "health questionnaire" used at a similar school-based sex clinic in Kansas City: "What is the total number of people living in your house/apartment? How far did your parents go in school? Most of the time, who fixes your meals at home? How many times a week do you have a meal at a fast food restaurant, like McDonald's or Kentucky Fried Chicken? Have you had sexual intercourse? How often did you or your partner use any kind of birth control? What kind do you or your partner usually use?"

One booklet distributed by a contraceptive-dispensing clinic is called "So You Don't Want To Be A Sex Object." It provides "rules" such as: "Don't diddle around about sex. Decide what it means to you, how you feel about it, what you want from it (if you want it), and with whom. Then be honest about it. What kind of sex are you interested in?" Then it discusses "sex between acquaintances," "sex between friends," "sex between buyers," "desperate sex," and "solo sex."

The booklet advises all to "get and use good contraception." It tells the "live-in mistress" to "get paid what you are worth. There is at least a minimum wage which you should be paid for every hour you are 'on duty.'"

Another pamphlet, called "Success With Condoms" reads like a commercial advertising brochure. It describes the advantages of condoms, how to buy them, and how to use them. It says that "it takes time to feel comfortable and at ease with condoms."

The promoters of sex clinics are not the educators; the promoters are the social service professionals and health care providers who see the opportunity to co-opt the schools and use them to subsidize an expansion of the social welfare bureaucracy. They are joined by those who want to use the schools as sales meeting places for the profitable commercial products of the contraceptive manufacturers and the abortion clinics.

Any public school with a sex clinic has lost its good name as an educational institution. It is also making itself socially, politically, and financially liable for the costly diseases that result from promiscuity.

COSTS AND LIABILITIES

The cost of installing and staffing school-based sex clinics is only one of its burdens. An even bigger cost factor may be the financial liability which is incurred by the schools and their school boards. Schools that dispense contraceptives to teenagers may be held financially liable for the venereal disease and other traumas of promiscuity in the same way that the tavern owner can be held liable for the auto accidents of persons to whom he serves liquor.

Venereal diseases are at an epidemic level in the United States as a consequence of the sexual revolution, the Playboy mentality, and the prevalence of pornography in entertainment media. Since "sex education" courses started in schools about 30 years ago, they have taught directly or indirectly the lie that antibiotics can cure all venereal diseases.

Today, 20 million Americans have incurable venereal herpes, 4.6 million have chlamydia (which causes infertility among women), and 20,000 have the incurable fatal AIDS. Teenagers who are given contraceptives so they can be "safe" from pregnancy are simply NOT safe from VD, and the school could be held liable for the horrendous costs of these diseases.

What about the financial liability for the abortions that may result from the failures of the contraceptives dispensed by the sex clinics? All contraceptives have an admitted percentage of failures, and the sex clinics dispense the devices to minors who may not use them correctly or regularly and who, in any event, cannot be held financially responsible themselves. Some clinic professionals admit that the high school girl who is given contraceptives uses them, on the average, for only about three months. Is abortion, then, the solution for teenage girls who have been taught at school that promiscuity is acceptable but having a baby is not?

The leaders of Women Exploited by Abortion (WEBA), an organization of women who have had abortions, describe their emotional devastation: the remorse, the loss of confidence in decision-making capabilities, the lowering of self-esteem, the preoccupation with death, the self-destructive behavior, the anger and rage, the helplessness and despair, the morbid desire to remember the death date every year, the lack of desire to enter into a relationship with a partner, the loss of interest in sex, the nightmares, the frustrations, the feelings of being exploited, and the memory of physical pain. Some WEBA members say they cannot vacuum their carpets because it reminds them of the powerful suction machine used in the abortion. Abortion is not the end of a problem; it's the start of a whole new set of problems.

A school which dispenses devices that facilitate and legitimize promiscuity may be held liable for many other consequences ranging from "wrongful births," to the long-range effects of contraceptives, to out-of-wedlock births and the poverty that follows. Remember, pregnancy is the side effect of the *real* problem, which is promiscuity.

Try asking schools and insurance companies about the financial liability of school-based sex clinics and you will find that previously loquacious persons suddenly become mute. They remind us of the old story about the chicken thief who answered the farmer's question "Who's there?" by saying "Nobody's here but us chickens." Everybody's ducking responsibility; but plaintiffs usually sue everyone and try to recover from what lawyers call the "deep pocket" (whoever has the most money and bears any responsibility at all).

Even before sex clinics and AIDS came along, public schools faced dramatic increases in the costs of their liability insurance. Many school districts and local government bodies have had their liability insurance canceled or their premiums increased tenfold as a result of a flood of lawsuits and large personal injury settlements. This rise in insurance costs means either curtailing services which some people regard as essential or whopping tax increases to pay the costs.

The sex clinic at DuSable High School sent home a parental consent notice which commits the School-Based Clinic "to provide comprehensive health services" including "Treatment of sexually transmitted diseases." The question Chicago parents are asking is, does existing school health insurance cover this sex clinic and the treatment of venereal diseases (including AIDS) and, if so, how much will school insurance costs skyrocket?

POSTSCRIPT

ARE SCHOOL-BASED HEALTH CLINICS AN EFFECTIVE AND SOCIALLY ACCEPTABLE WAY OF REDUCING THE INCIDENCE OF TEENAGE PREGNANCY AND STDs?

The newness and the rapidly changing variety of school-based health clinics (SBHC) have contributed much to the heated debate that surrounds them. Those who oppose sex education in the schools and believe that this value-laden area of child-rearing should be the sole responsibility of parents and churches are naturally disturbed by SBHCs that provide sexual counseling and contraceptives. Antiabortion advocates are understandably disturbed by the possibility of abortion referrals being made by SBHCs. Arguments about the rights and responsibilities of parents are equally heated, especially since many parents find it difficult to deal with the sexual maturation of their children and many adolescents find it equally difficult to discuss sex with their parents.

While the programs have the cooperation and support of students, teachers and principals, they are often started by an outside individual or group. They may be supported by the local community, but their long-term funding remains uncertain. To what extent will the state departments of maternal and child health, social services, and education be able to provide the necessary funds for expansion of the SBHCs in an era of constricting budgets? In late 1986, however, a bill to provide $50 million for school-based clinics in each of the following four years was introduced in both houses of Congress.

The short time in which SBHCs have been functioning leaves us with another important question. No studies have yet examined the effect of school-based health clinics on the incidence of various sexually transmitted diseases. This factor could become critical when one recalls these clinics are usually in low-income areas where street drugs are a common problem. Sharing of needles by IV drug users and multiple sexual partners are major avenues for the spread of AIDS. In October of 1986, the Surgeon General of the United States said that the best way to prevent the spread of the deadly AIDS virus is to begin teaching about AIDS and high risk sexual behavior "at the lowest grade possible" as part of a continuing sex-education curriculum. How might the SBHCs help in this effort? To what extent can education aimed at postponing adolescent sexual involvement and the availability in SBHCs of condoms for sexually active adolescents help reduce the spread of sexually transmitted diseases? Comparing the prophylactic advantages of condoms and spermicidal foams with the contraceptive pill raises questions about which contraceptives should be promoted.

All things considered, the debate over SBHCs is likely to continue as new questions arise and new data become available. See the bibliography for further readings on this subject.

PART 3
PRENATAL ISSUES

The Copernican revolution upset the Renaissance culture by declaring that the earth revolved around the sun. Darwinian evolution theory challenged the Victorian belief in the unchangeable nature of all species, while Einstein found relativity and flux everywhere beneath the surface appearances of familiar life. Each of these breakthroughs in the way we viewed the world wreaked havoc with our existing views, values, and eventually, our behavior. Today our contraceptive and reproductive technologies create a similar but much more personal revolution by reshaping some of most intimate experiences and relationships.

Within the past two decades we have experienced a technological revolution in human reproduction that introduces radical and novel ways of reproducing ourselves. This revolution has fundamentally altered the way we view the fetus in the womb and its relationship with the rest of the human world. It has created new ambiguities in the heretofore self-evident roles of motherhood and fatherhood. In the process, we have taken a quantum leap into a world of unprecedented and often undefined legal questions and ethical concerns.

The center of the storm is the embryo— the human fetus. For untold centuries the fetus developed in total secrecy, behind an impenetrable veil. But modern technology has lifted that veil with intrauterine television, ultrasound scans, genetic screening, amniocentisis and chorionic villi sampling to study the embryo when it is less than four weeks old. As the veil lifts, we are faced with a variety of new challenges, new questions and new dilemmas.

Is the Antiabortion Movement Based on a Belief in the Sacred Value of Human Life?

Is Surrogate Motherhood a Form of Prostitution?

Should Gender Predetermination Be Regulated?

141

ISSUE 9

IS THE ANTIABORTION MOVEMENT BASED ON A BELIEF IN THE SACREDNESS OF HUMAN LIFE?

YES: Senator Orrin G. Hatch, from "The Value of Life" (National Committee for a Human Life Amendment, Inc., 1986)

NO: James W. Prescott, from "The Abortion of 'The Silent Scream,' " *The Humanist,* September/October 1986

ISSUE SUMMARY

YES: Senator Orrin G. Hatch argues that abortion is a worldwide calamity. He supports a constitutional amendment that will overturn the US Supreme Court decisions legalizing abortion and halt the carnage of abortion by restoring respect for all human life as a right protected under our Constitution.

NO: Despite claims of the antichoice advocates that they are pro-life, James W. Prescott, a developmental neuropsychologist and cross-cultural psychologist, argues that their real motivation comes from an authoritarianism that consistently supports human violence, is indifferent to pain and suffering, and denies the personal right of self-determination, especially in sexual issues.

Abortion techniques are described in a 4000-year-old Chinese text, making it one of the oldest known medical procedures. Ancient Greece and Rome advocated abortion as an important method of population control. Today, abortion is worldwide the most common medical procedure, with an estimated 30 to 55 million abortions being performed each year, half of them illegally.

Since the 1973 Supreme Court decision legalizing first trimester abortions, a variety of attempts have been made to restrict abortion in America. In 1980, the Hyde Amendment forbade expenditure of any federal money for abortions under Medicaid, thereby making abortion for one third of a million poor women very difficult, if not impossible. In 1983, an effort to introduce a Human Life Amendment to our Constitution failed to gain necessary support of two-thirds of the Senate. Foreign aid programs to limit population growth were cut because they included abortion as an option. Federal funds for national and international programs sponsored by Planned Parenthood/World Population were prohibited because abortion was supported as an option. Local laws have been passed restricting abortion to hospitals, requiring a 24-hour waiting period, counseling by a doctor, and a court order or parental consent for minors seeking an abortion. Most of these have been ruled unconstitutional.

This perspective forces us to examine the consistency of arguments on both sides of the debate. To what extent are the antichoice and prochoice advocates consistent in their defenses of human life? Does the antichoice movement too frequently take on positions that are anti-family, pro-pain, and pro-violence in issues other than abortion, as Prescott maintains here? Or is there in fact a "seamless garment" of positions that respect human life across the board, as the Catholic bishops of the United States maintain?

In the two contrasting views presented here, as in any emotional debate, one has to be extremely careful about how words are used and their precise meanings. To what extent are key words or phrases used without precise definitions? What does a phrase like "Most women believe that life begins at conception" mean, and what does it imply without actually stating the hidden message? The key word in this sentence is obviously "life," but without a precise definition, "life," and the sentence it is used in here, can be very misleading. If most women believe that a full human life, a person, exists at conception, then obviously abortion is murder. If, on the other hand, most women believe that biological human life starts at conception but the fullness of human personhood only comes later in fetal development, in the last trimester for instance, then using this simple statement to imply that most women oppose all abortion is misleading. What is the message one should logically draw from the statement that "reliable polls show that 80 to 90 percent of all Americans consider abortion at some stage as the destruction of a living person"? What is the spread or range of views in this overwhelming majority? The key phrase "at some stage" can refer to conception, the end of the first or second trimester, or the eighth or ninth month of pregnancy. It is important to know how many Americans believe a fully human person exists at the various stages of pregnancy.

YES   Senator Orrin G. Hatch

THE VALUE OF LIFE

Sooner or later everyone involved deeply in the abortion controversy, as I have been, comes to realize that in this area, above all, myths conflict with facts, slogans with truths. In what follows I propose to contrast some of the myths with the facts, to scrutinize the emptiness of pro-abortion slogans when exposed to the truth. Only in this way, I am convinced, can the carnage of abortion be halted and respect for all human life be restored to the status of a right protected under our Constitution.

In 1983, a constitutional amendment to overturn the controversial Supreme Court decisions legalizing abortion on demand failed to secure the two-thirds majority necessary for Senate approval. Perhaps the major reason was public unawareness of the dimensions and implications of the brutal practice of abortion. Few realize that over 15 million children have been killed in the United States since abortion was legalized in 1973; that only one other country in the world—Communist China—has a more permissive abortion policy; that in our country two million unborn children a year fall prey to the tools of the abortionist's trade; that some of our nation's leading cities record more abortions than live births; or that at least 97% of these killings are performed solely for reasons of convenience. Furthermore, there are more than 50 million abortions worldwide each year. This is truly a calamity of catastrophic proportions.

Freedom of Choice
Ironically, this dreadful carnage takes place under the misleading banner

of a laudable principle: "freedom of choice." One day, while preparing for an important debate on the floor of the U.S. Senate, I learned that one of the Senate aides was pregnant. My immediate reaction was to enthusiastically congratulate her and to assure her of the joy of family life. As I told of the arrival of our first child and the joys Elaine and I had experienced as our family had grown to include six unique, challenging and rewarding children, my happy reminiscing was cut short by her uncharacteristically sullen demeanor. Stopping in mid-sentence, I asked if something was wrong. Indeed there was.

With an apology, she explained that she was considering the alluring option of abortion. Her career was just getting underway, and she felt that this interruption could disrupt her plans. Her hasty speech concluded with the most common justification for abortion: "After all, I must be able to choose, myself, what I will do with my body."

"The real question is not the freedom to choose," I replied, "but freedom to choose *what*?" We exercise freedom of choice when we elect to get out of bed, or play tennis, or eat lunch. Every deliberate action, good or bad, involves a choice. Mere freedom of choice does not justify any action, but only describes the process by which we weigh the pros and cons and arrive at decisions.

If freedom of choice were itself a justification for choice, then individuals could justify stealing, or pushing drugs, selling pornography, or even killing another human, on the basis that they were free to choose to do so. Anyone who drives a car, for instance, is free to exceed speed limits. Because of the threat to other drivers and innocent pedestrians, however, society has chosen wisely to protect itself against speeding by punishing that particular choice. Even tax laws favor some choices over others. Every governmental action in some way influences individual choices.

Choices must be governed by a careful and thoughtful search for the right course of action. The real question for you is not whether you are free to terminate the life of your infant, but what the moral significance and the consequences of that choice will be for you, your family—including your unborn child—and for society as a whole. From that vantage point, freedom of choice may have some meaning.

Ask yourself who is protecting your unborn child's freedom of choice. If we value freedom of choice, shouldn't we respect the choice the unborn child would obviously make—the choice to live? What I am saying is that, once a life begins within a woman, she isn't the only one involved. Just where does she get the right to "choose" someone else's death? None of us has absolutely unrestricted rights. Our rights are limited by the rights of other persons—preeminently, by this right to live.

Words of Scripture

Since then, I have often had occasion to reflect on the calamity of abortion. While presiding as chairman of the Senate's Constitution Subcommittee during nine lengthy hearings exploring every philosophical, legal, moral, medical, and social aspect of this crisis, I thought about the plain commands of scripture on this subject. Not that abortion is a sectarian or even uniquely "religious" issue; the public policy arguments against abortion are overwhelming. For a religious believer, however, religious considerations do add an extra dimension of concern.

If men strive, and hurt a woman with child,

145

so that her fruit depart from her . . . he shall surely be punished. (Exodus 21:22)

Can a woman forget her sucking child, that she should not have compassion on the son of her womb? Yea, they may forget, yet will I not forget thee. Behold, I have graven thee upon the palms of my hands. (Isaiah 49:15-16)

He (John the Baptist) shall be filled with the Holy Ghost even from his mother's womb. (Luke 1:15)

The baby (John the Baptist) leaped in her womb (when Mary, bearing the Savior, came into the presence of Elizabeth). (Luke 1:41)

So God created man in his own image, in the image of God created he him; male and female created he them. And God blessed them and God said unto them, be fruitful and multiply and replenish the earth. (Genesis 1:27-28)

While listening to the testimony of over 80 witnesses, I reflected on how our Father has shaped human history through the common miracle of sending children into the world. With Israel in bondage, He sent Moses and Aaron (Exodus 6:20). With the birth of the Saviour approaching, He sent John the Baptist. With the entire family of Adam in inescapable spiritual and physical bondage, He sent His own Son (John 3:16). Indeed, my wife Elaine and I have often thought that our greatest mission in life is to provide a home for the six special spirits He has sent to us. The simple phrase concerning Ruth, through whose lineage came the Savior, captures for us the Lord's hand in the birth process: "The Lord gave her conceptions" (Ruth 4:12). The birth of each child is indeed a small means by which the Lord can bring about great miracles.

Historic View of Abortion

The hearing process also gave me an opportunity to recall that, even during the times when the fullness of the gospel did not light the world, enlightened men still understood the sanctity of unborn life. John Calvin wrote:

> If it seems more disgraceful that a man be killed in his own home than in his field— since for every man his home is his sanctuary—how much more abominable is it to be considered to kill a fetus in the womb who has not yet been brought into the light. (John Calvin, *Commentaries on Exodus, 21,22.*)

Blackstone, the great eighteenth-century codifier of the common law, maintained that:

> Life is the immediate gift of God, a right inherent by nature in every individual . . . (Abortion) was by the ancient law homicide or manslaughter. (*1 W. Blackstone Commentaries, 129-130.*)

Our own Declaration of Independence decreed without equivocation:

> We hold these Truths to be self-evident, that all Men are created equal, *that they are endowed by the Creator with certain inalienable Rights, that among these are Life,* Liberty, and the Pursuit of Happiness. (emphasis added)

Most somber among my reflections, however, was that countless young women, like my friend, submit to abortion on the basis of a hollow "freedom of choice" without considering the consequences of that choice. Accordingly, I resolved to write this article to spotlight some of those consequences and, at the same time, to dispel some myths employed in the all too successful attempts to make abortion an acceptable choice.

The most tragic consequence of abortion, of course, is that more than 15 million children have been killed in the United States since the Supreme Court legalized abortion on demand. The war on the unborn has cost more than ten times the number of American lives lost in all our nation's other wars lumped together. Moreover, the death rate is still climbing. Over 1.5 million abortions a year are performed in America. Nearly one in every three pregnancies ends in abortion.

Supreme Court Error

These staggering totals have prompted many conscientious Americans to ask how abortion, banned for centuries by civilized cultures, could become legal. The sad truth is that on January 22, 1973, the Supreme Court declared that the Constitution includes a right to abortion. The effect was to overturn the prohibitions against abortion in each of the 50 states and substitute a more permissive policy than exists, or had ever existed, in any other nation except Communist China.

Indeed, this judge-created policy is so permissive that even during the last months of pregnancy, after the child is capable of surviving outside the womb, the mother may obtain an abortion by simply alleging any impediment to her "physical, emotional, or psychological . . . well-being." [*Doe v. Bolton,* 410 U.S. 179, 192 (1973).] In the words of Professor John Noonan, a woman's determination to abort her viable late-term infant is only curbed by "the necessity of a physician's finding that she needs an abortion" for any of the above reasons. [J. Noonan, *A Private Choice,* 12 (1979).] As the Senate Judiciary Committee reported, "it would be a rare physician who would be incapable of defending an abortion on the grounds that in his best medical judgment the 'well-being' of the mother demanded it." [Senate Report 98-149, Senate Judiciary Committee 6, 98th Congress, 1st Session (1983).]

Leading constitutional scholars immediately began to attack the Supreme Court's opinion. Even some who, like Professor John Ely, favored abortion, conceded that the ruling was a "very bad decision. . . . It is bad because it is bad constitutional law, or rather because it is not constitutional law and gives almost no sense of an obligation to try to be." [Ely, "The Wages of Crying Wolf," 82 Yale L.R. 920 (1973).] Another proponent of abortion who nonetheless felt the Court's decision had no basis in the Constitution was Professor Archibald Cox:

> Neither historian, layman, nor lawyer will be persuaded that all the details prescribed in *Roe v. Wade* are part of either natural law or the Constitution. [A. Cox, *The Role of the Supreme Court* 114 (1976).]

The frankest assessment of the constitutional question relative to abortion was made by Professor Ely: "The Constitution simply says nothing, clear or fuzzy, about abortion." [Supra at 927.] Therefore, under the Constitution the people in the states should have retained the authority to regulate abortion as they had for nearly two centuries prior to 1973. This proper interpretation of the Constitution could have prevented the loss of countless lives.

Protecting the Mother's Life

In discussing the cost in terms of human life, I must reiterate my concern for all human life. When the life of the mother is endangered in pregnancy, she is entitled to medical treatment even at the terrible cost of the life of the infant. There are cases—fortunately, rare ones—where dreadful choices may be necessary. But, even then the decision must be made by the mother after prayerful consideration.

I know of mothers who were told by doctors that without abortion they would die. After praying about this momentous decision, they opted not to terminate pregnancy. Both the mothers and babies survived.

Every state prior to 1973 protected the life of the mother by law. Protecting the life of the mother has little or nothing to do with today's indulgent regime of abortion. Preserving the mother's life is hardly at stake when abortions are performed at the rate of nearly 5,000 per day. Nor is the mother's life at stake when in some American cities—notably, both the nation's capital and its largest city—more children are aborted than are permitted to be born alive. The skyrocketing increase in the number of abortions since 1973 dispels the myth that our current abortion regime is somehow related to preserving the life of the mother. Risks to maternal health are declining with the advance of medicine, yet the number of abortions is growing at an alarming rate.

The Convenience Factor

The explanation for this dramatic increase is not related to maternal health. Only in extremely rare instances are abortions performed for health reasons. Indeed, even taking "health" in its broadest sense, an ardent advocate of abortion conceded that less than two percent of all abortions can be justified as medically expedient. [See Hearings on Abortion, Subcommittee on the Constitution of the Senate Judiciary Committee, 97th Congress, 1st Session (1981) (Statement of Dr. Irving Cushner).] Raising this estimate by fifty percent would still mean that only three percent of all abortions were really necessary to prevent medical complications. Several qualified physicians testified before my Senate Subcommittee on the Constitution that they had never encountered a case where abortion was necessary to save the life of the mother. Beyond a few medically expedient abortions, all the rest—at least ninety-seven percent—are performed for what amounts to reasons of convenience.

This convenience factor takes various forms. Perhaps the birth of a child will mean a financial burden; perhaps tests have disclosed that the unborn child is not of the sex which the parents prefer; perhaps the pregnancy will interrupt an education; or perhaps, as with my friend, it will simply interfere with other plans. In such instances abortion is a tool of convenience, not a medical necessity.

Handicaps and Hardships

Another myth used to justify the abortion ethic is that hardships, like poverty or the possibility of a handicap, make abortion necessary. The implications are tragic.

Consider the following case—a true one in its factual circumstances—of a mother weighing the consequences of her pregnancy. She announces to her physician that her husband is an alcoholic with a syphilitic infection; that one of her children was born dead; that another child is blind; and that another had tuberculosis. Finally, she confesses that she is living in abject poverty and that her family has a history of deafness. She is also past the normal child-bearing years. When this situation has been posed to classes of medical students, they have recommended abortion almost without exception.

The child described here is Ludwig von Beethoven. Yet this example does not just apply to Beethoven. Every child is unique and capable of making a contribution to family, community, and nation, which no other can make.

"Freedom of choice?" Where do we get the "freedom" to deny life to a potential Beethoven—or to any other human being?

Liberty of License

Again, religious convictions add an extra dimension for believers. The Lord Himself said to Jeremiah, "Before thou camest forth out of the womb I sanctified thee, and I ordained thee a prophet unto the nations" (Jeremiah 1:5). Do we enjoy the "freedom" to deny life to a potential Jeremiah or to any other child the Lord may have sanctified before birth? Such liberty is a license to kill. A society that cannot protect its own most defenseless and helpless members has lost sight of the basic purpose of our War for Independence in 1776: "To preserve these rights (including the right to life), governments are instituted among men, deriving their just powers from the consent of the governed." No society will long remain free which abandons the most fundamental purpose of societal bonds.

Unwanted Children?

There is yet another abortion myth—the myth that abortion is better than bringing an "unwanted child" into the world. Suppose Beethoven had been "unwanted?" What does "unwanted" really mean? In this context, it apparently means that whether one person "wants" another is sufficient to decide whether or not the other shall live. This is absurd. Each individual has his own inestimable worth, regardless of whether another person "wants" him or not.

Another question is—"unwanted by whom?" I know of several young couples who pray regularly that they might be permitted to adopt these supposedly "unwanted" children. Throughout the nation there are long waiting lists of couples who want to adopt children; in Utah there are nine couples who wish to adopt for every child available. As one adoptive parent stated the other day, "placing a child for adoption is a great act of love—both for the child and for the adoptive couple, who, without the child, would never have the joy of being parents." I find it unbelievably tragic that some individuals would justify the killing of their own unborn infant on the basis of their own fleeting wants.

Choosing to Take a Life

Here, then, is the real problem for those who advocate abortion as a way to avoid the passing difficulties that another child might create. Pope John Paul II summarized the moral aspects of abortion in two concise comments:

> Whoever attempts to destroy human life in the womb of the mother not only violates God's Law, but also attacks society by undermining respect for all human life.

> Human life is the basis of human dignity and human rights. If it can be destroyed in the womb of the mother it will be difficult to establish compelling safeguards at other times and in other circumstances.

Our wisdom is inadequate for us to judge that our own inconveniences or difficulties are more important than the life of another human being. President Ronald Reagan restated this same principle in haunting terms:

> Wholesale abortion has become a continuing prod to the conscience of the nation . . . We cannot survive as a free nation when some men decide that others are not fit to live and should be abandoned to abortion or infanticide. . . . Americans do not want to play God with the value of human life. It is not for us to decide who is worthy to live and who is not. [*Human Life Review,* Spring 1983.]

Infanticide

The President's characterization of the abortion crisis is not overstated. Our nation has regrettably witnessed hundreds of

149

thousands of late-term abortions since 1973. Over 15,000 abortions a year are performed after the mother's 20th week of pregnancy—the margin of viability, when the child might be delivered and survive on its own. It is not uncommon to abort a child very late in the pregnancy, even into the 7th or 8th month. Abortions after this point are more accurately described as judicially legalized infanticides.

Medical Science and the Unborn

Let us be specific about what is being aborted. I was very deeply impressed by the powerful story told by an obstetrician, an atheist, who presided for years over the largest abortion clinic in New York City. Indeed, he was one of four founders of the National Abortion Rights Action League (NARAL), the nation's leading abortion advocacy organization. A skillful and able physician, he began to study an advancing new field of medicine: fetology, the study of the unborn human. He described in detail how he learned of the humanity of the unborn:

- At three weeks, the new life has already developed its own blood cells;
- At four weeks, a muscle may flex—this will become a beating heart in a few weeks, a heart which is fully audible at eight weeks;
- At six weeks, the child's skeletal system is complete;
- At seven weeks, electrical brain patterns are discernible;
- At twelve weeks, all organ systems are functioning—stomach, heart, liver, kidney, brain—in fact, some infants have already developed a thumb-sucking habit;
- At twenty weeks, the fetus is kicking, punching, swimming, and recognizes his mother's voice;

- At twenty-two weeks the child can survive outside the womb.

Facing these realities day after day, Dr. Bernard Nathanson, for medical reasons, stopped performing abortions and began actively campaigning to tell the nation about the scientific facts which show that *the fetus is a distinct, living human being.* In his own words, "I changed my mind because of advances in the field of fetology which have allowed us to understand the fetus much more completely and much more carefully than we ever did before. This has posed a very severe philosophical problem, in that you can't be operating on the fetus and giving it drugs to cure it, and at the same time be destroying it." (*Washington Times,* page 3C, January 17, 1983.)

Fetal Pain

These scientific and medial facts refute the myth that the fetus is little more than a lump of tissue, without feeling, which can be extracted much like a bloated appendix. On the contrary, the unborn child is human, with human features, human behavior, human feeling. Medical experts now tell us that the neurological developments necessary for feeling pain are complete by the 13th week after conception and perhaps earlier. It is unbearable to contemplate the excruciating pain the unborn must feel as their lives are torn asunder. It is a wrenching nightmare to see in the mind's eye the delicate little hand of an unborn infant reaching out playfully to touch the very curette that is poised to rip him apart. We must ask again, "Freedom to choose what?" The answer is, "freedom to choose to exterminate a being whom science identifies as a unique, living person." The implications of that medical fact are frightening and far-reaching.

American Opinion

Given the advances in fetology, it is easy to see why reliable opinion polls show that 80 to 90 percent of all Americans consider abortion at some stage as the destruction of a living person. As to when the fetus becomes a living being, there is a slight gender gap. Most women believe that life begins at conception. This gender gap is exactly the opposite of current stereotypes, which claim that most women view abortion tolerantly. That is another myth. Women who personally experience pregnancy have a much stronger conviction than men that life begins at conception. A similar result has been demonstrated in other surveys, where women are more likely than men to oppose indiscriminate abortion on demand.

Having drawn special attention to the woman's point of view, let us examine another myth. It maintains that only legalized abortion can protect women from the merciless knife of the back-alley abortionist. On the contrary, legalization of abortion on demand should receive little, if any, credit for saving women's lives. Since 1941, the major factors contributing to a drop in maternal abortion mortality have been medical advances: sulfa drugs, penicillin, and finally the widespread use of the safer suction curette instead of the sharp curette, a 1970 innovation. The regime of elective abortion seeks something far different from maternal safety. As noted earlier, every state already acknowledged and permitted abortions necessary to save the life of the mother prior to the 1972 Court decisions.

A particularly insidious myth about abortion is that the majority of Americans want practically unrestricted access to abortion at any stage of pregnancy. To the contrary, a majority would favor a constitutional amendment to protect the unborn.

In reality, by a two-thirds margin, they are not only against abortion, but willing to adhere to those convictions should their 15-year-old daughters face an abortion decision.

Ironically, the Supreme Court stated recently that fifteen-year-olds may have abortions without even consulting their parents. [*Akron v. Akron Center for Reproductive Health,* (June 15, 1983).] If choice is really at stake in the abortion controversy, here is where it is relevant. Every state in the Union recognizes that minors must be protected against the consequences of immature choices. Accordingly, parental consent is required by law for marrying, attending certain movies, and in some cases even having one's ears pierced. Yet abortions performed on minors are allowed without proper parental protection against immature or poorly-considered choices.

After examining many of these myths with the pregnant Senate aide, I encouraged her to ponder the consequences of her choice before making it. We also discussed the horror many women experience years after their abortions, when they come to realize that they have killed their babies.

Indeed, a new organization with the name of Women Exploited By Abortion (WEBA), which has a rapidly growing membership of over 10,000, is dedicated to helping women avoid the mental anguish, the sleepless nights, and the inescapable guilt of making the wrong choice. These women are still suffering years after their own hasty decisions to have abortions; they wish only to warn others of the emptiness that accompanies the realization that they will never be able to teach, love, hold, or cherish the child they killed.

I also discussed with my friend the feelings of her family and their role in this decision. We discussed, although in terms new to her, the eternal consequences of her decision. At length we parted.

I hope our discussion helped her. It certainly strengthened my resolve to make the consequences of abortion known. I still trust that when Americans know that over 15 million children have already died (more than ten times all our war dead), and as many as 2 million more will become victims of convenience each year this policy continues, they will put an end to the slaughter.

The chance to make that case again came sooner than I expected. One of my own assistants, a member of our church, had repeatedly stated that she was personally against abortion, but felt that every woman should have the freedom to choose whether to terminate the life of her unborn infant. After she had listened to two days of testimony, pro and con, and considered what abortion really entails— what the choice really is—she came to me to say that she had not only changed her mind, but was horrified that she had based her position on a hollow slogan instead of considering this most important issue in depth. One human being simply cannot determine the value of another's life. A human being cannot exercise the power which God has reserved to Himself—the power to determine when men and women shall be born and when they shall die, the "bounds of their habitation" (Acts 17:26).

Since then, I have had the opportunity to take a constitutional amendment to reverse the Supreme Court's erroneous abortion decisions to the Senate floor and to appeal to the nation in terms similar to those that helped my assistant. Moreover I have had the opportunity to preside over Senate hearings which have disclosed a

new threat to the unborn, namely the proposed Equal Rights Amendment (ERA). In its current form, ERA would likely invalidate any state or federal laws, such as the so-called Hyde Amendment, that restrict taxpayer funding of abortion, because these laws deny funding to a "medical procedure" performed only on females. In 1980, the Supreme Court held that these funding restrictions were constitutional by the barest margin of five to four. [*Harris v. McRae*, 448 U.S. 227 (1980).] Yet even that narrow victory was based on the Court's reasoning that the Hyde Amendment does not disadvantage any "suspect class" of citizens who have been denied constitutional rights in the past. Both pro- and anti-ERA scholars agree that ERA will make sex-based classifications "suspect." Thus, using its former reasoning, the Court would be likely to strike down even modest limitations on abortion funding. Indeed a 1983 report by the Congressional Research Service concluded that "ERA would reach abortion and abortion funding situations," thus confirming the testimony of devoted pro-life advocates, like Congressman Henry Hyde and Professor John Noonan, that ERA could subject even more unborn children to jeopardy.

This last thin reason for denying the threat that the ERA poses to abortion restrictions disappeared, however, when the Commonwealth Court of Pennsylvania ruled on March 9 that two state laws restricting funding of elective abortions violated the state's ERA. That court stated that "[the ERA/abortion argument] is meritorious and sufficient in and of itself to invalidate the statutes before us in that those statutes do lawfully discriminate against women with respect to a physical condition unique to women." The warnings issued months earlier by numerous expert witnesses before my constitution subcommittee had been realized.

These advocates, as well as numerous dedicated pro-life Senators, have effectively and convincingly unmasked the moral and legal bankruptcy of a policy that allows the wholesale destruction of innocent human life. All of the insightful words from Senate debates on abortion, however, do not match the simple majesty of the Bible: "Thou shalt not kill."

NO

James W. Prescott

THE ABORTION OF
"THE SILENT SCREAM"

The antiabortion movement's members would have us believe that their concern for fetal life is derived from a broad base of respect for human life and a concern for human pain, suffering, and violence. The production of the film *The Silent Scream* is an attempt to dramatize those concerns by illustrating alleged fetal pain and suffering during an abortion procedure.

The perception of pain is a complex biological and psychological phenomenon that involves states of "consciousness" which can probably never be fully understood or known for certain stages of fetal development. Relevant to this inquiry are certain neurobiological and biobehavioral facts concerning states of "consciousness" and "pain" perception during fetal development that should be known by all concerned citizens.

Patricia A. Jaworski has produced an audio tape, "Thinking About the Silent Scream," in which she interviews several internationally renowned neuroscientists on fetal brain development, the alleged fetal perception of "pain," and alleged fetal "personhood." Some of the highlights of those interviews are summarized in the following paragraphs.

Dr. Michael Bennett, chairman of the neuroscience department of Albert Einstein Medical School, when asked whether a brain exists at conception and whether there can be a person without a brain, answered with an unequivocal *"no"* to both questions. It was pointed out that the human brain has approximately *100 billion brain cells* and that there are an estimated *100 trillion* connections between neurons in the brain. This extraordinary neuronal "interconnectivity" provides the neurostructural foundation for complex perceptions and "personhood" and takes many months and often years to fully develop and function.

Dr. Patricia Goldman-Rakic, professor of neuroscience at Yale University Medical School, emphasizes that brain neurons do not exist prior to *four weeks in utero,* that the *peak* period for brain neuron development is from *two to five months in utero,* and that the existence of neurons, per se, does not

From, "The Abortion of 'The Silent Scream': A False and Wrongful Cry for Human Pain, Suffering and Violence," by Dr. James W. Prescott, *The Humanist,* September/October 1986. Reprinted by permission of *The Humanist.*

indicate the existence of a developed, functioning brain. Once the brain cell is born, there is a long process of migration of brain cells that occurs mainly from *two to six months in utero* during which the brain cells move (migrate) to their final destination in the brain. An even longer process of development makes possible the "interconnectivity" of brain cells which is absolutely essential for sensation, perception, conscious experience, thought, and behavior. The formation of brain synapses that make possible brain cell communication does not begin until about the *third month in utero*, and most are formed after birth.

Dr. Clifford Grobstein, former chairman of the Department of Biology at Stanford University and now at the University of California at San Diego, highlights the complexity of brain development by noting that the brain does not develop uniformly. For example, certain parts of the brain develop earlier and some later. The cerebral neocortex that is responsible for complex perceptions is one of the last to develop.

Dr. Dominick Purpura, dean of Albert Einstein Medical School, has been studying human brain development since 1974 with his research on mental retardation. Dr. Purpura emphasizes that there are a minimum number of neurons and synaptic connections that are necessary before the qualities of "humanness" and "personhood" can be developed and that this capacity *begins to occur* in the middle of the last trimester. Thus, about *twenty-eight to thirty weeks in utero* is the *minimal time* for the beginning of this capacity—"It can't begin earlier," according to Dr. Purpura.

Dr. Purpura also emphasizes that critical changes are seen in the fetal brain wave pattern at thirty-one weeks when the brain waves become more organized and, thus,

meaningful; the first signs of sleep and wakefulness are not observed until a few weeks later. It is emphasized that all cells have electrical potentials and that the mere presence of such signals, per se, does not mean that the capacity for complex perceptions or "personhood" exists. How these neuronal signals become *organized* and reflect underlying neuronal and structural *organization* is fundamental to understanding the basic neurobiological principle that *structure precedes function.*

Thus, it can be concluded that neither pain perception nor personhood exists *at conception* and that the *beginning* capacity for personhood may only begin at *twenty-eight to thirty weeks in utero.* Why, then, the film *The Silent Scream,* with all its deliberate distortions and errors of fact? It is the intent of this socio-psychological study to address the producers and supporters of *The Silent Scream*—a film which has been offered as a manifestation of their compassion for human pain, suffering, and violence—to illustrate through a review of both previous and new data that their motivation for *The Silent Scream* was not fetal well-being. This study will show that the antiabortion motivation behind the producers and supporters of *The Silent Scream* resides in an authoritarian control and denial of the fundamental human right of self-determination and the sexual expression of affection and love as a basic right of all persons.

In the production of *The Silent Scream* questions must be raised as to the elements of compassion and malevolence that made that film possible. Presumably, those who abhor abortion under any circumstances would not support any abortion, including participation in filming an abortion they consider to be a murder! Why did the antiabortionists not stop the filming of the abortion and the abortion itself which made the film possible? Or is the fetus simply an object to be exploited for ulterior motives—like the children of the antiabortion cultures?

Is it appropriate to compare from a *moral perspective* the production of *The Silent Scream* and the production of "snuff" films in which women are enticed into a sexual encounter and, unbeknownst to them, are scheduled for sexual torture, mutilation, and murder? Assuming that abortion is murder and "snuff" is murder, do the producers and supporters of these two kinds of films share a *certain common morality?* If so, what would be the nature of that common morality?

When the Reverend R.L. Hymers, Jr., pastor of the Fundamentalist Baptist Tabernacle in Los Angeles, called Supreme Court Justice William J. Brennan, Jr., a "baby killer" and led his four-hundred-member congregation in prayer to ask God to kill Brennan so that President Reagan could replace him with a judge who opposes abortion, does this not reinforce a common morality of violence in the antiabortionist mentality as it is reflected in The *Silent Scream* and the fire-bombings of abortion clinics and personnel? (See *The Washington Post*, June 2, 1986.)

Since the morality of pain and pleasure reside at the core of the abortion controversy, it may be helpful to reflect upon the following data as these moral questions are addressed.

In an attempt to clarify the ideological and motivational structure of the antiabortion personality and "subculture," this writer published a series of research articles that addressed these issues (Prescott, 1975; 1978; Prescott and Wallace, 1978). A summary of these findings would appear helpful as a background to the new studies reported herein which will shed further light on the lack of compassion for human pain, suffering, and violence that is a salient characteristic of the militant antiabortion movement.

The question of whether abortion represents a "murderous" act or a "benevolent" act is addressed in the 1975 article in *The Humanist* by examining the social-behavioral characteristics of primitive cultures that permitted or punished abortion and by examining the relationship between voting patterns in the Canadian Federal Parliament on abortion and capital punishment legislation.

It was hypothesized that, if abortion reflected a "murderous" violent act, then the cultures which permitted abortion should be similarly characterized; conversely, if abortion reflected a benevolent act, then the cultures which permitted abortion should also be benevolent and peaceful. Similarly hypothesized was whether votes on abortion rights correlated positively or negatively with votes on capital punishment.

In brief, the following relationships were obtained from twenty-one primitive cultures where coded anthropological information was available on abortion and other behaviors:

1. 55% of cultures that punish abortion practice slavery. 92% of cultures that permit abortion prohibit slavery.

2. 73% of cultures that punish abortion also torture, mutilate, and kill enemy captured in warfare. 80% of cultures that permit abortion do not torture, mutilate, and kill enemy captured in warfare.

3. 78% of cultures that punish abortion punish premarital coitus. 67% of cultures that permit abortion permit extramarital coitus.

4. 88% of cultures that punish abortion punish extramarital coitus. 67% of cultures that permit abortion permit extramarital coitus.

5. 70% of cultures that punish abortion exploit children. 78% of cultures that permit abortion do not exploit children.

With respect to the voting patterns in the Canadian Parliament on abortion and capital punishment, the following relationships were established:

1. 59% voted for abortion rights and against capital punishment.

2. 21% voted against abortion rights and for capital punishment.

3. 80% supported a statistically valid relationship between antiabortion and antilife voting patterns, and vice versa.

These voting patterns in the Canadian Parliament were consistent with the data obtained from primitive cultures that established a strong relationship between antiabortion and antilife sentiments. It was concluded that the above data did not support the antiabortion movement's claim to be a "Right to Life" movement and, in fact, supported the opposite.

In a further effort to validate the above relationships, this writer examined the voting patterns in the United States Senate on bills involving abortion, capital punishment, support of the Vietnam War, support of the "no knock" law (police did not need a court order to break into a private home), and opposition to gun control legislation (Prescott, 1978).

In summary, the following statistically significant relationships were obtained between abortion and bills on human violence:

1. 71% valid relationship between antiabortion beliefs and support of capital punishment and its converse relationship.

2. 72% valid relationship between antiabortion beliefs and support of the Vietnam War and its converse relationship.

3. 65% valid relationship between antiabortion beliefs and support of the "no knock" law and its converse relationship.

4. 71% valid relationship between antiabortion beliefs and opposition to handgun control and the converse relationship.

The preceding data are fully consistent with and cross-validate the findings obtained from primitive cultures and from the Canadian Parliament that established a strong relationship between antiabortion beliefs and support of human oppression and violence, and the converse relationship.

In a further examination of these relationships, this writer utilized the National Farmers Union ratings of US senators on a scale from zero to one hundred to study the senators' support of legislation that helped families and their children—such as support of school lunch and milk programs. This rating was based upon the senators' voting records on fifteen different bills and was interpreted by this writer as a valid and reliable measure of family nurturance. It was found that the average Family Nurturance Score of senators who supported abortion rights of women and opposed capital punishment was *ninety-six out of one hundred.* The average Family Nurturance Score of senators who opposed abortion rights of women and supported capital punishment was *forty-four out of one hundred*—less than half of the Family Nurturance Score of the pro-choice senators.

It was concluded from the above data that the antiabortion ideology did not reflect compassion and respect for human life but, rather, an ideology of authoritarian control over the personal lives of individuals that included violent means of human oppression.

In the final article on the abortion issue, which was coauthored by my associate, Dr. Douglas Wallace, the major motivation force underlying the antiabortion ideology that was suggested from the primitive culture data was examined—namely, anti-sexual pleasure (Prescott and Wallace, 1978).

An analysis of the voting patterns of the Pennsylvania House on abortion and on a bill that made fornication and adultery a felony yielded the following results: 85 percent who supported abortion rights supported rights of self-determination of sexual expression; and 86 percent who opposed abortion rights opposed rights of self-determination of sexual expression.

Similarly, the voting patterns in the Pennsylvania Senate with respect to abortion and a bill that would prevent homosexuals from being hired by the state government were examined. These evaluations yielded the following results: 73 percent who supported abortion rights supported homosexual rights of employment; and 89 percent who opposed abortion rights opposed homosexual rights of employment.

In addition to the above findings, extensive questionnaire data were reported from 688 males and 1,178 females from various walks of life on abortion ideology and other life values. Based upon the fifty-six-item questionnaire, the following items were the most highly and statistically linked to the statement, "Abortion should be punished by society" (Prescott and Wallace, 1978):

1. Prostitution should be punished by society.

2. Unmarried persons having sex with their lovers is wrong.

3. Sexual pleasure helps build a weak moral character.

4. Physical punishment and pain help build a strong moral character.

5. Society should interfere with private sexual behavior between adults.

6. Nudity within the family has a harmful influence upon children.

The above findings taken collectively from primitive cultures, modern cultures, and legislative bodies strongly support an "anti-sexual pleasure" ethic as a major driving force underlying the antiabortion ideology.

Although the above data have been available over the past eight to eleven years, they have not been utilized in confronting the increasing virulence and violence of the antiabortion movement—that is, the numerous fire-bombings and violent attacks against medical clinics and personnel providing abortion services to women and the increasing legislative attacks on the fundamental right of women to be mothers by choice.

The production of *The Silent Scream* by the antiabortion movement is another attempt to mislead the public and legislators into believing that the antiabortion movement has a fundamental concern and compassion about human pain, suffering, and violence. Since the publication of the above studies, additional statistics on voting on bills before the U.S. Congress have become available, making possible the direct examination of the antiabortion movement's claims of compassion for human pain, suffering, and violence, as it is purportedly reflected the *The Silent Scream,* and for the cross-validation in the U.S House of Representatives of certain relationships that had been previously established in the U.S. Senate.

The following analyses of voting patterns evaluate the one hundred pro-choice congressmen and one hundred anti-choice congressmen identified by Catholics for a Free Choice as *totally supporting* or *totally opposing* abortion rights of women (Catholics for a Free Choice, 1985). I have characterized the three legislative bills evaluated for this study as: (1) Human Pain and Suffering Bill (H.R. 5290); (2)

Jeopardizing Human Lives Bill (H.R 4332); and (3) Promoting Human Violence Bill (H.J. Res. 540).

The Human Pain and Suffering Bill was the bill to permit the use of parenteral diacetylmorphine (heroin) for the relief of intractable pain due to terminal cancer (H.R. 5290: Compassionate Pain Relief Act). The vote analyzed was on the Hughes Amendment and other amendments to H.R. 5290 which specified circumstances when pain "may not be effectively treated with currently available analgesic medications." The Hughes Amendment was defeated 231 to 178, with 22 not voting on September 19, 1984.

> 72% (68 of 94) of pro-choice congressmen support human pain relief.
> 95% (88 of 93) of anti-choice congressmen oppose human pain relief in dying cancer patients!

The Jeopardizing Human Lives Bill was on gun control legislation, specifically the Federal Firearms Law Reform Act of 1986 (H.R.4322). The vote analyzed was on the Hughes Amendment, which limited the serious weakening of the 1968 Gun Control Act under H.R. 4332. If H.R. 4332 was passed without the Hughes Amendment, it would have significantly increased the danger to lives of the public and law enforcement officers. (It is worth noting that police organizations supported the Hughes Amendment.) The vote was taken on April 9, 1986, and the Hughes Amendment was defeated 242 to 177, with 15 not voting.

> 69% (47 of 680) of pro-choice and anti-pain congressmen support gun control legislation.
> 82% (63 of 77) of anti-choice and pro-pain congressmen oppose gun control legislation.

The Promoting Human Violence Bill was the vote on "Contra Aid" (H.J. Res. 540) which "approves the additional authorities and assistance for the Nicaraguan democratic resistance that the President requested pursuant to the International Security and Development Cooperation Act of 1985, not withstanding section 10 of Public Law 91-672." The vote was taken on March 20, 1986, Roll No. 64, and was defeated 222 to 210, with 3 not voting.

> 95% (60) of pro-choice and anti-pain congressmen oppose Contra Aid—that is, oppose support of human violence.
> 77% (67) of anti-choice and pro-pain congressmen support Contra Aid—that is, provide support for human violence.

The above data contravene the claims of the antiabortion movement that they have a basic compassion for the victims of violence, which the attempt to portray in *The Silent Scream*.

In summarizing previous and current data on the antiabortion "personality" and "subculture," a profile emerges from these scientific studies with the following characteristics:

1. *Authoritarian control over the personal lives of individuals,* as it is reflected in the practice of slavery in primitive cultures, the legislative denial of freedom for women in modern cultures to be mothers by choice, and the imposition of arbitrary police arrests and seizures.

2. *Support of human violence and its associated disregard for the dignity and integrity of the human body,* as it is reflected in support of such physical assaults against the human body as: torture, mutilation, and killing of enemy captured in warfare; support of the war in Vietnam and violent revolution (Contra Aid); opposition to gun control legislation; violent

attacks on medical clinics and personnel providing abortion services to women; and participation in the exploitation of a fetus in an abortion procedure to produce a false film "documentary" to serve authoritarian political and religious objectives.

3. *Indifference to human pain and suffering,* as it is reflected in the refusal to provide effective medicine to control excruciating pain in dying cancer patients.

4. *Authoritarian control and denial of the fundamental right of self-determination in sexual expression,* as it is reflected in the punishment of prostitution and premarital and extramarital sexuality, in mandating fornication and adultery as felonious crimes, and in punishment of homosexuality.

5. *Indifference to the quality of life of children,* as it is reflected in the economic exploitation of children (primitive cultures) and failure to provide basic medical care, food, education, and clothing for poor children and their families (legislative actions).

6. *A moral value system that equates human pain, suffering, and violence with moral strength and, conversely, equates sexual pleasure and relief from pain and suffering with moral weakness.*

It is emphasized that the foregoing does not apply to certain individuals who represent 3 to 13 percent of the populations studied. These individuals are characterized by opposition to abortion and physical violence; they respect rights to sexual privacy and choice and have high child and family nurturance scores.

Given the profound moral, psychological, and political dimensions of the abortion controversy, it is unlikely that "data alone" will resolve it. The solution is *prevention,* with which women have complete control over their reproductive state. The prevention of all unintended and unwanted pregnancies should be our common goal.

POSTSCRIPT

IS THE ANTIABORTION MOVEMENT BASED ON A BELIEF IN THE SACREDNESS OF HUMAN LIFE?

The issue of abortion would not exist if men and women were not engaging in sexual intercourse at times when they are not in a position to have a child or do not want a child. That situation, however, is only likely to exist in Alice's Wonderland. Millions of American teenagers are sexually active, as are millions of married couples who do not want a pregnancy to occur. Some use contraceptives, but there are failures. More do not use any contraceptives. The result is unwanted pregnancies.

Given this situation, it is unrealistic to believe that abortion can be eliminated by making it illegal, or by establishing "chastity centers" for teenagers as Congress did a few years ago. However, behind any solution to the abortion problem is a more basic issue, namely our attitude toward sexual relations which are engaged in by unmarried couples and which are not oriented to reproduction. Sexual intercourse for pleasure, communication, exploration, friendship, and other reasons is a reality we must face.

In this context, confusion is compounded when the term "pro-abortion" is set in opposition to "pro-life" and "antiabortion." Since no rational or sensible human being maintains that abortion is an unalloyed good, the issue goes beyond the simplicities of pro-abortion and antiabortion or pro- and antilife camps.

In reality, two basic questions emerge. The first question is whether abortion should be outlawed or left to the choice of a woman and her physician, a pro- or antichoice issue. Despite their varying uneasiness with abortion in different circumstances, the majority of Americans appear to favor leaving the decision to the individual woman. Still the battle continues.

Achieving a consensus answer to the second question is proving more difficult. If no one really advocates abortion as a good solution to unwanted pregnancies, then how can be effectively reduce the flood of unwanted pregnancies? What can our families, education system and society do to motivate and educate teenagers and married women toward abstinence or contraceptive use? It appears impossible to transport today's unmarried teenagers and adults back to the days of Victorian morality when sex outside marriage was severely punished, especially for "good girls." The growing population of sexually mature single persons, the lack of an effective, safe and aesthetically acceptable contraceptive, and the growing desire of married couples to limit their pregnancies are factors that cannot be avoided. See the bibliography for further readings on this subject. Pro and con views of the film "The Silent Scream" are recounted on page 322.

ISSUE 10

IS SURROGATE MOTHERHOOD A FORM OF PROSTITUTION?

YES: Susan Ince, from *Test-Tube Women* (Pandora Press, 1984)

NO: Lori B. Andrews, from *Family Advocate* (American Bar Association, 1981)

ISSUE SUMMARY

YES: Women's health counselor Susan Ince recounts her personal experience of being interviewed for surrogate motherhood. She believes surrogate motherhood for pay should be banned because it exploits women and is a form of reproductive prostitution.
NO: Lori B. Andrews, a research attorney at the American Bar Foundation, argues that despite the many legal conflicts and complications of surrogate motherhood, society must consider the right to privacy and self-determination of a childless couple.

Aldous Huxley's *Brave New World* of human reproduction fascinated the general public as science fiction for nearly half a century before it became reality on July 25, 1978. On that day in 1978, after weeks of media hype, a healthy Louise Joy Brown was born. Six years later, there were over 700 in vitro fertilized (IVF) babies, including 56 sets of twins, eight sets of triplets and two sets of quadruplets. In 1985, the number of IVF babies went over the 1,000 mark.

Years before IVF, embryo transplants and surrogate motherhood became a reality, other less striking advances in reproductive technology were developed. Artificial insemination was first developed in 1776 by the Italian embryologist Lazarro Spalanzani. A woman was first artificially inseminated in 1800. Human sperm were first frozen without damage in 1942, but twelve years passed before the first human infant was born following artificial insemination with frozen sperm. By the mid-1970s, artificial insemination with fresh or frozen semen from the husband or a donor was widely used as remedy for infertility. Sperm banks opened up as commercial ventures.

Then IVF became a reality and society became aware of a frightening array of perplexing questions. The technologies of human reproduction bounded beyond the primitive simplicity of Huxley's *Brave New World* with a speed few experts expected. Worldwide, by the end of 1985, there were well over 200 IVF clinics, with 120 of them operating in the United States. In 1984, techniques for freezing one-to-two-day-old embryos for later use in embryo transfer allowed infertility specialists to take full advantage of the ability to induce superovulation of a dozen eggs or more in a single cycle. All the eggs ovulated can now be fertilized, two or three selected for immediate transfer, and the remaining embryos held in liquid nitrogen to be used in case the first transfer fails.

Various voices have challenged the use of surrogate mothers. Ethicists and lawyers question payment for surrogate mothers. Several now-famous court cases have brought notoriety to embryo transplants and surrogate mothers. In May 1982, Judy Stiver, a 26-year-old Michigan woman, agreed to be artificially inseminated and serve as a surrogate mother for Alexander Malahoff and his wife of Long Island, New York. When the child was born in January 1983, it suffered from a severe strep infection and microcephaly, a smaller-than-normal head and a sign of mental retardation. Contending the child was not his, Malahoff filled a $50 million law suit against the surrogate mother. After a sensational appearance on television's *Phil Donahue Show,* Mrs. Stiver agreed to raise the child and Mr. Malahoff dropped his suit. In 1986, Mary Beth Whitehead, a New Jersey surrogate mother, violated her contract and sued in court to keep her child and not give it up for adoption by the couple who hired her.

How should society respond to surrogate motherhood today? Some of the most vocal opposition to surrogate motherhood comes from members of the Feminist International Network on the New Reproductive Technologies. In the two essays in this section, Susan Ince speaks as a member of FINNRET while Lori Andrews deals with the legal aspects and the right to privacy.

YES

Susan Ince

SURROGATE MOTHERHOOD
REPRESENTS
REPRODUCTIVE PROSTITUTION

> This is not a nine-to-five job. It demands enormous commitment and understanding. It requires your total thought and consciousness, full-time, twenty-four hours a day.

The job was for the key position in one of the "growth industries" of the 1980s, and involved rigid application processes, including thorough medical examination, intelligence testing, psychological evaluation, and even genetic screening if indicated. I had just applied to become a surrogate mother.

From reading the glowing newspaper reports and seeing the self-satisfied lawyers on television, I had been uneasy about the idea of a surrogate industry. I had played out lively and humorous "what if" scenarios with friends, but had no substantive answers to the questions of proponents: what's wrong with it, if that's what the women want to do? Are you against them making money? Are you saying the industry should be regulated by the state? The questions were naggingly familiar, the same ones asked by apologists of the sex-buying industries, prostitution and pornography.

In order to get a first-hand look, I answered an advertisement placed in a local newspaper by a surrogate company considered reputable and established. Two weeks later, I met with the program's director and psychologist in their basement office on a street filled with small businesses and discount shops. The office looked newly occupied, and the director struggled with the unfamiliar typewriter and telephone system. Decorations included pictures of Victorian children; plump, white, and rosy-cheeked. Missing from sight were file cabinets, desks with drawers, and other standard office paraphernalia.

The director did most of the talking. I was touched by her stories of infertile couples—the woman who displayed the scars of multiple unsuccessful surgeries creating a tire-track pattern across her abdomen; the couple, now infertile, whose only biological child was killed by a drunk driver, the couples who tried in good faith to adopt an infant, and were kept on waiting lists until

From, *Test-Tube Women: What Future for Motherhood*, Rita Ardetti, Renate D. Klein and Shelley Minden, eds. Copyright © 1984. Reprinted by permission of Methuen, Inc., publishers.

they passed the upper age limit and were disqualified. Stories like these, said the director, inspired her to offer a complete surrogate mother service to combine all the administrative, legal, and medical aspects of this modern reproductive alternative.

The screening and administrative procedures were outlined by the director as simple and proven successful. As a potential surrogate, I had to pass an interview with the director and psychologist, history and physical examination, and finally meet with a lawyer who would explain the contract before I signed to officially enter the program. Parents desiring surrogate services also had to pass screening by the director and psychologist, and pay $25,000 at contract-signing. Surrogate and purchasers never meet, although information about them is described so that both parties can determine if the match is acceptable. Complete anonymity is stressed as a benefit of going to this company instead of making private arrangements through a lawyer.

While pregnant, the surrogate receives approximately $200 to purchase maternity clothing, and is reimbursed 15%ct/mile for transportation costs. It is her responsibility to enter the program with medical insurance that includes maternity benefits. The company will pay her medical and life insurance premiums and non-covered medical costs while she is in the program. After delivery of the baby to the father, the surrogate receives her $10,000 fee.

I tried to ask my many questions about the procedure in a curious and enthusiastic manner befitting a surrogate. The answers were not reassuring.

What happens if you don't become pregnant? Artificial insemination is tried twice a month for six months. If the surrogate has not conceived, she is then re-moved from the program and the father begins again with a different surrogate.

And she receives no money for her participation? "No. Look at it this way. We pay all the fees and medical expenses. What has it cost you? Unless you start putting a value on your time."

What if she has a miscarriage? Again, no money is paid to the surrogate. "The father decides if he will take a chance with her." Then if the surrogate also wants to try again, there is a second attempt.

What if the baby is born dead, or something is wrong with it and the father doesn't want it? In this case, the surrogate has fulfilled her contract and is paid $10,000. "We are not in the business of paying for a perfect baby. We are paying for a service rendered." Possible fine-line distinctions between a late miscarriage (no fee to surrogate) and a stillborn premature baby (full fee paid) are made by the primary physician provided by and paid for by the company.

What qualities are you looking for in a surrogate? Ideally, they would like her to be married and to already have children. A healthy child provides "a track record. It's as simple as that." And the husband is a "built-in support system." They hastened to assure me, however, that there were exceptions (I am single with no children). "Why, we just entered a single woman who had never been pregnant before. And the next couple that came in *demanded* a single donor. Things just always match up. It's a miracle!"

The director chatted on about the enthusiasm and good spirit of the "girls" in the program so far. Many of them, it seemed, had added to the program by inventing creative ways to include the fathers more in the pregnancy and birth process. The women with infertility, who provide the basis for the industry's foundation, and who will become the adoptive mothers, are notably absent from consideration. It is expected that surrogates will "write a nice note" to the father after conception, and many plan to follow this with a tape recording of the baby's heartbeat. One "girl" even invited the father to be in the delivery room, and this was applauded as an altruistic gesture beyond anyone's expectations. "But wait," I asked wide-eyed. "I thought everything was completely anonymous." She looked at me as if I were a simple-minded child. "Well, he's not going to be looking at her face! He's just there to see his baby come out."

I was nervous two weeks later when I went to meet the psychologist who I thought would administer IQ tests and probe into my motivations to judge whether I was an acceptable surrogate. My plan was to offer no unsolicited information, but to tell the truth about all questions asked (except for my intention to become a surrogate). When I arrived, the psychologist was borrowing Kleenex from the tailor next door. I made a small wisecrack, "What's a psychologist without Kleenex, right?", and he acted as if this was unusually clever. "Boy, that's funny," he said, continuing to chuckle as he returned to the office. "You are really sharp." Either he was attempting to put me at ease, or this was going to be easier than I thought.

We settled down for the actual interview. I was asked my name, address, phone number, eye color, hair color, whether I had any birth defects (no), whether I had children (no), whether I had relatives or friends in the area (yes, friends), whether I had a boyfriend (male friends, yes), whether I expected to someday marry, settle down, have babies and live happily ever after (no). He inquired as to my religious upbringing (Protestant) and began reminiscing about a college sweetheart ("Oh,

I used to be so in love with a Protestant girl. . . .") Ten minutes later, we got back on track and I was surprised to find he had no more questions, "I just needed to be sure you're still positive 100 per cent. You are, aren't you?" Without a nod or a word from me, he continued, "You seem like it to me."

Because I was "obviously bright," there would be no IQ testing. I was never asked whether I had been pregnant before, whether I was under medical or psychiatric treatment, or how I would feel about giving up the baby. To lower costs, and save time, the medical exam would take place after I had signed the contract, while a match was being made. The psychologist pronounced me "wonderful" and "perfect," and I awaited my next call.

Soon the phone rang and the director solemnly said she had two serious questions to ask me. "It's not easy but I think it's important for us to lay our cards on the table. . . ." I gulped, thinking she was suspicious. "I just want to ask you this straight up, right now, yes or no, are you going to have any trouble making appointments?" (I had rescheduled the last visit because of car trouble.) When I assured her that there would be no problem, she asked her second question. "What are you going to do with the money?" This, I later heard her say, was asked of each surrogate to weed out those women who had frivolous motivations, such as "buying designer jeans." My answer was deemed acceptable, and screening was complete.

Although I was repeatedly assured that there had never been a problem with legal and financial arrangements made through the company, it was acknowledged by all concerned that this was a largely uncharted and confusing legal area. The contract itself repeated three times that a surrogate might seek her own legal counsel, fee to be paid by the program, to further her understanding of the concept, rules and regulations, rights and liabilities involved. After I was deemed ready to "enter the fold," I inquired about the independent legal consultation. There had been problems with that, the director said. Some of the "girls" had submitted bills up to $500 for legal fees, which program members thought was exorbitant. Of even greater concern, surrogates had come back from their consultations with new doubts and questions. Because of this, I was strongly encouraged to see a nearby lawyer "not associated" with the program, but already familiar with the contract, and selected and paid by the company to provide "independent" consultations to all of the surrogates. When I said that I had my own lawyer in mind, she reiterated strenuously that she advised against it. As an example, she said, one girl had come back to her from an outside lawyer, saying "He's asking me all these questions and he's really driving me crazy." The director said, "and after I sent her to see *our* lawyer, and he explained it *our* way, she felt much better and thanked me."

I decided to hear how this independent company lawyer would explain the contract and our meeting was arranged. Before then, the director called to say she was eager for me to sign the contract on the same day as my consultation. A couple had been found who, after she had taken the liberty of describing me, said that they were very interested in me as a surrogate. More hesitant than I had ever heard her, she cautioned that we needed to discuss "certain issues" which might be a problem. The father, she explained, was very bright, but Oriental, and would that be a problem? His wife was Caucasian. I said I couldn't see any problem, since the wife ought to be the one I was matching. She said that

was *exactly right,* and that the couple could have easily adopted an Oriental child but they wanted a half-Caucasian. We would talk more at our next meeting.

To my surprise, the independent consultation was held within earshot of the director, who was called on by the lawyer to interpret "various clauses" of the contract, and who kept a record of questions I asked. The interview was held at the new corporate office, on a block filled with elegant fur and clothing shops in one of the richest counties in the United States. The move was explained as necessary for the convenience of the buying parents.

The director took me first into her office for a private chat before meeting the lawyer. A new couple was described—in the petroleum business, very wealthy, and building a new house in anticipation of my baby. She explained that this was a very common and positive sign, the parents "inevitably building, remodeling, adding wings, buying new houses, not because they don't live in perfectly lovely homes, but because they want to be doing something for the baby during the pregnancy." I asked if she had any plans to write a book including some of her interesting observations about the surrogate process. She nodded enthusiastically,

> Oh yes, we are collecting data right now— if for nothing else than to dispel the misconceptions people have about surrogates. I'm very sorry to say it, but they don't think our surrogates are nice girls like you. When people think surrogate, they think tight black satin slacks. I don't know why, but they do.

By this time, the lawyer had arrived and we settled down with the contract. Three areas were of greatest concern to me: the extensive behavioral controls over the surrogate, her precarious legal/financial position should something go wrong, and the ill-defined responsibilities of the company itself. Each of these was broached during this interview with what I hoped were sincere and non-threatening requests for clarification. Briefly, the rules governing surrogates' behavior are as follows (quotation marks indicate exact language of contract):

Sex: The surrogate must abstain from sexual intercourse from two weeks before first insemination until a conception is confirmed.
The surrogate must not engage in "sexual promiscuity."

Drug use The surrogate must not "smoke nor drink any alcohol [sic] beverage from the time of initial insemination until delivery."
The surrogate must not use illegal drugs.

Medical: The surrogate must keep all scheduled administrative, medical, psychological, counseling or legal appointments arranged for her. These may be "set by the physician in accordance with his schedule and, therefore, may not always be convenient for the surrogate mother."
The surrogate must use the services (medical, psychological, etc.) which are chosen and provided by the program.
The surrogate must submit to all standard medical procedures and "any additional medical precautions and/or instructions outlined by the treating physician."
The surrogate must finish medical and psychological records to the company and the parents.

In general, any action that "can be deemed to be dangerous to the well-being of the unborn child" constitutes a breach of contract which means the surrogate will forfeit her fee, and be subject to legal action from the buyers.

The company lawyer responded to my questions about these restrictions by denying their importance and reiterating the good will of all concerned. On alcohol— "You're on the honor system. No one is going to care if you have a glass of wine now and then." On sexual promiscuity— "Who cares? I don't know what that means. I don't know why that's in here." When asked if there was a legal definition, he said, "They just want to be sure who the father is. Intercourse doesn't hurt the baby, does it? Don't worry about it."

I was worrying a lot, mostly about the company's complete control over the surrogate. There was no limit to the number of appointments that could be scheduled requiring the surrogate's participation. If she should become uncooperative, they could simply schedule more psychological visits. If they didn't want to pay her, they could schedule so many that she couldn't possibly keep them. The medical controls seemed particularly ominous: all standard procedures PLUS ANY OTHER precautions or instructions. This could include bedrest, giving up a job, etc. A medical acknowledgment attached to the main body of the contract advised that "there are certain medical risks inherent in any pregnancy. Some of these may be surgical complications, such as, but not limited to, appendix and gall bladder." Of course, these surgical complications would most likely arise from a caesarean delivery, major surgery which is not mentioned at all in the conversation or contract. if the doctor should request one, the surrogate would have no contractual right to object.

Complications could also arise after birth. I learned that names of both surrogate and father would appear on the birth certificate, compromising promised anonymity, and that the certificate would only be destroyed several weeks, months or years later when the child was adopted by the "the potential stepmother" (in the same way a new spouse can adopt a child if the former spouse wished to relinquish her/his rights and responsibilities). "Why not right away?" I asked. The law yer recommended a reasonable waiting period because an immediate adoption "could be construed, by someone who wanted to construe it that way, as baby-selling."

In fact, he elaborated, the baby-selling argument could also be used by a court to declare the entire contract illegal and void. It is acknowledged in the contract itself that its *rights and liabilities may or may not be honored in a Court of Law should a breach arise.*" The document further states that, in a lawsuit, it could be used to assist "a court of competent jurisdiction in ascertaining the intention" of surrogate and parents.

If the surrogate breaches her contract, by abortion, by violation of rules, or by refusal to relinquish the child, the father may sue her for the $25,000 he paid into the program, plus additional costs. If the parents breach by refusal to accept delivery of the child or failure to pay medical expenses, the surrogate may sue them for her $10,000 fee, plus the expenses of child support or placing the child up for adoption. "What about the company?" I asked. "If something went wrong and I had to sue the parents, would they help me or pay my legal expenses?" "No," he replied. "When the shit hits the fan you're on your own." Indeed, each party is required to sign a "hold harmless" clause which says that no matter what happens the company is not responsible. The lawyer explained this clause away as meaningless—everyone would, of course, sue everyone else if there should be a problem.

As we perused the contract, the lawyer discovered a new clause had appeared since his last consultation, the "Amniocentesis Addendum" which stated that, should the treating physician request, the surrogate would submit to amniocentesis for prenatal diagnosis. If results were ab-

normal, she would consent to abortion at the parents' request. To my surprise, this clause out of the entire contract was worrisome to the lawyer. Why, he asked, should the surrogate abort at 2-4 weeks gestation and receive no fee, when she could carry the pregnancy to term and fulfill her contract regardless of the infant's condition? I was more concerned about what might be considered an abnormality sufficient to request abortion. What about a sex chromosome abnormality? What about just the "wrong" sex? I was also concerned that this again allowed for the total discretion of the treating physician. Why was it left ambiguous in the contract when there is no legitimate indication for amniocentesis that couldn't be known before the pregnancy started? My suspicion was that it would always be requested, as an unacknowledged "quality control" measure.

The lawyer called the director into the room, and asked about this clause's financial disadvantage to the surrogate. Any woman, she stated flatly, who would knowingly carry a defective fetus to term to cheat the parents out of $10,000 would not be acceptable to the program. Nevertheless, the lawyer suggested that I not sign until he spoke with the author of the contract, to suggest that a small fee be paid to the surrogate if there was such an unfortunate occurrence. My one request before signing was to see a copy of the parents' contract, to compare responsibilities, and to "make sure they hadn't been promised something I couldn't fulfill." The request was never honored.

The lawyer called the next day to say the Amniocentesis Addendum must remain as written. He paraphrased the company officials: "The program works because it works the way it is. We cannot make big changes for the surrogate or the parents." We arranged to meet a week later, after I had received the parents' contract, for final signing.

Before then, however, I was called by the director who had become concerned while listening in on my legal consultation. She admonished me for asking too many questions:

> The program works because it is set up to work for the couple. You have to weigh why you are participating in the program. For the money only, or to do the service of providing the couple with a baby. To be very frank, we are looking for girls with both those motivations. I felt after the last visit that this is a gal looking for every possible way to earn that money, and that concerns me. . . . We are playing with peoples' lives, with people who are desperately looking for a child. They have made an emotional investment . . . emotionally and in every other way that baby is not yours. . . . No contract is perfect for anyone, for anything.

She urged me to take an extra week before signing, and if I was still interested to arrange to be reevaluated by the psychologist.

When I called to schedule the interview, I was informed it would not be with the original psychologist (who thought I was perfect) but with a new "more convenient" one. I was very apprehensive about the visit, and when I knocked on the psychologist's door, about five minutes late, I expected to be confronted about my tardiness as yet another sign of my "bad" behavior. No one answered my knock, but I could hear someone coming down the hallway. A woman approached and let me in the unlocked door. I stood in the waiting room a few moments and the doctor arrived. As we shook hands, he said, "I hear you've been knocking at my door."

"Yes."

"And you didn't even think to open it."

This was not a question but a statement: I felt my every move was open for analysis.

The doctor was in charge for the next one-and-a-half hours. It seemed he pried into every aspect of my family background. He was extremely interested in my romantic life, and my intention not to marry was considered unusual and an indication of not planning for the future. He also wondered how, with no man in town, I managed to "feel loved and affirm my femininity." ("By having this baby, of course!", I didn't say.) As the session went on, I felt violated and bullied by this man, and too intimidated not tell the truth. Only two of his inquiries obviously concerned becoming a surrogate mother. "How will you feel if you aren't accepted for the program?" and "Are you the kind of person who can start a task and complete it, or do you lose interest in the middle and abort the project?" ("Great choice of words, doctor.") He concluded the encounter with a short analysis of my psyche, explaining that he felt that I deserved this as payment for putting time and thought into the session. Again, I had gone through a psychological evaluation with no questions about whether I was under psychiatric care, whether I used medications or drugs, or how I would feel about carrying an anonymous man's child and giving it up after birth. He also seemed uninterested in my friends, emotional supports, living or employment situations. Only my relationships to men were probed.

About two weeks later, I received the verdict from the director: I was acceptable to the program and could start as soon as possible. I was embarrassed to find myself pleased to have "passed" my analysis. I decided I could find out nothing further without signing the contract. Using a possible job transfer as an excuse, I asked to have my file put on hold a few months.

A few days following my last psychological evaluation, the director and lawyer for the company appeared on a holiday talk show, smiling and discussing at length the "blessing" of this reproductive alternative. They were treated with deference by the host as they told the identical infertility stories, and outlined the tried and true professional process. At the time of my interviews, the "tried and true" process had yet to result in even one pregnancy, so all hospital, contractual, emotional, and financial arrangements were untested.

The careful screening process was a myth. I encountered no evidence of real medical or psychological safeguards, just enough hurdles to test whether I would be obedient. The minimal questioning I did was labelled as selfish, dangerous, and unique in their experience. My impression was that there was a serious shortage of available surrogates and that any appropriate (white and compliant) woman would be rushed into contract-signing and immediately told her perfectly matched couple had been located.

Anonymity was also a myth, since the father would know the city where I lived, my name from the birth certificate, and my physical characteristics from required baby pictures, from company files and medical and psychological reports. He would have visitation rights to the hospital nursery, and perhaps to the delivery room. Company files were said to be confidential, but it was acknowledged that they would be opened upon court order.

It is a myth that women are easily making large sums of money as surrogates. The director of this program acknowledges that the woman who goes through a lengthy insemination process may end up being paid less than $1.00/hour for her participation. To earn this sum, she is completely "on-call" for the company. She may be required to undergo invasive diagnostic procedures, forfeit her job, and perhaps undergo major surgery with its attendant morbidity and mortality risks. Of course, should there be a miscarriage or failure to conceive, the surrogate receives no compensation at all.

The flow of money is also interesting. I was told that the surrogate's $10,000 fee would be held in an escrow account until delivery, but this was not confirmed by the lawyer or contract. If the parents breach the contract, why must the surrogate sue them for her fee, which the company already holds? And if she breaches the contract, shouldn't the couple be entitled to a refund from the company without taking the surrogate to court? The company holds all of the funds, makes the profit, and attempts to take a minimum of the financial/legal risks.

Control by contract is a crucial element of this surrogate program, with power clearly in the hands of the company officials. Besides the explicit demands in the contract, an additional clause yielding staggering control to the company was brought to my attention by an unaffiliated lawyer I later consulted. She pointed out Item Nine in a list of rules for surrogates which reads: "Surrogate mother and her husband must sign all documents provided by the (company) including but not limited to the surrogate mother agreement and contract," plus addendums listed. In essence, at any time I could be handed any new document and be obligated to sign it, no matter what its effect on my well-being or best interests.

It came as no surprise, then, when I later read in the newspaper that the first surrogate to become pregnant was to have none other than the program director as her childbirth coach. I could imagine a surrealistic scene with the director by the woman's side, the father at the foot of the bed to see "his baby come out," perhaps even a bag over the surrogate's head to preserve someone's anonymity. In the interest of delivering a perfect child, all birth technologies would be employed, and at the first sign of fetal distress or maternal complaint the coach could encourage or insist on a cesarean delivery.

Who is this baby for? It is clear from contract and practice that the purchasing father is the key figure of the industry. From the first phone contact, I was told "the child is the child of the natural parents. That means the father." The contract requires delivery of the child to the father, and every effort is made to include him in the procedures. This is in sharp contrast to the invisible woman who will become the adoptive mother of the child. She is referred to only rarely, as the "wife" of the father, and the "potential stepmother." There were no plans mentioned to try and include her in the process, although it would seem she might have a greater need for company sensitivity and an active role.

The fathers, as described by the industry representatives, are largely upper middle class and well-educated. As the director explained it, "to be able to come up with $25,000 cash, they *have* to be well-educated." They share a desire to biologically father an infant: some have tried adoption and turn in desperation to the surrogate alternative to begin a family; others are already rearing children from their wives' previous marriages, but want a child of their own. The need to continue patriarchal lineage, to make certain the child has the sperm and name of the buyer, is primary.

The public image of the surrogate mother is important to the reputation of the companies who must distinguish their "reproductive service" from both sexual prostitution and baby-selling. The new surrogate image is bright, altruistic, and feminine. She is a very special girl next door, a plucky pioneer in a new industry, a girl who loves being pregnant and is able to give a man what his wife can't. While company spokespersons promote the surrogate as on a par with the buyers, able to provide good genes and a clean prenatal environment, there is also an attempt to place her in a slightly different moral class from the prospective parents. They state the logical economic and convenience incentives to becoming a surrogate, then readily disclose that many have had previous abortions or have given up children for adoption. These surrogates, approximately one-third of applicants according to a Michigan psychologist, may participate in order to atone for their previous abortions. Such public announcements, although seemingly in contrast to the desired altruistic image, and based on spurious research citing a statistic no different than general population estimates, may have at least two positive results for the companies:

1. It may ease the conscience of liberal prospective buyers, who can more easily accept the financial misuse of the surrogate if they believe she is receiving invisible psychological/moral gains.
2. It may lure some prospective surrogates who have unresolved abortion experiences, perhaps exacerbated by new anti-abortion propaganda.

In general, surrogates may be deterred from demanding better treatment, if convinced that giving up this child is part of a moral punishment or therapeutic process.

There is a need for feminists to pay attention to the surrogate industry and to structure debate in feminist terms. There have, of course, been outspoken critics of the surrogate companies, but they have primarily questioned the industry's effect on traditional business dealings and family structure. For example, the only ethical issue raised in a lengthy *Wall Street Journal* article was whether participants might be taking unfair advantage of insurance companies offering maternity benefits. Robert Francoeur, in his 1974 book *Utopian Motherhood,* (p. 102) envisioned a gloomy world in which so-called "mercenary mothers" would jeopardize the traditional "monogamous family structure."

The metaphors of description and criticism are fascinating. Is the surrogate mother a prostitute, or is she instead a modern extension of the wet nurse? Is the surrogate arrangement like donating sperm, simply giving women the right to sell their reproductive capacity as men have done for years? Or is the arrangement more like building a house, where the father furnishes half the blueprint and materials and the labor is contracted out? Is it baby-selling? Or is it organ-selling, morally equivalent to allowing the needy to sell their kidneys to rich patients? Each metaphor frames political/ethical discourse in different terms. Even the use of the term "surrogate mothering," or the more recently popular euphemism "surrogate parenting," begins by labeling the biological mother as artificial. Allowing the debate to be structured by the industry has slowed criticism from the feminist community. In California, after an educational session from an industry representative, a NOW chapter passed a resolution supporting efforts to have the surrogate contracts recognized and enforceable under California law.

Our recognition of the problems of infertile women may also be delaying a strong feminist opposition to the surrogate industry. We must not only offer support to women in the painful emotional situation of being involuntarily childless, but we must examine its broader historical basis. The infertility was largely brought to us from the manufacturers of other types of reproductive control, birth control pills and IUDs. The same laws which make it difficult for many infertile women to adopt children will make the surrogate alternative equally unavailable unless she is part of a wealthy married heterosexual couple. Older children, children of color, and those with special needs will remain unadoptable, and the traditional patriarchal family system will remain intact.

In *Right-Wing Women* (1983), Andrea Dworkin has placed surrogate motherhood in the center of her elegant model of the systematic exploitation of women. In it, she describes the brothel model and farming model. Simply stated, in the brothel model women are used efficiently and specifically for sex by groups of men. In the farming model, women are used by individual men, not so efficiently, for reproduction. The surrogate industry provides a frightening synthesis of both which

> enables women to sell their wombs within the terms of the brothel model. Motherhood is becoming a new branch of female prostitution with the help of scientists who want access to the womb for experimentation and for power. A doctor can be the agent of fertilization; he can dominate and control conception and reproduction. Women can sell reproductive capacities the same way old-time prostitutes sold sexual ones but without the stigma of whoring because there is no penile intrusion.

This system will become increasingly efficient with the refinement of other reproductive technologies such as embryo transplanting. As Genoveffa Corea points out, we are not far from being able to use a combination of artificial insemination and embryo transplant to allow Third World women to become the prenatal carriers of completely white children (at the same time that Depo-Provera and other exports are compromising these women's ability to conceive their own children).

The language and process encountered in my experience within a surrogate company is consistent with the reproductive prostitution model described by Dworkin. The surrogate is paid for "giving the man what his wife can't." She "loves being pregnant," and is valued solely and temporarily for her reproductive capacity. After she "enters the fold" she is removed from standard legal protections and is subject to a variety of abuses. She is generally considered to be mercenary, collecting large

unearned fees for her services, but the terms of the system are in reality such that she may lose more permanent opportunities for employment, and may end up injured or dead with no compensation at all. Even the glowing descriptions of the surrogates sound remarkably like a happy hooker with a heart of gold.

The issue of prostitution has been a difficult one for feminists; so ancient and entrenched a part of the patriarchal system that it seems almost impossible to confront. We must not now participate in a quiet liberal complicity with the new reproductive prostitution. It is our challenge to pay attention to our feminist visionaries, and to expose the surrogate industry during its formation.

NO

Lori B. Andrews

OUR LAWS SHOULD REFLECT
THE NEW MORAL REALITIES
OF SURROGATE MOTHERHOOD.

One day last year, a young couple sat around a dinner table calmly discussing how they would raise money by selling their child. A few days later they gave the child to a stranger in exchange for $2,000. The stranger happened to be cooperating with police, and they were tried and convicted under a statute that prohibits the selling and bartering of children.

Around the same time, 38-year-old Elizabeth Kane (a pseudonym), a pregnant, married mother of three, was receiving money to be a surrogate mother. She had agreed to be artificially inseminated with the sperm of a man whose wife was infertile, carry the child until birth, and then turn it over to the couple for adoption.

In the first situation, the couple selling the child was greeted with disdain and legal action. In the second instance, Kane was a favored talk show guest and heralded by some as admirable for sharing her body. But how different is selling an existing child from contracting for a fee to bear one and then turning the child over to a paying couple? Increasingly, lawyers, judges and legislators are asking themselves this question as they are approached by infertile couples who want to arrange contracts with surrogate mothers.

There are no state laws applying directly to surrogate motherhood, although Michigan State Representative Richard Fitzpatrick plans to introduce legislation to allow payment of up to $10,000 to a surrogate who allows the genetic father and his wife to adopt the child. Until such legislation is passed, however, attorneys must consult various laws for guidance in deciding whether a woman may contract in this way to bear a child.

SEARCHING THE STATUTES

A lawyer who represents a couple wanting to hire a surrogate mother finds that every step of the process, including the initial artificial insemination, may be affected by the language of certain state laws not drafted to deal directly

From, "Removing the Stigma of Surrogate Motherhood," by Lori Andrews, *Family Advocate, 20*(2) 1981. Copyright © 1981. Reprinted by permission of the American Bar Association and the author.

with this procedure. When artificial insemination began being widely used in the United States, it was feared that the sperm donor would be held liable for the costs of raising the child. So some states—California, Connecticut, and Oregon—passed laws saying that when a man donates sperm for artificial insemination of a woman who is *not* his wife, that donor is *not* the legal father of the child.

Obviously, these laws impede the surrogate mother's arrangement where the donor of the semen *does* in fact want to be considered the father. Other states passed laws with a similar effect, which declare that the man who consents to his wife's insemination is the father of the child. In all, at least 19 states have legislation governing the use of artificial insemination.

In states that have no statutes on artificial insemination, other problems might arise. Some early cases held that the use of artificial insemination constituted adultery. The more recent (and better) approach is typified by a judge who notes the absurdity of that viewpoint. "Since the doctor may be a woman, or the husband himself may administer the insemination by a syringe, this is patently absurd: to consider it an act of adultery with the donor, who at the time of insemination may be a thousand miles away or may even be dead, is equally absurd," wrote the judge. *People v. Sorensen,* 437 P.2d 495, 66 Cal. Rptr. 7 (1968).

In addition to the artificial insemination laws, other statutes governing paternity might affect whether the sperm donor is considered the legal father. What would happen, for example, if the surrogate is married? In a number of states, even if there is no artificial insemination law, the husband of any woman who gets pregnant during the marriage is presumed to be the child's father. Thus, the husband of the surrogate could exert legal rights to the child, while the natural father would have to bring a paternity proceeding to try to establish his own parental rights.

APPLICATION OF ADOPTION LAWS

The most extensive laws applicable to a surrogate mother arrangement, however, are the adoption laws. Provisions governing payment, consent, and the transfer of custody to a stepparent come into play.

In many states, payment to the surrogate mother for her services would be forbidden. For example, in Florida, no payment may be made in connection with an adoption beyond the medical and living expenses of the mother through the pregnancy and 30 days after the birth.

Another common provision invalidates a mother's consent to release her child for adoption if the consent was given prior to the child's birth or within a certain time period after birth. In Kentucky, for example, the law provides that a woman may not consent to give her child up for adoption, nor file a petition to relinquish her parental rights, until five days after the baby's birth. Both provisions are designed to give the mother a cooling-off period to ensure that her decision is carefully made.

Therefore, any contract the woman makes before her pregnancy is void, since it was made before the waiting period ended. Yet a contract for a fee made after the waiting period also would be illegal—it would be considered "child selling" since the child would have already been born.

Certain laws governing stepparent adoptions may also apply to the surrogate situation. Some states have streamlined adoption procedures when the biological parent's spouse (i.e., the stepparent) wishes to adopt the child. For example, Oklahoma law allows the court to waive the waiting period when the child is related by blood to one of the petitioners.

Several other states exempt stepparent petitioners from suitability investigations or reports of expenditures connected with the adoption process. California has an unusual statute exempting stepparent adoptions from the ethical prohibitions against one lawyer representing both the natural parents and the adoptive parents.

However, a stepparent provision apparently would not be applicable unless the sperm donor is considered the legal father. This is difficult to establish if the artificial insemination statute or other paternity laws deny him that status.

Other laws not traditionally the domain of a family lawyer might also affect a surrogate contract. For example, some states have anti-slavery laws which prohibit buying or selling of "people." The California penal code provides that giving or receiving money or anything of value in consideration of placing one person in the custody of another is punishable by two or four years imprisonment. Such a law could be used to prevent a surrogate from accepting a fee to bear the child and turn him or her over to the couple.

REGULATING THE ATTORNEY'S ROLE

The legal liabilities in connection with surrogate mothering extend beyond the couple and the surrogate, however. In surrogate arrangements where the attorney serves as a sort of "matchmaker" for the parties, and charges accordingly, the attorney may find that he or she is subject to certain laws.

Under Arizona law, attorneys are prohibited from receiving a fee for helping place a child for adoption. A Nevada statute prohibits any person, other than a parent or guardian, from assisting in the arrangement to place a child for adoption without securing a license as a child placement agency. The provision explicitly applies to physicians and attorneys.

All in all, few states leave the intermediary role unregulated. Even if any person or agency is allowed to act between the parent or parents and the adoptive parents in arranging an adoption placement, state courts supervise such unlicensed agencies with great care. The courts still look on profit made by the mother or large fees charged by an attorney or other middleman as symptoms of a "black-market" transaction.

CIRCUMVENTING THE LAW

. . . Legal action is [currently] in the works in Michigan. In that state, a couple wants to pay the husband's secretary to be inseminated with the husband's sperm and bear a child for them. The payment will be $5,000 plus medical expenses, sick leave, pregnancy disability insurance, and medical insurance. Since Michigan law prohibits the payment of money in connection with either an adoption or the termination of parental rights, the couple's attorney, Noel Keane, has brought suit to declare the law unconstitutional.

CONSTITUTIONAL QUESTIONS

He maintains that a prohibition against surrogate motherhood is an unconstitutional infringement on the participants' right of privacy, which protects personal decisions regarding marriage and reproduction. This right to privacy, he argues, covers the infertile couple's decision to bear a child in this manner and the natural mother's right to sell her services as a surrogate.

In January, 1980, the Wayne County (Michigan) Circuit Court in *Doe v. Kelly,* 6 Fam. L. Rep. 3011, approached the issue narrowly, holding that no fundamental right exists to pay someone to give up a child for adoption. The judge also held that Michigan's long-established policy against "baby bartering" prevents such conduct. He wrote, "Mercenary considerations used to create a parent-child relationship and its impact upon the family unit strikes at the very foundation of human society and is patently and necessarily injurious to the community."

Reviewing the case, the Michigan Court of Appeals stated that the plaintiffs had a fundamental right to decide to bear a child by using a surrogate. The court, however, did not find that the statutes at issue would interfere with the conception of a child through the insemination of a surrogate.

"The statute in question does not directly prohibit John Doe and Mary Doe from having the child as planned," said the court. "It acts instead to preclude plaintiffs from paying consideration in conjunction with their use of the state's adoption procedures. In effect, the plaintiffs' contractual agreement discloses a desire to use the adoption code to change the legal status of the child—i.e., its right to support, intestate succession, etc. We do not perceive this goal as within the realm of fundamental interests protected by the right to privacy from reasonable governmental regulation."

Appealing the case to the Michigan Supreme Court, Keane is again asserting his clients' right to privacy. He is also arguing that the laws prohibiting payment to a surrogate are a violation of the equal protection clause of the Fourteenth Amendment, since payment to a sperm donor is permissible.

But the sperm donor is merely turning over a gamete (as would a female donating an egg), while the surrogate is relinquishing her rights to a living individual. Even if the surrogate mother were not viewed as selling a child, donating sperm is just not comparable to providing nine months of prenatal care and childbearing. The former could be characterized as a product, sold at a uniform price, while the latter is a personalized service. The surrogate is, in effect, entering into an employment contract. Thus Keane's equal protection argument is unpersuasive.

The Michigan Court of Appeals did not give the constitutional issues raised the careful attention they deserve. The court should have analyzed whether the statutes infringed on a fundamental right, and whether that infringement was justified by a compelling state interest. . . .

STATE INTERESTS

Even if the right to use a surrogate is found to be a fundamental right, the statues interfering with that right could be held constitutional if they advance substantial state interests and are closely tailored to effectuate only those interests. The Michigan Court of Appeals made no attempt to analyze what the state interests were in a statute prohibiting payment to a surrogate mother.

The state interests regarding surrogate mothers might not be the same as those responsible for the initial passage of the laws prohibiting payment in connection with an adoption. For example, the legislatures might have aimed to protect already-pregnant women from being coerced into giving up their children for a fee, and to protect children from being sold to the highest bidder, who might not necessarily be the best parent.

The surrogate mother situation, however, is clearly distinguishable from such instances. Since the surrogate contract is made before pregnancy, there is less chance that the woman will be taken advantage of. And since the man paying a fee to gain custody is the natural father, it is at least arguably more likely that the child will be given a better home than if he or she were merely "sold" to a stranger.

Nevertheless, there are several interests that the state could advance to attempt to justify prohibiting payment even in the surrogate situation. These include a public policy against treating children as property, evidence that such an arrangement might not be in the child's best interest psychologically, the desire to protect potential surrogates from economic coercion to bear children, and the possibility of surrogate arrangements being used for eugenic purposes.

Moreover, the state may point to the practical difficulty of distinguishing surrogate mother situations from typical "black-market" adoptions, where unwed mothers decide to sell their children rather than undergo abortions. If a surrogate can get paid for bearing a child, women who have become pregnant through intercourse, rather than artificial insemination, may present themselves as surrogates to the courts so that they may sell their children to infertile couples who desperately want to be parents. All of these issues deserve close attention when presented in future court cases.

CONCLUSION

Attempts to develop a surrogate mother policy have been stifled by the use of terms like "baby buying" without a close analysis of what is behind them. The possibility of using a surrogate clearly was not considered when the laws governing ar-

tificial insemination, adoption, and presumptions about paternity were passed. The key issue to be faced is not whether these laws as drafted do prohibit surrogate motherhood, but whether they should. For even if the laws were not initially drafted to limit surrogate motherhood, there may be valid policy reasons for such restrictions.

Ultimately, the surrogate mother issue will have to be resolved in the legislature, not the courts, for, as the Supreme Court stated in the abortion funding case, *Maher v. Roe,* 432 U.S. 618 (1977), "[w]hen an issue involves policy choices as sensitive as those implicated here, the appropriate forum for their resolution in a democracy is the legislature."

A SURROGATE MOTHER'S VIEW

Last February 5, Carol Pavek gave birth to a ten-pound son. The delivery was routine, but when the baby arrived, Mrs. Pavek did not get to hold him. Instead, he was handed to a second woman in the delivery room. Mrs. Pavek had served as a surrogate mother—a role that had just ended.

By profession, Carol Pavek is a midwife. A few years ago, she wanted to have her own son at home, but last-minute complications forced her to change to a hospital delivery. She decided to become a surrogate so that she could have another chance at home birth.

Her husband was supportive, helping her compose a letter to Noel Keane, an attorney who had talked about surrogates on the *Phil Donahue Show.* Two weeks later, a couple wanting her services arrived at the Paveks' Amarillo, Texas, home. Mrs. Pavek performed the artificial insemination herself, using a syringe. She asked for no payment beyond medical expenses.

Mrs. Pavek had agreed to terminate her

parental rights to the baby so that the genetic father and his sterile wife could take custody. But since Mrs. Pavek was married and, under Texas law, her husband was presumed to be the child's father, she was unsure whether a judge would approve the arrangement. Because of the uncertain legal status of surrogate motherhood, the Paveks and the couple made a pact.

"We were all horrified at the thought of the baby ending up in foster care," says Mrs. Pavek. "So, we all agreed that if the couple couldn't keep the child, my husband and I would. The current law seems so strange. Why should the actual father have to adopt his own child?"

Mrs. Pavek may be facing these issues again in another nine months, as she recently met a New Jersey couple for whom she hopes to bear a child.

SETTING STANDARDS

While the law as yet has not required screening of the couples, Mrs. Pavek has her own standards for the type of couple she will enter into contract with. For various reasons, she has turned down about 200 couples who have called her.

"I want to feel that I've personally selected a good home for my baby," she says. "I don't want to worry for the next 18 years whether the couple is financially and emotionally stable."

Mrs. Pavek has refused to serve as a surrogate to a couple who wanted a child just because they needed an heir, and for a couple whom she didn't think would spend enough recreational time with the child. She has also turned down couples who already have children through adoption or previous marriages.

Even if the New Jersey couple meets Mrs. Pavek's standards, the arrangement will proceed differently than her first surrogate pregnancy.

"I certainly want life insurance this time," she says, "and I want decision-making power over the baby's medical care for the first 24 hours." The latter requirement will ensure that doctors know where to turn in case they need consent for emergency medical services to the child and will allow her to refuse tests on the baby that she, as a midwife, feels are unnecessary.

FEE CHARGING

Mrs. Pavek is also considering charging a fee for her services. Other women purportedly have received as much as $10,000 for bearing a couple's child. "At first I was horrified at the idea of asking for money," says Mrs. Pavek. "But then my husband got out his calculator and figured out that $10,000 works out to approximately $1.5 an hour, which seems reasonable for full-time child care."

What does she think about the bill Michigan State Representative Fitzpatrick is planning to introduce setting a $10,000 limit on the fees a surrogate can charge?

"I'm just furious about it," says Mrs. Pavek. "Why should they set a financial limit? Either payment is legal or it's not.

"Instead of setting limits on what a surrogate can get paid, they should set a limit for what psychiatrists, attorneys and medical doctors can get," she continues. "After all, there is a ceiling on attorneys' fees for adoption. And once you get a precedent set, it shouldn't be that tough to handle additional surrogate cases."

PUTTING IT IN WRITING

Where legally permissible, lawyers who have been active in the surrogate mother area have developed contracts which spe-

out the rights and responsibilities of each party—the husband who will be the natural father, the sterile wife, the surrogate, and the surrogate's husband—at each stage of the process. They offer the following advice concerning the drafting of such a contract.

The contract should include the basic agreement that the surrogate agrees to be inseminated with a particular man's sperm, carry the baby and turn it over after its birth to the man and his wife. If the surrogate is to be paid, the contract should also spell out when she will receive the payments— for example, $3,000 when the pregnancy is confirmed, $3,000 midway through the pregnancy, and $3,000 after the baby has been adopted by the couple. Some attorneys also feel the contract should provide that the surrogate's husband agrees not to claim that he is the child's legal father.

Specific provisions to help assure that the baby is healthy have also been included in these contracts. Some stipulate, for example, that the surrogate mother should not smoke, drink, or take drugs (other than on a doctor's recommendation) during pregnancy.

The agreement might also provide that the surrogate must undergo amniocentesis at an appropriate point in the pregnancy. Thirty-eight-year-old Elizabeth Kane was asked to undergo amniocentesis since the chances of giving birth to a Down's Syndrome child are greater in older mothers.

PREPARING FOR MISHAPS

Kane's test showed she was carring a normal fetus, but what if it hadn't? If a contract is to be used, it might describe the rights of the various parties if the fetus is found to have a genetic defect. For example, it could answer the following questions: Does the surrogate agree to abort the child on the couple's request? Does she agree to continue to carry the baby if the couple decides they want the child despite the defect? If she decides to have the genetically defective child, despite the couple's wish that she abort, can she then keep the child herself?

The agreement might also include what would happen if the natural father died before the child were born. The contract could tell whether the natural father's wife (not genetically related to the child) would be given custody of the child, or whether an altogether different arrangement would ensue. At Surrogate Parenting Associates (SPA), for example, if the natural father dies, the doctor is given custody of the child until he or she is placed for adoption.

The contract might make other provisions for the welfare of the surrogate and child. The SPA's contract provides that the natural father must pay for an insurance policy on the life of the surrogate, to remain in effect until six months after the baby's birth. It also requires that the natural father take out a policy on his own life, payable in trust to the unborn child.

There might also be some sort of testing provided for in the contract to assure that the child was actually fathered by the man who contracted for it, rather than another man. For example, the contract could state that the child must undergo blood tests, and that if the blood type didn't match, the surrogate must pay back the money she was given and the couple would not have to accept the child.

Provisions for anonymity of the various parties could also be included. The agreement might state that the natural father and his wife will not try to find out the identity and whereabouts of the surrogate (and vice versa) and that the couple will not advise the child about the surrogate's identity.

WHAT THE CONTRACT MEANS

A detailed contract can be a valuable way to explain exactly what the surrogate situation entails. Any confusion about what a certain party's rights are, or any doubts about whether the arrangement should be undertaken, can thus be cleared up before the pregnancy begins. It is fairly clear, however, that courts will not use the existence of a contract to force a surrogate mother to give up a child. Under traditional contract law, the right of specific performance is not available.

One Philadelphia lawyer, Burton Satzberg, explains to prospective parents that if the surrogate changes her mind, she cannot legally be required to terminate her parental rights. Satzberg believes, however, that a court might be willing to accept the contract as proof of paternity, which would allow the genetic father to bring a custody suit. The issue would then become whether the environment the natural father and his wife could provide would be more in the child's best interest than that which the surrogate could offer.

Lawyers involved in surrogate arrangements thought they would have the opportunity to see the custody issue tested in the courts last June. A New York couple, James and Bjorna Noyes, had entered into a simple twelve-line "statement of understanding" with Nisa Bhimani, from California. Bhimani had agreed to be inseminated, long distance, with Mr. Noyes' sperm, and then turn over to the Noyeses legal custody of the child born nine months later.

A few months into the pregnancy, however, Bhimani decided she wanted to keep the child. James Noyes brought suit to win custody and made a motion to prevent Bhimani from naming the child when it was born. He lost the motion, and, a few weeks later, withdrew his suit minutes before it was to be heard.

The status of contracts to bear a child is thus still in legal limbo. However, lawyers involved in such arrangements believe that a contract will ensure that a couple can at least recover the money paid to the surrogate for her services, her medical expenses, and perhaps their own out-of-pocket expenses as well, including their attorneys' fees.

POSTSCRIPT

IS SURROGATE MOTHERHOOD
A FORM OF PROSTITUTION?

Two old adages come to mind in discussions of surrogate motherhood. "Let the consumer—the buyer—beware" obviously needs to be expanded in the case of surrogate mothers to include all the parties affected by this new possibility. At the same time, the reality that "Money is the root of all evil" has application when we ask whether payments should be allowed for surrogate mothers.

The dilemma of contract law, when applied to surrogate motherhood, will not be easily resolved. Legal tradition allows that when a contract is violated or not fulfilled as specified, the injured party can seek either damages or "specific performance." If a surrogate mother decides to keep her child instead of giving it up for adoption as she contracted to do, the genetic father and his childless wife are not going to be interested in her paying monetary damages when what they really want is "their" infant. On the other side of the dilemma, the courts cam compel the defaulting party to perform the work agreed to under the contract. Suppose, a couple of months into the pregnancy, the surrogate mother decides she doesn't want to go through with the pregnancy and seeks an abortion. What court would think of compelling her to continue the pregnancy to term? Unlike a builder's contract, the surrogate mother contract involves the "services" of the surrogate's body for nine months, and enforcing the contract in this case borders on slavery.

On March 1, 1987, a superior court judge in New Jersey granted exclusive custody of "baby M" to the natural father. Mary Beth Whitehead, the surrogate who had refused to give up her child for adoption by the couple who had contracted with her, was stripped of all parental rights. This decision is likely to be appealed and the impact on surrogate mother programs is still unclear.

Equally perplexing is the question of how might society and legislation control this approach to parenthood when the surrogate mother can be artificially inseminated by the husband whose wife is childless?

Ethicist Peter Singer and Deane Wells, a concerned member of the Australian Parliament, suggest that ". . . it is too early to produce a detailed blueprint of how regulated surrogacy might work. In this area, piecemeal social engineering is the way to make progress." This means that the debates and controversies are going to continue for some years, until surrogate motherhood is incorporated into our legal system the way adoption and simple artificial insemination of a childless wife with donor semen is now. See the bibliography for further readings on this subject.

ISSUE 11

SHOULD GENDER PREDETERMINATION BE REGULATED?

YES: Gena Corea, from *The Mother Machine: Reproductive Technologies from Artificial Insemination to Artificial Wombs* (Harper and Row, 1985)

NO: Peter Singer and Deane Wells, from *Making Babies: The New Science and Ethics of Conception* (Scribner's, 1985)

ISSUE SUMMARY

YES: Gena Corea, founder of the Feminist International Network on the New Reproductive Technologies, argues that the immediate and most socially devastating outcome of the new techniques for predetermining or selecting the sex of fetuses is gynicide.
NO: Peter Singer, Director of the Centre for Human Bioethics at Monash University in Australia, and Deane Wells, a member of the Australian Parliament, emphasize that the benefits these techniques would have in promoting population control outweigh alarmist claims about unbalanced sex ratio.

We have known since 1923 that sperm are the key to sex determination in the fetus, and that there are, in fact, two different kind of sperm, androsperm carrying a Y sex chromosome and gynosperm which carry an X sex chromosome. The problem is how to separate these two sperm types without harming them or reducing their ability to fertilize an egg. Thus far, sex preselection has focused on that problem.

In 1971, a popular book by Shettles and Rorvik suggested ways to time intercourse to coincide with or precede ovulation, use douches of baking soda or white vinegar, ejaculate deeply or shallowly in the vagina, and avoid or have female orgasm in order to shift the balance in favor of the androsperm or gynosperm.

Scientists have worked on a variety of ways to separate the androsperm and gynosperm. They let them race through a gelatin column, in order to enable the androsperm to finish first because they are lighter and swim faster. They spin semen samples in high-speed centrifuges to collect the heavier gynosperm. They use ultrasound to explode the heads of one or the other type of sperm with just the right frequency of sound waves. Then, the woman is artificially inseminated with the desired gynosperm or androsperm.

A variation on sex predetermination involves the sophisticated technique of inducing the woman to ovulate several eggs instead of the usual single egg, in vitro (test tube) fertilization (IVF) of several eggs, and then checking the sex of all the embryos before transfering one or two of the desired gender into the woman for a normal pregnancy and discarding the surplus embryos.

In the second approach, a variety of techniques can be used to ascertain the gender of the fetus after pregnancy is underway. If the fetus turns out to be of the "wrong" gender, it can be aborted. Fetal cells can be aspirated from the cervix of the pregnant woman in the second month of pregnancy. The chromosomes of fetal cells in the pregnant woman's saliva or blood can also be used to learn the sex of the fetus. Chorionic villi sampling in the second month of pregnancy and amniocentesis in the third month are the more conventional ways of learning fetal gender today, but both techniques carry some risk. Ultrasound scans can be used to check the genitalia of the fetus in the fourth month, but abortion at that time is more risky than it would be in the first trimester.

How do Americans respond to these possibilities of selecting the sex of their children? In 1986, a Media General/Associated Press poll of 1,464 adults revealed that a total of 49 percent opposed sex preselection. Of this 49 percent, 19 percent said gender selection is wrong or unnatural. Thirteen percent said it violates their religious or moral beliefs. Five percent objected because it takes away the mystery and surprise of having a child. Three-and-a-half percent opposed it because they thought it would upset the balance of males and females. The remaining 8.5 percent gave other reasons for opposing it.

YES

Gena Corea

SELECTING THE GENDER
OF HUMAN FETUSES
PROMOTES GYNICIDE

In 1955, four research groups working independently in Copenhagen, Jerusalem, New York and Minneapolis developed amniocentesis, a procedure involving the insertion of a long, hollow needle through a pregnant woman's abdomen and into her uterus. Through the needle, physicians withdraw some of the amniotic fluid, which surrounds the fetus and contains embryonic cells. Technicians can distinguish between XX (female) and XY (male) cells in this fluid. So amniocentesis can be and is used as a prenatal sex detection test.

Sociologists studying the record of two hospitals in a large city in western India for a twelve-month period in 1976 and 1977 found disturbing evidence of the consequences of this use. In the first hospital, all ninety-two women who sought amniocentesis for sex detection wanted to abort the fetus if it were female; all wanted to retain the fetus if it were male. In the second hospital, 700 predominantly middle-class women underwent amniocentesis for sex detection. Of these, 450 were told they would have a daughter and almost all (430) aborted the female fetuses. The remaining 250 mothers were told they were carrying male fetuses and every single one of them elected to carry the babies to term, even those who were advised of a possible genetic defect in the child.

The sociologists conclude: "The pattern we have documented of inducing abortion when the foetus is female continues the traditional practice of female infanticide" (Ramanamma and Bambawali, 1980).

Clearly, the technology of sex control can translate sexual prejudice (a "preference" for male children) into a sexist reality. The number of women relative to men could well be reduced. This is what one medical ethicist terms "previctimization"—women being destroyed and sacrificed before they are even born (Raymond, 1981). This can be accomplished today by *sex determination* (evaluation of fetal sex through such a technique as amniocentesis followed by abortion of female fetuses) and may someday be accomplished through *sex predetermination* (techniques, such as sperm separation, to ensure that a male embryo is formed in the first place).

Sociologists rarely see the previctimization of females as a problem. In studying sex preference, they seldom question its morality. "Rather," according to sociologist Jalna Hanmer of England's Bradford University, "one can detect a tendency to cope with possible criticisms by implying or stating that all is not as bad as it might be." The researchers, for example, tell us that when sex predetermination methods are available, the anticipated increase in males over females will decline after a few years (an assertion others have effectively challenged) or that only a minority will use these techniques.

Despite the widespread misperception that reliable sex predetermination techniques are already available, no such methods have had their effectiveness convincingly demonstrated. But if such techniques do become available, are we so sure that males will be valued over females? Yes. Folk customs expressing male preference, the sex preference studies, and social and economic structures that select on the basis of sex, all indicate this.

First, folk customs. The notion that boys are better is implicit in ancient beliefs on the prediction or determination of a child's sex. An age-old belief that the right side of the body is the more valuable side and that right-handedness is associated with strength and justice coincided with innumerable theories that boys emanated from the right. Sons were produced by the right testicle, under one theory, and by the right ovary under a later one. Left-handedness was associated with weakness and evil. Girls came from the left. It was popularly believed in antiquity that men copulating with the left testicle tied up would produce a boy.

Certain ways of predicting fetal sex revealed the presumption that sons were superior to daughters. For example, according to Arabian, Indian and Jewish traditions, if the woman was particularly happy and untroubled, the fetus was male (Cederqvist and Fuch).

P.J. McElrath argued in his 1911 book, *The Key to Sex Control,* that boys were made of superior stuff. Fresh, vibrant sperm and newly released eggs produced sons. Aged, weak sperm and stale eggs produced daughters (Whelan 1977).

From the scripture of Father-God religions, from the folk sayings and practices of peoples around the world, I could present an endless list showing that sons are more highly treasured than daughters. A sample:

—A German adage goes: "A house full of daughters is like a cellar full of sour beer."

—A Chinese proverb: "Eighteen goddesslike daughters are not equal to one son with a hump."

—The Talmud states: "When a girl is born, the walls are crying."

—In India shortly after a Hindu marriage, the husband performs the ceremony *Garbhadhana,* in which he and his wife pray for the conception of a son. Three months after the conception, they perform another of the sacred domestic ceremonies, the *Pumsavana,* for obtaining a son. Mantras prescribed in a Hindu sacred text can also be chanted in an attempt to transform a female fetus into a male (Ramanamma and Bambawali, 1980).

—In the past in Korea, rituals designed to produce sons were common. They were called "son praying." A drastic form involved burning the woman's navel through cautery. Blue salts and musk powder mixed with wheat dough were placed over the woman's navel and cauterized with salt moxa. This was generally done two hundred to three hundred times on a sonless woman. According to researchers

Chung, Cha and Lee (as cited in Williamson, 1976), this "seeding of sons" through cautery was practiced widely into the 1920s or 1930s. They write: "Sometimes cautery was carried to an extreme by zealous husbands who believed that the more salt burned, so much the better. Instead of burning mox on the navel, the husband brought a red-hot iron rod against the navel of his wife and held it there while the wife screamed in unbearable pain."

Studies confirm what the folk customs tell us. Sociologist Dr. Nancy E. Williamson has reviewed the sex preference research around the world and conducted her own studies. The evidence that parents in many countries would rather have a predominance of boys over girls is "overwhelming," she writes. Daughter preference is so rare she refers to it as "this deviant preference."

An example: In a 1954 study of American college students, 92 percent of males and 66 percent of females surveyed wanted a son for an only child, while 4 percent of males and 6 percent of females wanted a daughter. Twenty years later, other researchers replicated the study with similar results (as cited in Williamson, 1976, p. 31).

Son preference prevails in the United States and in developing countries but the degree differs vastly. In developing countries, son preference is "much, much stronger," Williamson said in an interview. "It borders on obsession." Studies show that couples in the United States often want a balanced family—one child of each sex. But there is a decided son preference here as well, expressed as much in birth order as in numbers. Studies have consistently found that people want the first-born to be a son and, if they want an uneven number of children, more sons than daughters (Westoff and Rindfuss, 1974).

Men desire sons much more strongly than women do, the studies reveal. Women, however, still want a first-born son and, if the number of children is not even, more boys than girls.

Professor Gerald Markle, a sociologist from Western Michigan University, examined sex preference studies, conducted his own and concluded: "There is a consensus among most scientists that the adoption of sex-choosing by the general population would lead to an excess of male infants" (Markle and Nam, 1971).

On a worldwide basis, girl preference is rare. In fact one study of factory workers from six nations found that the alternative to boy preference was not girl preference but was, rather, a desire for "either." Those wanting a girl did not exceed 5 percent among any of the six groups of workers (Williamson, 1978, p. 9).

Women would also choose sons over daughters, though their son preference is weaker than men's. But is it really a "choice" they would be making? Choice, one commentator has noted, is intrinsically connected with the *power* to choose, a power systematically undermined by patriarchal values. "The fact that women 'choose' male children in a culture where women are programmed not to value themselves can hardly be termed choice," she wrote (Connors, 1981, p. 206).

A woman's son preference may not be a "preference" at all, but rather something that is maintained by force and ideology. Within the traditional patriarchal family, women are rewarded for bearing sons and punished for failing to do so. Women may "prefer" a son because they prefer not to live as outcasts, poor and despised.

A wife's status increases when she produces sons who will carry on her husband's name and inherit his wealth (Williamson, 1976, p. 19). A married woman in Taiwan, according to a 1968 sex preference study, gets her first bit of security in her husband's family when she bears a son and the quality of her life will largely depend on the ties she develops with that son. "Until a woman bears a male child," the researcher observed, "she is only a provisional member of her husband's household, merely a daughter-in-law; with the birth of a son, she becomes the mother of one of its descendants, a position of prestige and respect" (quoted in Williamson, 1976, p. 143).

Women in many cultures who failed to produce a man-child have been subjected to pity, contempt, social disapproval and social displacement. They have suffered a lack of personal security. Some have been physically beaten, some divorced, deserted, some even killed. The severity of the punishment varied with the time and culture:

—In traditional Korea, a man would desert his wife if she bore no son (Williamson, 1976, p. 96).

—Henry VIII annulled his marriage to the aging Catherine of Aragon because he wanted a male heir. Another wife, Anne, disappointed him by bearing a daughter, Elizabeth, and then bringing forth a stillborn son. He had her beheaded.

—In 1982, the controlled Chinese press began publicizing the abuse of wives who gave birth to daughters, noting that the offending husbands and in-laws had been punished for their actions. In one case, a teacher from northeastern China, Gao Lihua, married a soldier, Chen Xudong, and subsequently bore a daughter. Her in-laws advised their son to divorce her. Chen came home on furlough and beat his wife, leaving her with a brain concussion and facial injuries (Wren, 1982).

—In the United States, pressure— though in a different form—can also be exerted on women to produce sons. The husband's "disappointment" at the birth of a series of daughters can place a "strain" on the marriage, arousing fear in the wife that she might not be able to hold onto her man (see Rorvik and Shettles, 1971, pp. xvii-xxiii).

In addition to folk customs and sex preference studies, the presence of social and economic structures that select on the basis of sex also indicate that males will be valued over females once sex control techniques are fully developed.

Boy preference is not simply a personal preference but something embodied in institutions, in customs and in laws. For example, in rural areas in many countries, parents have often felt the need for a son who will take over the family farm and provide for them in their old age, society being so structured that a daughter could not do that for them.

Sons and daughters have different access to goods, services, status and power because they live within a sexual caste system. Sex selection technology, then, cannot be seen as an isolated phenomenon. "Sex selection takes place every day in this society without a specific biomedical technology," Dr. Janice Raymond notes. "These procedures merely carry out, on a technological level, what happens on other levels" (Raymond, 1981, p. 209). We see the results of sex selection every time we read the list of male names on the masthead of *The New York Times* or look at the composition of the Soviet Politburo, OPEC, the American Medical Association or the Pittsburgh Pirates.

There is yet another reason why sons are valued, especially, by men. The sons, through whom men pass on their name and property, assure men a form of immortality. The father transmits his name to his son as a way of signifying that his life has been transmitted to the child; surnames have become male "life lines" (Stannard, 1977, p. 302). A daughter cannot build a father's immortality; she will go off and help another man build his by bearing children who will carry his surname.

In view of the importance of sons and the pressures that can be exerted on women to bear them, I want to examine a statement a medical ethicist made in justifying the abortion of "wrong sex" fetuses. Dr. Karen Lebacqz of the Pacific School of Religion argues that aborting a fetus because of its sex rather than because of a genetic defect like Down's syndrome is only a difference of degree. Parents, she adds, have a right to abort a child for a serious reason, including a threat to the integrity and unity of the family. "And I can see instances in which to abort a child because it's the unwanted sex is done because that child would be a threat to the integrity of the family unit," she said (Chedd, 1981).

Lebacqz fails to ask Background questions before arriving at her analysis: Why might the "unity" and "integrity" of the family be threatened by the birth of, say, a female: Is it threatened because the husband is intent on a male heir to carry on his name and bring him immortality and perhaps, through a relative's will, an inheritance? Is family unity and integrity threatened because the wife fears that if she does not bear a son, a "strain" will be placed on the marriage and her husband might divorce her, leaving her and her daughters to fend for themselves in a society where child support payments are meager and, after the first two years, seldom paid and where women earn 59 cents to every dollar a man earns? Is it that the parents have a set of gender stereotypes they want to impose on the child

born to them and if the "wrong sex" is born, they will have to switch and impose a less desired stereotype? What does Lebacqz mean by "unity" and "integrity" anyway? Are those words here anything but platitudes obscuring the power difference between men and women in the family?

If we need further evidence that patriarchal cultures value males over females, it presents itself in the history of infanticide. Sociologist Jalna Hanmer came to examine infanticide from what at first seems a roundabout way. Something puzzled her when she considered polyandry, the system under which a woman is married to several men at the same time: If certain women have numerous husbands, what happens to all the women who must be left without any husbands at all? She learned that those women do not exist. They were destroyed at birth. As one encyclopedia informs us: "Polyandry . . . seems to be associated with scarcity of women owing to the practice of infanticide of females."

Infanticide, which usually involves the murder of girl children, is, Hanmer believes, more properly called femicide or gynicide. Since "gynicide" is not in the dictionary, my definition of it is adapted from Webster's for "genocide": The use of deliberate systematic measures (as killing, bodily or mental injury, unlivable conditions, prevention of births) calculated to bring about the extermination of women or to destroy the culture of women.

Societies that practiced infant gynicide include: the Greeks, Romans, Chinese, Tibetans, Eskimos, Arabs, Japanese, Indians and the Maori of New Zealand.

From antiquity into the Middle Ages there was a statistical imbalance of males over females. One method of limiting population is the destruction of females, the "breeders," reported classical scholar Sarah B. Pomeroy, "and the most likely reason for sexual imbalance in a population is female infanticide" (Pomeroy, 1975, p. 46).

It was the father, in many places, who decided to keep or to kill the infant. During the "lifting up" ceremony of many patriarchal primitive tribes, the father either lifted up the infant, acknowledging it as his own, or did not, leaving the child to be killed or to live as an outcast. Similarly, according to an ancient Roman custom, a newborn was placed on the ground and was allowed to live only if the father raised it. This is the origin of the expression "to raise a child" (Stannard, 1977, p. 299).

Collier's Encyclopedia informs us that infanticide "cannot be classed as callous brutality." No? This is how girl children were killed: thrown in ditches; suffocated; skulls smashed against a hard surface; exposed on a mountaintop; abandoned on the bark basin onto which they were born; drowned; buried alive. In the Hellenistic period in Greece, exposure of infants was widely practiced. Sometimes people would collect the exposed infants who, in most cases, would automatically have slave status. Some slave dealers took these girl babies and sold them as prostitutes (Pomeroy, 1975, pp. 140-141).

Another form of sex selection did not involve outright destruction of females. Systematic neglect of female infants— underfeeding them and denying them needed medical care—sometimes co-existed with the practice of infant gynicide. When infanticide was illegal, neglect alone could lead to the desired result without any law violation.

Neglect could be responsible for suspiciously low rates of survival among female infants in ancient Greece and Rome and in some countries today. Studies cited by Williamson report evidence of female neglect in modern times in Pakistan, India, Ceylon (Sri Lanka) and Bangladesh. Additionally, in northern Algeria, where strong son preference prevails, female infanticide or female neglect are reputedly practiced today. . . .

Proponents of sex predetermination have offered several rationales for its use, including population control. In 1973, John Postgate proposed, as the solution to the world's alleged population problem, the distribution of a pill assuring the birth of boys. This "man-child" pill, made freely available to all, could be used mostly in Third World countries where the desire to breed male children "amounts to an obsession," according to Postgate. The resulting deficiency of females (breeders) would limit the number of babies who could be born in the following generation, thereby reducing population growth. Further, couples would stop producing child after child in an attempt to get the desired number of sons.

Postgate describes how women would live in a world in which many of their kind had been eliminated. "All sorts of taboos would be expected and it is probable that a form of purdah would become necessary. Women's right to work, even to travel alone freely, would probably be forgotten transiently. Polyandry might well become accepted in some societies; some might treat their women as queen ants, others as rewards for the most outstanding (or most determined) males." . . .

What are [the potential] consequences [of this]? The sex preference studies indicate that, globally, sons will be sought more often than daughters and the proportion of men to women (the sex ratio) will likely rise. How life is structured in future, female-scarce societies would vary with the cultures. Commentators speculate that in

191

such societies, several men might share one wife in a polyandrous marriage, and rises might occur in homosexuality and prostitution. The scarce women might be secluded and pressured into marrying and reproducing, further reducing the control women have over their bodies. During a militaristic buildup, males might be regarded as cannon fodder and their conception planned with that purpose in mind. The government might legislate the circumstances under which people could use sex predetermination technology and occasional scandals in the administration of the laws might surface. Black markets in "boy-pills" and "girl-pills" could arise (Postgate, 1973; Luce, 1978; Etzioni, 1968; Hanmer, 1981; Pohlman, 1967). Since women read more books, see more plays and visit more museums than men, less culture would be "consumed," as one sociologist phrased it (Etzioni, 1968). Criminality, he noted, would increase because males are a disproportionate percentage of criminals. . . .

Other potential consequences of the use of sex determination are the radical reduction of the number of women in the Third World and increased poverty among women in developed countries. Postgate, as noted, has advocated a policy that would lead to the first consequence. As for the second, if selective abortion were the primary means of sex determination, poor people would have less access to that means. The availability of abortion for poor women is already severely restricted, Steinbacher points out. So more firstborn males would be born among the privileged while the number among the poor would remain the same. This, Steinbacher noted, would ensure that throughout the world "increasing numbers of women in the future are locked into poverty while men continue to grow in numbers, in positions of control and influence. Whatever

selection method is utilized, the end result will carry with it the lasting opportunity for institutionalizing sexism in birth order."

Finally, the burden of the technology itself falls on the woman. It is women who must take their temperatures daily, chart their menstrual cycles and douche before intercourse. It is women who must bear the physiological effects of amniocentesis. It is women who face the risks of abortion for sex selection in the second trimester when the procedure is six times as life-threatening as in the first trimester. It is women who must endure repeated, and occasionally painful, courses of artificial insemination.

Commentators on sex predetermination assume that only those who want the technology will use it. But we cannot assume it will not be used coercively, perhaps on an unknowing people. Theologian Emily Culpepper has pointed out that DES (diethylstilbestrol) was given to some pregnant women who were told they were receiving vitamins. The drug has since been associated with serious abnormalities in the children of such women. (To convey that the decision on use of the technology may be made by someone other than the mother, sociologist Hanmer and colleague Hilary Rose use the term "sex predetermination" rather than the liberal terms "sex choice" or "sex selection.")

Dr. R.G. Edwards, co-progenitor of the world's first test-tube baby, has given some indication of how he views the coercive use of sex predetermination technology. As we saw earlier, he correctly determined the sex of rabbit embryos by analyzing the outer cells. He described the technique's potential use in humans and commented "Imbalance of the sexes could probably be prevented by recording the sex of newborn children, and *adjusting the choice open* to parents" (my emphasis) (Edwards, 1974).

In discussing sex predetermination, most scientists focus on foreground issues (the expansion of options; disease prevention; population control) and ignore the Background question: Gynicide. If many women in the Third World are eliminated through sex predetermination, if fewer first-born females exist throughout the world, if the percentages of poor women and richer men rise in the overdeveloped nations, then it is indeed gynicide we are discussing.

Hanmer observes: "A new offensive against women may be opening up in the sex war, one that social scientists seem determined to ignore in the pursuit of choice for happy families" (Hanmer, 1981).

REFERENCES

Cederqvist, L.L. & Fuch, F. (1970). Antenatal sex determination: A historical review. *Clin. Obstet. Gynec.* 13, 159-177.

Chedd, G. (Producer). (1981). *Hard choices: Boy or girl?* Copyright by KCTS/9 and The Regents of the University of Washington, Seattle.

Connors, D. (1981). Sex preselection response. In H. Holmes, B. Hoskins & M. Gross (Eds.), *The Custom-Made Child?* Clifton, NJ: Humana Press.

Edwards, R.G. (1974, March). Fertilization of human eggs in vitro: Morals, ethics and the law. *Quarterly Review of Biology, 49,* 3-6.

Etzioni, A. (1968, September). Sex control, science and society. *Science.*

Hanmer, J. (1981). Sex predetermination, artificial insemination and the maintenance of male-dominated culture. In H. Roberts (Ed.), *Women, Health and Reproduction.* London: Routledge & Kegan Paul.

Luce, C.B. (1978, August 6). Fewer moms would slow pop clock. *Seattle Times.*

Markle, G.E. & Nam, C.B. (1971). Sex predetermination: Its impact on fertility. *Social Biology, 18*(1), 73-83.

Pohlman, E. (1967). Some effects of being able to control sex of offspring. *Eugenics Quarterly, 14* (4), 274-281.

Pomeroy, S.B. (1975). *Goddesses, Whores, Wives and Slaves.* New York: Schocken Books.

Postgate, J. (1973, April 5). Bat's chance in hell. *New Scientist.*

Ramanamma, A. & Bambawali, U. (1980). The mania for sons: An analysis of social values in South Asia. *Social Science and Medicine, 14B,* 107-110.

Raymond, J. (1981). Sex preselection: A response. In H.B. Holmes, B. Hoskins & M. Gross (Eds.), *The Custom-Made Child?* Clifton, NJ: Humana Press.

Rorvik, D. & Shettles, L.B. (1971). *Your baby's sex: Now you can choose.* New York: Bantam.

Stannard, U. (1977). *Mrs. man.* San Francisco: Germainbooks.

Westoff, C.F. & Rindfuss, R.R. (1974, May). Sex preselection in the United States: Some implications. *Science.*

Whelan, E. (1977). *Boy or girl?* New York: Pocket Books.

Williamson, N.E. (1976). *Sons or daughters: A cross-cultural survey of parental preferences, 31,* Sage Library of Social Research. Beverly Hills and London: Sage Publications.

Wren, C.S. (1982, August 1). Old nemesis haunts China on birth plan. *New York Times.*

NO

Peter Singer
and Deane Wells

PROJECTIONS ABOUT FETAL SEX SELECTION ARE HIGHLY QUESTIONABLE DUE TO VARIATIONS IN DIFFERENT CULTURES

Since ancient times, we have tried to choose the sex of our children. Aristotle advised those wanting a boy to wait until the wind is in the north before having intercourse. Every folk culture has its own techniques, from sex with boots on to hanging one's trousers on the left side of the bed for a girl, and the right side for a boy. Recently some supposedly more scientific methods have been suggested. Landrum Shettles, the controversial New York gynecologist whose attempt to produce the world's first IVF baby was frustrated by his hospital chief, has claimed that by correct timing of intercourse and the use of vaginal douches (acidic for girls, alkaline for boys) any couple can give themselves an 80 percent chance of getting a child of the sex they desire. Shettles has coauthored a book, *Choose Your Baby's Sex*, setting out his method. The other coauthor is David Rorvik.

If we succeeded in cloning adults, one side effect would be a 100 percent reliable way of selecting the sex of one's child. A cloned child would always be the same sex as the person from whom it was cloned. Of course, it would also be the same in so many other respects that for many parents this method would be a severe case of overkill. Technically, too, cloning adults to select sex is a bit like using a laser beam to open letters. Simpler methods are either already feasible or soon will be.

One way of selecting sex presents no technical difficulties at all. When a pregnant woman has a higher than normal risk of bearing a defective child—for example, if she is over thirty-five—it is now standard practice to check the fetus by a procedure known as amniocentesis. This involves drawing off a small amount of the amniotic fluid surrounding the fetus. The amniotic fluid will contain cells from the fetus, and these can be examined for abnormalities. The examination also reveals the sex of the fetus. If a serious defect is revealed, the woman will be offered an abortion. If no abnormalities are detected, the doctor will often ask the woman if she wishes to know whether her child is a boy or a girl. Many prefer to wait until the baby is born, and those who do wish to know are generally motivated by nothing more significant than the desire to begin knitting booties of the right color. There have been cases, however, of couples who have sought amniocentesis precisely in order to find out the sex of the fetus, with a view to aborting it if it is not the sex they want.

Many doctors will not perform amniocentesis if they believe it is being requested with a view to sex selection; but how can one prevent deception? A couple may claim that one partner has a family history of hemophilia, and so they do not want to risk a male child (only males suffer from hemophilia). If a male child is in fact what they want, then after the amniocentesis report assures them that the child is female, they can go elsewhere for an abortion. It seems, however, that such behavior is rare. One American genetics center announced that it was prepared to perform amniocentesis for sex selection if, after counseling, the client requested it. Six months later the center had received only one request. The lesson appears to be that while many couples would like to select the sex of their offspring very few are so determined to do so that they are prepared to abort a healthy fetus of the "wrong" sex.

Couples might be more inclined to reject an embryo of the unwanted sex if it could be done without abortion. Cloning by dividing the early embryo would make this possible, for we can already determine the sex of the newly fertilized embryo. One embryo of each divided pair could be used to reveal the sex of the other member of the pair, which could then be transferred to the womb or discarded, as the couple wished. The woman is spared an abortion; on the other hand she has to submit to all the complications of IVF. Unless IVF becomes easier, less expensive, and more reliable, this method would not be attractive to couples who can conceive in the normal way.

This method of embryo sex selection might be of more interest to infertile couples, who in any case need IVF if they are to have children. Of those responding to our questionnaire, however, only about a quarter said that they would like the scientists to be able to select the sex of the embryo before transfer. Nearly all the remainder—72 percent—did not want this done. Scientists at several different centers around the world are close to finding a simpler method, applicable for all couples. The sex of the child is determined by the sperm that fertilizes the egg. Sperm carrying an X chromosome produces girls, and sperm carrying a Y chromosome produces boys. The female-producing sperm are larger than the male-producing sperm and also give out slightly different electrical charges. From time to time, scientists announce promising results in separating the sperm. The methods of separation include spinning in a centrifuge, using a weak electrical current to attract sperm of one electrical charge, and suspending the sperm in a fluid in the hope that the female-producing sperm will settle nearer the bottom. In May 1983,

11. SHOULD PREDETERMINATION BE REGULATED?

Professor Hiroshi Nakajima of the Tokyo Medical and Dental University claimed the best results so far: using electrical separation, he had produced 100 percent pure X-sperm and 83 percent pure Y-sperm. If these results are confirmed, sex selection by means of sperm separation and artificial insemination would not be far ahead; and since artificial insemination is easy and painless, this method would be much more likely to be widely used than methods requiring either abortion or IVF.

Another technique, already in use although still of uncertain efficacy, has been developed by Ronald Ericcson, the founder of Gametrics Ltd. of Sausalito, California. Ericcson, who has a Ph.D. in reproductive physiology, claims to have developed a new method for selecting the sex of children. His technique is based on the fact that the sperm carrying the Y chromosome travel more quickly than the sperm carrying the X. A sperm sample is placed at the top of a glass column containing albumin, a sticky protein. The sperm begin to migrate down this albumin "racetrack." After an hour, the faster Y-containing sperm will in theory have moved to the bottom of the column, while the majority of the X-containing sperm will remain on top. The Y sperm are concentrated further by treks along increasingly dense albumin solutions. Prospective mothers are then artificially inseminated with the concentrated Y-containing sperm.

Gametrics has licensed its patented technique internationally to twenty-four fertility clinics, and initial tests show promising results. The procedure costs between $225 and $350, and three or four inseminations may be necessary before the prospective mother becomes pregnant. Critics of Gametrics' procedure claim that the data are not yet significant, but Ericcson's technique may yet prove effective.

Should sex selection be allowed? The major objection is that it would lead to an imbalance of the sexes, most likely a preponderance of males. This would, of course, vary from society to society. Some cultures have taken their preference for boys to such lengths that unwanted female babies were killed at birth. Others are indifferent between the two sexes. Surveys of American families indicate a slight preference for boys. Amitai Etzioni, professor of sociology at Columbia University, estimates that if reliable sex-selection methods were available in America, at least 54.75 children in every hundred born would be males. This means a surplus of males over females of 9.5 percent. The imbalance would probably be much greater in countries that place a higher value on having a son. On the other hand, once the shortage of females became apparent the value placed on daughters might rise.

The only evidence about the effects of an uneven sex ratio comes from societies affected by special factors. Throughout the early period of white settlement, Australia had substantially more males than females: the same is true of the American West and of Israel in the early immigration periods. Conversely, after World War II both the USSR and Germany had many more females than males. One might tentatively conclude that more males means a higher crime rate and good business for prostitutes; but it is virtually impossible to generalize across diverse historical and cultural circumstances.

Is the satisfaction of the desire of parents for children of a particular sex worth the cost? Etzioni points out that even if we are not alarmist about the overall social consequences, we have to consider the surplus males—some 360,000 born every year in the United States, if Etzioni's figures are right—who, unable to find a mate would have to make do with prostitution, homosexuality, enforced celibacy, or polyandry. The joys experienced by parents who would have children of the sex they wanted would, Etzioni believes, be much less intensely felt than the sorrows of the males who could not find mates.

Landrum Shettles has denied that sex selection will lead to any long-term imbalance of the sexes. He thinks most couples want evenly balanced families, and an abundance of one sex would soon lead to the other sex becoming more popular. Moreover, Shettles sees positive advantages in sex selection as a means of controlling population growth. In this he is supported by Paul Ehrlich, author of *The Population Bomb,* who has urged the setting up of a Bureau of Population and Environment, which would, among other things, encourage research into sex determination. As Ehrlich puts it:

> . . . if a simple method could be found to guarantee that first-born children were males, then population control measures in many areas would be somewhat eased. In our country and elsewhere, couples with only female children "keep trying" in hope of a son.

No doubt some families with only male children also "keep trying"! Sex selection would have an especially pronounced effect in countries like India, where many couples try to have at least two sons; sex selection would halve the number of children the average couple needs to produce in order to have two sons. In China, too, the "one-child" policy has been threatened by the traditional belief that only a male child can carry on the family line. Many families refused to stop at one child if the first child proved to be a girl. When officials took punitive measures in order to enforce the policy, reports started coming in

of female infanticide. Since the population explosion is arguably the greatest problem facing the world today, any method that offers a hope of containing it should not be rejected except on the clearest and most serious grounds.

One way of obtaining the gains offered by sex selection without suffering the disadvantages would be the use of the method to be monitored and steps taken to prevent any significant imbalance. If the method of sex selection were available only through registered medical practitioners, control could be kept by setting up waiting lists for those who wanted a child of the sex that was being chosen too frequently. Couples who were more interested in having a child soon than in having one of the right sex would drop off the waiting list, and an even sex ratio would be restored without frustrating the desires of those prepared to wait.

It would be less easy to control a "do-it-yourself" method like that recommended by Shettles. This is not a problem with Shettles's method itself since the measures required are irksome and its efficacy is doubtful. It could become a problem, however, if some future technique should prove both simple and reliable. Then the government would have to try publicizing the developing imbalance and warning parents of the risk that a child of the sex in demand would be unable to find a mate. If this did not work, as a last resort couples might have to be taxed in accordance with the number of children they have of the preponderant sex.

Monitoring the sex ratio and warning of imbalances might be enough to avoid most of the problems of a grossly uneven ratio of males to females. In any case, the seriousness of these problems is difficult to estimate, whereas the seriousness of continued population growth is undeniable. Countries facing famine as a result of over-population might choose unfettered selection as a means of stopping population growth. In this way, the good achieved by a convenient method of sex selection is likely to be more significant than any harm it would cause.

POSTSCRIPT

SHOULD GENDER PREDETERMINATION
BE REGULATED?

Regardless of the arguments offered for or against sex predetermination and fetal gender selection, a point alluded to by Peter Singer and Deane Wells appears to be crucial. If the United States, or any group of nations, decided to outlaw sex preselection, how would these laws be enforced?

Amniocentesis is commonly recommended for pregnant women over 35, and ascertainment of fetal sex is included in the findings. Abortion is legal in the United States and many countries. How, then, could the government prevent pregnant women from using this information and aborting a fetus simply because it is not of the desired gender?

Even more difficult to eliminate or control effectively would be do-it-at-home gender predetermination kits. In 1986, 100,000 Gender Choice kits were sold over-the-counter in American pharmacies. The cost was $39.95 for a set of instructions that could be found free in any one of several books available in public libraries. The other components in the Gender Choice kit are also easily obtained. The test strips for the Billings test for ovulation and monthly temperature charts are used by women practicing natural birth control and those wanting to become pregnant. Could these be controlled to prevent their being used for sex preselection?

A 1980 study published in the *International Journal of Gynecology and Obstetrics* reported that diet can be used as a factor in shifting the odds of a boy or girl being conceived. Eighty percent of the 280 women studied reported success in getting the gender they wanted, using a diet high in calcium and low in salt and potassium for a girl or a diet high in salt and potassium, and low in calcium and magnesium if they wanted a boy. There is no way to regulate this approach to sex selection.

If we decided to outlaw fetal gender selection, how could this be accomplished? But the more basic question seems to be: who and how many prospective parents would really be interested in this possibility? See the bibliography for further readings on this subject.

PART 4
SOCIAL ISSUES

Every society evolves its own unique combination of formal and informal guidelines designed to regulate the structure of society. As a result, most societies also consider certain behaviors as unacceptable and deviant. Every society has its taboo behaviors and relations. However, standards of behaviors and attitudes do change with time. Cultures respond to outside and internal influences. Until recently, cultural changes occured very gradually, almost imperceptibly, from one generation to the next.

As the twentieth century draws to a close, social scientists and students of human behavior, along with the average man and woman on the street, have realized that the pace of our social change has greatly accelerated. Margaret Mead, the cultural anthropologist and pioneering student of sexual behavior in many cultures, has called America a pre-figurative society, a society in transition without clear concepts of what our society accepts and believes in. As a society, we have abandoned many, but not all, of the sexual roles, expectations and values of the prior eras. At the same time, we have yet to spell out our new roles, expectations and values. The debates and issues in this volume are evidence of our lack of agreement in a pre-figurative culture.

If any society or culture is to survive in a changing world, it must learn to balance stability with flexibility. It must maintain orderly social functions and still show an ability to adapt to new circumstances and new environmental demands. In this section, we examine a variety of contemporary issues which involve changes in our taboo and value systems.

Does Government Have a Constitutional Right to Prohibit Certain Kinds of Sexual Conduct?

Should Legislation Protect All Citizens Against Discrimination Based Solely on Sexual Orientation?

Does Pornography Promote Sexual Violence?

Does the Attorney General's Report Clearly Document the Harm Pornography Does?

Would It Be a Mistake to Decriminalize Prostitution?

Does Christianity Promote an Antisexual Culture?

Is the Sexual Revolution of the 1960s and 1970s Over?

201

ISSUE 12

DOES GOVERNMENT HAVE A RIGHT TO PROHIBIT CERTAIN KINDS OF SEXUAL CONDUCT?

YES: Justice Byron R. White, Majority Opinion with concurring opinions by Chief Justice Warren E. Burger and Justices Lewis F. Powell, William H. Rehnquist, and Sandra Day O'Connor, from *Bowers v. Hardwick,* 1986

NO: Justice Harry A. Blackmun, Dissenting Opinion, joined by Justices William J. Brennan Jr., Thurgood Marshall, and John Paul Stevens, from *Bowers v. Hardwick,* 1986

ISSUE SUMMARY

YES: Justice White, arguing the majority opinion, claims that, unlike heterosexuals, homosexuals do not have a constitutional right to privacy when it comes to engaging in oral or anal sex even in the privacy of their homes because of the traditional social and legal condemnation of sodomy.
NO: Justice Blackmun, dissenting from the majority opinion, argues that since the right to be left alone is the most comprehensive of human rights and the most valued by civilized men, that state has no right or reason to prohibit any sexual acts engaged in privately by consenting adults.

When Michael Hardwick's friend answered the door, the police officer said he just wanted to serve Michael with a warrant because he had not paid a fine for carrying an open can of beer in public. The friend invited the officer in and said Michael was somewhere in the house. When the officer peered into the bedroom, he saw Michael Hardwick engaging in oral sex with another man. Michael was arrested, but not prosecuted. When a federal appellate court in Atlanta held that the Georgia law, enacted in 1816, "infringes upon the fundamental constitutional rights of Michael Hardwick" to engage in private sexual relations, his case went to the United States Supreme Court.

In July 1986, a bitterly divided Supreme Court ruled 5 to 4 that the Georgia law prohibiting all people from engaging in oral or anal sex could be used to prosecute such conduct by homosexuals. Contrary to tradition, the dissenting opinions were read along with the majority opinion.

The majority opinion draws a sharp line between those choices that are fundamental to heterosexual life—whether and with whom to marry, whether to conceive a child and whether to carry the pregnancy to term—and the decision to engage in sexual acts considered to be homosexual. Yet Justice Stevens admitted the Georgia law applies to sodomy "regardless of whether the parties who engage in it are married or unmarried, or of the same or different sexes." The Court did not rule on whether the Constitution protects heterosexual couples, although Justice Stevens stated that previous Court decisions clearly protect heterosexual couples.

The majority opinion cited history as a reason why the constitutional boundary on privacy does not extend to homosexual acts. They noted a traditional condemnation or oral and anal sex with deep roots in English common law reaching back to the days of King Henry IV. All 13 colonies had outlawed sodomy as did all 50 states until 1961. Since 1961, however, 26 states have removed their laws against oral and anal sex between consenting adults.

The four dissenting justices took a drastically different view of the right to privacy. Justice Blackmun said the issue is more profound than merely the choice of a sexual act. It encompasses the "fundamental interest individuals have in controlling the nature of their intimate associations with others." He offered a strongly worded plea for expanding the zone of privacy to include human sexuality in all its forms, traditional or not, approved by society or not, as long as the parties involved are consenting adults. "The right of an individual to conduct intimate relationships in the intimacy of his or her own home seems to me to be the heart of the Constitution's protection of privacy." Society protects the citizen's rights in private consensual acts, Justice Blackmun argued, "not because they contribute, in some direct and material way, to the general public welfare, but because they form so central a part of an individual's life. . . . What the court really has refused to recognize is the fundamental interest all individuals have in controlling the nature of their intimate associations."

YES

Justice Byron R. White

STATES HAVE A CONSTITUTIONAL RIGHT TO PROHIBIT CERTAIN SEXUAL CONDUCT

This case does not require a judgment on whether laws against sodomy between consenting adults in general, or between homosexuals in particular, are wise or desirable. It raises no question about the right or propriety of state legislative decisions to repeal their laws that criminalize homosexual sodomy, or of state court decisions invalidating those laws on state constitutional grounds. The issue presented is whether the Federal Constitution confers a fundamental right upon homosexuals to engage in sodomy and hence invalidate the laws of many states that still make such conduct illegal and have done so for a very long time. The case also calls for some judgment about the limits of the court's role in carrying out its constitutional mandate.

We first register our disagreement with the Court of Appeals and with respondent that the Court's prior cases have construed the Constitution to confer a right of privacy that extends to homosexual sodomy and for all intents and purposes have decided this case. Three cases were interpreted as construing the Due Process Clause of the 14th Amendment to confer a fundamental right to decide whether or not to beget or bear a child.

Accepting the decisions in these cases and the above description of them, we think it evident that none of the rights announced in those cases bears any resemblance to the claimed constitutional right of homosexuals to engage in acts of sodomy that is asserted in this case. No connection between family, marriage, or procreation on the one hand and homosexual activity on the other has been demonstrated, either by the Court of Appeals or by respondent. Moreover, any claim that these cases nevertheless stand for the proposition that any kind of private sexual conduct between consenting adults is constitutionally insulated from state proscription is unsupportable.

From, Majority Opinion, by Justice Byron White, *Bowers v. Hardwick*, US Supreme Court, 85-140, 1986.

WHAT RESPONDENT SEEKS

Precedent aside, however, respondent would have us announce, as the Court of Appeals did, a fundamental right to engage in homosexual sodomy. This we are quite unwilling to do. It is true that despite the language of the Due Process Clauses of the Fifth and 14th Amendments, which appears to focus only on the processes by which life, liberty, or property is taken, the cases are legion in which those clauses have been interpreted to have substantive content, subsuming rights that to a great extent are immune from Federal or state regulation or proscription. Among such cases are those recognizing rights that have little textual support in the constitutional language.

Striving to assure itself and the public that announcing rights not readily identifiable in the Constitution's text involves much more than the imposition of the Justices' own choice of values on the states and the Federal Government, the Court has sought to identify the nature of the rights qualifying for heightened judicial protection. In Palko v. Connecticut, (1937), it was said that this category includes those fundamental liberties that are "implicit in the concept of ordered liberty," such that "neither liberty nor justice would exist if (they) were sacrificed." A different description of fundamental liberties appeared in *Moore v. East Cleveland*, (1977) (opinion of Powell, J.), where they are characterized as those liberties that are "deeply rooted in the nation's history and tradition." See also *Griswold v. Connecticut. ticut.*

ANCIENT ROOTS
OF PROSCRIPTIONS

It is obvious to us that neither of these formulations would extend a fundamental right to homosexuals to engage in acts of consensual sodomy. Proscriptions against that conduct have ancient roots. Sodomy was a criminal offense at common law and was forbidden by the laws of the original 13 states when they ratified the Bill of Rights. In 1868, when the 14th Amendment was ratified, all but 5 of the 37 states in the Union had criminal sodomy laws. In fact, until 1961, all 50 states outlawed sodomy, and today, 24 states and the District of Columbia continue to provide criminal penalties for sodomy performed in private and between consenting adults. Against the background, to claim that a right to engage in such conduct is "deeply rooted in this nation's history and tradition" or "implicit in the concept of ordered liberty" is, at best, facetious.

Nor are we inclined to take a more expansive view of our authority to discover new fundamental rights imbedded in the Due Process Clause. The Court is most vulnerable and comes nearest to illegitimacy when it deals with judge-made constitutional law having little or no cognizable roots in the language or design of the Constitution. That this is so was painfully demonstrated by the face-off between the Executive and the Court in the 1930s, which resulted in the repudiation of much of the substantive gloss that the Court had placed on the Due Process Clause of the Fifth and 14th Amendments. There should be, therefore, great resistance to expanding the substantive reach of those clauses, particularly if it requires redefining the category of rights deemed to be fundamental. Otherwise, the judiciary necessarily takes to itself further authority to govern the country without express constitutional authority. The claimed right pressed on us today falls far short of overcoming this resistance.

PRIVACY OF THE HOME

Respondent, however, asserts that the result should be different where the homosexual conduct occurs in the privacy of the home. He relies on *Stanley v. Georgia* (1969), where the Court held that the First Amendment prevents conviction for possessing and reading obscene material in the privacy of his home: "If the First Amendment means anything, it means that a state has no business telling a man, sitting alone in his house, what books he may read or what films he may watch."

Stanley did protect conduct that would not have been protected outside the home, and it partially prevented the enforcement of state obscenity laws; but the decision was firmly grounded in the First Amendment. The right pressed upon us here has no similar support in the text of the Constitution, and it does not qualify for recognition under the prevailing principles for construing the 14th Amendment. Its limits are also difficult to discern. Plainly enough, otherwise illegal conduct is not always immunized whenever it occurs in the home. Victimless crimes, such as the possession and use of illegal drugs do not escape the law where they are committed at home. *Stanley* itself recognized that its holding offered no protection for the possession in the home of drugs, firearms, or stolen goods. And if respondent's submission is limited to the voluntary sexual conduct between consenting adults, it would be difficult, except by fiat, to limit the claimed right to homosexual conduct while leaving exposed to prosecution adultery, incest, and other sexual crimes even though they are committed in the home. We are unwilling to start down that road.

Even if the conduct at issue here is not a fundamental right, respondent asserts that there must be a rational basis for the law and that there is none in this case other than the presumed belief of a majority of the electorate in Georgia that homosexual sodomy is immoral and unacceptable. This is said to be an inadequate rationale to support the law. The law, however, is constantly based on notions of morality, and if all laws representing essentially moral choices are to be invalidated under the Due Process Clause, the courts will be very busy indeed. Even respondent makes no such claim, but insists that majority sentiments about the morality of homosexuality should be declared inadequate. We do not agree and are unpersuaded that the sodomy laws of some 25 states should be invalidated on this basis.

Accordingly, the judgment of the Court of Appeals is reversed.

BY CHIEF JUSTICE BURGER, CONCURRING

I join the Court's opinion, but I write separately to underscore my view that in constitutional terms there is no such thing as a fundamental right to commit homosexual sodomy.

As the Court notes, the proscriptions against sodomy have very "ancient roots." Decisions of individuals relating to homosexual conduct have been subject to state intervention throughout the history of Western civilization. Condemnation of those practices is firmly rooted in Judeo-Christian moral and ethical standards. Homosexual sodomy was a capital crime under Roman law. See Code Theod. 9.7.6; Code Just 9.9.31. See also D. Bailey, Homosexuality in the Western Christian Tradition 70-81. During the English Reformation when powers of the ecclesiastical courts were transferred to the King's Courts, the first English statute criminalizing sodomy was passed. 25 Hen. VIII, c.6. Blackstone described "the infamous crime against nature" as an offense of "deeper malignity" than rape, an heinous act "the very mention of which is a disgrace to human nature," and "a crime not fit to be named." Blackstone's Commentaries *215. The common law of England, including its prohibition of sodomy, became the received law of Georgia and the other colonies. In 1816 the Georgia Legislature passed the statute at issue here, and the statute has been continuously in force in one form or another since that time. To hold that the act of homosexual sodomy is somehow protected as a fundamental right would be to cast aside millennia of moral teaching.

This is essentially not a question of personal "preferences" but rather of the legislative authority of the state. I find nothing in the Constitution depriving a state of the power to enact the statute challenged here.

BY JUSTICE POWELL, CONCURRING

I join the opinion of the Court. I agree with the Court that there is no fundamental right—i.e., no substantive right under the Due Process Clause—such as that claimed by respondent, and found to exist by the Court of Appeals. This is not to suggest, however, that respondent may not be protected by the Eighth Amendment of the Constitution. The Georgia statue at issue in this case authorizes a court to imprison a person for up to 20 years for a single private, consensual act of sodomy. In my view, prison sentence for such conduct—certainly a sentence of long duration—would create a serious Eighth Amendment issue. Under the Georgia statute a single act of sodomy, even in the private setting of a home, is a felony comparable in terms of the possible sentence imposed to serious felonies such as aggravated battery, first degree arson, and robbery.

In this case, however, respondent has not been tried, much less convicted and sentenced. Moreover, respondent has not raised the Eighth Amendment issue below. For these reasons this constitutional argument is not before us.

NO

Justice Harry A. Blackmun

GOVERNMENT HAS NO COMPELLING REASON TO MAKE LAWS REGULATING PRIVATE SEXUAL ACTS

This case is no more about "a fundamental right to engage in homosexuality sodomy," as the court purports to declare, than *Stanley v. Georgia* (1969) was about a fundamental right to watch obscene movies, or *Katz v. United States* (1967) was about a fundamental right to place interstate bets from a telephone booth. Rather, this case is about "the most comprehensive of rights and the most valued by civilized men," namely "the right to be let alone." *Olmstead v. United States* (1928) (Brandeis, J., dissenting).

The statute at issue, Ga. Code Ann. section 16-6-2, denies individuals the right to engage in particular forms of private, consensual sexual activity. The Court concludes that section 16-6-2 is valid essentially because "the laws of many states still make such conduct illegal and have done so for a very long time." But the fact that the moral judgments expressed by statutes like section 16-6-2 may be "natural and familiar ought not to conclude our judgment upon the question whether statutes embodying them conflict with the Constitution of the United States." *Roe v. Wade* 410 U.S. 113, 117 (1973).

Like Justice Holmes, I believe that "(i)t is revolting to have no better reason for a rule of law than that so it was laid down in the time of Henry IV. It is still more revolting if the grounds upon which it was laid down have vanished long since, and rule simply persists from blind imitation of the past." Holmes, The Path of the Law (1897). I believe we must analyze respondent's claim in the light of the values that underlie the constitutional right to privacy. If that right means anything, it means that, before Georgia can prosecute its citizens for making choices about the most intimate aspects of their lives, it must do more than assert that the choice they have made is an "abominable crime not fit to be named among Christians." *Herring v. State* 119 Ga. 709, (1904).

From, Dissenting Opinion, by Justice Harry Blackmun, *Bowers v. Hardwick,* US Supreme Court, 85-140. 1986.

DISTORTION IS DISCERNED

In its haste to reverse the Court of Appeals and hold that the Constitution does not "confe(r) a fundamental right upon homosexuals to engage in sodomy," the Court relegates the actual statute being challenged to a footnote and ignores the procedural posture of the case before it. A fair reading of the statute and of the complaint clearly reveals that the majority has distorted the question this case presents.

First, the Court's almost obsessive focus on homosexual activity is particularly hard to justify in light of the broad language Georgia has used. Unlike the court, the Georgia Legislature has not proceeded on the assumption that homosexuals are so different from other citizens that their lives may be controlled in a way that would not be tolerated if it limited the choices of those other citizens. Rather, Georgia has provided that "(a) person commits the offense of sodomy when he performs or submits to any sexual act involving the sex organs of one person and the mouth or anus of another." Ga. Code Ann. section 16-6-2(a).

The sex or status of the persons who engage in the act is irrelevant as a matter of state law. In fact, to the extent I can discern a legislative purpose for Georgia's 1968 enactment of section 16-6-2, that purpose seems to have been to broaden the coverage of the law to reach heterosexual as well as homosexual activity. I therefore see no basis for the Court's decision to treat this case as an "as applied" challenge to section 16-6-2, see *ante*, at 2, n. 2, or for Georgia's attempt, both in its brief and at oral argument, to defend section 16-6-2 solely on the grounds that it prohibits homosexual activity.

Michael Hardwick's standing may rest in significant part on Georgia's apparent willingness to enforce against homosexuals a law it seems not to have any desire to enforce against heterosexuals. But his claim that section 16-6-2 involves an unconstitutional intrusion on his privacy and his right of intimate association does not depend in any way on his sexual orientation.

DISAGREEMENT OVER LAW

Second, I disagree with the Court's refusal to consider whether section 16-6-2 runs afoul of the Eighth or Ninth Amendments or the Equal Protection Clause of the 14th Amendment. I need not reach either the Eight Amendment or the Equal Protection Clause issues because I believe that Hardwick has stated a cognizable claim that section 16-6-2 interferes with constitutionally protected interests in privacy and freedom of intimate association. But neither the Eighth Amendment nor the Equal Protection Clause is so clearly irrelevant that a claim resting on either provision should be peremptorily dismissed. The Court's cramped reading of the issue before it makes for a short opinion, but it does little to make for a persuasive one.

"Our cases long have recognized that the Constitution embodies a promise that a certain private sphere of individual liberty will be kept largely beyond the reach of government." *Thornburgh v. American Coll. of Obst. & Gyn.* (1986). In construing the right to privacy, the Court has proceeded along two somewhat distinct, albeit complementary, lines. First, it has recognized a privacy interest with reference to certain decisions that are properly for the individual to make. *E.g., Roe v. Wade* (1973). Second, it has recognized a privacy interest with reference to certain places without regard for the particular activities in which the individuals who occupy them

209

are engaged. The case before us implicates both the decisional and the spatial aspects of the right of privacy.

The Court concludes today that none of our prior cases dealing with various decisions that individuals are entitled to make free of governmental interference "bears any resemblance to the claimed constitutional right of homosexuals to engage in acts of sodomy that is asserted in this case." While it is true that these cases may be characterized by their connection to protection of the family, the Court's conclusion that they extend no further than this boundary ignores the warning in *Moore v. East Cleveland*, (1977) (plurality opinion), against "Clos-(ing) our eyes to the basic reasons why certain rights associated with the family have been accorded shelter under the 14th Amendment's Due Process Clause."

WHY RIGHTS ARE PROTECTED

We protect those rights not because they contribute, in some direct and material way, to the general public welfare, but because they form so central a part of an individual life. We protect the decision whether to marry precisely because marriage "is an association that promotes a way of life, not causes; a harmony in living, not political faiths; a bilateral loyalty, not commercial or social projects." *Griswold v. Connecticut*. We protect the decision whether to have a child because parenthood alters so dramatically an individual's self-definition, not because of demographic considerations or the Bible's command to be fruitful and multiply. And we protect the family because it contributes so powerfully to the happiness of individuals, not because of a preference for stereotypical households.

Only the most willful blindness could obscure the fact that sexual intimacy is "a sensitive, key relationship of human existence, central to family life, community welfare, and the development of human personality," *Paris Adult Theatre I v. Slayton,* (1973). The fact that individuals define themselves in a significant way through their intimate sexual relationships with others suggests, in a nation as diverse as ours, that there may be many "right" ways of conducting those relationships, and that much of the richness of a relationship will come from the freedom an individual has to choose the form and nature of these intensely personal bonds.

In a variety of circumstances we have recognized that a necessary corollary of giving individuals freedom to choose how to conduct their lives is acceptance of the fact that different individuals will make different choices. For example, in holding that the clearly important state interest in public education should give way to competing claims by the Amish to the effect that extended formal schooling threatened their way of life, the Court declared: "There can be no assumption that today's majority is 'right' and the Amish and others like them are 'wrong.' A way of life that is odd or even erratic but interferes with no rights or interests of others is not to be condemned because it is different." *Wisconsin v. Yoder* (1972). The Court claims that its decision today merely refuses to recognize a fundamental right to engage in homosexual sodomy; what the Court really has refused to recognize is the fundamental interest all individuals have in controlling the nature of their intimate associations with others.

PRIVACY OF THE HOME

The behavior for which Hardwick faces prosecution occurred in his own home, a place to which the Fourth Amendment attaches special significance. The Court's treatment of this aspect of the case is symptomatic of its overall refusal to consider the broad principles that have informed our treatment of privacy in specific cases. Just as the right to privacy is more than the mere aggregation of a number of entitlements to engage in specific behavior, so too, protecting the physical integrity of the home is more than merely a means of protecting specific activities that often take place there.

The Court's interpretation of the pivotal case of *Stanley v. Georgia* (1969), is entirely unconvincing. *Stanley* held that Georgia's undoubted power to punish the public distribution on constitutionally unprotected, obscene material did not permit the state to punish the private possession of such material. According to the majority here, *Stanley* relied entirely on the First Amendment, and thus, it is claimed, sheds no light on cases not involving printed materials. But that is not what *Stanley* said. Rather, the *Stanley* Court anchored its holding in the Fourth Amendment's special protection for the individual in his home. The right of an individual to conduct intimate relationships in the intimacy of his or her own home seems to me to be the heart of the Constitution's protection of privacy.

First, petitioner asserts that the acts made criminal by the statute may have serious adverse consequences for "the general public health and welfare," such as spreading communicable diseases or fostering other criminal activity. Nothing in the record before the Court provides any justification for finding the activity forbidden by section 16-6-2 to be physically dangerous, either to the persons engaged in it or to others.

The core of petitioner's defense of section 16-6-2, however, is that respondent and others who engage in the conduct by section 16-6-2 interfere with Georgia's exercise of the "right of the nation and the states to maintain a decent society." Essentially, petitioner argues, and the Court agrees, that the fact that the acts described in section 16-6-2 "for hundreds of years, if not thousands, have been uniformly condemned as immoral" is a sufficient reason to permit a state to ban them today.

THE FREEDOM TO DIFFER

I cannot agree that either the length of time a majority has held its convictions or the passions with which it defends them can withdraw legislation from this Court's scrutiny. As Justice Jackson wrote so eloquently for the Court in *West Virginia Board of Education v. Barnette* (1943), "we apply the limitations of the Constitution with no fear that freedom to be intellectually and spiritually diverse or even contrary will disintegrate the social organization. (F)reedom to differ is not limited to things that do not matter much. That would be a mere shadow of freedom. The test of its substance is the right to differ as to things that touch the heart of the existing order." It is precisely because the issues raised by this case touches the heart of what makes individuals what they are that we should be especially sensitive to the rights of those whose choices upset the majority.

The assertion that "traditional Judeo-Christian values proscribe" the conduct involved, cannot provide an adequate justification for section 16-6-2. That certain, but by no means all, religious groups condemn the behavior at issue gives the State no license to impose their judgments on the entire citizenry. The legitimacy of secular legislation depends instead on whether the State can advance some justification for its law beyond its conformity to religious doctrine. Thus, far from buttressing his case, petitioner's invocation of Leviticus, Romans, St. Thomas Aquinas, and sodomy's heretical status during the Middle Ages undermines his suggestion that section 16-6-2 represents a legitimate use of secular coercive power. A state can no more punish private behavior because of religious intolerance than it can punish such behavior because of racial animus.

PEOPLE AND MORALITY

Nor can section 16-6-2 be justified as a "morally neutral" exercise of Georgia's power to "protect the public environment," *Paris Adult Theatre I,* 413 U.S., at 68-69. Certainly, some private behavior can affect the fabric of society as a whole. Reasonable people may differ about whether particular sexual acts are moral or immoral, but "we have ample evidence for believing that people will not abandon morality, will not think any better of murder, cruelty and dishonesty, merely because some private sexual practice which they abominate is not punished by the law." Petitioner and the Court fail to see the difference between laws that protect public sensibilities and those that enforce private morality. Statutes banning public sexual activity are entirely consistent with protecting the individual's liberty interest in decisions concerning sexual relations; the same recognition that those decisions are intensely private which justified protecting individuals from unwilling exposure to the sexual activities of others. But the mere fact that intimate behavior may be punished when it takes place in public cannot dictate how states can regulate intimate behavior that occurs in intimate places.

This case involves no real interference with the rights of others, for the mere knowledge that other individuals do not adhere to one's value system cannot be a legally cognizable interest, let alone an interest that can justify invading the houses, hearts, and minds of citizens who choose to live their lives differently.

I can only hope that the Court soon will reconsider its analysis and conclude that depriving individuals of the right to choose for themselves how to conduct their intimate relationships poses a far greater threat to the values most deeply rooted in our nation's history than tolerance of nonconformity could ever do. Because I think the Court today betrays those values, I dissent.

POSTSCRIPT

DOES GOVERNMENT HAVE A RIGHT TO PROHIBIT CERTAIN KINDS OF SEXUAL CONDUCT?

What did the writers of the American Constitution intend when they said the individual liberty of citizens should be protected from government infringements? If we have, as the Court has previously ruled, a constitutional right to marry and live with whomever we wish, to sell and purchase contraceptives openly, to have an abortion, to use pornographic material in our homes if we so choose, and to engage in whatever private acts we choose related to family, marriage, and procreation, then why are not oral and anal sex included in this right to privacy? This question was not developed by the majority opinion.

Mr. Hardwick and his defenders argued that given the importance of the freedom of a citizen to chose and decide freely the nature of the intimate associations he or she has within the privacy of one's home, a homosexual's right to private consensual sexual relations is an element of "ordered liberty." The Court's majority opinion saw this claim as "at best, facetious."

The public response to the Court's 5 to 4 decision is interesting. In a *Newsweek* magazine-sponsored Gallup Poll, 47 percent of those surveyed disapproved of the Supreme Court decision to uphold the Georgia law while 41 percent approved. Fifty-seven percent believed that states should not have the right to prohibit certain private sexual practices between consenting adult homosexuals while 34 percent said they should have this power. When asked if states should have the right to prohibit sexual acts between consenting heterosexual men and women, 74 percent said no and 18 percent said yes.

The Supreme Court decision leaves many questions unanswered. Are laws restricting sexual behavior between consenting adults wise or desirable? Many state laws, like that in the Hardwick case, pay lip service to religious values, but how often are these laws applied, when are they used, and whom are they used against? The question of how the Georgia law affects heterosexual couples may be answered in an appeal of another Georgia case in which a jury acquitted a man on rape charges but convicted him of engaging in consensual sodomy with the woman. It is clear that this debate has only begun. See the bibliography for further readings on this subject.

ISSUE 13

SHOULD LEGISLATION PROTECT ALL CITIZENS AGAINST DISCRIMINATION BASED SOLELY ON SEXUAL ORIENTATION?

YES: Robert Nugent, from an essay written for this volume

NO: Terry Teachout, from *National Review,* November 11, 1983

ISSUE SUMMARY

YES: Robert Nugent, a Catholic priest who has worked with homosexual men and women since 1971, sees no valid basis for opposition to civil rights for homosexuals based on concerns about homosexuals in sensitive positions being blackmailed, the role models that would be provided by homosexual teachers, or the influence of homosexuals who would be allowed to adopt children or retain custody of children after a divorce.
NO: Terry Teachout, a student of psychology at the University of Illinois, warns advocates of gay rights legislation that the conservative majority in this country has no philosophical objection to certain kinds of intolerance, and that this majority has a right to preserve its integrity, which it will do if pushed far enough.

In the American colonies, homosexuals were condemned to death by drowning and burning. In the later 1770s, Thomas Jefferson joined other progressive political leaders in suggesting reduction of the punishment for homosexual acts to castration.

Today, the position of homosexuals in society has changed radically, along with our attitudes about different types of sexual activity. After a ten-year study, the 1957 Wolfenden Report maintained there was no evidence that homosexual behavior contributes to "social decay." This British committee also recommended that personal revulsion with homosexuality was not a justification for laws regulating sexual behavior between consenting adults in private. On December 15, 1973, the Board of Trustees of the American Psychiatric Association voted to remove homosexuality from its official list of psychiatric disturbances. They also adopted a position statement deploring "all public and private discrimination against homosexuals in such areas as employment, housing, public accommodations, and licensing." In january 1975, the American Psychological Association followed suit, urging "all mental health professionals to take the lead in removing the stigma of mental illness that [has] long been associated with homosexual orientations."

In the years since these recommendations, much has changed in terms of laws and the civil rights of gays and lesbians. A high school opened in Greenwich Village, New York City, to serve adolescent homosexuals who find little support or understanding for their orientation and lifestyle in the ordinary public school. Congressman Gary Studds (D-Mass.) revealed his homosexual orientation and won reelection. On the other hand, Congressman Robert E. Bauman (R-Md.) fell from power after almost two decades of outstanding service to the conservative cause when he was arrested for soliciting sex from a teenage male prostitute.

In 1985, a referendum concerning homosexuals in Houston was defeated in a bitter fight by a margin of more than 4 to 1. Corporations and the Chamber of Commerce argued that an ordinance protecting homosexuals from discrimination in city employment would turn Houston into a "homosexual mecca" infested with AIDS that would stunt the city's economic future. About the same time, New York City finally passed its ordinance protecting homosexual persons from discrimination in employment and housing, despite strong opposition from Orthodox Jews and the Catholic hierarchy. The Gay Men's Chorus began giving Christmas concerts in New York City's prestigious Carniege Hall while the Gay Veterans Association joined the Veterans Day Parade down Fifth Avenue.

Following several court cases, a state-appointed commission recommended that Massachusetts reverse its policy of not placing foster children in the care of homosexual and lesbian couples or single people. On Long Island, New York, a divorced homosexual father was awarded custody of his child.

In late 1986, the American Civil Liberties Union (ACLU) announced that it would seek elimination of legal barriers to homosexual and lesbian marriages. If successful, gay and lesbian "life partners" would enjoy the same the economic benefits as heterosexual spouses, including employee fringe benefits, insurance coverage, income tax benefits, and visitation, child custody and next-of-kin rights.

Still, homosexual men and women are far from the "complete legal equality" advocated by the ACLU. The debate remains heated, as the following essays demonstrate.

215

YES
Robert Nugent

RACISM, SEXISM, AND SOCIAL HOMOPHOBIA—WHAT ARE THE COSTS OF DENYING CIVIL RIGHTS TO HOMOSEXUALS?

INTRODUCTION

In 1969, in the city of New York, history was made on a hot Friday night in June when the city police routinely attempted to raid a popular bar on Christopher Street which was a meeting place for homosexual men. The bar was located in Greenwich Village, a haven for decades for poets, beatniks, hippies, artists, writers and dozens of other kinds of people whom society often pushes to the fringes. The name of the bar was the "Stonewall Inn," a name that is associated with one of the turning points of the modern homosexual liberation movement in the United States.

At the "Stonewall Rebellion" the patrons of the bar decided, spontaneously it seems to resist the harassment of the police. Resistance from the "sissies" and the "queers" caught the police unprepared. At one point the police found themselves locked inside the bar and the patrons on the outside throwing bottles and calling names. Reinforcements were called in and the crowds were dispersed. On the following night, however, a large crowd of homosexual men and their supporters gathered in Sheridan Square to protest the police action. When the police arrived another confrontation took place and continued for several days. Eventually things returned to normal. Both for the people who had experienced that event, and for thousands of homosexual men and women ever since, the "normal" life of pretending, hiding and denying would never be the same again.

The gay liberation movement came to prominence in 1969 and is commemorated each June with the Christopher Street Parade in New York and marches, cultural events and celebrations of "gay and lesbian pride" in almost all major U.S. cities. Before 1969, however, separate organizations of lesbians and gay men both on the east and west coasts were already attempting to obtain fairer treatment from society. Timid at first, these early pioneers through their educational projects and support groups helped break ground for later political and social gains which gay and lesbian citizens enjoy today.

RELIGION, LAW AND MEDICINE

Homosexual people have had to contend with three major institutions in our society which shape and mold our thinking and feelings about homosexuality. It is understandable why, for example, the gay-lesbian liberation movement turned its attention to medicine which judged homosexuality as a "sickness," to religion which said homosexuality was "sinful" and to the law which called homosexual behavior "criminal." Since the Stonewall Rebellion major changes have taken place in medicine, religion and the law. Although these institutions still evidence great ambiguity about homosexuality, all of them have modified their former judgments.

The majority of psychiatrists and psychologists, although not all, do not believe that being gay or lesbian is any form of mental illness or emotional disturbance. Some major Christian denominations include reputable teachers who do not believe that all homosexual behavior is immoral, and there are also Jewish leaders who would share this same opinion. In only 24 states and the District of Columbia is "sodomy" still a felony or a misdemeanor. Other states either have repealed the law or have not had such a law on the books. Although "sodomy" is generally understood to mean anal intercourse between two males, historically and legally it has also included anal and oral sex between a husband and wife and forms of sexual behavior which are other than heterosexual, genital intercourse. When discussing homosexuality we need to avoid the error of equating sodomy with "homosexual behavior" (there are gay men who do not engage in anal intercourse) or assuming that heterosexual people cannot also engage in "sodomy" less strictly defined.

MINORITY RIGHTS

The gay/lesbian liberation movement has concentrated in the past few years in securing and furthering protection for gay and lesbian people the same kinds of legal rights which are enjoyed by other groups in our society called "minorities." One way has been to obtain legal protection against arbitrary discrimination in several areas such as employment, housing, and public accommodations based on the concept of "sexual orientation." In the media this struggle is usually called the "gay rights" movement. Legislation on both federal and state levels is called "gay rights laws." There is a common misunderstanding (deliberate or accidental) that homosexual people are asking for special consideration or special laws which other groups or individuals in our country do not enjoy. This is not true. Gay and lesbian people involved in the campaign for their civil rights are asking for the same protections and guarantees that blacks, women, Hispanics and others have sought. Homosexual people see themselves as members of a "minority" group just as blacks and women do because gay and lesbian people compose only ten percent of our society. While being numerically a minority does not necessarily imply discrimination (left-handed people and redheads are also minorities who do not experience discrimination), when the majority characteristic such as whiteness, maleness or heterosexuality is judged superior or considered the norm for full acceptance or equality, then the minority status does evoke discrimination.

Some people find the analogy between race and homosexuality difficult to understand. They acknowledge the injustice of discrimination against blacks and women because people have "no choice" in their race or gender. The hidden assumption in this objection to "gay rights" is that homosexual people chose their homosexuality. But from what we know about the genesis of sexual orientation at this point in time, it seems that a person's sexual identity is established perhaps as early as age three when the language skills are also formed. A child is born with the biological or physical capacity to speak, but has to learn how to speak a "native" or fundamental language. Likewise it is thought by most theorists that there is both a biological and an environmental component of homosexuality.

It is important not to confuse a homosexual "orientation" where there is no choice with homosexual "behavior" where there is personal choice. A homosexual orientation means that a particular individual is attracted predominantly and persistently to some individuals of the same gender. The attraction is not only an erotic, physical attraction, but even more importantly, an inner, emotional or romantic attraction. A true homosexual orientation has more to do with the gender of the person one falls in love with rather than the gender of the person one has sex with.

People who understand why society ought not to discriminate against people because of race or gender can also understand why citizens should not suffer discrimination or persecution because of their sexual orientation. Likewise those who oppose rights for lesbian and gay people often use the same arguments and tactics against homosexual people as were (and are) used against women and blacks. These minorities were required by criminal law to keep within limited boundaries of "acceptable" behavior. The extreme form of this kind of discrimination can be found in South Africa's apartheid system which attempts to keep certain groups even physically limited by imposing geographical boundaries affecting place of residence.

There are strong analogies between the movement for racial equality and the movement for equality among gay and lesbian people, although there are also some striking differences. Before considering particular areas of discrimination against homosexual people which can and ought to be eliminated by sound legislation, it will be important to anticipate one objection which is commonly heard from those groups and individuals who oppose "gay rights."

COMMON OBJECTIONS

Homosexual people have often been called "the invisible minority." Despite the popular belief that "you can always tell a homosexual" by their walk, dress, occupation, etc., the vast majority of lesbian women and gay men remain hidden from society at large and, may times, from their own families and friends. With the advent of the Stonewall Rebellion and the Gay-Lesbian Liberation movement, more and more homosexual people are identifying themselves as gay or lesbian ("coming out of the closet"). But pressures are still strong for them to remain hidden. Those who object to "gay rights" legislation contend that the only time homosexual people suffer from discrimination or persecution is when they identify themselves as such. "If no one knew they were homosexual, then they would have no problems."

This kind of reasoning is essentially saying that in order to be treated fairly and justly a homosexual person must constantly deny or hide a part of his or her humanity that is central to living a full, rich, human life. It is comparable to telling black people or Jewish people that the only way they can be treated equally is for them to "pass" as white people or as Gentiles, and to deny their racial identity. Some light-skinned blacks attempted to do this in order to fit into US society. In Nazi Germany some Jewish people did the same in order to escape the death camps. The cost of such denial, however, to one's sense of integrity and self-worth cannot be measured.

Up to this point it has been argued that individuals ought not to suffer discrimination in our society because of something over which they have no choice (race, gender, sexual orientation) and which is important to them as they live out their human lives. People of good will can see the logic and the probity of this approach. When it comes to lesbian and gay people, however, there are other considerations which enter into the thinking of those opposed to laws protecting homosexual people against discrimination in employment, housing and other areas of life.

The objection that is often heard against "gay rights" laws, especially as they apply to certain jobs, is that such legislation could be seen as condoning, justifying or approving of homosexual behavior or a "lifestyle" that many people oppose on religious grounds. Same-sex behavior, for some people, is "against nature," "immoral," or "condemned by the Bible." These people are concerned that legal approval or protection of gay and lesbian persons will also imply societal approval of homosexual expressions. According to this position homosexual behavior is harmful to society, and we ought not to give it any kind of approval.

If our laws embody certain moral beliefs and principles, then they also teach people what is right and wrong. Society, it is said, has a stake in heterosexuality and family life and ought to promote these values whenever possible. Laws protecting homosexual people in jobs and housing will send signals to young people that homosexuality is perfectly all right—something we ought not do.

While this position merits serious consideration and dialogue in a pluralistic society which claims a Judaeo-Christian basis and value system, it is also marred with serious flaws which need to be pointed out. First of all, the laws which protect gay and lesbian people in jobs and guarantee them protection against discrimination in housing are clearly written to protect a person's sexual orientation if it becomes a matter of public knowledge—and not sexual behavior which is a private matter.

A comparison might be made with laws guaranteeing freedom of religion. The state can take a neutral stance toward particular religions while protecting and promoting freedom of religious belief and practice. The only time the state cannot maintain neutrality is when the practice of a certain religion would cause serious harm to individuals or the public order. The state might want to intervene if a particular religion practicing "snake handling" were to expose young children to such a ceremony.

Can the state, while promoting the value of human sexual identity, including sexual orientation, through the enactment of legislation which protects heterosexual, bisexual and homosexual orientation of individuals, also maintain a neutrality as to the concrete expressions of these orientations in so far as they do not harm the common good? This is not to deny the right and responsibility of religious groups to promote certain values and concepts of sexuality, marriage and family life in society, but only to assert that others might come to different conclusions about sexuality and even the definitions of "marriage" and "family" which will eventually have to be tested in the marketplace of a free and pluralistic society. It is rather unlikely that homosexuality will ever replace or even equal the heterosexual mode of human sexuality. Given the strength of the heterosexual impulse in humanity and its strong support in laws, culture, religions, etc., it is surprising to hear the opponents of "gay rights" argue in such a way as to imply that the homosexual urge is so strong in so many people that only constant vigilance embodied in laws, taboos and prohibitions will serve as a floodgate to stem the homosexual tides that threaten to drown the human race!

A second flaw in the argument of many who oppose any protection for homosexual persons is the unproven assumption that homosexual behavior is harmful or destructive to individuals or society and that homosexuality will increase if we protect homosexual persons and/or condone homosexual behavior. Contrary to popular belief, no society or culture (including Greece, Rome, Sodom and Gommorah) have ever collapsed because of homosexual behavior. Societies and cultures react differently to the phenomenon of homosexuality. In Greece and Rome high culture flourished alongside a certain toleration of and openness to rather carefully circumscribed homosexual relationships. No society has ever held homosexuality to be an ideal. Sodom and Gommorah were "destroyed" for gross injustices toward the poor, for inhospitality and, perhaps, for gang rape—a reprehensible crime whether homosexual or heterosexual!

There is no proof that those societies which tolerate certain forms of homosexuality evidence a higher percentage of homosexual persons. Likewise those countries which exhibit particularly hostile and punitive attitudes towards homosexuality, including the communist and socialist nations, show no decrease in the percentage of homosexually oriented individuals. In cities and states where protective legislation for homosexual citizens has been enacted, there has been no increase in the homosexual population.

It might be proven, however, that those geographical areas which are respective of the rights of homosexual citizens would be a natural draw for lesbian and gay people because their lives could be much easier in such a climate. But the fear often voiced in small towns across the country ("If we pass this gay rights bill [insert name of town or city] will become a 'gay Mecca' ") is humorous. While gay and lesbian people might move to San Francisco, Washington, DC or even New York in significant numbers for educational and career reasons, it is doubtful that civil rights legislation in Eugene, OR, Norristown, PA or Maywood, NJ would precipitate a major influx of homosexual people to those places! What such legislation will do is to make life for gay and lesbian people already living in certain locales more secure and more pleasant.

With the advent of the AIDS crisis, the argument against "gay rights" legislation that homosexual activity causes demonstrable damage both to society and to individuals has received apparent confirmation. Apart from confusing protection for orientation with protection for sexual behavior, the simple response is first of all that, globally at least, AIDS is a heterosexual disease; secondly, it is a virus that causes AIDS—not sexual behavior. Society has never outlawed heterosexual intercourse because of sexually transmitted diseases. Society has, however, taken both medical and legal steps to curtail and eliminate such diseases. In the same way, society can and should take steps to control and eliminate AIDS, but not by disenfranchising ten percent of the population of their sexuality.

Even this would not include policies and procedures which threaten the privacy and basic human rights of individuals. Enforced testing, imposed quarantine, denial of insurance coverage or benefits and public disclosure of people with AIDS or those who test positive are invasions of the basic right to privacy. There is a serious personal and communal responsibility for gay males to alter their sexual practices not only for their own personal interests, but also as part of an effort to prevent further spread of the disease in the population.

EMPLOYMENT

In proposing legislation for homosexual individuals in the area of employment, there are some issues which need to be addressed more specifically. Protection in employment generally implies legislation which makes it illegal either to fire someone solely on the grounds of a homosexual orientation or to refuse to hire an individual for the same reason. Most of the discrimination that gay and lesbian people face in this area has to do with being fired rather than being hired. Very few job applications today inquire specifically about an applicant's sexual orientation. Some military and government agencies, however, might scrutinize this area of an applicant's life more than others in the interviewing process.

What most gay and lesbian people fear is possible dismissal from a position simply for being discovered to be homosexually oriented. Even in those cities and towns which have enacted anti-discrimination ordinances or in those firms which have incorporated similar clauses in their policies, homosexual people often find themselves in a Catch-22 situation. For the person who does not want his or her homosexuality a matter of public record, such protection is not very comforting. If such an individual wishes to fight to retain a job, then he or she eventually has to initiate a formal complaint or undertake legal action, both of which involve either a hearing or a court trial. In either case, there is little chance of preserving one's anonymity. Military personnel officers Lieutenant Leonard Matlovitch and Ensign Vernon Berg and school teacher Joseph Acanfora are individuals who felt it more important to fight for principle than to preserve their anonymity.

The fundamental insight underlying job protection is that a homosexual orientation is never sufficient reason for depriving a person of his or her ordinary rights to employment, advancement, equal benefits, etc. Homosexual orientation is a personal and private matter (like heterosexual orientation) and, ordinarily, has no effect on a person's job performance unless an individual chooses to make it an issue.

But what of homosexual behavior? External behavior which is not a matter of public record should not of itself be the bias for discriminating against employees. Even if an employer learns about private sexual behavior of an employee, that information ought not be used against the employee unless it can be proved that the behavior in question seriously affects the ability of the person to fulfill the duties of his or her position.

It is often objected that it should not be illegal to fire some homosexual persons because of the danger of blackmail, for example, in some sensitive government intelligence-related positions. Yet the only reason at present for the possibility of blackmail is the fact that society judges homosexuality so negatively. If, in fact, homosexuality were regarded by society as a variant of human sexuality for at least ten percent of the population, then the very grounds for any blackmail opportunity would be eliminated. No one would have to fear being known as a homosexual person if there were no stigma or opprobrium attached to this sexual identity; there would be no possibility for blackmail attempts or threats. In fact, homosexual individuals who are already "out" claim that the grounds for blackmail, i.e., making a fact public, have been eliminated.

HOMOSEXUAL TEACHERS

One of the most sensitive and emotional topics about gay rights and job protection involves homosexual school teachers and child care workers. The concern about teachers is less a fear of child molestation or even seduction since current statistics show that the large majority of such cases involve heterosexual offenders. The more serious concern expressed by some is the question of the appropriateness of having gay or lesbian "role models" for young students.

At the bottom of this question, however, is the unspoken fear that the sexual orientation of the teacher might have some effect on the sexual orientation of the student. The few studies that have been done indicate that the sexual orientation of the teacher (or the parent, for that matter) does not influence the development of the sexuality of the child in any appreciable way. If the sexuality of the adult did influence the sexual orientation of the child, then how does one account for the 10% of the children who, having been exposed all their lives to heterosexual role models

(parents, teachers, clergy, etc.), developed nevertheless as homosexual individuals?

While healthy role models for impressionable young people is of crucial importance to parents and educators, there is an additional need for healthy role models for those students who are developing with homosexual orientations. Although homosexual students will always comprise the minority in the educational and social settings of our society, their needs and problems are no less worthy of our serious personal concern and institutional resources.

Civil rights protection for jobs such as teaching does not mean that society might not have to dismiss some gay or lesbian employees because of inappropriate or unprofessional behavior. But if this is the case, then the problem is one of a serious disturbance of the public order (of the workplace, for example) and not simply one of homosexual orientation. The restrictions placed upon homosexual teachers, in fairness, ought to be the same as those required of heterosexual teachers. Without legal protection of their orientation, gay and lesbian teachers live in constant fear of discovery and subsequent dismissal. No matter how talented or how dedicated to their profession, their careers can end in disaster not because of their personal and private lives, but simply for acknowledging honestly their human sexual identity. Teachers, students and the entire educational system would be much better off if mature and responsible homosexual teachers could be relieved of this unnecessary burden.

The psychologist Carl Jung theorizes that homosexual people are drawn— almost instinctively—to those professions which require a special capacity for nurturing the healing and growth of others. Among the professions where there is an unusually high percentage of lesbians and gay men are nursing, the clergy and teaching.

No one will deny that, historically, the teaching profession has embraced large numbers of homosexual people and many will admit that among the most creative teachers in their own lives have been homosexually oriented ones. These are living proof of the ability of gay and lesbian teachers and others in similar positions to exercise their professional responsibilities in a manner that justifies legal protection against arbitrary dismissal.

With the recent spate of child sexual abuse coming to light in this country, there is a need to separate an adult and mature homosexual orientation from the psychological disturbance called "pedophilia," which manifests itself both in heterosexual and homosexual child abuse. Employers for child care institutions have a right and responsibility to inquire into the backgrounds of potential employees to determine if there is any history of pedophilia. They have the right to dismiss employees who evidence such behavior or to investigate reasonably founded suspicions or charges. But in all these cases, it must be remembered, the issue is pedophilia, not homosexuality.

ADOPTION AND CHILD CUSTODY

Two other issues require additional comment because they raise concerns from people opposed to "gay rights." These are the issues of foster care and adoption by homosexual individuals or same-sex couples and custody rights of gay or lesbian parents. There are no legal precedents established in either of these issues. Individual jurisdictions, states and agencies render decisions and make policies based on a variety of circumstances including the political makeup of the geographical area in which the decisions are being made.

Individuals and groups working for legal reform in these areas assert that the simple fact of being gay or lesbian is not, in and of itself, sufficient reason for denying foster care, adoption or custody rights. Battles have been waged, especially by lesbian mothers, across the nation to protect their right to retain and raise children after legal separation or divorce. Gay fathers also seek court orders to keep their children claiming, at times, that they are more competent to raise the children than the biological mother.

The question that is asked in all these cases is what effect will the homosexual orientation of the parent, foster-parent or adoptive-parent have on the sexuality of the child. The younger the child is, the more concern that is expressed. We have already noted that there is no proof that the sexual orientation of the parent affects that of the child. A related question raised by some judges has to do with the "moral tone" or "moral climate" of the home in which one of the parents is homosexual. For example, if there is a strong belief that the homosexual lifestyle is "immoral," then the judgment will generally go against the homosexual person who is not considered as a fit parent. This is usually true when there are two homosexual individuals present in the home, but also even in the case of a single gay or lesbian person who applies for foster care, adoption or child custody.

There are no simple answers to any of these complex questions. What gay and lesbian advocates suggest is that the law should not automatically decide these cases simply on the basis of the sexual orientation of the parent. A same-sex, responsible and stable male couple would make a much better environment, for example, for raising a child than would a home with an alcoholic, abusive mother;

two lesbian women raising children from a previous marriage is a much healthier social situation than awarding custody of children to a biological father who is a drug or gambling addict.

On the other hand, the age, maturity and wishes of the child need to be considered seriously in making such a judgment. While some children might be able to cope with the situation of living in a home with one or two homosexual parents, the same situation might cause great stress for others. Even those who thrive in such situations also need help in coping with misunderstanding, ridicule and even rejection by classmates, friends and peers.

While the ideal home environment for sexual and social maturing has traditionally been the presence of a heterosexual male and female, the instances of heterosexual family breakdown, child abuse, incest and other serious problems make us less able to judge negatively the parenting skills of lesbian and gay individuals. The real needs for the healthy growth of children are non-possessive love, responsible affection, religious values, and caring discipline. The ability to embody these qualities does not depend on one's sexual orientation. Given the number of unwanted children (including older gay and lesbian children) and the proven ability of many homosexual people to provide good environments, society cannot afford to be blinded by unfounded biases and unproven assumptions about the "dangers" of placing adopted and foster-care children with lesbian and gay individuals and couples.

CONCLUSION

The struggle for "gay rights" will continue and expand in the coming years. This discussion has not touched on many other civil rights for which some homosexual people are working. All of them are both emotional and controversial. Should same-sex couples be afforded the same rights to civil and religious marriage ceremonies? Should individuals be entitled to "palimony" or something comparable to the support that people receive following a divorce? Should homosexuality be taught in the schools simply as an "alternative lifestyle?" Should students have gay clubs in schools as do black and Hispanic students and be allowed to take a same-sex partner to the senior prom? Should gay and lesbian employees have a legal right to exactly the same work benefits (health and insurance coverage) for their "spouses" as married heterosexual partners already enjoy? Positive responses to these questions require a much different definition of both marriage and family than society, influenced by religious beliefs and values, has been willing to make. Legal protection for jobs and housing for homosexual people might be among the least controversial or threatening topics for many people to consider and even support. Some of the other issues being raised by the gay liberation movement raise further challenges to traditional values and societal structures.

The outcome of the movement for gay and lesbian rights is unpredictable. Like any social movement it will experience times of victory and acceptance and times of social rejection and defeat. The political, religious and social climate all interact with the homosexual liberation movement both to modify it and, in turn, be modified by it. It is doubtful that the gains won thus far will be lost or that the social tolerance for homosexuality will change drastically. Legal equality will not necessarily bring about personal or social acceptance. But at least legal equality will prevent individuals and groups from acting out their irrational fears against homosexual people by firing them from jobs, refusing them accommodations or denying them the opportunity for parenting as foster parents, adoptive parents or natural parents.

Society has really little to fear from homosexuality. It is neither a threat to the family nor an attack on marital values. But society has much to fear from bigotry, ignorance and hostility as responses to a form of human sexual identity that is different from the vast majority of people. If we have learned our lesson from the experiences of generations past who fled to our country for religious and other freedoms which were threatened by totalitarianism, we will hesitate to deny or restrict the responsible sexual freedom of a small minority of those who live among us and who deserve our respect and friendship on this spaceship earth.

NO

Terry Teachout

GAY RIGHTS AND STRAIGHT REALITIES

"Gay Rights" is currently a big issue—which is merely to say that a good deal of thought on several levels is being given to the question. To what extent is the American polity willing to tolerate the increasingly vehement demands of this country's homosexuals for explicit statutory guarantees of their civil rights? This is also an issue on which comparatively little clear thinking has been done by conservatives—and yet it is a very important issue for the Right. For the whole problem of civil liberties and the homosexual (and it is, by any reckoning, a problem) is likely to drive a wedge into the conservative movement—and not the trusty old libertarian/traditionalist hatchet that mainstream right-wingers buried years ago, but a more unpleasantly divisive one with thoroughly disagreeable implications. It therefore wants discussing; and the purpose of this essay is to make a start. How, I shall ask in due course, should a conservative think about gay rights? The answer is, Constitutionally; but we have certain amount of groundwork to lay before we get that far.

THE DISCREET YEARS

Prior to 1969, the issue of gay rights was, to all intents and purposes, nonexistent, for the very good reason that as far as the law was concerned there was, *sensu stricto*, no such thing as a homosexual. There were, rather, "homosexualists" (to borrow Gore Vidal's handy expression)—that is, people who engaged in proscribed sexual activities with other people of the same sex. The *people* were not illegal, in the sense that, say, a Jew was illegal in Nazi Germany; only the sexual acts they chose to perform were. Thus, the civil-rights question was irrelevant, since the law did not recognize the homosexual as a legal entity subject to discrimination.

A legal fiction? Certainly; but, like all legal fictions of long standing, it served an invaluable purpose: In this case, it permitted the judicious interposition of hypocrisy, that typically Anglo-Saxon social lubricant, in order to defuse "the homosexual problem." Briefly stated, the homosexual problem consists of two contradictory axioms:

1. *Homosexuality falls decisively outside the protective sanctions of the American consensus.* This consensus, as defined by such commentators as John Courtney Murray, is Judaeo-Christian in its orientation; and the Judaeo-Christian strictures against homosexuality (which is considered immoral, both *per se* and because of the promiscuity that has been shown to be characteristic of the "average" homosexual) have been incorporated into our legal framework via the statutes outlawing sodomy and other so-called unnatural acts. It seems unlikely that those states which have repealed their sodomy laws have, in doing so, reflected the sense of the polity, which has traditionally held that minority practices that are at once immoral and illegal are simply not protected by this country's guarantees of individual liberty.

2. *homosexuals, nevertheless, play an undeniably important part in the workings of society.* Sheer numbers alone suggest this to be true; according to the Kinsey surveys (which are, even at this late date, the only statistically reliable bodies of data indicating the incidence of homosexuality in a large Western population), some 13 percent of the adult male and 7 percent of the adult female population of the United States were primarily or exclusively homosexual as of the mid- to late Forties, and these figures are widely considered to be approximately valid for today's population as well. It stands to reason that so large a group would play a significant role in the society of which it is a part and, while most Americans are at least partially aware of the extent to which homosexuals influence their everyday lives, it remains the case that, in George Steiner's words,

Neither sociology nor cultural history, neither political history nor psychology has even begun to handle authoritatively the vast theme of the part played by homosexuality in Western culture since the late nineteenth century. The subject is so diffuse and of such methodological and emotional complexity that it would require a combination of Machiavelli, Tocqueville, and Freud to produce the great missing book. There is hardly a branch of literature, of music, of the plastic arts, of philosophy, of drama, film, fashion, and the furnishings of daily urban life in which homosexuality has not been crucially involved, often dominantly.

Now one may argue that, after all, the world would probably be better off if *Myra Breckinridge* or *The General Theory of Employment, Interest, and Money* had never been written; but can the same be said of *A Streetcar Named Desire?* Or *Peter Grimes?* Or *Cakes and Ale?* Or *Remembrance of Things Past?* Or, for that matter, "Night and Day"?

Thus, two axioms arise, one morally imperative and one pragmatic, the operational consequences of which stand in direct opposition. There is, of course, no way to solve a conflict like this; but, as I say, there is a time-honored way to avoid the necessity of facing so painful an issue directly—hypocrisy.

In this context, hypocrisy may be defined as an arrangement in which two parties, each acting out of self-interest, privately agree 1) not to stand on certain principles that would affect the other party to the arrangement, and 2) not to explicitly discuss their agreement in public, so as to preserve the minimum appearances of rectitude. This is not quite the same thing as the hypocrisy described in La Rochefoucauld's maxim ("the homage that vice pays to virtue"): The hypocrisy I am discussing presupposes *mutual* gains for *mutual* concessions; and here, the legal fiction of "homosexualism" enters into the picture. Recognizing that American society was highly unlikely to tolerate the open practice of homosexuality, American homosexuals agreed to be discreet; and recognizing that the wholesale persecution of homosexuals would have been both impractical and unprofitable, the law left those homosexuals who chose to be discreet alone. homosexuals who broke this "tolerance contract" by flaunting their sexual preferences in inappropriate venues were arrested and allowed to serve as scapegoats for the discreet—but they were arrested for engaging in proscribed sexual acts rather than for "being homosexual."

This contract served to purpose admirably: It kept the homosexual problem out of the unyielding area of fixed statute and allowed it to be worked out in what conservative theorist L. Brent Bozell has called "the fluid channel" of socio-political consensus. The resulting solution was by no means ideal; but it *worked*. homosexuals who abided by the contract were, in the main, allowed to live out their lives with a minimum of legal harassment, while the "straight" community was allowed to remain more or less ignorant of the "gay" community in its midst.

'HOMOSEXUAL' TO 'GAY'

Over the last two decades, however, the moral climate in this country has shifted dramatically, moving toward considerably freer standards of heterosexual conduct; and, in a parallel development, the civil-rights movement provided homosexuals (and others) with the twin examples of group awareness and political activism to steer by. With the 1969 homosexual "riots" in New York, where gays actively resisted police harassment for the first time in this country's history, a new and important so-ciopolitical force emerged: Gay Liberation.

This movement essentially repudiates the terms on which our society's accommodation of homosexuality has rested. It stands, unequivocally, for "gay rights": the right of American homosexuals openly to acknowledge and practice their sexual preferences without fear of harassment or discrimination. And it strongly advocates the corollary doctrine of "coming out of the closet": that is, presenting oneself to the world as a homosexual, an individual whose entire system of values is significantly shaped by his sexual identity, rather than as a homosexualist, an individual who says (in effect) that his sexual activities are a function separate from his personality. The inherent intransigence of this stance, tending as it does to take discussion of the homosexual problem out of the fluid channel and into the public arena of statutory debate, is rapidly leading to a total breakdown of the tolerance contract—one with dire implications for the American homosexual, implications that are apparently not understood by those in the forefront of the gay-rights movement.

STRAIGHT TALK

For we have also seen over the past few years a markedly conservative shift in values on the part of the American public. This shift is, of course, symbolized by the presence in Washington of Ronald Reagan and a Republican Senate; but it is also symbolized by an increasingly visible conservatism in moral attitudes. And our new-found tolerance of open homosexuality, based as it is on a widespread middle-class ignorance of the gay social order, is bound to be among the first tenets of the "new" moral code to be jettisoned

Most Americans "know" what they know about homosexuality on the basi of such modern phenomena as, say, the once-a-season gay TV episode in which a clean-cut male homosexual, whose appearance and on-screen demeanor have been scrupulously vetted by the influential gay lobby, stands up successfully for his "constitutional rights." (A notable exception: *Hill Street Blues*, the only dramatic series on TV that could be described as conservative, takes up the topic from time to time with a typical blend of good humor and surprising candor.) Needless to say, the unsanitized truth normally remains either on the cutting-room floor or, as is more likely, unfilmed and undiscussed; for as one of the present author's homosexual acquaintances once remarked, "If Anita Bryant ever got hold of the 'pink pages' of *The Advocate* [the explicitly sexual personal advertising supplement of a prominent gay magazine], it would set gay rights back twenty years."

BREAKING THE CONTRACT

In abandoning their end of the tolerance contract, American homosexuals have forgotten that in any agreement based on hypocrisy, virtue inevitably holds the upper hand should vice renege: the power of public consensus. Society is willing to put up with a certain amount of immorality so long as the immoralists contribute to the general good and keep quiet about their leisure-time activities. But for American homosexuals to declare unilaterally that, contrary to all prior understandings, they now expect to live openly and be treated without prejudice or legal reprisal—that breaks the lease, as it were, and obligates the moralists to stand once again on their principles; at this point, a quiet return to the old tolerance contract becomes difficult if not impossible.

The consequences have already be-

come clear. As homosexuals militantly insist on a holistic view of their sexuality, conservatives frequently prove only too willing to oblige them—by putting forward statutes abridging the civil rights of homosexuals. These statutes, popularly known as Anita Bryant laws, are a message from the conservative majority to the homosexual minority that says: "Unless you are willing to be properly discreet, we have no real choice but to withdraw our tolerance of your activities and replace it with statutes consistent with the values of the community and appropriate to your argument that 'homosexuals' should be treated as responsible persons whose sexual practices are merely the outward expression of their moral values."

This situation obviously has the potential for developing into outright repression; and mainstream conservatives, who flatly reject the notion of an "open society," are not philosophically opposed to repressive measures taken against subversive elements of society. The classic statement of this doctrine is to be found in Willmoore Kendall's essay "McCarthyism: The Pons Asinorum of Contemporary Conservatism": Conservatism":

> Now, such a consensus, conceived of as a body of truths actually held by the people whose consensus it is, is incomprehensible *save as we understand it . . . to exclude ideas and opinions contrary to itself.* Discussion there is and must be, freedom of thought and freedom of expression there are and must be, but not anarchy of thought and anarchy of expression. In such a society by no means are *all* questions open questions; some questions involve matters so basic to the consensus that the society would, in declaring them open, abolish itself, commit suicide, terminate its existence as the kind of society it has hitherto understood itself to be.

It is crucial to remember that Kendall was talking both theory and practice in this passage. He believed that an ideal good society would act decisively to defend its shared orthodoxy—arguing elsewhere, for instance, that Plato's "Apology" was really a defense of Athenian conduct in the matter of Socrates. He also believed that the American public unconsciously subscribed to this doctrine ("they carry it," he would have said, "in their hips"), that the Constitution codified it implicitly but unmistakably, and that our society was quite capable of acting on it if circumstances warranted.

In short: If present-day America is, indeed, a conservative society in the process of rediscovering itself, then homosexuals committed to fighting openly for their civil liberties are asking for it—becasue the conservative reading of American history and tradition, which 1) places homosexuality outside the American consensus and 2) allows the community the right to exclude contrary ideas and opinions that threaten the consensus, is in effect a charter for repression of the publicly defiant homosexual. Of course, it is by no means clear to what extent the average American perceives gay rights as a fundamental threat to the consensus; but I, for one, would not care to put too much faith in the continuing tolerance of the public for an essentially alien presence whose rhetoric grows more militant daily—a public, we would do well to recall, that took in the story of Sodom and Gomorrah with its mother's milk.

It is here that the potential fissure that the gay-rights issue threatens to open in the conservative movement can be found. There are a great many conservatives who would like nothing better than institutionalized repression of the homosexual community, abandoning altogether any vestige of the tolerance contract; and there are a great many conservatives who,

though they have no particular sympathy for the gay-rights advocates, would very much prefer to let the matter take care of itself in a more sensible and less strident way. These latter conservatives would prefer not to immanentize the eschaton, so to speak; would prefer not to try to judge the question whether or not all homosexuals are going to Hell. If, indeed, they are all bound for Hades, then there is surely no need to pack the discreet ones off to prison first. In a difficult situation exacerbated by noisy demands for Gay Rights Now, the two points of view summarized here will become increasingly difficult to reconcile.

COMMUNITY STANDARDS

Which brings us back to the previous question: How should a conservative think about gay rights? At the beginning of this essay, I answered: Constitutionally. Let me answer more fully now. *A conservative position on the matter of civil liberties should accord with four factors: the Constitution of the United States; the sense of the community; the religious orientation of the American consensus; and a decent regard for the lot of certain citizens who, to the best of our knowledge, are fundamentally unable to change their offensive ways.*

To my mind, the best way of reconciling these four factors is for individual communities to settle the matter through local referendums; and, to this end, I would encourage homosexuals and antihomosexuals alike to put the question of mandated tolerance or institutionalized repression (depending on whose petition makes it onto the ballot) to the voters in as many citywide elections as they please. Past experience suggests that, in this matter as in most others, community sentiment will vary as widely as Miami varies from San Francisco; and, in time, one will find both a number of cities in which the question is closed one way or the other and a number of cities that have elected to leave the matter in the "fluid channel."

From the constitutional viewpoint, such a policy is impeccable. Individual states are free to pass or repeal sodomy laws as they see fit, since there has never been any serious challenge of the state's right to regulate certain kinds of sexual conduct; and even if the Supreme Court should at some point decide that public homosexuality falls under the category of symbolic speech and merits First Amendment protection, such a decision would not affect citywide Anita Bryant statutes, since the First Amendment's guarantee of free speech applies only to actions by Congress and (as a result of the long series of Supreme Court decisions that have "incorporated" the entire Bill of Rights into the Fourteenth Amendment) the state governments, with room left for the application of "community standards" in obscenity-related cases.

From the twin viewpoints of community and religion, this is as satisfactory a solution as can be devised, since it simultaneously allows the community to express its views on the homosexual problem and gives religious leaders and their organizations the opportunity to mobilize public support in whatever direction they see fit. And the realistic homosexual, recognizing that there is no possibility of his mobilizing a national consensus in support of gay rights, will no doubt accept with alacrity the chance at least to preserve his favored status in a few communities, such as New York and San Francisco. Indeed, if good sense prevails, the operating slogan of the gay-rights movement may well become, "Keep it local and keep it quiet," a change that most Americans, regardless of sexual preference, would probably greet with relief.

THE AMERICAN WAY

I want to stress that my personal inclinations with regard to the homosexual problem tend pretty strongly in the direction of tolerance. Anyone who has spent a goodly part of his formative years as part of an artistic community (as I did) is bound to take a more reasoned view of the homosexual, since the chances are high that he has known and worked with quite a few. Offhand, I can think of few things more disagreeable than a decisive move toward wholesale repression of the American homosexual; I am advocating no such thing here.

I am, however, warning those who wish to avoid such a move that, regardless of their personal feelings, conservatives have no *philosophical* objection to certain kinds of intolerance. Ultimately, the whole question boils down to whether or not the community has a right to preserve its conception of the American consensus by repressing those whose actions would tend to undermine it; and on this point the answer is clear. I'm put in mind of what Willmoore Kendall said when asked whether he was for or against freedom of speech:

> Temperamentally, like most Conservatives, I happen to be a man who in any given situation would always favor letting everybody have his "say"—temperamentally, I repeat, which is to say, *not* on principle but partly out of a selfish wish to satisfy my curiosity about what there is *to* say on whatever question happens to be up . . . in a certain kind of community, where people have in some sense *contracted* with one another to conduct their affairs on a freedom-of-speech basis or to treat each other as equals. . . . I recognize, *other things being equal* (recognize not just "temperamentally" but *to some extent* as a matter of principle), a *presumption* in favor of the let-'em-speak contingent and against the shut-'em-up contingent. . . . [But] one

231

begins to suspect that the true American tradition is less that of our Fourth of July orations and our constitutional law textbooks, with their cluck-clucking over the so-called preferred freedoms, than, quite simply, that of riding somebody out of town on a rail.

In much the same sense I am "for" tolerance; but I am also very much "for" the American polity's right to ride the gay-rights movement out of town on a rail, too, assuming that enough people deem such an action appropriate, and I happen to believe that the second right is considerably more important than the first one. The sooner homosexuals in America realize just how widespread that belief is, the better for everyone—gay *and* straight.

———

POSTSCRIPT

SHOULD LEGISLATION PROTECT ALL CITIZENS AGAINST DISCRIMINATION BASED SOLELY ON SEXUAL ORIENTATION?

The conservative views of Terry Teachout offer an interesting counterpoint to those of Father Nugent. However, his argument carries haunting echoes of the white racists of the 1960s. One can easily transpose his arguments back to that era of the civil rights movement when white racists argued that "blacks should be tolerated, but only if they keep their place and don't ride our buses, try to live in our neighborhoods, or attend our schools." While Teachout believes the conservative majority of Americans still finds this argument acceptable when applied to homosexuals, one cannot help but wonder how accurate his appraisal is.

At the same time, Father Nugent may be exposing the real fear behind the opposition to civil rights legislation for homosexuals in his conclusion where he lists even more perplexing and pragmatic questions which acceptance of gay civil rights would unleash. Like it or not, many of these questions are already being raised, even without civil rights legislation. In the early 1980s, a gay Connecticut high school student tried to bring his male friend to the senior prom. Many school districts with mandated sex education programs are facing the question of how to present homosexual and bisexual orientations. Gay students at several Catholic colleges have gone to court to force the administration to allow a gay and lesbian student support group. Even so, it may be, as both Nugent and Teachout seem to agree, that our society just isn't ready yet to face these kinds of practical questions. See the bibliography for further readings on this subject.

ISSUE 14

DOES PORNOGRAPHY PROMOTE SEXUAL VIOLENCE?

YES: Hilary Johnson, from "Pornography: A Humanist Issue," *The Humanist,* July/August 1985

NO: Carole S. Vance, from "Pornography Panel Discussion," *Vogue,* September 1985

ISSUE SUMMARY

YES: Hilary Johnson says lawyers and feminist organizations are beginning to compile evidence that they believe link pornography and male violence irrefutably.

NO: Carole S. Vance, an anthropologist, argues that large-scale studies have failed to demonstrate a clear relationship between pornography and violence against women.

What is the role and place of pornography in our culture? Is it obscene? Why, in our culture, does so much pornography depict violent sex and the degradation and victimization of women? Is Susan Brownmiller on target when she contends that "pornography promotes a climate of opinion in which hostility against women is not only tolerated but ideologically encouraged"? Is pornography a symptom of a sick society, or is it a healthy safety valve in a society that is basically uncomfortable with sexuality? If we had a more accepting and positive view of sex that allowed it a natural place in our daily lives, would pornography continue to sell?

How do we control pornography in a free society, which holds the First Amendment dearer than any other freedom guaranteed by the Constitution? Is regulating or suppressing pornography censorship of freedom of the press and speech, or only a necessary means of protecting the innocent? Should victims of rape or sexual abuse be allowed to sue the publishers of pornographic magazines or movies on the claim that their sexual assaulters were incited to rape by reading or viewing pornographic material?

More basic than all these perplexing questions is a fundamental, seemingly irresolvable issue. In a pluralistic society, how do we define pornography? Married couples who rent a sexually explicit film to show on their VCR to inspire variety in their loveplay do not consider the film they watch pornographic or obscene. Others, however, would denounce the same videotape as obscene, degrading to women, and even an inspiration for males to rape. In 1986, a group of Tennessee parents objected to their children being exposed to the *Wizard of Oz* and a scientific explanation of tidal waves in a public school because the former encouraged children to use their imagination and the latter did not praise God as the ultimate cause of all natural phenomena. Defining the limits and extent of individual freedoms in a pluralistic, democratic society is not easy.

Ten years ago, when the *New York Times* reported on a workshop the editor of this volume directed as part of a human sexuality course, he was accused of showing pornographic films. Members of Morality in Media charged that the films shown were obscene and pornographic because they showed frontal nudity of men and women. Of course, the educational films used also showed various forms of sexual relations including intercourse, oral sex, and masturbation, but critics did not need to go that far. Simple nudity was obscene. That judgment may be an extreme, but it illustrates the problem of defining pornography and obscenity, and the subsequent problem of applying that definition in law or court.

Outside of abortion, few sexual topics today provide more fuel for public debate and emotions than pornography. As you read each of the following statements, see if you can pick out the strongest single argument in each essay, as well as the weakest argument. Lay them out and compare them as you form your own judgment on this critical issue.

YES

Hilary Johnson

THE NEW RESEARCH
IS COMPELLING

A young woman is bathing. She seems lost in a reverie of sensual plea-sure. Suddenly, a man wearing a mask and carrying a rifle breaks into the room. In the next five minutes, she is sexually attacked, shot in the stomach, and finally, shot point blank in the forehead. It is scene from *Tool Box Mur-ders*, one of thousands of pornographic films available for rental or purchase in video stores across North America. The fusion of sex and violence in *Tool Box Murders* is hardly an anomaly in pornographic films. In the last decade, the nature of pornography—in books, magazines, and film—has changed rad-ically, and a surprisingly high percentage of contemporary pornography depicts women as victims of rape, torture, and sadistic domination by men.

Neil Malamuth, a professor of communication studies at the University of California at Los Angeles and coeditor with Edward Donnerstein of *Porno-graphy and Sexual Aggression,* has been researching the effects of violent pornography for nearly a decade. He uses this film clip to illustrate the tenor of today's violent pornography. Thirty percent of pornographic books, 10 per-cent of pornographic magazines, and 15 percent of pornographic movies, Malamuth says, convey a message of brutal disregard for the value of women as human beings. The result, he and his fellow researchers believe, may be the creation of a society that is increasingly accepting of aggression toward women. He adds, "In a culture that celebrates rape, the lives of millions of women will be affected."

Malamuth is among a widening circle of at least two dozen academic researchers who are studying the effects of pornography on society. Their per-suasive findings ultimately may dispel the notion that pornography has a sex-ually liberating effect. Malamuth and other researchers have found that men exposed under laboratory circumstances to violent pornography become both more tolerant of the idea of violence against women and more aggressive toward women. They also more easily accept the myth that women secretly want to be raped and will enjoy it. Researchers have found as well that a certain percentage of men in the population are aroused by aural or visual representations of women being assaulted.

These results have failed to surprise anti-pornography feminists, who have argued many of the same points in their efforts to protect women from violence. Says Pauline Bart, a feminist and sociology professor at the University of Illinois College of Medicine who is publishing a study of rape victims, "I didn't start out being against pornography; but if you're a rape researcher, it becomes clear there is a direct link. Violent pornography is like an advertisement for rape." Many of the women Bart interviewed said their attackers expected them to respond as rape victims do in pornography, that is, to enjoy the rape, to look upon it as a "date" rather than an assault, and in some cases, to have orgasms—even though during one rape, the rapist held a gun to his victim's head. "Men are not born thinking women enjoy rape and torture—it's not carried on the Y chromosome," Bart says. "They learn it from pornography."

Bookstores, hotels, supermarkets, convenience stores, and drugstores all sell these publications. Readership in the spring of 1985 was 11,839,000 for *Playboy* and 7,647,000 for *Penthouse*. The FBI estimates that the American pornography industry, which includes books and magazines as well as videos and films, is worth $2-$4 billion a year, much of it financed by organized crime.

The rise in violent, sadistic pornography has been charted in a number of studies. In one, researchers P.E. Dietz and B. Evans assessed pornographic magazine covers between 1970 and 1981. They found that covers depicting bondage and domination of women, though rare in 1970, increased markedly over the decade. By 1981, such depictions constituted close to one-fifth of the covers of 1760 porn magazines studied.

Much of this new research runs counter to the findings of the Commission on Obscenity and Pornography that was convened by Congress, in 1967, to determine what, if any, social harm derived from pornography. Commissioners reported, in 1970, that they were unable to find evidence of harm. When the Commission did its work, however, the flood of violent pornography had not yet begun.

The assumption that violent pornography is tucked away in publications with small circulations is proving to be in error. In the February, 1979, issue of *Penthouse*, an article called "Snatch" chronicled the kidnap and rape of a woman; the accompanying photographs showed her assailant having sex with her while she was bound. In a 1982 issue, the magazine pictured naked women brandishing straight-edge razors inches from their own breasts. In a more recent issue (December, 1984), there were several pages of nude women tied and hung from trees in postures of death.

Penthouse has recently introduced a second glossy men's magazine, *Newlook*. *Newlook* specializes in photographs of naked women interspersed with graphically illustrated articles about carnage and death, like a piece on cockfighting or one on the viciousness of hyenas. In the premier issue, one spread showed photographs of a woman whose pubic hair had been shaved off and of a gloved hand holding a straight razor: the text, by Anais Nin, described the shaving, which the woman struggled against but ultimately found arousing. Malamuth finds it interesting that "*Penthouse* calls this the 'new magazine of contemporary man.' What it shows on its pages is either violence, women's bodies, or a fusion of both."

Films and videos may be more pernicious than other pornography because their violence is so lifelike. "There is considerable research that the more realistic the image, the greater its ability to influence people," Malamuth says. "The distinction between reality and fantasy becomes smaller." Malamuth believes that R-rated "slasher" films like *Friday the 13th* and *The Texas Chainsaw Massacre* are as violent as the so-called "snuff" films of the 1970s, in which women reportedly were murdered on camera. "These films fuse sex and violence in a very disturbing way," Malamuth says, citing the slick production values of the Hollywood films, which, compared with the crudeness of the "snuff" genre, make them seem more real.

The implications of this change in tenor are as troubling as the material itself, but explanations—aside from the catchall cry of misogyny—are elusive and tend to be speculative. Catharine MacKinnon, a University of Minnesota law professor who drafted a law that would enable women to sue pornographers for damages if they can prove that pornography has harmed them, writes, "More and more violence has become necessary to keep the progressively desensitized consumer aroused to the illusion that sex is (and he is) daring and dangerous." Malamuth agrees: "There's a need to break taboos to increase sales—people get satiated."

"Initially, I was interested in the feminist notion that rape is not really a deviant thing, that it is rooted in the society," Malamuth says. One of his early experiments used a series of questionnaires to measure men's "likelihood of raping." "When I didn't use the word 'rape,'" Malamuth says, "when I asked, 'How likely would you be to force a woman into sexual acts against her will if you knew you wouldn't be caught or punished?' 57 percent said there was some likelihood they

would do so." When Malamuth used the word "rape," the percentage dropped to 35—still a daunting figure. Malamuth and others have repeated this study numerous times on thousands of men around the country and found the results to differ only slightly. In later studies, Malamuth found that men exposed to films in which physical abuse was shown sexually to arouse the victim were increasingly accepting of violence against women.

For a more complicated study, Malamuth exposed three groups of men to three kinds of material: violent pornography, nonviolent pornography that emphasized positive feelings of mutuality during sex and equal power relationships between men and women, and non-sexual illustrations—photographs of scenery from *National Geographic,* for instance. Afterward, the men were asked to participate in another study, this time a phony one involving ESP. Each man was assigned a female "partner," who was secretly in league with the researchers. After interviewing each other, the partners each filled out a questionnaire, supposedly to determine characteristics in common. The women had been instructed to write insulting comments, such as "It seems to me this person is kind of shallow," or "he's confused in his thinking," or "he's not a person I would want to date or be friends with." Each partner was then given the other's responses to read. Next, the men were divided into two groups. Both groups were told that if their partners failed to pick up the telepathic message, they could punish them by the ostensible delivery of electric shocks. Men in one group were told it was permissible to behave as aggressively toward the women as they wished. Those in the other group were given a warning designed to make them somewhat self-conscious about administering the shocks.

The men inhibited by the warning showed no significant differences in aggression, regardless of the category of material they had been exposed to. Among the disinhibited group, those men who had been exposed to violent pornography were more willing to shock the women than were those who had been exposed to neutral material or non-violent pornography. Malamuth points out that this research indicates, among other things, that pornography that emphasizes positive feelings between men and women might reduce aggressive tendencies in men. Men who were exposed to such pornography were even less willing to shock their partners than were men exposed to neutral material.

According to Malamuth, the study also shows that although violent pornography may strengthen some men's aggressive tendencies, the actual expression of those tendencies may be deeply affected by "situational factors as well as *internal* variables—the background and psychological makeup of the persons exposed."

Internal variables encompass a man's own values. "We cannot predict who will commit a rape," Malamuth says, "but there are several factors that when combined seem to be very powerful indicators." Among those factors are a tendency to become sexually aroused by rape depictions or rape fantasies; a belief that male dominance is justified; general sex-role rigidity; acceptance of rape mythology; and hostility to women. Researchers have found, too, that a man for whom dominance is the prime motivation for sex (a desire to have power over someone rather than to feel physical pleasure or to express love and affection) is at greater risk of becoming a rapist. Another factor is acceptance of violence against women. "Any factor alone seems to make a 5 or 10 percent difference in a man's likelihood to

rape. A combination may make about a 40 percent difference," Malamuth says.

Research indicates that violent material in which women are attacked without being sexually assaulted takes its toll, too. Male sensitivity to a rape victim's plight was diminished after viewing a series of five R-rated "slasher" films in experiments by psychologists Dan Line and Edward Donnerstein at the University of Wisconsin. Each film contained graphic violence against women. After a week of viewing these films, the men were shown a reenactment of a rape trial and asked to evaluate the rape victim. According to Donnerstein, "They saw less injury, more responsibility, and more worthlessness on the part of the victim in comparison with a control group that had not seen the five films."

What makes the new research compelling is the current level of violence against women in America. Although many of the statistics about violence against women are controversial, it is clear that, by any measure, a great deal of violence exists. The Los Angeles-based Women Against Violence Against Women, for example, believes women in that county suffer rape at the rate of one assault for every 2.2 women, although some observers believe this estimate to be exaggerated. The frequency of rape is particularly difficult to estimate: numbers vary depending on how many unreported rapes the statistician figures into the equations, and the ratio varies from three to ten for each reported one. The FBI recently stated that in America a woman is raped every six minutes.

The National Institute of Mental Health recently released a survey on the incidence of battery of women. According to NIMH-supported researchers, one in five women admitted to hospital emergency rooms is the victim of a beating from her spouse or boyfriend. One of the authors of the study reports that "Battering may be the single most common source of injury to women—more common than auto accidents, mugging, and rape combined."

Malamuth stresses that violent pornography's proven area of influence has been in reinforcing aggressive attitudes among men: actual violence is a result of a complicated set of interactions. "It appears that cultural factors create the potential in many men to commit violent acts. Certain aspects of an individual—having an antisocial personality, a difficult home background, or an inability to cope with certain types of stress—may take that potential and translate it into an actual act of violence," Malamuth says. "In a healthy culture, in which people are brought up with sex education and a lot of internal controls against violence, violent porn would not have the same influence as in a culture in which people have little information about sexuality." Malamuth adds that rapists often come from home backgrounds where sex is considered taboo. He points out that "A lot of people wind up getting their information about sex through pornography. Unfortunately, in pornography there are myths about women. People who have a lot of accurate information

about sex will be less likely to be influenced. They have a better basis for seeing the myths."

Lawyers and feminist organizations are beginning to compile evidence that they believe links pornography and male violence irrefutably. Two years ago, in two days of testimony before the Minneapolis City Council for the ordinance drawn by feminist attorney MacKinnon with feminist author Andrea Dworkin, women described the ways in which pornography was used by their boyfriends, husbands, and by rapists as a kind of textbook of abuse against them. The ordinance resembles product-liability and sex-discrimination law in an attempt to sidestep First Amendment issues. "There's a massive amount of sexual abuse connected to pornography, most of it invisible," says MacKinnon, who was present at the Minneapolis hearings. "Women who have been exposed to it are silenced by their exposure—by just plain devalidation."

Anti-porn activists and feminists embrace the research emanating from universities. Yet, perhaps not surprisingly, there is a begrudging aspect to their embrace. "If people believed women, we wouldn't need to have all this research," suggests sociologist Pauline Bart.

NO
Carole S. Vance

ORDINANCES RESTRICTING PORNOGRAPHY COULD DAMAGE WOMEN

Alison Humes: *Is porn harmful to women?*

Carole Vance: Large-scale studies have failed to demonstrate a clear relationship between pornography and violence against women. At best, recent psychological studies show a short-lived change in attitude among men exposed under artificial, laboratory conditions to sexually explicit films that contain violence. If anything, convicted rapists appear to read less pornography than "normal" men.

There's no question, however, that pornography—or as I prefer to call it, sexually explicit representation—contains a very heavy dose of sexism. But is sexism in pornography worse than sexism in mass media, in government, in electoral politics, in the Bible? And if so, why?

Sexism in pornography is a serious issue, and violence against women in all forms—rape, sexual harassment, sexual abuse—is a serious issue. Feminists have addressed these issues and must continue to address them. I'm critical, though, of approaches that focus only on sexual danger to women without also looking at the sources of sexual pleasure for women. The fight against pornography picks up on a cultural theme that sees sex as very dangerous for women, and sex *is* dangerous for women. But if we look only at danger, we distort women's experience, and inadvertently make women more victimized than they are. We also deprive women of knowledge about their own sexual power, which actually does exist in this culture.

AH: *Does porn serve any useful purpose?*

CV: Commercially available sexually explicit material has both progressive and regressive elements. In part, it functions as the poor man and woman's sex education, to ill and to good. When it's sexist, it can reinforce sexist values. But the messages in pornography are complex and contradictory; even ordinary commercial porn has a lot of messages about female autonomy, female desire, about women acting on their own desire. If we look at societies besides our own, we see some cultures—for example, Iran—in which sexually explicit representation is completely banned as offensive to morals, yet the position of women, from an American feminist point of view, is extremely poor; in other societies, such as those in Scandinavia, sexually explicit materials are widely available, and women's status is relatively good.

From, statements by Carol Vance in "Pornography Panel Discussion," *Vogue* magazine, September 1985. Courtesy *Vogue*. Copyright © 1985 by the Condé Nast Publications, Inc.

AH: *Why has pornography become the focus of feminist debate?*
CV: I think the media have been somewhat irresponsible in making it seem as if feminists are agreed on the issue of pornography. In fact, there's considerable diversity of opinion about pornography and what it means, and even more difference of opinion about whether any legislative attempt to regulate pornography is a good idea for women. It has taken some time to break through this media simplification of *the* feminist position, *the* feminist point of view, when feminists actually disagree.

Women have a great deal of sexual anger at men, and rightly so. The feminist movement should speak to that anger, to what women are dissatisfied about. I mean not only rape and violence but also dissatisfaction in sexual relations, not getting what they want, being subject to acts they object to, being kept ignorant, being constrained. These issues are much more difficult to talk about and much more explosive and controversial. Targeting porn just becomes a symbolic way to get at all this dissatisfaction.

The women's movement has been concerned with female sexuality since its beginnings. This has taken a number of forms: discussions about the importance of orgasm for women, about vibrators and masturbation; and a great deal of political action on lesbian rights, sex education, availability of contraception, abortion rights. Over the course of these fifteen years, we started to narrow things down. First, to a critique of sexism in the media. Then, the critique was narrowed to violence and sexism in the media. Then, it was narrowed even further, to a critique of violence and sexism in pornography. Now, it has been totally narrowed to a focus on pornography—as if pornography represented the locus of sexism in our culture. I don't see that it does. T think it represents our seeing, culturally seeing, sex as very dangerous. I think it's connected with the notion that sex is some kind of drive, this beastly quality that impels people to act—which we don't believe about ourselves for a minute in any other realm.

The controversy over pornography almost always centers on visual images, much more than on written texts. This reflects a class bias, that those who can read are less corruptible; a concern that visual materials are now widely disseminated; as well as our unsophistication in knowing how to deal with images.

AH: *Are the efforts to restrict porn a way of thwarting men's perceived sexual drive?*
CV: In the end, the fight against pornography is a campaign against male masturbation, in that pornography is used for that purpose. It's a slippery slope. One thing leads to another: so masturbation leads to pornography, pornography causes violence, and all of a sudden, we've posited this kind of male monster who consumes pornography, but we need to know much more about what pornography means to men.

AH: *Hasn't pornography become increasingly violent over the last ten years?*
CV: I think the amount of violence in both written and visual material is really quite low. We'd have to define what we mean by violence, because people understand the word differently. But to use the most commonly quoted figure, 85 percent of commercially available pornographic film and video is not violent. There's more violence in mainstream films that no one would call pornographic. There's pornography, which is sexually explicit material; and then, there are these "slasher films"—I stalk you by night and slit you throat, and I'm a man and you're a woman. These are not sexually explicit, yet some would argue that they are much

more misogynistic than films that show sexual relations.

When you walk into your average adult bookstore, you find that most commercially available pornography is not violent. It's sexually explicit representations of consensual sexual relations. It may be poorly produced. It may look silly. It may not meet your taste. It may be sexist: some of it isn't; a lot of it is, but so is any other magazine I can think of on the stand. But it's not violent. The best way to make up your mind about pornography is to go and look at it.

AH: *What about sado-masochistic porn?*
CV: Sexually explicit material that's about sadomasochism is the sexual literature of a sexual minority. It's very poorly understood by other people, who take it to be violent, when, in fact, it's not. What's being depicted is a consensual fantasy that attempts to approximate being overpowered, being dominant, being submissive.

The whole convention of SM porn is resistance at the beginning followed by acceptance at the end. According to people who are participants in SM practice, consent and safety are major, major themes. All pornography has its own conventions, which let the viewer know what it means. For example, most would grant that the sexual material women produce for one another is erotica—that it is not being produced to arouse men to do horrible things to women. Yet what if some nasty man get hold of it and uses it for another purpose? Does this not transform good erotica into pornography?

AH: *Is material that shows a woman in a sexually dominant role feminist?*
CV: A lot of SM porn features female domination, which doesn't fit with this neat analysis of porn's singular purpose, to oppress women. Some would argue that SM represents nonegalitarian power relations that ape a patriarchal model; so any way you cut it, it's bad and all of it should go. The popular understanding of SM is today where the popular understanding of homosexuality was twenty years ago.

AH: *How can we tell erotica from porn?*
CV: In practice, this distinction is impossible to make. I would say that erotica is what you like, and pornography is what the other guy likes. I call it Vance's one-third rule: Show any picture that you like to other people, and one-third will find it ridiculous, one-third will find it disgusting, and one-third will find it hot. That's why we'd better off to use a phrase like "sexually explicit representation," which could run the gamut from art to *Playboy* to sex-education materials, all of which can contain some sexual explicitness.

AH: *Is there an effort by feminists to create an erotica that emphasizes egalitarianism?*
CV: Feminists would like a world in which gender is not the basis for social inequality. But our quest for the real sexuality is like a quest for something that doesn't exist. Perhaps it's a mistake to think that egalitarian sex means that every person does the same thing in equal amounts, as if equality could not encompass difference. Surely our vision of the future is not sex that's devoid of passion or juice.

If feminists were to apply a definition so stringent that the only cultural products available were egalitarian, most of Western culture would have to go in the trash bag. We would end up with the feminist version of Socialist Realist art.

What women are trying to do is redress the balance between sexual pleasure and danger and develop a way of looking at sex that admits both at the same time with all the contradiction.

AH: *Why is sex connected to power?*
CV: Many more psychoanalytically based theorists would argue that sexuality is intrinsically connected to power. Many believe that sexuality draws on infantile

experience—being small and, in a certain sense, overpowered. The infant and the young child's fantasy is, in turn, of overpowering others. That this leaves residues in adult psychology is not the same as sexism.

For many people, what's erotic on the level of fantasy is not what they necessarily want to do in sex. In fact, many enjoy fantasizing about precisely what they would *not* want to do in sex. Some would argue that fantasy is a very good place to deal with what's frightening, to deal with what's risky, even to repair earlier psychological damage. The much-touted finding that women do have rape fantasies was initially used by opponents of the stop-rape movement to somehow legitimize rape, by confusing fantasy with reality. If you have a rape fantasy, it in *no* way means you want to be raped. In fantasy, you are in control, you imagine the actor, you're in charge; when you're tired of it, when it's unpleasant, you stop it.

AH: *Are women consumers of pornography?*
CV: The invention and dissemination of video is changing the porn market quite radically. People are moving away from the Times Square adult theater, where you bring your raincoat and where a woman wouldn't be caught dead, to porn that's seen more privately at home. Women are increasingly renting this stuff; and they're creating a new market. In the past few years, there have been a lot of new porn producers, some of whom are women. Porn films have typically been very male-authored: the women are gorgeous in a plastic way and the guys look like shlepps. Well, whose fantasy is that? Some of the porn produced by women has gorgeous men and ordinary-looking and plausible women.

AH: *How could ordinances restricting pornography damage women?*

CV: First of all, the proponents of the ordinance argue that their approach is novel, that it's not moralistic, that it's not obscenity-based, that it's feminist. It asserts that pornography is a kind of discrimination against women. Feminist opponents (among whom I count myself) point out that it's actually a very old approach because it reasserts that women are sexually different from men and in need of special protection. Yet special protection inadvertently reinforces the ways in which women are legally and socially said to be different from men.

The ordinance's definition of pornography is extremely vague. The push to restrict material is very mistaken in this political climate: any ordinance is going to be used primarily by right-wing groups against women. A great deal of writing and art and films produced by women will be prosecutable under these laws. Proponents argue that this ordinance would empower women to object to, to bring suit against, to have injunctions brought against sexually offensive material. Yet those who interpret what falls under the definition of the law are going to be local officials, usually male conservative court judges who do not view these things the way feminists do. For that reason, and given the state's general track record on matters of sex, many feminists think the net effect will be negative.

Finally, pornography is not uniform, even though we use the word as if it were. It's very diverse. There are different markets. There are different producers. There are different audiences. Porn is not uniformly about sexism. A lot of heterosexual porn may be sexist, but so are other available things in the culture. Why are we targeting pornography in particular? What makes sex so special? The anti-porn approach privileges sex as the cause of women's oppression, which I think is wrong and misguided.

POSTSCRIPT

DOES PORNOGRAPHY PROMOTE SEXUAL VIOLENCE?

Symbolic of the pornography debate in recent years was the undraped appearance of Vanessa Williams, Miss America, in the pages of *Penthouse* in the summer of 1983. Americans were outraged at the photographer and publisher who exploited an inexperienced and novice model, and equally angry at the pageant committee for demanding that Miss Williams relinquish her crown. But Vanessa Williams was also denounced because she fractured our mythic image of an innocent, pure Miss America. Yet six million Americans rushed to their newstands to buy and contemplate the pictures of the first nude Miss America.

Social critics, feminists, church leaders and members, artists and film makers, civil libertarians and average citizens will continue to debate the place and role pornography plays in our culture. Yet, in the midst of the debate, one needs to avoid ethnic or cultural myopia. In discussing the Attorney General's Commission on Pornography in Issue 15, Robert Staples, a student of black family sociology, reminds us that pornography is primarily a white problem and concern. It will be interesting to see how, in the years ahead, the growing and visible number of immigrants from Southeast Asia, Latin America, and the Islamic Middle East will add new tones and color to our debate over pornography. The Hindu temples of northern India are world famous for the sexually explicit sculptures that cover their interiors and exteriors. The Chinese and Japanese have venerable and stylized traditions of erotic art that reach back centuries that would shock or embarrass many Americans. Asians are now the majority population in a number of American cities. Will they continue their traditions, or abandon them in the process of acculturation? What will our debate over pornography look like five or ten years from now? See the bibliography for further readings on this subject.

ISSUE 15

DOES THE ATTORNEY GENERAL'S REPORT CLEARLY DOCUMENT THE HARM PORNOGRAPHY DOES?

YES: Commissioner Bruce Ritter, from "Summary of the Official Report of the Attorney General's Commission on Pornography" (Covenant House, 1986)

NO: Shadow Commissioners Larry Baron, Barbara Ehrenreich, Barry Lynn, John Money, Robert Staples, Murray Straus, and Bernard Zilbergeld, from *United States of America vs. SEX: How the Meese Commission Lied About Sex* (Minotaur Press, 1986)

ISSUE SUMMARY

YES: Commissioner Bruce Ritter, founder of Covenant House for runaway teenagers, describes the Meese Commission Report on Pornography as a cautious, reasoned and balanced documentation of the national problem of pornography and a needed remedy to the invalid conclusions of the 1970 commission.
NO: The Shadow Commissioners argue that the Meese commission was totally biased from the start, carefully selected its witnesses, and ignored or distorted the testimony of witnesses who did not confirm their previous conclusions.

In the 1950s, pornography was an American social taboo, restricted to red-light districts and furtively passed from one male to another. Kinsey's surveys of American sexual customs, which many considered shocking and pornographic, were still kept in the closed collections of libraries and often circulated only to doctors and psychologists. Then, in 1957, the US Supreme Court created a new definition of obscenity in the *Roth* case. Henceforth, a work could be considered legally obscene only if its dominant theme appealed to obsessive and depraving sexual interests, was offensive to the average community member, and also totally lacked any redeeming social value.

In the next decade, the *Roth* decision was followed by the first Playboy Club, Lenny Bruce's onstage sexual dialogues, explicit sex advertisements in the Los Angeles *Free Press, Berkeley Barb* and *Rolling Stone. Fanny Hill—Memories of a Woman of Pleasure* and *The Valley of the Dolls* were best-sellers and *The Graduate* a popular movie. The Woodstock Rock Festival was followed by the on-stage nudity in *Oh! Calcutta* and *Hair.*

In 1970, after two years of study with a budget of $2 million, the Presidential Commission on Obscenity and Pornography recommended the abolition of obscenity laws. Working with a staff of 22 to support pioneering research, the 15 commissioners found that neither hard-core nor soft-core pornography leads to antisocial behavior. Three commissioners disagreed in a minority report. President Nixon found the conclusions "morally bankrupt" and the Senate disapproved of the finding in a 60-5 vote.

In 1979, the Williams Committee of England and Wales concluded that "Given the amount of explicit sexual material in circulation and the allegations often made about its effects, it is striking that one can study case after case of sex crimes and murder without finding any hint at all that pornography was present in the background." In 1984, Canada's Fraiser Committee reported that it was "not prepared to state, solely on the basis of the evidence and research it has seen, that pornography is a significant causal factor in the commission of some forms of violent crimes, in the sexual abuse of children, or the disintegration of communities and society."

Meanwhile, men's magazines became more explicit. *The Joy of Sex, More Joy of Sex,* live sex shows and movies such as *Deep Throat* and *Debbie Does Dallas* influenced many. Rock music moved from Elvis Presley to Prince. Cable television and videocassettes put sexually explicit films into millions of homes. In 1984, an estimated 54 million X-rated tapes were rented from 14,000 national outlets—a $400 million business. New types of hard-core pornography appeared including "kiddie porn" and "snuff" films showing violent sadistic sex murders.

Responding to pressure from many sources, President Reagan used the occasion of signing the Child Protection Act of 1984 to announce a national war on pornography and a new commission to document the connection between the pornography plague and child abuse, incest and rape.

The eleven commissioners* chosen by United States Attorney General Edwin Meese were given a budget of $500,000 and one year to come up with a report. Criticisms were widespread and immediate, as the following statements of the "Shadow Commissioners" show.

*See page 323 for brief biographies of the members of the commission.

YES

Bruce Ritter

THE 1986 MEESE COMMISSION CLEARLY DOCUMENTS THE HARM PORNOGRAPHY DOES

THE BACKGROUND

D.H. Lawrence called modern pornography a "beastly and dangerous thing," and said "you can recognize it by the insult it offers, invariably, to sex, and to the human spirit." Yet sincere Americans have long disagreed over how, and whether, pornography should be attacked. In 1970 the President's Commission on Obscenity and Pornography recommended that all laws against pornography be repealed, except for those preventing sale of pornography to children.

The findings of that commission were unanimously rejected that same year by a vote of the United States Senate, and have been strongly attacked by scholars and other concerned citizens. Some pointed out, for example, that the commission's logic would allow child pornography to circulate freely. And indeed, in the decade and a half after 1970, sexually explicit materials of every description (including child pornography) flooded the American marketplace.

By 1985 new concern over the effects of pornography was being voiced by representatives of women's organizations, by social scientists and by citizens living in neighborhoods bombarded by images of sex. In response to these concerns, the President of the United States asked the Attorney General to create a new federal commission to re-examine the problem.

THE COMMISSION AND ITS MANDATE

Appointed on May 20, 1985, the Attorney General's Commission on Pornography was chartered by the U.S. Department of Justice to "study . . . the problem of pornography" and to "make specific recommendations to the Attorney General." Eleven commissioners, from widely diverse backgrounds, were given one year to wrestle with an issue that has plagued Americans for over a century: Is pornography harmful, and, if so, what can we do about it?

To address those questions the Commission conducted six public hearings in six cities, receiving oral testimony from well over 200 witnesses, and written testimony from scores of others. All published scientific studies on the effects of viewing pornography were carefully reviewed. The work of previous commissions was closely examined, and law enforcement officials throughout the country helped provide extensive information about the underground workings of the major American sex industry.

Defining "pornography" was, not surprisingly, one of the Commission's most difficult tasks. The Commission recognized that *any* definition of that term is controversial, but ultimately used a definition which had been adopted by previous national commissions in Britain and Canada. Thus the Report defines "pornography" as material which is "predominantly sexually explicit and intended primarily for the purpose of sexual arousal."

Through the year the eleven unpaid Commissioners engaged in long and sometimes heated discussions, all of them fully open to the public. The result was a 2-volume, 2000-page report presented to the Attorney General—and the American people—on July 9, 1986.

"This report provides an abundance of information and the conclusions of a community of eleven citizens. The American people must now decide what to with it."
Commissioner Diane Cusack

PROTECTING FREEDOM OF SPEECH

The starting point for the Commission's Report was, simply, the "special power of the First Amendment" in American life.

Rather than treating concerns about freedom of speech as a technical legal issue, the Report begins with a thorough analysis of the protection provided to sexually oriented speech under the Constitution.

The Supreme Court has ruled that "hard-core" pornography may be outlawed—if it patently offends local community standards, if it appeals to a morbid, unhealthy interest in sex, and if it does not have serious literary, artistic, political or scientific value. The Commission agreed with this standard, and urged all government and law enforcement officials "to enforce the existing principles of the First Amendment as conscientiously and vigorously as they enforce the obscenity laws." The Commission recommended *no* shrinkage of the area protected by the First Amendment.

"We find it difficult to understand how much of the material we have seen can be considered to be even remotely related to an exchange of views in the marketplace of ideas. . . . We believe it necessary for this society to ensure that the First Amendment retains the strength it must have when it is most needed."
Report, Chapter 3

THE CHANGING NATURE OF PORNOGRAPHY

When the previous Commission on Obscenity and Pornography issued its Report in 1970, "hard-core" pornography scarcely existed. Child pornography was virtually unknown, and the 1970 Report voiced no concern over it. Sado-masochistic materials, explicit portrayals of bestiality, and materials showing the extreme sexual degradation of women were largely unheard of.

The Report of the current Commission describes how thoroughly the situation has changed. Child pornography is now a large and underground problem. Sexually violent material has become a major segment of the adult pornography market, and depictions of sexual bestiality are now common. Further, material depicting sexual degradation, domination, and humiliation has become, in the words of the new Report, "the largely predominant proportion of commercially available pornography."

Dramatic changes in technology have also occurred. Pornography, once confined to books, magazines and film, is now transmitted directly to the home through cable television and telephone ("dial-a-porn") networks—both accessible to children. The VCR revolution has made it possible for hard-core pornography on video cassettes to be played on home TV. The Report thus concluded that the 1970 Commission's descriptions of pornography are now "starkly obsolete," and that a fresh examination of the problem is necessary.

"More than in 1970, when the President's Commission on Obscenity and Pornography issued its Report, and indeed more than just a year ago in 1985, we live in a society unquestionably pervaded by sexual explicitness."
Report, Chapter 4

THE PORNOGRAPHY INDUSTRY . . .

Making, packaging and selling "hard-core" pornography has become an enormous business—and has come out of the closet. The Commission's research disclosed a wide range of crucial facts about the sex industry and its operations, including:

• 80 percent of the production of "hard-core" material occurs in the Los Angeles area.

• Profit margins in the pornography in-

dustry are extremely high, from 200 to over 1000 percent depending on the nature of the material.

• Videotape is rapidly replacing film in the "hard-core" industry because it is far cheaper and produces extraordinary profits.

• Hundreds of "hard-core" pornographic magazines are published each month, with over 50,000 titles currently available.

• Performers used to make commercial pornography are generally young and economically desperate, are sometimes recruited and managed through use of physical force, are generally "used up" quickly and left with heavy drug habits, little money, and no means of emotional or financial support.

"After consideration of the evidence presented, we conclude that those who exploit women's vulnerability in the production or consumption of pornography are inflicting harm that profoundly violates the rights of women, damages the integrity of the American family and threatens the quality of life for all men and women."
Commissioners Judith Becker, Ellen Levine, and Deanne Tilton-Durfee

. . . AND ORGANIZED CRIME

Perhaps the Commission's most important finding of all with regard to the pornography industry centered on the dominant role of organized crime. The Commission found that "significant parts of the pornography industry are controlled by organized crime." More specifically, the Report declares that "major portions" of the industry "seem to be as much a part of La Cosa Nostra as any of their activities." Reuben Sturman, operating out of Cleveland, was found to head perhaps the biggest organization to distribute pornography, but members of the Columbo, De

Cavalcante, Gambino and Luchese "families" are also actively involved.

To reach these conclusions the Commission relied on extensive reports from the F.B.I. and state law enforcement officials, as well as information from inside informants. An appendix to the Report includes a complete description of the largest federal investigation of the pornography industry—the "MIPORN" investigation from 1977 to 1980—which exposed the link to organized crime. Ultimately the Report flatly rejected the conclusion of the 1970 Commission that organized crime was not involved in the pornography industry. And it listed other crimes, ranging from murder to drug trafficking to money laundering, that have been committed by elements of organized crime to preserve its control over the industry.

> "Organized crime involvement in pornography is indeed significant, and there is an obvious national control directly, and indirectly by organized crime figures of that industry in the United States. Few pornographers can operate in the United States independently without some involvement with organized crime."
>
> F.B.I. Report (1978)

THE HARMS OF PORNOGRAPHY

The most difficult, the most controversial, and the most important task which the Commission faced was determining what harms, if any, are "caused" by pornography. The Commission stressed in its Report that every social "harm"—for example, an increase in crime or a decrease in family stability—has many "causes." The question considered was, therefore, only whether pornography plays *some* role in causing harm.

Certain harms were easy to see. The brutal exploitation of children, teenagers, and vulnerable adults in the *making* of pornography is fully described and strongly condemned in the Report. The domination of the industry by organized crime means that it is a center of violence and fraud. The display of pornography to unwilling or unsuspecting viewers—or worse, to children—was condemned as harmful by all Commissioners.

A more difficult issue was whether the wide circulation of sexually explicit material in this country contributes to violence—and especially to violence against women. The Commission concluded (by a vote of 9 to 2) that two different types of pornography are likely to increase sexual violence against women: (1) sexually explicit material which includes scenes of violence; and (2) sexually explicit material which shows the degradation, humiliation or subordination of women. In reaching this conclusion the Commission relied heavily on evidence from the social sciences as well as evidence from a wide range of law enforcement officials and victims of violence.

These types of materials—which in the Commission's view represent the bulk of commercial pornography—were also found to foster harmful attitudes toward women. Violent and degrading pornography teaches that women are inferior beings, created only to satisfy the sexual needs of men. The Commission, based on the evidence from social science and other sources, found this teaching to be a powerful shaper of attitudes which promote (along with many other factors) discrimination against women.

On other questions of "harm" resulting from pornography, the Commissioners did not reach full agreement. Many found the attitudes promoted by pornography to be a serious threat to family life. Many feared that pornography threatens the concepts of privacy and intimacy in sex—thus

251

threatening all healthy sexuality. And many believed, finally, that pornography harms the moral environment of American life. All agreed that non-degrading depictions of simple nudity are harmless, and that sexually explicit materials may be useful in legitimate sex education and sex therapy.

"There is a direct casual relationship between exposure to aggressive pornography and violence against women."
Professor Edward Donnerstein

"The type of material found in mass circulation sex magazines may encourage or legitimate rape."
Dr. David Jaffee & Professor Murray Straus

"Pornography's greatest harm is caused by its ability — and its intention — to attack the very dignity and sacredness of sex itself."
Commissioner Bruce Ritter

RECOMMENDATIONS FOR ACTION

The Commission found clear harms in most current pornography, but it also found that there is "striking underenforcement" of the laws against obscenity. While not recommending any change in the standards for judging sexual material, the Commission did urge a broad range of actions against harmful pornography that is not protected the First Amendment. Among its recommendations to legislatures, law enforcement officials, and citizens are the following:

Government Officials
• Impose stricter penalties on those who regularly traffic in obscene pornography, particularly violent and degrading pornography.
• Enact laws to keep hard-core, obscene pornography off home cable television and off home telephone service.

• Amend federal and state laws to allow forfeiture of profits from, and property used in, illegal sale of obscene pornography.
• Prosecute obscenity cases more vigorously, while providing badly needed training to prosecutors and police.
• Coordinate federal, state and local law enforcement efforts carefully, especially in cases involving organized crime.
• Provide protection for performers against exploitation in making pornography.

Private Citizens
• Assert First Amendment rights of private citizens to condemn material he or she believes offensive or harmful.
• Protest, where appropriate, near establishments selling harmful pornography.
• Consider use of consumer boycotts as a method to discourage marketing of harmful pornography.

"Those who find the image of women portrayed in some pornography to be a grotesque caricature, those who feel its message of casual sexuality to be inconsistent with their cherished values, and those who resent the overt display of activity they consider private, have the right to critique the material and to urge its disuse by all persons."
Barry Lynn, American Civil Liberties Union

"A great deal of contemporary pornography constitutes an offense against human dignity and decency that should be shunned by the citizens, not because the evils of the world will thereby be eliminated, but because conscience demands it."
Commissioner Park Elliot Dietz

CHILD PORNOGRAPHY

In considering the issues presented by most pornography, the Commissioner were faced with raging debate and some times doubtful evidence. In one area, though, they found nearly universal agreement: children and teenagers should not be sexually abused to make pornography. Evidence from law enforcement officials indicated that a large underground traffic in child pornography still exists in this country. Children who are seduced or forced to have sex with adults often are photographed for purposes of blackmail and for the later gratification of their abuser and others. Adult and child pornography are used to lower the inhibitions of children: If the people in the picture are having sex, why don't you?

Over half of the Commission's recommendations, consequently, focused on protection of children. Stronger law enforcement, stricter sentences, and far greater levels of sensitivity and services to child victims were strongly urged. Most importantly, new laws against *possession* of child pornography were recommended to prevent is use as a tool of seduction and blackmail. The existence of child pornography in the hands of pedophiles guarantees that more children will be sexually abused in the future.

The Commission also made a dramatic call for outlawing the use of any young person under age 21 in pornography. If older teenagers are not old enough to drink or to serve as officers in the military, the Commission reasoned, they are not old enough to make a decision—appearing in a pornographic movie or magazine—that may haunt them forever.

The Commission found that children and youths used in pornography are extremely vulnerable and are likely to suffer severe long-term damage from the experience. Young children are generally helpless in the hands of a determined abuser, and teenagers who turn to pornography are usually runaways who are alone and desperate. Calling child pornography a "special horror," the Commission's Report asked those who are divided on other aspects of the problem of pornography to put aside their differences in this area. The Report, declared, finally, that "dealing with child pornography in all of its forms ought to be treated as a governmental priority of the highest order."

"[Child] pornography literally makes the child's body 'available' for anyone willing to pay the price anywhere in the world."
Dr. Ulrich Schoettle, Child Psychiatrist

"I can't tell you how tragic their lives are."
Commissioner Bruce Ritter,
on children used in
prostitution and pornography

NO

Shadow Commissioners Baron, Lynn, Money, Staples, Straus, and Zilbergeld

THE MEESE COMMISSION REPORT DISTORTS THE SCIENTIFIC EVIDENCE

BARRY LYNN

Fathers Who Know Best

I spent much of the last year stalking the pornography commission, commenting regularly on their inadequacies and criticizing the civil liberties dangers posed by many of their proposals. The zaniness of the pornography commission was, of course, so inspired that it will provide the grist for a lifetime of my censorship lectures. Who can forget the FBI agent detailing the photographs he seized in his career, including the terrifying one of a "woman surrounded by a vagina"? How about the commissioner discussing a recently viewed bestiality slide of a man and a chicken and who queried, after noting it was but a "small point," whose penis was in whom (or what)? When the laughter ends, though, the real tragedy of the commission starts to become visible.

This body was not encumbered with the need to accept Supreme Court-articulated limitations on the availability of sexual material. They were writing on a clean slate and could have chosen to repudiate, as did their predecessor commission, the archaic constraints of "obscenity" law and let consenting adults see what they choose, regardless of whether their neighbors would be offended by it.

Instead, they tried to breathe new life into "obscenity" regulation. They applauded the most dangerous reasoning of all to suppress speech—that it generates bad "attitudes." I'm convinced that much pornography does generate bad attitudes, along with much in cartoon shows, floor-wax advertising and network sitcoms. But when in this battle against "bad attitudes" we abandon what we view as affirmative alternative speech and turn instead to use of governmental censorship or moral mob rule, we are all the losers.

The commission could not really discover much more than a smidgen of science to bolster the claims of real-life sexual violence caused by pornography. No matter. They simply filled in the gaps of science with the legion of their own preconceptions and intuitions buttressed with some Gestalt derived from the sometimes plaintive, sometimes pathetic, voices of alleged "victims" of pornography.

Many of their "victims" were obsessed "addicts," one of whom claimed to have seen a deck of pornographic playing cards and then became obsessed with stealing *Playboy* and, finally took to sexually abusing the family dogs; and the rapists who sought to explain away their crime and guilt by scapegoating a medium more contemporary than comic books and more plausible than the Twinkies which drive Dan White to murder. The *victims* also included women so mired in abusive relationships steeped in pathology, substance abuse and family crisis that claimed causality from pornography was so tangential as to be nearly an invisible afterthought.

They could have endorsed things which would have made a difference to real "victims" of the rampant abuses of a still sexist culture—strengthening sexual harassment laws; removing spousal immunity in sexual-assault cases; providing real help to those actually coerced into pornography. And then to prevent the creation of future "victims," they could wholeheartedly have embraced a serious sex-education program in our schools. Instead, they launched a national crusade against dirty pictures, as if they had some magical powers to corrupt the young, obliterate the values taught by the other institutions in our culture and preserve a dying patriarchy. I am underwhelmed by pornography's power to do any of these.

They were, on balance, quintessential censors, sharing all the arrogance of censors throughout the world and throughout our history. They truly believed that they knew best what all should see about sex—and most even knew how all should "behave" sexually as well. Moreover, although they have wallowed in the worst of pornographic muck for a year and been apparently unaffected, they remain convinced that the average American would be led down the path to criminality or deviance by his or her chosen encounters with the same material.

Here is a group that says it would be "socially harmful" if people picketed the bookseller hawking [James Joyce's] *Ulysses*—a book nearly as unreadable as the turgid prose of the commission's report—but embraces with all their hearts the boycotters of stores which hustle *Penthouse* from behind the counter. Let the elite read; keep the masses from even looking. Historically, there was no "obscenity" law before the printing press finally gave average people a chance to see the sexually explicit material previously available only to the wealthy and powerful, who undoubtedly thought only they could handle it.

The 1,000-page report they wrote was so predictable, it could have been drafted the day after the commission convened and saved the taxpayers a good $500,000. But the particular way it was styled is clever to a fault, slippery enough to be cast [aside] if it becomes too much of a personal or professional embarrassment. It sometimes reads like a scientific discourse and occasionally like a legal treatise. Mostly, though, it crows like some elephantine moral tract passed out at the bus station. . . .

I believe it was the commission which ultimately neutralized itself—its methods for gathering evidence, evaluating it and finally reporting it were so intellectually indefensible that it sank from its own irrelevance and irresponsibility.

DR. JOHN MONEY

A Conspiracy Against Women

The Meese commission report purports to be a modern-day Saint George, slaying the evil dragon of pornography to protect women from its violent and degrading effects. But the real intent of the report is not to protect women, but to exploit them. By adopting the militant-feminist rhetoric of Catharine MacKinnon and Andrea Dworkin, the Meese commission affirms that women have no right to be sexual. They are obliged only to be loving wives committed to their men, whom they must treat not as sex, but as status and success, objects.

The Meese report turns out to be a conspiracy against women—the most furtively sexist and antifeminist document of our time. It declares that women are so morally delicate that they may not partake with men of the explicit depiction of the frankly erotic. Can you believe it? Even the sexual normalcy of the naked human body and of healthy, happy people having joyful sexual intercourse must be suppressed, lest it lead the viewer downward on the ladder of degeneracy to the warped and pathological sex of violence and degradation.

With women excluded, men will not, of course, relinquish pornography, for by nature's decree they are dependent on their eyes more than women are to get turned on sexually. As they did with alcohol under Prohibition, men will simply take pornography back to where it used to be, distributed commercially by bootleggers on the nontaxable underground market and seen in locker rooms and at stag parties restricted to men only. Women once again will be divided into Madonnas and whores, lust belonging only to the whores, not to the sexually neutered Madonnas. The deceptive purpose of the Meese report is to deny women's equality with men; and to put women back in their traditional place, unliberated, dependent on men and under men's patriarchal protection.

It is not surprising that the commission

split, 9-2, and that the two dissenting voices are those of two of the four women commissioners. Ellen Levine and Judith Becker had the wit to perceive the overall effect of the report in subjugating women, and the wisdom to recognize that it is just plain foolish to attribute all the injustices of women's inequality in society to dirty pictures.

That does not mean that the two dissenting voices condone the kind of pornography which the report classifies as violent and degrading and which medicine and science classify as paraphilic and pathological. This kind of pornography is erotically useless to people who do not have the particular paraphilia that it depicts. The report singles out for special mention urophilia, the paraphilia in which a man or a woman is turned on and climaxes sexually not in the usual way, but by being urinated upon and drinking urine. People who are not urophiliacs could be locked in a viewing room and forced to watch 50 hours—or 500 hours—of urophilic movies, but they would not be turned into urophiliacs as a result of the experience. If you don't believe that statement, then try the experiment.

Paraphilias are not contagious. They are not caught from books, films or videotapes. The contagion theory is as old as the theory of witchcraft. Less than three centuries ago, people, mostly women, were being burned at the stake because of it. Today they are imprisoned—at exorbitant taxpayer expense, one should be reminded. The commission was given expert testimony on the falsity of the contagion theory, but it elected to disregard the evidence of its own experience. If the contagion theory were correct, then the commissioners should by now all be imprisoned as sex criminals, for they have been exposed to large quantities of all varieties of pornography, violent, degrading and otherwise.

By clinging to the ancient falsehood of the contagion theory, the report evades what should have been its major responsibility, namely, finding out how to prevent the development of paraphilias, especially those that it classified as violent or degrading, in the generation of children now growing up. A boy does not need to look at pornography to know what turns him on sexually. Nature presents him with his own personal pornography in his wet dreams. Developmentally, the sequence is from wet dreams and masturbation fantasies to homemade pornography that copies the dream content and possibly, as he grows older, to commercial pornography—but only if he finds the type of commercial pornography that matches his own wet-dream and masturbation fantasies. Any other type, no matter how much it may stimulate someone else, will leave him cold.

Girls at puberty do not have the same dramatic experience of seeing pornography vividly and visually as the accompaniment of a wet dream. Only a few girls have explicit sexual dreams with orgasm, at the time of puberty. This is one reason, and a very powerful one, why females, by and large, do not understand the male's interest in and arousal by visually explicit pornography. Women's pornography is different. It is more verbal, more romantic and centered more on cuddling, hugging, kissing and the sense of touch.

Children who grow up sexually healthy develop a healthy, usually heterosexual, mental "lovemap" in their brains (see J. Money, Lovemaps, New York, Irvington, 1986). They become the future purchasers of normal, healthy pornography. Children, especially boys, who fail to develop a healthy lovemap are those who are sex-

ually traumatized while growing up. The greatest single source of traumatization is the brutal punishment and humiliation of children who are discovered playing with their own genitals or engaging in normal sexual rehearsal play with playmates. Traumatic punishment of children for obeying nature's way of preparing for healthy sexuality in maturity vandalizes the lovemap and either destroys it or turns it into a paraphilic one. Not unexpectedly, brutal punishment of childhood sexual rehearsal play introduces brutality and violence into the lovemap, thus creating a person who will grow up to be dependent on violence for sexual arousal and climax. This is the person who becomes a patron of violent pornography.

Because the commission does not address the issue of the origins of pornographic imagery, and because it advocates an escalation of punishment related to pornography, its report will prove to be self-defeating. Instead of protecting women, the report will have the long-range effect of actually producing an ever-expanding epidemic of violence and degradation presently evident not only in pornography, but also in reality. The next generation, and the next, will hold us all accountable.

DR. ROBERT STAPLES

The Black Response
As the black member of the "shadow commission," I am indebted to the opponents of sexual fascism for giving me a chance to express the black view on pornography—an opportunity denied by the government-formed commission. Although we represent 35 million American citizens or one in nine inhabitants of this country, the attorney general did not see fit to include one of us among his carefully selected commission. This is hardly sur-

257

prising considering that Ed Meese is a known adversary of the black community. Perhaps he thought blacks were too perverse to ever agree that porn debased women, destroyed the family and caused violent rapes and sexual promiscuity. More likely he realized that it would be difficult to find a black representative of his/her community who viewed porn as a major issue. In one sense, we were relieved that Meese's attention was diverted from restoring us to our nineteenth-century status and that instead he had decided to concentrate on regulating what all Americans can do in the privacy of their own homes. To that extent, he has become an equal-opportunity enforcer of the denial of human rights to all members of this society.

Most blacks would agree with Dr. Morris Lipton, one of the experts on the 1970 presidential report on pornography, that "given the major issues of the day, pornography is a trivial issue." Blacks would add to that analysis the caveat that porn is a white man's problem—a particular kind of white man's problem. The presidential commission Dr. Lipton served on found that the typical consumer of porn was a white male and that blacks were under-represented among the purveyors of erotica. However, blacks were not total abstainers from porn consumerism. Nor did they harbor any particular antipathy toward it. Indeed, many today do buy sex videocassettes, purchase *Penthouse* and enjoy risqué jokes, cartoons, etc. But as a group that earns only 56 percent of the income whites do, they often do not have the discretionary income with which to purchase erotica.

As for the black position on porn, it would certainly differ from that arrived at by the Meese commission. Meese and his minions reflect a particular white world-view that there is something inherently damaging and sinful about sexual activity and interest outside the marital bedroom, and that any participation in other kinds of sexual behavior should produce enormous amounts of guilt in the errant individual. Blacks have traditionally had a more naturalistic attitude toward human sexuality, seeing it as the normal expression of sexual attraction between men and women. Even in African societies, sexual conduct was not the result of some divine guidance by God or other deities. It was secularly regulated and encompassed the tolerance of a wide range of sexual attitudes and behaviors. Sexual deviance, where so defined, was not an act against God's will but a violation of community standards.

Rather than seeing the depiction of heterosexual intercourse or nudity as an inherent debasement of women, as a fringe group of feminists claims, the black community would see women as having equal rights to the enjoyment of sexual stimuli. It is nothing more than a continuation of the white male's traditional double standard and paternalism to regard erotica as existing only for male pleasure and women only as sexual objects. Since that double standard has never attracted many American blacks, the claim that women are exploited by exhibiting their nude bodies or engaging in heterosexual intercourse lacks credibility. After all, it was the white missionaries in fourteenth century Africa who forced African women to regard their quasi-nude bodies as sinful and placed them in clothes. This probably accounts for the rather conspicuous absence of black women in the feminist fight against porn. Certainly black men were unlikely to join with the likes of lunatic feminists such as Catharine MacKinnon and Andrea Dworkin, who treat pornography as discrimination against women.

The black community represents organic evidence against some of the assumptions of the Meese commission on pornography. If porn is alleged to lead to male sexual aggression, that is, rape, why are the lowest consumers of porn (blacks) so over-represented among those arrested for and convicted of rape? A porn commission without a political axe to grind might have concluded that when other expressions of manhood such as gainful employment and economic success are blocked, those men will express their frustration and masculinity against women. In other words, it is the denial of economic rights, not porn, that is in large part responsible for rape in this country. Such a conclusion would not go down well with the Reagan administration, whose policies have led to the burgeoning number of unemployed black males.

As for the Meese commission view that porn is related to sexual promiscuity, it is almost a laughable finding in the black community. One man's sexual promiscuity is another man's definition of sexual freedom. In most cases it refers to keeping women in their sexual straitjackets so that sexual pleasure remains a male domain. The black community has exhibited a lusty sexual appetite while obeying certain rules of common sense and propriety in its sexual conduct. The kinds of kinky sex favored by a small minority of whites is almost unknown among the black population. Group sex, and sexual crimes other than rape, were and are rare among us. And a recent survey commissioned by the National Institutes of Health found that sexually active black women were more likely to be involved in long-term "serious" relationships than were sexually active white women, and that their serious relationships lasted longer than the relationships of white women.

Still, it is one of the ironies of American life that the one racial group in the U.S. whose image is so strongly linked to sexuality in the public mind should be excluded from a commission dealing with the sexual aspects of human behavior. Ranging from the thousands of lynchings of black men for the dubious sin of lusting after white women to the segregation of races in the South to prevent interracial sexual contact, we now have the more recent variation on the theme of black immorality.

While there may be cause for concern over the high rate of out-of-wedlock births occurring among black women in their teenage years, the Meese commission refused to endorse the best weapon against teenage pregnancy—sex education. The same National Institutes of Health survey discovered that twice as many single black women as white women hare having sex through their 20s without contraceptives. Nationally, a majority of all out-of-wedlock births occur among black women. Ultimately, blacks suffer more and are the chief victims of white sexual guilt. They are denied sex education in the public schools because a white-controlled bureaucracy either denies it to the school system or forces it to contain a largely moral content. However, in those few public schools that have decided to provide contraceptive services to their students, only schools with a predominantly black student body have chosen to do so. Using black high-school students as the first guinea pigs in these experiments is akin to the same kind of white colonialism that tested birth-control products on Puerto Rican women to see if they would be safe for white women.

Teenage pregnancy is a problem in the black community because the unwed mothers keep their children and many become dependent on public assistance. The

N.I.H. survey found that half of the white women surveyed and only one-tenth of the black women aborted their first pregnancies. Young black women seldom resort to shotgun weddings, because their pool of potential husbands largely consists of young and unemployed black males. Were they to be provided a sound sex education or safe contraceptives, many would never face this dilemma.

The kinds of morals that Ed Meese and Ronald Reagan understand are related to nineteenth-century notions of sin. . . .

Their past record is one of supporting racial segregation and black deprivation. Therefore blacks can only hope they will cease to interfere with the private lives of American citizens and adopt a real moral posture toward the conditions of poverty, nuclear disarmament and the conduct of government. Permitting poverty to exist and escalating the nuclear-arms race are the real sins and major issues of today.

DR. BERNIE ZILBERGELD

Porn As Therapy

Pornography has one great value that is often overlooked—its use in enhancing marital sex. Pornography can help to strengthen not only individual marriages, but perhaps the very institution of marriage itself. The importance of satisfaction in a good marriage is supported by scientific research and is recognized by many Christian ministers. Millions of ordinary married Americans benefit from erotica and will suffer if it is taken away from them.

Why do so many people refuse to admit that keeping sex interesting, exciting and satisfying in a long relationship is not easy? Couples have to work at it, using whatever aids they can find. Vacations without children, sharing fantasies and open communication are reliable ways to rejuvenate a marriage. Equally valuable is the sharing of erotic materials. It would be tragic if this loving opportunity were denied them.

Dr. June Reinisch, director of the Kinsey Institute, frequently gets letters like this: "My wife and I belong to the church, have three children and do everything right. But once a week we like to spice up our private lives with an erotic video. Why are people trying to take them away from us?" I hear similar things all the time from clients and others who talk to me about sex.

Many people in traditional marriages have turned to erotic films, books and magazines to enhance their sex lives. These people recognize that it is no easy matter to keep ennui at bay over a long period. Before turning to erotica, these spouses made love infrequently, found it either boring or unexciting and realized that much of their sexual desire was directed at people other than their partner. But they did not want to have affairs. Rather they preferred to rekindle passion for their own spouse.

Such couples often report that watching an erotic film, usually on a VCR in their own bedrooms, or reading sexual letters and articles in magazines like *Penthouse* or *Playboy*, leads to more frequent and more intense sex.

Obviously, erotic materials are not for everybody. Some people are turned off by them rather than on. I simply want to emphasize the popularity of erotica among many traditional couples.

Other benefits of pornography include learning specific sexual techniques and getting ideas about how and where to have sex with their partners.

Exposure to sexually explicit materials also leads to more open communication about sex. "I've always wanted to try that," or "Have you ever fantasized anything like this?" are common reactions to viewing pornography. Such honest conversations usually lead to increased closeness and better sex. I have found that exposure to erotica is one of the best ways to improve sexual communication between a man and a woman. Even if a person's initial reaction is "I could never imagine doing that," a useful dialogue often results. It's a scientifically proven fact that talking about sex plays an important part in a good sex life.

Most of what I have learned about the benefits of erotica comes from middle-aged churchgoers who believe strongly in monogamy and family. Some acknowledge that they would be tempted to have affairs if they failed to put some zest into their marital sex. Contrary to what the critics of erotica maintain, these people are using pornography to strengthen their marriages. But all the negative publicity about pornography causes them to be apologetic or embarrassed about discussing it. Even though they know its value in their own lives, they still feel that perhaps it indicates a defect in their personalities or in their love for one another.

Therapists who work with couples' sex problems are also familiar with the benefits of erotica. It's probable that more than half of all sex therapists recommend explicit sexual materials to their clients. A fair amount of research indicates that exposure to sexual materials increases both a couple's tolerance of the sexual behavior of others and desire for one another.

Personally I find the vast bulk of erotica to be poorly presented and boring. But I cannot deny the rewards it has brought to many American couples. It is sad to think that this gift may be taken away.

DR. LARRY BARON
AND DR. MURRAY A. STRAUS

Two False Principles

In 1970 the President's Commission on Obscenity and Pornography concluded that there was no evidence demonstrating that sexually explicit materials caused sex crimes. In the intervening years, those who wanted to limit pornography claimed that sex magazines and movies had become increasingly explicit and violent and that new research has invalidated the finding of the 1970 president's report. On the basis of this assumption, Attorney General Meese mandated his 11-member commission to study a wide variety of pornographic materials, document adverse effects and devise new strategies to curb its proliferation. True to its assignment, the Meese commission concluded that pornography is harmful and urged law-enforcement agencies to crack down on those engaged in the production and sale of obscene materials.

Ironically, the new and more sophisticated research reviewed by the commission makes a causal connection between sexually explicit materials and rape even *less* plausible than it was when the 1970 commission was examining this issue. How then could the Meese commission come to this conclusion? The answer is fairly clear. It is based on two principles.

The first principle is that explicit depiction of sex is offensive and harmful in and of itself. Based on this principle, there is no way of coming to any other conclusion than that pornography should be forbidden. Although the two commissioners (Judith Becker and Ellen Levine) who dissented from the final report lamented that the commission was not granted sufficient time and money with which to properly assess the testimony and reports made available to them, in light of the principle that sexually explicit materials are inherently offensive, more time and money would not have made much of a difference.

The second principle underlying the commission's conclusions and its recommendations to vigorously prosecute those who produce and sell obscene materials is to base conclusions on the "totality of evidence." This is a code phrase which means that the commission gave as much credence to the testimony of fundamentalist preachers, police officers, antipornography zealots and putative victims of pornography as it did to the results of carefully conducted social research. The "totality of evidence" also gave the commission an escape hatch to disregard the warnings and interpretations of researchers whenever they suggested that the findings do not support a causal connection between pornography and rape, In fact, that was the fate of our own research at the hands of the Meese commission.

We found that rape rates are higher in states with a large readership of sexually explicit magazines. That impressed the commissioners. However, they were not impressed by our explanation that this correlation was most likely the result of a common factor which underlies both sex-magazine-readership rates and rape, nor by our recent demonstration that when appropriate statistical controls are introduced, the correlation between sex-magazine-readership rates and rape rates no longer holds.

There are many such "spurious" (i.e., noncausal) correlations. For example, there is a very high correlation between the reading ability of children and their shoe size, but having big feet does not cause children to read better. The underlying factor is the child's age—older children read better and also have bigger feet. If age is statistically controlled, then the correlation between shoe size and reading ability does not hold. Similarly, we pointed out that there are underlying social and demographic factors which cause both high rape rates and high sex-magazine readership. How does the commission report deal with such information? By ignoring our warnings and arguing that: "The absence of evidence should by no means be taken to deny the existence of the causal link." The commission is so bent on showing harmful effects that when the research shows none, they argue that harm simply has not yet been uncovered.

Our view of the totality of the *scientific* evidence is that it shows no causal relationship between pornography and rape. Indeed, Donnerstein's experimental studies show a *reduction* in aggression following exposure to pornography without violent content; and Berle Kutchinsky's recent studies of nations that have removed restrictions on pornography shows either no increase in the rape rate for the years after the legalization of pornography, or a decrease in the rape rate. Of course, there are aggressive and violent people who use sex as a means of expressing aggression, but images of sex do not cause such violence.

The commission probably began its inquiry assuming that the research conducted since the 1970 pornography report would support its belief in the harmfulness of pornography. Instead it was confronted by evidence which shows that the roots of violence are to be found in violence, not in sex, no matter how explicit or "offensive" it may be. The commission ignored or distorted that evidence because, in our opinion, it was more concerned with censoring sexual depictions than with eliminating violence against women.

POSTSCRIPT

DOES THE ATTORNEY GENERAL'S REPORT CLEARLY DOCUMENT THE HARM PORNOGRAPHY DOES?

Comparisons between the 1970 and 1986 presidential commissions on pornography are inevitable. The contrasts are clear in their mandates, in the commissioners themselves, in the ways in which they conducted their hearings and gathered evidence, and in their conclusions.

One of the most controversial aspects of the Meese commission began with the testimony of the Reverend Donald Wildmon, founder of the National Federation of Decency, implicating 26 major American corporations in the "distribution of pornography." His conclusions became part of a staff-prepared draft document circulated by the commissioners. The draft briefly chronicled the alleged involvement of CBS, Ramada Inns, Coca-Cola, *Time* Inc., and other companies in "marketing" pornography through their associations with cable television. Rite-Aid, K-Mart, 7-Eleven and other firms were alleged to be involved in marketing pornographic magazines. A letter including these charges was sent to all the companies named, stating that a failure to respond within 30 days would be taken by the commission as agreement that the charges were valid. The letter also stated that the final report of the commission would contain a specific listing of purveyors of pornography. Shortly after the letter was sent, several companies, including 7-Eleven, Rite-Aid and People's Drugs announced they would no longer sell *Penthouse, Playboy* and *Forum* magazines. In May 1986, *Penthouse, Playboy* and the American Booksellers Association sued the commission.

At present, the only data available on the alleged causal connection between sexual violence and exposure to pornography is either incomplete or inconclusive. In one study, Shadow Commissioners Baron and Straus compared rape rates with the availability of pornography measured by the circulation rates for eight leading men's magazines state by state. Utah and Missouri which rank the lowest, 50th and 49th, in the availability of pornography rank 25th and 18th respectively in the incidence of rape. In contrast, New Hampshire ranks 9th on the availability of pornography and 44th in rape. As Dr. Straus warned the commission, a simple connection between pornography and sexual violence cannot be made. Japan has 2.4 reported rapes per 100,000 population while the United States has 34.5 rapes per 100,000. Yet general circulation magazines and television in Japan show much male and female nudity, though showing the genitals or pubic hair is legally prohibited. At the same time, recurring themes of bondage and rape are common in Japanese pornographic films and novels. Both the Netherlands and Sweden have legalized pornography, and yet both countries have very low rates of rape, child sexual abuse, and teenage pregnancy.

Obviously, neither the 1970 nor the 1984 presidential commissions have settled the question of pornography. See the bibliography for further readings on this subject.

ISSUE 16

WOULD IT BE A MISTAKE TO DECRIMINALIZE PROSTITUTION?

YES: Charles Winick, from "Debate on Legalization of Pornography," *Medical Aspects of Human Sexuality,* September 1979

NO: Depaul Genska, from an essay written for this volume

ISSUE SUMMARY

YES: Charles Winick, coauthor of *The Lively Commerce: Prostitution in the United States,* argues that it would be "extremely foolhardy to base public policy on the temporary or neurotic needs of a very small element of the population." Whether prostitution is legal or illegal, it is always surrounded by an array of socially undesirable third parties, such as pimps, as well as violence, blackmail and drugs.
NO: Depaul Genska, a Franciscan priest, disagrees with Winick and is firmly convinced that the present criminalization of prostitution is immoral, ineffective, and carries an excessive financial price. Decriminalization of prostitution, Genska argues, is the least immoral and most acceptable alternative.

Roman men attending sporting events in the local coliseum also found prostitutes plying their trade under the lower arches or fornixes of the stadium. Their customers became known as fornicators. In Greece, Rome, and medieval Europe, fornication and prostitution were socially tolerated, regulated and taxed.

While fornication may not have been socially accepted in the early 1600s, neither English nor American common law recognized it as a crime. In Pilgrim times, Massachusetts made fornication a crime in 1692, and "street walking" by single women a crime in 1699. In the 1800s, bawdy houses could be closed as public nuisances, but prostitution was usually taken for granted and tolerated, particularly in the frontier West. In San Francisco, the Gold Rush of 1849 resulted in mansions on Nob and Telegraph Hills where "soiled doves" sold sex to the successful miners while women in one-room cribs took care of those still seeking their fortune.

After the Civil War, a series of laws were proposed to segregate and license prostitutes to operate only in "red-light" districts. The emerging women's suffrage movement stalled this effort, and some states passed laws prohibiting fornication and adultery, but not prostitution. In spite of this, all the states found ways of punishing sex for pay by applying statutes prohibiting "open and gross lewdness." Bawdy houses could be closed as a "public nuisance" and prostitutes arrested for "loitering" or "soliciting." By 1900, prostitution was well-organized with at least one union, the Independent Benevolent Association, organizing pimps and panderers and arranging police protection.

In the early 1900s, Americans were alarmed by the "flood of oriental criminals" entering the United States and setting up opium dens where they could entice or force innocent young ladies into "white slavery." In 1910, this paranoia led Congress to pass the Mann Act, prohibiting any male from accompanying a female across a state border for the purpose of prostitution, debauchery, "or any other immoral purpose."

By 1925, every state had enacted an antiprostitution law. Still, the effectiveness and the social/economic cost of making prostitution a crime has been continually questioned. There are still a few local communities in the West, particularly in Nevada, where houses of prostitution operate as legal businesses. This reality, and the legalization or decriminalization of prostitution in many European countries, provide fuel for the ongoing debate. In the Netherlands and West Germany, prostitutes do not need pimps because they can count on the police for protection. Local physicians and health departments provide prostitutes with regular medical tests and treatment when needed. Like any other citizen, the prostitutes in these countries pay income tax on their earnings. Organized crime, then, has little, if any incentive to become involved as it does in the United States.

In the 1970s, several guilds or unions of prostitutes were organized: a national union, COYOTE (Call Off Your Old Tired Ethics), and sister organizations like CAT in California, DOLPHIN in Hawaii, and PONY (Prostitutes of New York). At an international conference of prostitutes in 1986, considerable attention was paid to the issue of "safe sex" practices which can reduce the spread of AIDS, herpes and other sexually transmitted diseases.

Should the United States keep its present laws making prostitution a criminal offense? Or should we legalize, or at least decriminalize, the world's oldest profession? A serious, honest comparison of prostitution in Europe and the United States and a careful examination of the arguments pro and con could help answer this question.

YES   Charles Winick

LEGALIZING PROSTITUTION WOULD BE EXTREMELY FOOLHARDY

Since prostitution has always been with us, it is often argued that it is an exercise in futility to try to control it. However, the argument that something has existed for a long time and meets human needs is a very questionable one. Merely because something has existed does not make it in any way socially desirable. For centuries slavery was in existence and it appeared to be a very important service in many different countries. However, we now recognize that slavery is unacceptable. . . .

Prostitution has been described as a crime without a victim, but I say the women are victimized. First of all, the call girl, however attractive she may be to writers and movie-makers, represents a very small part of the prostitution population. It's also the part of prostitution which is of least concern to the public, since call girls operate away from where they offend the citizenry.

I've interviewed over 2,000 prostitutes in the United States during the last ten years. It's not a very good job, by and large. The gross income is about what a good secretary might earn, of which they keep a very small percentage.

And while a good secretary may look forward, as her career develops, to various kinds of upward mobility, the prostitute is in one of the very few occupations where the mobility is all downward. She does not become more valuable and more sought after as she becomes older. Her most important asset is her youth.

Furthermore, whether or not it is legal, any business in which there is a large flow of cash invites the attention of a variety of elements connected in some way with the criminal world. There's a large group of people eager to take away her money, and a large group of people that she may be eager to give money to, such as pimps, because of the barrenness of her emotional life.

So we have a situation where the income is relatively low, where a lot of people are interested in taking away much of what money there is, and where the working life, in terms of years, is relatively brief. The prostitute is clearly a "victim."

From, statements by Dr. Charles Winick in "Debate on Legalization of Prostitution," *Medical Aspects of Human Sexuality*, September 1979. Copyright © 1979. Reprinted by permission of Hospital Publications, Inc.

As she gets older, a prostitute will find herself essentially without friends, surrounded by exploiters who have been living off her but who want nothing to do with her once her income begins to decline. She will not have a salable occupation or vocation; she will not have an experience on which she can build, she does not have the opportunity for putting aside money in a conventional way by pension benefits or unemployment insurance or workmen's compensation and the like.

Where is this woman at the age of 30? It's hardly any wonder that every study of prostitutes has reported an enormously high suicide attempt rate. This hardly seems a desirable career line that society should encourage.

There can be little doubt that legalized prostitution would encourage more women to give up relatively poorly paid jobs, perhaps as typists, in favor of the new career. A woman office worker has the possibility of promotion, becoming more valuable to her employer, acquiring new skills, and increases in pay and benefits as she grows older. A prostitute has little likelihood of promotion, of becoming a more valuable employee, or of increasing income as she grows older. If she works as a prostitute only when she is relatively young, what will she do when she reforms, perhaps at 30 or so, to more conventional work? How will she be able to compete with the women who have been developing career skills? . . .

Pimps and other persons profiting from prostitution have existed and do exist whether or not prostitution is legal or decriminalized. In Germany, Holland, and England today, where prostitution is accepted, pimps and procurers flourish. In fact, no twentieth century community has experienced prostitution without an array of third persons who profited from it. It is chimerical to suggest that legalization of prostitution can eliminate exploiters.

Another chimera is that prostitutes can effectively organize themselves into a guild or other regulatory apparatus that will exclude amateurs and freelancers. Whether in London, Paris, Hamburg, or Honolulu, no such machinery has worked. It is too easy for outsiders to find clients, and enforcement of restrictions on client activity is next to impossible.

At one time, up to the 1940s, pimps were indeed necessary for protection from violent clients, for provision of bail and legal assistance, and other supportive services. Today, they seldom carry out such functions. Pimps are seldom available near where prostitutes are working, unless they appear to urge her to greater efforts or check to see if she has slipped into a coffee shop or is other wise taking a break. The pimp is not a social but an emotional necessity because of the thorough demoralization and psychological incapacitation of prostitutes. . . .

I think it would be extremely foolhardy to base public policy on the temporary or neurotic needs of a very small element of the population. There has never been any society where regulated prostitution has worked. Prostitution has never been a completely aboveboard transaction. Many women prostitutes are drug-dependent and enter the vocation in order to get money for drugs. A substantial proportion of other prostitutes use drugs in order to deal with the difficulties and problems of their vocation, often seeking to anesthetize themselves while they are working. Such needs would exist whether or not prostitution were legal. Indeed, legalizing prostitution would foster such tragic adaptations. Furthermore, I would suggest that at the very time that sexual attitudes in general are apparently becoming more liberal, our attitudes toward prostitution should be hardening because of our increasing concern with equality. There is a desire not to encourage people to enter into exploitative and degrading relationships, and prostitution is an exploitative relationship.

Why should we have laws regulating it? Very simply, where you have laws which are enforced reasonably there is a minimum amount of prostitution; it is minimally offensive to the citizens and there is a minimum amount of police corruption and graft in connection with prostitution. Where the laws are on the books but not enforced, there is the most overt streetwalking, with thousands of people accosting persons at all hours of the day and night. . . .

We have a recurrent theme—the difference between what we might deem desirable and what is humanly possible to achieve. If we could get prostitutes to testify against pimps and other exploiters in the courts, that would be very good. Then we could address ourselves to implementing the laws against abuses such as blackmail, forced labor, and the like rather than regulating the mere sale of sex. But in fact because of the emotional ties which prostitutes have with pimps and similar persons, it is almost impossible to get a prostitute to testify against a pimp even after he has rejected her, beat her up, thrown her out, taken all her money, and will not even talk to her.

So, in principle, we should have laws regulating the exploitation of these women, but we know that such laws would not be enforceable because it is important to the woman to be beaten, assaulted, have her money taken away, be supplied with heroin, and so forth. These are part of her complicated emotional relationship with her pimp. So if we eliminated the laws against prostitution and encouraged police to implement the laws against exploitation, nothing would happen. . . .

Prostitution is so emotionally freighted that it seems to me very unlikely that it will ever become an ordinary service occupation like barbering or being a beautician or anything like that. The stigma attracts a type of personality that is often prone to criminality.

There has always been a predatory attitude among many prostitutes toward their clients which legalization is not likely to alter. For decades there's been the "Murphy game," where the customer hands his money over to an intermediary who guarantees to hold it for him while he is with the woman, and then disappears with the money. There's the long history of the "creeper," the person who creeps in while the prostitute is engaged in sexual activity with the client, and goes through his pockets. During sexual activity most men's sensory apparatus is functioning minimally and hearing and vision are severely depressed. We don't as yet have an occupation of providing sexual pleasure to others in an altruistic, devoted spirit. Given the values of our culture, this strikes me as an impossibility. . . .

The contention that some men *need* prostitutes is like the old argument that prostitution is the sewer that the city needs in order to remain clean. We have several studies of what happened to communities before and after prostitution was eliminated. The closing of the brothels had no particular effect on anything, except that the general level of law enforcement increased. The incidence of all crimes appeared to go down, because the existence of prostitution carries with it a certain amount of acceptance of other illegal activity. Therefore, when prostitution ceased many other forms of illegal activity also ceased. As for increases in sex crime— promiscuity, availability of pornography, rape, and so forth—none of that happened. So I don't think we can say that prostitution is a necessary outlet for needs that are not being met in other ways.

Current enforcement of laws against prostitution is indeed hypocritical by being selective and chauvinistic. In 24 states, "customer amendments" make the client as guilty as the prostitute. In most such states, however, the law is not enforced. The woman is arrested, tried, and convicted, but the client is usually set free. Were such laws enforced properly, our ability to control prostitution would be substantially enhanced.

I agree that "social control and rehabilitation" should be the foci of our policy toward prostitution. It is particularly disturbing that rehabilitation is so generally unavailable for those women who wish to leave prostitution. Countries like England have been able to mount and develop dignified and effective programs of resocialization of prostitutes. In this country, "rescue" operations often imply the sinfulness and guilt of the woman and are not set up toward realistic goals. We possess knowledge to conduct thoughtful programs of resocialization, but community ambivalence over such programs has led to their generally being moralistic and underfunded, and of low priority.

The reason for a prostitute's downward mobility is that customers prize youth. As a woman grows older, she is less desirable to customers and less able to earn money. The typical prostitute working in a legal context in Nevada is in her 20s because clients do not want older women. Organization into guilds or unions is not going to force customers to take what they do not want . . . .

NO
Depaul Genska

OUR SOCIETY WOULD BE BETTER OFF IF PROSTITUTION WERE DECRIMINALIZED

. . . THE PRESENT SITUATION: PROSTITUTION IS A CRIME

The present penal code in every state of the United States (with some exceptions in Nevada as regards houses of prostitution), says very clearly that prostitution is a criminal offense. Prostitution is illegal and what leads to it: soliciting, pandering, loitering for the purposes of prostitution (these too are also illegal in Nevada). In every city where I have lived—New York City, Paterson (NJ), Washington (DC), Boston, and now Chicago—hardly a year goes by without the passage of more laws against prostitution in almost every part of the world. And the same reports also confirm that instead of reducing prostitution by more legislation, prostitution proliferates. The present situation is toward prostitution to continue its illegality.

The main obstacle to eliminating or reducing prostitution is finding jobs for prostitutes where they can earn the same amount of money as in prostitution. Most prostitutes cannot obtain other jobs because they are lacking in education or skills. The select group of very highly paid call girls also cannot legitimately equal their earnings.

Other factors are involved in the economics of the prostitution network. There are the houses or hotels used primarily for prostitution, massage parlors, referral agents, recruiters, pimps, hotel clerks, cab drivers, doormen, and rental agents. Often, bribes are paid to many of these people as well as to local police officers. In some cities, prostitution is big business and controlled by organized crime.

To get a better idea of the prostitution business, consider the following facts regarding prostitution.* There are more than 450,000 female prostitutes in the United States, 40,000 working in New York City and 2500 in mid-Manhattan. In 1980, it cost the City of New York $285 to prosecute a woman each time she was picked up on prostitution charges. More than 50 percent of the women in city prisons are convicted prostitutes, and each woman in

*Unfortunately, no financial figures are available more recent than those given here for 1980.

From, an original essay written for this volume by Depaul Genska, OFM. Copyright © 1986 by Depaul Genska. Reprinted by permission of the author.

prison cost the taxpayer $15,000 a year! While the prostitution network derives a staggering income from this "profession," the state and city governments also pay exorbitant sums of money trying to control prostitution. This is one of the major reasons why decriminalization or legalization is strongly supported by many groups.

The fines and prison sentences attached to prostitution are other aspects to consider. About a dozen states have laws with penalties for persons who patronize and use the services of prostitutes. In most of these states the customer's penalty is at the discretion of the judge. In only two or three states can the customer face the remote possibility of a stiff fine, $500 to $1000, or more than a year in jail. The prostitute, on the other hand, is regularly penalized in every state, with prison sentences usually between 1 and 12 months and fines between $100 and $1000. Depending on the state, pimps can get up to 10 or 20 years and stiff fines up to $2000. In the statutes, the operators of brothels or "house of ill-repute" may also, if convicted, be given fines and prison sentences. Usually the fines listed in the statutes are between $100 and $500, although in Indiana it may be only $10 and in Alaska a whopping $5000. Six months to a year is the usual statutory penalty for running a brothel. Overall, the prostitutes are the persons who bear the brunt of these statutory penalties. But, even when convicted, the fines never compensate for the financial cost to the public of prosecution and imprisonment.

A VIEW TO THE FUTURE; LEGALIZATION OR DECRIMINALIZATION

The immediate future regarding prostitution seems to be more laws against it.

There have been, however, efforts and discussion toward other legal ways to cope with the existence of prostitution. Two of the main legal ways are: legalization and decriminalization.

Legalization would make prostitution, now substantially an illegal activity in the United States, a legal activity. The American Bar Association, in discussing what would be necessary to make illegal prostitution a legal activity, lists three essential elements: licensing, taxation, and the taking of a medical examination.

Licensing: to license a prostitute would require some kind of "test." We know what one has to do to get a driver's license. To get a prostitute's license, what kind of "road test" would be required? The thought of this boggles my imagination! That is, perhaps, a rather flippant way to dismiss the licensing aspect. But more seriously and important is that by licensing a prostitute it is established for all time that this particular woman is a prostitute and known to "big brother." No matter what happens to the woman in later life—she retires from prostitution—but there is always the "trump card"—the license to use against her! We know even from personal experience how one's past can come back to haunt.

Taxing: to tax a prostitute would also be counterproductive. Taxes are hardly ever known to decrease, they usually increase (it is almost the nature of a tax to increase). And where does the prostitute get the tax money? She would charge more for her services to pay the government tax. By taxing prostitutes, for all practical purposes the government then becomes the pimp who "lives off of her earnings." How virtuous would a society be living off a "sin-tax"?

Medical examination: the onus of a

medical exam for prostitution would fall on the women only. And if they were examined one day, who knows if they are sexually "safe" the next day? I cannot imagine any man who frequents prostitutes, voluntarily or compelled by law, to submit himself to a medical examination for any sexually transmitted diseases.

And the medical exam of the women prostitutes is, I believe, based on the misinformation that prostitutes are the prime spreaders of venereal diseases. In study after study, the United Nations, among others, state very emphatically that prostitutes are responsible for only 3-5% of the venereal diseases! Prostitution is a prostitutes' profession and if she "isn't safe/fresh, she is out of business!" Many prostitutes take better care of themselves sexually than most other people. Some prostitutes have doctors as clients who as part of the client's payment check out the women medically, perhaps more often than any law would compel them to do.

These three requirements—licensing, taxation, medical examination—in order to make prostitution legal would, I believe, require an enforcement agency far in excess of what the taxpayer is willing and able to support. We cannot now enforce the laws against prostitution, how then can we reasonably suppose that an enforcement agency could enforce the legalization of prostitution? Who would collect the taxes? What would the taxes from prostitution be used for? Who would pay for the medical examination of prostitutes—would it be covered by Blue Cross? Would there be enough medical personnel to examine the "world's oldest profession"? Who would issue the license for prostituting? Would all prostitutes subscribe to the licensing: Wouldn't some women prostitutes fear being licensed lest they be known as prostitutes? Licensing of prostitutes

would not, I think, make prostitutes more socially acceptable to the public. By licensing, some prostitutes would be more widely known, and hence more vulnerable to public harassment.

It is my opinion that legalization of prostitution is not only not the way to proceed with the "world's oldest profession," but legalization would in many ways be worse than what we have now—the criminalization of prostitution in the United States.

DECRIMINALIZATION

By decriminalization of prostitution, I mean the repealing of criminal statutes specifically against prostitution. All laws regarding prostitution as prostitution between *consenting adults* should be nullified. Also here I make a caveat: decriminalization of prostitution in no way implies approval or encouragement for prostitution. Decriminalization is only a way of dealing with prostitution legally. As I stated above, as a Catholic priest from a *moral* perspective, I do not approve of prostitution. From a *legal* perspective however, I believe firmly in not making prostitution a criminal offense. In other words, prostitution should be decriminalized. The present situation now where prostitution is criminalized, I believe it is also immoral; and I would hold the same to be true if legalization of prostitution were enacted against adult forms of prostitution.

Several Catholic organizations already advocate decriminalization of prostitution: NETWORK, Jesuit Prison Chaplains, National Coalition of American Nuns.

I advocate decriminalization of prostitution for several reasons which, to me, are more cogent than those proposed to continue the present criminalization of prostitution, or the legalization of prostitution:

1. Decriminalization already exists at several levels of prostitution—mainly among call girl and escort service types of prostitution, and with the clients (johns) of prostitutes across the spectrum of all forms of prostitution. Most frequently, men (johns) are never arrested, convicted, nor incarcerated for prostitution. When police "busts" are made for prostitution, in the present illegalness of prostitution, 99% of the time, only the women prostitutes are arrested. I have been witness on several occasions when such police raids were made for prostitution, and the men (johns) were told "get lost"; the men faced some harassment, but were never arrested. Prostitution is, however, not something that you do all by yourself; it takes at least two persons—a woman *and* a MAN! By law, prostitution is illegal for both the women and the men, but in the enforcement of the law, there is gross discrimination. Decriminalization would help eliminate this double standard.

2. Some argue, however, that since prostitution is presently illegal for men and women, both then should be arrested. But even if the laws against prostitution were equally enforced, I still do not believe that laws are effective against prostitution—neither for the women nor the men. The laws do not address significantly nor sufficiently the underlying causes of prostitution.

3. Eliminating laws against prostitution, there would be more chances for the persons who really wanted to leave prostitution to do so. Once a woman is arrested for prostitution, let alone convicted and incarcerated, it becomes more difficult—virtually impossible—for her to leave prostitution. She has now been branded with the label (scarlet letter!) of criminal. Her criminal record prohibits her from obtaining legitimate (by society's definition)

employment. Without an arrest record—because prostitution is not a criminal offense in decriminalization—she does not have to admit she is or was a prostitute to anyone.

4. Decriminalization would lessen the need for a woman prostitute to have a pimp. The use of a pimp further compounds a woman's stay in prostitution. Reliance on a pimp to act in her defense (to pay court fees, to take care of business when she is in jail) would be reduced if prostitution were decriminalized. The woman would not be in court nor in jail.

5. My main reason, however, for supporting the decriminalization of prostitution, lies in the fact that in taking away the laws that now prohibit prostitution, society in general and the churches in particular would be faced with the challenge of providing viable alternatives to women who now feel compelled or forced into prostitution. As long as laws against prostitution are on "the books," many persons feel that prostitution is the government's business, the police force task to control this situation. As long as society in general shirk their duty to provide gainful, equitable, equal opportunity for the employment of all its citizens—men and women; and as long as the churches fail to empathize with the "anxieties and agonies" (Gaudium et Spes, Vatican II document, paragraph I) of their sisters and brothers in their struggles to survive (and often are driven to prostitution as their way to do so), and leave to others (government, police) their (the churches') responsibility, and to lean on laws against prostitution as crutches, then prostitutes will continue to prostitute. Until it becomes evident that persons in female prostitution also have a God-given RIGHT to churches' ministrations as so many other groups have (and often after many years!), then

prostitution will proliferate. Until women prostitutes can turn to the churches filled with compassion—and not condemnation nor condescension—then they will have no other places to turn to other than the streets, the brothels, massage parlors for their survival. Places and environments like Genesis House (Chicago) which provide a safe, non-judgmental, nourishing atmosphere for women forced into a de-escalating web of prostitution must increase as viable ways for women to get their shattered lives together—shattered by family violence, societal criminalization, church condemnation. Self-righteous religious people often create an atmosphere in which "Jack-the-ripper and L.A. strangler" types grow to rid society of the "scum-sluts" condemned by church and marginalized by *criminal* laws! Who really is sinning?

As long as law is used as a "wal(l)" law spelled backwards) "protecting" us—the virtuous-non-prostitutes, from them—the sinners-prostitutes, then there will be persons who prostitute. Until we *realize* we are *all* sinners—some in one way, some in other ways, but all sinners nevertheless, we won't *stand together*—women with men, men with women—not some standing/lording it over others, and "throwing stones" at those below. Stones are meant for building, building blocks for more human and humane relationships. Women prostitutes are exploited by men, condemned by men and often by the very men who use the services of prostitutes. And the women prostitutes exploit the loneliness and sexual inadequacy of men. The "battle of the sexes" continues. If there are to be any laws, when do we outlaw "the battle of the sexes," laws making it a "crime to be lonely"? When does love for all men and women become *the* reality so we will stop our charades with one another, and settling for mere illusions?

POSTSCRIPT
WOULD IT BE A MISTAKE
TO DECRIMINALIZE PROSTITUTION?

In summing up this issue some years ago, a United Nations study team came up with a sophisticated list of arguments for and against the treatment of prostitution as a crime.

In support of the prohibition of prostitution, the United Nations team cited the following arguments:

1. It is the responsibility of the government to regulate public morals in the interest of public good; hence, to declare prostitution a punishable offense.

2. If prostitution *per se* is not made a punishable offense, the abolition of the regulation of prostitution will merely replace controlled prostitution by clandestine prostitution.

3. It will be difficult to enforce strictly legal provisions proscribing the exploitation of the prostitution of others when prostitution itself is not considered a punishable offense.

4. Many women and girls on the borderline may be encouraged to take up prostitution if the law does not proscribe such a calling.

5. The absence of any legal provision against prostitution may be interpreted by the public as meaning that the government tolerates commercialized vice as a "necessary evil."

The arguments for decriminalization were summarized as follows:

1. To make prostitution a crime requires defining this activity. If the term "prostitute" is given a wide scope, the fact of making prostitution a legal offense could entail unwarranted interference in private life which would be contrary to the Universal Declaration of Human Rights. If, on the other hand, the term is given too restricted a legal connotation, then it would be difficult to establish the charge against the culprit.

2. Laws against prostitution, even when written to include both parties, in practice penalize only one party, the woman.

3. There is only a difference of degree between prostitution and other sexual relations outside wedlock, and it is unjust to limit the penalty only to persons who meet the arbitrary criteria set forth in the legal definition of prostitution.

4. While laws are needed to maintain public order and protect minors, penal law should not take cognizance of all adult moral violations nor single out adult prostitution for punishment apart from other adult moral violations.

5. Criminalization of prostitution does not reduce or eliminate it. Instead it promotes a ruthless underworld organization that increases exploitation and crime.

6. The prohibitionist policy depends for its effectiveness on a system of police espionage and entrapment which is itself harmful to society.

7. Criminalizing prostitution creates a collective and individualistic antagonism among the perpetrators which hampers the chances of their rehabilitation.

As always with any controversy, the pros and cons need to be weighed and balanced against each other. See the bibliography for further readings on this subject.

ISSUE 17

DOES CHRISTIANITY PROMOTE AN ANTISEXUAL CULTURE?

YES: Vern L. Bullough, from *Sin, Sickness, and Sanity* (New York: New American Library, 1977)

NO: Peter Gardella, adapted from *Innocent Ecstasy: How Christianity Gave America an Ethic of Sexual Pleasure* (New York: Oxford University Press, 1985)

ISSUE SUMMARY

YES: Historian Vern Bullough believes that most of the antisexual attitudes in Western culture can be traced to Christianity's traditional discomfort with sexuality and sexual pleasure, particularly because of its acceptance of a dualistic view of our world.
NO: Peter Gardella, professor of religion, argues that, while sexual pleasure was often condemned as sinful by Christian writers in the past, our recent sexual revolution grew in part from the surprising interaction of Protestants and Roman Catholics within American culture.

Tracing the development of ideas in fragmentary writings scattered across centuries of history can be a fascinating adventure in detective work, but it seldom leads to a definite conclusion about how a particular concept or belief was born and developed over the years or what its influence has been. This is very evident in the debates among historians and theologians over why Western civilization has been so uncomfortable with human sexuality and so ridden with sexual anxieties, taboos and guilt. Why is the Jewish tradition much more comfortable with sexuality than the Christian tradition? What are the differences in sexual attitudes between Protestants and Catholics and where did these differences originate?

Although there are numerous allusions to sexuality in the Bible, there is no single word in Hebrew or Greek for what we know as sex. The Israelites who wrote the books of what later became the Old Testament spoke openly about sexual matters. In the Jewish tradition, sex is not associated with some original sin nor with the exaltation of virginity and celibacy as a way of life. Sexual relations and sexual pleasure were openly viewed as a blessing, a *mitzvah*. Adultery, rape and seduction of virgins are condemned, but not masturbation or contraception. Sex is natural and is not raised into some sacred realm as it is by Christians. Still, the Jewish tradition is very patriarchal. Like every other religious tradition, Judaism and its sacred writings grew out of its own unique ethnic and cultural environment. The prominence of sexual practices in the pagan cults around them, social and economic considerations, a strong respect for women, and care for religious and cultic purity all helped shape Jewish regulations about sexual relations.

Christian attitudes toward sex have likewise changed over the years, as both Bullough and Gardella clearly show in their essays. These changes must be seen against the background of the politics, economics and social structures of the particular eras in which they occurred. Sexual attitudes are but a single thread in a tapestry that brings together a variety of other threads of different hues to create a particular culture.

Jesus often associated with women he met while traveling, ignoring the usual concern of Jewish men for menstrual taboos and cultic purity. He spoke of divorce, adultery and marital fidelity, affirming the rabbinical stand that before God there is no distinction between male and female, but said nothing about contraception, abortion, masturbation, or homosexuality.

The opinions of the Fathers and Doctors of the early Christian Church were nearly unanimous in their condemnation of sex and of women. Methodius said women were naturally "carnal and sensuous," the "irrational half of the human race." For Jerome, woman was "the devil's gateway, a scorpion's dart, the outpost of hell." A medieval couplet recorded by one Cardinal Hugues de St. Cher echoes this antisexual Christian view: "Woman pollutes the body, drains the resources, kills the soul, Uproots the strength, blinds the eye, and embitters the voice."

Is Christianity then responsible for American sexual inhibitions?

YES
Vern L. Bullough

WHY IS CHRISTIANITY
SO HOSTILE TO SEX?

Western culture, at least since the advent of Christianity, has been looked upon as a sex-negative culture, one in which sexual activities have been regarded with suspicion if not hostility. Such attitudes did not emerge full bloom with the advent of Christianity but rather have roots that go much further back into the past and are based upon intellectual assumptions that few could accept today. The major source of these ideas is not so much the Jewish Scriptures known to the Christians as the Old Testament (which in comparison is perhaps more open about certain aspects of sexuality), as it is some of the philosophical beliefs of the pagan Greeks and Romans. In this respect Christianity did not make the world ascetic but rather, in the words of biblical scholar Morton Enslin, the "world in which Christianity found itself strove to make Christianity ascetic."

The source of this Western hostility to sex has been traced to Greek dualistic thought which divided the world into two opposing forces, the spiritual vs. the material, resulting in man having two natures, the higher and the lower, or alternately, in having a soul and a body. Put in its simplest terms, dualism held that the soul was undergoing punishment by being incarcerated in a human body. Man's purpose in life was to achieve salvation, to allow the soul to escape the domination of the flesh. Sex was bad because sexual activity represented the assertion of the bodily needs over the spiritual and by creating children continued the imprisonment of future souls. The origin of these dualistic ideas has been the subject of rather intense scholarly investigation over the past several decades, but as yet there is no unanimity, in part because so many of the earliest references are shrouded in myth and legend. It is quite possible that the ideas go deep into the consciousness of the earliest Indo-European peoples, since both the ancient Persians and the ancient Greeks have some of the same concepts. Though failing to agree on the starting point of this dualistic thought, most scholars believe that the concept became fixed in the Greek-speaking world through the Orphic religion and the cult of the god Dionysus.

Orpheus is usually remembered as the famed musician who so charmed Hades, the god of the underworld, that he was allowed to bring his wife, Eurydice, back from the dead. Through the surviving fragments of information, we believe the Orphic religion taught that the soul was undergoing punishment for sin with the body serving as an enclosure or prison in which the soul was incarcerated. Release and immortality could be achieved by leading a pure life and by engaging in the secret rituals of the Orphic religion. . . .

Though the Orphic mysteries were never officially incorporated into the state religion of classical Greece, they enjoyed a great vogue and exercised considerable influence on the Pythagoreans, on Plato, as well as on the later Greek philosophical-mystical writers, all of whom purged the Orphic dualism of some of its grosser superstitions. Pythagoras, who lived in the sixth century B.C., taught that the universe was ultimately divisible into two opposing principles, one of which he described as Unlimited Breath, the other as Limited. It is with the nature and operations of the latter that the famous Pythagorean teachings that all things are numbers is concerned. Limited and Unlimited are opposites, and this opposition is expressed also in light and darkness, odd and even, one and many, right and left, male and female, resting and moving, straight and curved, good and bad, square and oblong, and so on. Limit, light, odd, and male are right and good, whereas the unlimited, darkness, even, and female are wrong and evil, or at least one set is superior and the other is inferior.

Salvation was to be achieved through a *katharsis;* this required the observance of certain taboos based upon the Orphic concepts that the soul is imprisoned in the mortal body, and the body itself is governed by evil passions which are our indwelling Furies. Pythagoras taught that individuals should not be the slaves of their own bodies but should improve and save their souls by escaping from the domination of the flesh. Since sexual consummation was the prime pandering to the indwelling Furies, every symbol relating to it had to be repudiated. Though Pythagoras himself apparently did not advocate total abstinence, some of his followers did. . . .

The most influential transmitter of these dualistic ideas was Plato (427-347 B.C.) who rejected the cultic aspects of the Pythagoreans while elevating their philosophical ideas. Plato had only contempt for those who taught or believed that a god could be persuaded or bribed to confer blessed immortality upon an initiate merely because he performed special ceremonials, or because he accepted certain doctrines or revelations, or even because he adopted a way of life involving ascetic renunciation. Instead he taught that the moral law was fixed and immutable, that our fate depended upon our actions during life, and that each of us had the power to rise above his Titanic nature. To this end, Plato postulated the existence of two universal principles, Ideas and Matter, which he equated with the intelligible and sensible worlds. Ideas were eternal and immutable, present always and everywhere, self-identical, self-existent, absolute, separate, simple without beginning or end. They were complete, with perfect existence in every respect, without taint of sense or imagery, invisible to the eye, accessible only to the mind. Matter, or the material world of sensible objects, existed only insofar as it caught and retained the likeness of the Idea, but in any case it was always an imperfect imitation.

Most philosophers (following Aristotle) have regarded Plato's concept of the Idea (or Form) as a metaphysical principle existing in and for itself apart from the sensible world and possessing the incorporeal yet quasi substantial sort of being commonly attributed by theologians to Deity. In fact, Christianity adopted so many of the Platonic concepts that Justin Martyr, an early Christian Father, never tired of reiterating that Plato must have been versed in Christian prophecy. Thus Plato, at least through his Neoplatonic interpreters, can be looked upon as the dominant force in Early Christian theology.

Following the lead of Pythagoras, Plato taught that the soul, an immaterial agent, was superior in nature to the body, and was hindered by the body in its performance of the higher psychic functions of life. Reality for Plato had two components—the phenomena, the changeable world of bodies which man can know through sense perception, and the Ideas, the timeless essence or universal realities. It was only the world of Ideas that contained the ultimate realities after which the world of sensible things had been patterned. This world could not be known through the senses but through the *nous,* the mind or soul, which knows because it is the essence of the divine being and had existed before the body. Though the soul had been born with true knowledge, the encrustation of bodily cares and interests made it difficult to recall the truth which was innately and subconsciously present. Sense perception might aid the soul in the process of reminiscence, but only by intuitive thought, only by clearing the mind of bodily concerns, by probing ever deeper by the Socratic method of questions and answers, would it be possible to evoke the necessary recollection.

Plato conceived of love in dualistic terms, dividing it into the sacred and profane, the former occupied with the mind and character of the beloved, the latter with the body. It was only through the higher love, the nonphysical, that true happiness could be found. To reach this highest form there was a step-by-step progression starting with the body of the beloved, then physical loveliness in general, then contemplation of the beauties of the mind and soul, and finally the pure form or essence of loveliness in itself—absolute, separate, simple, and everlasting—which without diminution or increase or change was imparted to the continually growing and perishing beauty of all things.

He compared the types of love to a charioteer driving two winged steeds, one of which (true love) was a Thoroughbred, gentle and eager to bear its driver upward into the presence of the ideal, the other (physical love) vicious and refractory, forever bolting in pursuit of physical satisfaction. The discipline of love lay in training the unruly steed to run in harmony with its Thoroughbred mate. If the charioteer was successful in his training, the team would bear the lover and beloved away from the world of sense to the vision of absolute loveliness that alone made them truly lovely and lovable in each other's eyes. Love, in essence, implied the mutual attainment of self-mastery that cured the disease of physical craving. Copulation lowered a man to the frenzied passions characteristic of beasts, and for this reason Plato relegated sexual desire to the lowest element of the psyche (i.e., soul).

Many other Greek philosophical writers, even those who started with assumptions different from Plato's, seemed to assume that the true state of goodness was one devoid of physical sexual activity. Democritus, the fifth-century proponent of the atomistic nature of the universe, taught that enjoyment of pleasure was the end naturally sought by man. Democritus, however, was no hedonist since he believed that all pleasures were not equally good. . . . Since sexual activity tended to interfere with the pleasures of the mind, he disapproved of such activity. . . . Epicurus, the fourth-century B.C. disciple of Democritus and the founder of the Epicurean school, became even more specific in his condemnation of sex. Sexual intercourse, he held, "never benefitted any man," and he believed that the good life could not result from "sexual intercourse with a woman." . . .

Some Stoics, such as the first-century A.D. Musonius Rufus, went so far as to claim that marital intercourse was only permissible when the purpose was procreative; sexual intercourse for pleasure even within the marriage bed was reprehensible. His contemporary, Seneca, urged the wise man to love his wife with judgment, not with affection. "Let him control his impulses and not be borne headlong into copulation." Seneca cautioned husbands to imitate the beasts and not copulate when their wives were pregnant, to avoid loving a wife like she was an adultress. . . .

By the first century B.C. the center of philosophical speculation in the Graeco-Roman world had shifted to Alexandria in Egypt, and it was here that philosophical speculation became incorporated into religious teaching. Particularly influential on later Christian writers was Philo, an Alexandrian Jew born in the last quarter of the first century B.C. Though Philo accepted Jewish teaching on the necessity to procreate and replenish the earth, he followed the Graeco-Roman philosophic tradition that sexual intercourse could only be justified when there was hope of legitimate offspring. He described those who mated with their wives with no intent of begetting children as being "like pigs or goats." Such an attitude led him to hold that those who mated with barren women deserved condemnation because in their pleasure-seeking they destroyed the "procreative germs" with deliberative purpose. Following Plato, Philo conceived of sex in dualistic terms. The highest nature of man was asexual, in imitation of God, and it was only the irrational part of the soul that contained the categories of male and female and existed in the realm of the sexual. For him the original sin of Adam and Eve was sexual desire, and sexual pleasures were the "beginnings of wrongs and violation of the law." He justified circumcision as necessary to curb man's sexual desires. . . .

It was in this intellectual setting that Christianity appeared, while these ascetic ideas are not particularly influential in the New Testament, the later disseminators of the Christian message drew heavily from these pagan writers. So did the rivals of Christianity, particularly the Gnostics, and since Christianity was competing with Gnosticism and other redemptive cults, it was both influenced by and exercised influence upon its rivals. In fact, it might be suggested that within any particular Christian community—they were spread all over the Mediterranean world—the degree of sexual repression among the Christians was dependent upon the practices of their leading rivals. This helps explain why within Christianity there was a range, if only a slight one, between permitting copulation if motivated by a desire for children to an outright demand for celibacy for all church members. At times it seems that Christian communities tried to gain status and adherents by outdoing their pagan rivals at ascetic practices. Such a hypothesis might also serve as a possible explanation for the ambiguous statement of the physician Galen that the Christian community in Rome during the second century included men and women who, like the philosophers, refrained from "cohabitating all through their lives." . . .

By the end of the second century, the organizational ability of the more orthodox Christians had begun to win the battle for control of Christianity over the group we now associate with Gnosticism. By insisting upon the importance of the community as opposed to individuals, by emphasizing the teachings of the Hebrew Scriptures, yet incorporating pagan philosophy, orthodox Christianity eventually succeeded in overcoming the extremes of Gnosticism. Still, the Christian Church retained a strong undercurrent of hostility to sex, and in this respect was more like the ascetic Gnostic than the earthy Jews who were willing to accept the joys of sex, at least for men. The extent of the Gnostic influence is indicated by the fact that one of the most avid opponents of Gnosticism, Tertullian, stopped just short of condemning intercourse in marriage, actually appearing to be uncertain why God ever permitted it. The Gnostic appeal rested in part on the similarity of the Gnostic attitude to the Christian stress on virginity, with the Gnostics only carrying to logical conclusion what many orthodox Christians seemed to want to believe. Orthodox Christianity, however, hesitated to go quite so far, if only because of the biblical sanction given to marriage.

With the decline of Gnosticism, it would seem that Christianity should have been able to go through a reassessment of its position and tone down some of its extreme antisexuality. That this did not happen was mainly due to the influence of St. Augustine, who was responding to a new religion, Manicheanism, a sort of Gnostic synthesis which for a time presented a renewed threat to Christian dominance. Manicheanism was based upon the teachings of the prophet Mani (216-277 A.D.) who lived and was crucified in southern Babylonia. Mani incorporated into his religious beliefs the teachings of the Gnostics, the Christians, the Zoroastrians, as well as the Greek philosophical ideas of the Neo-Pythagoreans and Neoplatonists. By the time of Mani's death his religion had spread to Egypt, Palestine, Rome and soon afterward it appeared in Asia Minor, Greece, Illyria, Italy, and North Africa. Manicheanism was similar to Christianity in that it had a savior (Mani) and a canonical scripture (the seven books of Mani), claimed to be a universal religion, and had a hierarchy and apostles. Similarly it was a missionary faith and one of its converts, St. Augustine, was for better or worse later to become the most influential teacher in the Western Christian Church about sexuality and marriage. Manicheanism was a dualistic religion combining science, philosophy, and religion in a new synthesis. Although claiming the authority of revelation, the Manicheans also paid the highest deference to reason. . . .

St. Augustine was an adherent of the Manichean faith for some eleven years but never reached the Adept stage, in part because of his difficulties with sex. He remained an Auditor, living with a mistress, and feeling uncomfortable about his inability to control his lustful desires. When he eventually renounced Manicheanism for Christianity, he carried over many of his Manichean ideas about sex; sexual intercourse for him came to be the greatest threat to spiritual freedom.

I know nothing which brings the manly mind down from the heights more than a woman's caresses and that joining of bodies without which one cannot have a wife.

With such attitudes Augustine had difficulty in accepting any kind of sex even though it had biblical justification. He finally concluded that sexual intercourse could only be justified in terms of procreation. Celibacy was the highest good, while intercourse was essentially only animal lust; in marriage, however, and only in marriage was intercourse justified because of the need for procreation. Marital intercourse itself was both good and evil, and it was only through procreation that the evil act became good. All other kinds of intercourse were evil.

With St. Augustine the basic sexual attitudes of the Christian Church were set. Virginity was the preferred state of existence, but for those unable to adapt to this state, marriage was permitted. Within marriage intercourse was tolerated, but only for the purpose of procreation. Although the Christians never quite rejected sex altogether, they felt uncomfortable accepting it, largely because of the biblical sanction. Christian ideas on sex, however, were not primarily derived from any biblical teaching but were based upon the intellectual and philosophical assumptions of the period of its birth, assumptions that must be regarded as the value system of a people lacking any real scientific knowledge. Inevitably Christians became—in spirit if not always in practice—ascetics, justifying sexual activity only in terms of progeny. Inevitably any kind of sexual activity not resulting in procreation had to be condemned. Moreover, even when children resulted from an act of intercourse, sex itself was not necessarily something to be enjoyed but rather engaged in because it was God's will. The Church Fathers regarded sex as at best something to be tolerated, a necessary evil out of which procreation resulted. The dominant Western attitudes have been conditioned by these beliefs ever since. Americans, whether or not they are Christians, are heirs to this tradition, and understanding this background might help us to come to terms with our own ambiguous feelings about sex.

Though Christian theologians have periodically attempted to rid Christianity of its Gnostic-Manichean-Stoic outlook on sex, they have not been entirely successful. Thus, though the Puritans did emphasize the joys of married sex, they continued to condemn all sexual pleasure outside of marriage, including masturbation, as sinful. In fact, despite its embrace of the joys of marital sexual union, New England Puritanism seemed to have the same Christian obsession with sex that was present in the early Church Fathers. It is only as Christian theologians have tried to break with traditional Christian interpreters that they have been successful in undoing some of the Christian ambivalence about sexuality. Even so, Christianity cannot avoid accepting a major responsibility for much of the psychological harm and guilt anxieties its traditional antisexual attitudes still cause today for too many men and women.

NO
Peter Gardella

CHRISTIANITY HAS GIVEN US A POSITIVE ETHIC OF GENDER EQUALITY AND SEXUAL PLEASURE

Every religion regulates sex. Any serious reflection on life affects sexual behavior, because sex is basic to life. Apart from ethical or supernatural concerns, the health of a community requires laws and customs regarding marriage, the sexual initiation of children, and the responsibilities of sex partners to each other.

We should not, then, make the mistake of unconsciously comparing the sexual attitudes of societies with a Christian heritage to the attitudes that might prevail in some imaginary realm of freedom. Such culture-blind observations prove nothing. Many critics have noticed, for example, that St. Jerome (320-420) wrote letters reminding women that sin came into the world through them; but few have considered that the mere act of writing letters of spiritual advice to women distinguished Jerome as more of a feminist than the Greek philosophers or Jewish rabbis of his day. St. Augustine (354-430) believed that all sexual pleasure entailed some sin, even for the married; but Augustine also wrote the most frankly sexual autobiography to appear in the West for seven hundred years, contributing mightily to what historian Vern Bullough has described as a "Christian obsession with sex." Readers of romances know how easily such negative obsessions become positive.

Another common error, selective comparison, isolates one feature of a religion (for example, the erotic temple decorations or the *Kama Sutra* of the Hindus) to demonstrate the deficiencies of Christianity, without considering how much more repressive that religion is than Christianity with regard to the sex lives of ordinary people, the role of women, etcetera. If the liberality of Christian cultures on these issues results from the defeat of religion by modernization and secularization, a question arises as to where the modernizers learned their values.

Where have we in the United States acquired our high expectations of sexual pleasure, our visions of justice between men and women, and our impatience with sexual abuses and inhibitions? America has witnessed increasingly tolerant standards for sexual display in clothing, public expressions of affection between the sexes, the subjects allowed in polite conversation, and the freedom of women to seek sexual pleasure. Has all this happened despite universal opposition from Christians, or without co-operation from organized Christianity? Of course not. I would argue that Christianity has fostered the sexual revolution of our century in four ways: (1) by providing textbooks for confessors that discussed the details of sexual acts; (2) by furnishing ideas and symbols for the ministers and doctors who carried on the discussion of sex in mass culture; (3) by teaching that ecstatic experience leads to spiritual perfection; and (4) by representing women as naturally superior beings in the moral and spiritual realms. These factors came together in the United States between 1830 and 1930 to produce an ethic I call "innocent ecstasy," which I will describe in my conclusion.

Of course, the Christian influence on sex has not been without cost. I do not contend that modern Americans practice the best possible sexual ethic. I do not deny that Christianity has inculcated a great deal of repression and guilt. On the other hand, I insist that the positive values we hold with regard to sex, and even the concrete ways in which we make love, grow directly out of our Christian heritage.

CHRISTIAN DISCUSSIONS OF THE DETAILS OF SEXUAL BEHAVIOR

Since the 1930s, books of sexual advice have taught Americans that intercourse should include orgasm for both partners. The dogma has become so well established that evangelists representing the Campus Crusade for Christ insist on it in their sermons on marriage. Mutual orgasm is a physiological bottom line by which people judge the success of lovemaking and for which they accept moral responsibility.

Usually, commentators assume that this ethic of orgasm arose from recent advances in the study of sexuality—perhaps from the work of Freud, or Havelock Ellis, or Kinsey, or Masters and Johnson. Most doctors of a century ago certainly denied or ignored female orgasm. But the obligation to mutual orgasm appeared hundreds of years ago in Catholic moral texts.

The first American writer to prescribe orgasm was the Right Reverend Francis Patrick Kenrick, Roman Catholic bishop of Philadelphia. In the third volume of his *Theologiae Moralis,* a textbook for priests published in 1843, Kenrick wrote that a married woman had the right to bring herself to orgasm "by touches" after intercourse, if she had experienced no climax during lovemaking. Kenrick also ruled that a husband should continue lovemaking until his wife reached orgasm; neglect of this duty was a venial sin. It was mortal sin for a wife to distract herself during sex in order to avoid having an orgasm.

Kenrick inherited these conclusions from five centuries of development following a breakthrough by St. Thomas Aquinas (1225-1274), who learned from Aristotle that pleasure could not be sinful in itself because pleasure was involuntary. Pleasure derived its moral character from the action that produced it; pleasure in a good act was good, and pleasure in a sinful act was sinful. Since the Bible and natural law both allowed intercourse to the married, taking pleasure in marital intercourse was good. So ended the era of Augustine's dominance.

Whatever Catholic theology defines as good, it eventually makes obligatory. "Nature does nothing in vain," reasoned St.

Alphonsus Liguori (1969-1787), whose writings guided Catholic thinking about sex into the twentieth century. Liguori was concluding his discussion of female orgasm, a subject of speculation for Catholic theologians since St. Albert the Great (1193-1280), the teacher of Aquinas. Because female orgasm was part of nature, Liguori gave it a place in natural law as part of the perfection of the sexual act. Liguori's argument supported the rights and obligations to orgasm that Kenrick, and all other moral theologians published in America until 1946, reported in their textbooks.

Often, moral theology permitted greater freedom than law or custom. For example, Liguori told priests not to disturb the consciences of peasant husbands who thought that their adulteries were venial sins. Aquinas ruled that the church could collect rent from houses of prostitution. Catholic advice on women's fashions, on attending the theater, and on dancing always allowed some expression of sexuality, depending on community standards and the intentions of the individual, even when Protestants rejected all plays and denounced the waltz and the décolleté gown.

Of course, all this leniency appeared only in Latin, to train celibate priests to hear confessions. Catholics never preached in public on the obligation to orgasm or the usefulness of whores. Yet, the church had an elaborate body of teaching on sex, including recommendations about positions for sexual intercourse, frequency of intercourse, stimulation with the hand or mouth, sexual fantasy, transvestism, homosexuality, and many other issues. Catholic teaching gained incalculable influence through the confessional, where priests answered the questions of penitents and asked questions of their own. Before psychoanalysis, newspaper advice columns, and television talk shows, the confessional was the only formal context for discussing sex in Western culture. Moral theology developed out of that context, in dialogue with science and sexual experience. Contrary to the stereotype, that dialogue clearly did not end with "Thou shalt not."

CHRISTIAN IMPACT ON SEX IN AMERICAN MASS CULTURE

Mass culture began in the 1830s, when the application of steam power to the printing press made large editions of books and magazines possible. The United States led the world into the age of mass culture, partly because of our aptitude for industrialization and partly because the weakness of traditions in America gave the new media more influence than they could obtain in Europe. Among the first to use this influence were experts, especially ministers and doctors, writing about sex.

Protestant ministers made the Catholic moral theologians more famous than they ever wanted to be. At least twelve editions of excerpts from Catholic moralists, translated as far as prudery allowed and highlighted by editorial expressions of shock, came from American presses in the nineteenth century. Sermons and articles attacking the licentiousness of Catholic teaching reached large audiences.

When the first waves of Catholic immigrants came to the United States, between 1830 and 1860, cities like Boston, New York, Cincinnati, and St. Louis abruptly became half Catholic. The resulting cultural transformation still has not been entirely understood. Among the immediate effects was the emergence of many purported exposés and works of fiction filled with charges of Catholic immorality. Maria Monk's *Awful Disclosures of the Hotel Dieu Nunnery*, which described seduction in the confessional and the rape and torture of women in convents, sold more copies (about 300,000) than any book written in America before *Uncle Tom's Cabin*. Suspicions of the same kind led to the burning of a convent in Charlestown, Massachusetts by a mob in 1834. Even in the 1980s, when *The Thorn Birds* and Andrew Greeley's novels and *Agnes of God* entertained millions, portrayals of Catholic misbehavior have found a ready reception in America. Writers as distinguished as Nathaniel Hawthorne (in *The Marble Faun*) and Harriet Beecher Stowe (in *Agnes of Sorrento*), and writers as vulgar as Ned Buntline (the inventor of Buffalo Bill and author of *The Beautiful Nun*) all contributed to the genre. Anti-Catholic writing became the first American pornography, effectively increasing the amount and the explicitness of cultural discourse about sex.

More direct influence on sexual behavior came from the doctors and health experts who began to address the public in the 1830s. Most of them wrote from deep Christian convictions. For example, Sylvester Graham (1794-1851), the inventor of the Graham cracker and the first professional crusader for change in American sexual mores, began his career as a Presbyterian minister. John Harvey Kellogg, M.D. (1852-1943), the inventor of the cornflake and an advocate of nearly total abstinence from sex, ran a sanitarium for the Seventh-Day Adventists who had nurtured him and sent him to medical school. Both Graham and Kellogg believed that passion weakened people and injured their children in the womb. Passion gave them a biological basis for the Christian doctrine of original sin: Adam disobeyed through sensual desire, and the effects of his sin continued through sensuality. If people would adopt a vegetarian diet (including Graham flour and cornflakes), they could control their passions and limit their sexual activity (to once a month following Graham; to nothing beyond procreative necessity following Kellogg). The resulting improvements in health and heredity would reverse the curses of Eden and redeem the race. Although these hopes seem ludicrous today, similar projects appear in virtually all nineteenth-century medical writing on sex.

Health experts usually aimed at repression, but their warnings also focused attention on orgasm. Orgasm swept along the nerves "with the tremendous violence of a tornado," lamented Sylvester Graham; the "venereal paroxysm" stimulated the heart to drive blood "in fearful congestion, to the principal viscera," damaging every organ of the body. Unlike theorists of earlier centuries, who concentrated on the relations between semen and blood, nineteenth-century doctors saw sensation as the central thing in sex.

Convinced that passion caused all sin and suffering, doctors investigated sex with profound urgency. Their accomplishments matched the damage that they did. J. Marion Sims, an Alabama country doctor, invented the speculum and the speciality called gynecology in the 1840s. By the 1880s, though American doctors still went to Europe for training in most fields, the United States had eleven regional societies of gynecologists, more than all of Europe and Russia combined. Clitoridectomies and ovariotomies came into fashion as "cures" for masturbation and for passion; the last clitoridectomy in the United States was performed in 1948. Even those gynecologists who rejected such radical measures generally understood themselves as the protectors of women and of unborn generations from the ravages of passionate sex.

To reduce original sin to an hereditary effect of sex, however, invited a reversal of the argument: perhaps redemption hinged upon healthy passion. In upstate New York in the 1870s, a former divinity student named Andrew Ingersoll healed men and women by teaching them a breathing exercise and telling them to let go of their repressions. "Sexual life is the sustaining force of body and mind," through which "the Creator will work the regeneration of body and soul, which is the second birth," Ingersoll wrote. He urged thankfulness to Christ for every stirring of desire. . . .

The most influential expert writing on sex was not a doctor, but a nurse and a sexual mystic who owed most of her zeal to Christianity. Margaret Sanger (1879-1966), the inventor of the phrase "birth control" and the main proponent of legal contraception, admitted that in her girlhood she "stole money to buy flowers to put at the feet of the Virgin Mary." After her father clashed with the local priests in Corning, New York, Margaret fled Catholic persecution and entered a Methodist college, where she encountered freedom of thought, participatory worship, and the hope for complete deliverance from sin in this life.

For Margaret Sanger, the cause of birth control became a religious mission. In hired halls and on street corners, in illegal clinics and in prison, in her own newspaper and in books that sold hundreds of thousands of copies, Sanger preached that the redemption of the race would come through properly managed sex. "Through sex, mankind may attain the great spiritual illumination which will transform the world," she wrote in *The Pivot of Civilization* (1923). Birth control

prepared the way for this illumination. Husbands and wives needed practice—men to learn self-control and regard for their wives' pleasure, women to learn how to release their inhibitions. If women connected with the power of sex, the "passionate intensity" of their love would ennoble their children. "Great beings come forth at the call of high desire," wrote Sanger in *Woman and the New Race* (1920). "When the womb becomes fruitful through the desire of an aspiring love, another Newton will come forth . . . There will come a Plato who will be understood a Jesus who will not die upon the cross."

Original sin was just as central to Margaret Sanger as it was to Sylvester Graham and John Harvey Kellogg. For her, the essence of sin was shame; but the framework of Fall and Redemption shaped her thinking just as effectively as it shaped the advice of any minister or doctor.

Sanger even clothed her specific sexual advice in Christian terms. Rarely did she refer to intercourse as anything but "sex communion." A husband who initiated his wife successfully into sex took on the power of "a veritable god—worthy of her profoundest worship." In simultaneous orgasm, which Sanger held forth as the goal of sex, she promised "a true union of souls" that "takes on the nature of a sacrament."

Before Margaret Sanger died, the major Protestant denominations in the United States all endorsed birth control. In a sense, these churches were simply accepting a new application of their own traditional hopes.

CHRISTIAN TEACHING ON ECSTASY AND SPIRITUAL PERFECTION

Over the last sixty years, experts have urged Americans to explore mutual an simultaneous orgasm, vaginal (as opposed to clitoral) orgasm, multiple orgasm, the role of masturbation in developing a capacity for orgasm, and the G-spot. Christian teachers prepared us for this concentration on the moment of ecstasy.

Religions can organize emotions in many ways. The moods induced by Gregorian chant, by Quaker silence, by martial hymns, by the narrowly reasoned arguments of a fundamentalist sermon, and by a Christmas eve candlelight service differ dramatically, and these moods seem likely to result in different modes of action. If religions are nothing else, they are effective systems of applied psychology. And for the last century and a half, many evangelical Christians in America have been preaching that lives can change in a moment, and more, that the qualitative change people need can *only* come in a moment. Ecstatic emotion—a sense of being carried away, beyond the self, of surrendering control—distinguishes these moments. Those who have never known ecstasy, the argument implies, have not been born again. Evangelicals offer the choice between letting go to ecstasy and living in sin. . . .

In the 1980s, no Americans more eagerly praise ecstatic sex than the evangelicals. "Pastor, I never dreamed when I accepted Christ that He would invade our sex life," a young husband told the Rev. Tim LaHaye, cofounder of the Moral Majority, "but we had never been able to make my wife's bells ring until after we were converted. Now she has a climax most of the time." Improving sex through Christ fits perfectly with the instant salvation and complete deliverance from sin that modern evangelicals seek.

It was not always so. The first great revivalists, Jonathan Edwards and his con-temporaries in the Great Awakening of the 1740s, told people that they would struggle with sin until death, and they never said a word about enjoying sex. The current optimism stems from the Methodists, founded by John Wesley (1703-1791), who made freedom from sin a point of dogma and who encouraged women to lead prayer groups. His message and his methods sold very well in America. Before Aimée Semple McPherson, Wesley's heritage yielded Phoebe Palmer (1807-1874), whose followers turned Martha's Vineyard and the New Jersey shore into summer resorts. Since McPherson, evangelicals like Anita Bryant and Marabel Morgan (author of *The Total Woman*) have explicitly linked rebirth and sex. Popular singers like Donna Summer, Michael Jackson, and Marie Osmond have exemplified the new evangelical personality: healthy, obedient to their Lord, sexually attractive, and free from guilt.

Of course, mystics since the Desert Fathers of the third century have described their communion with God in sexual terms. Four factors gave American evangelicals their unique impact: (1) the audience provided by mass media; (2) the doctrine that full deliverance from all sin and guilt could happen immediately; (3) the affinity between this expectation of instantaneous conversion and the more general American penchant for instant gratification; and (4) the prominence of women in the evangelical movement. The last factor belongs to a larger part of the story.

CHRISTIAN IMAGES OF WOMEN

Churches dedicated to Mary have not always stood on every corner. In fact, only one such church stood in Europe in the year 1000. But today in the United States, there are more Catholic churches named for Mary than for her Son. This change has softened the patriarchal bias of Christianity and altered Christian doctrine on sex.

During the twelfth and thirteenth centuries, just before Albertus Magnus and Thomas Aquinas liberated Catholic teaching on sex from its Augustinian roots, Mary rose to prominence in the West. Her devotees included St. Bernard of Clairvaux (1091-1153), who claimed that Mary had inspired sexual desire (the same "concupiscence" that Augustine saw as the effect of sin) in God the Father. Followers of Bernard like St. Amadeus of Lausanne (died 1154) preached that Mary was "burning, dissolved by heavenly fires" when God impregnated her, and that she "took strength from the fire" so that she might "always burn, and again dissolve." Bernard and Amadeus urged the monks they led to emulate Mary by retiring to their cells and reading the prophets until God overshadowed them. By the fifteenth century, St. Bernardino of Siena (1380-1444) was admiring Mary for her seduction of God.

> One Hebrew woman invaded the house of the eternal King; one girl, I know not by what caresses, pledges or violence, seduced, deceived and, if I may say so, wounded and enraptured the divine heart and ensnared the Wisdom of God.

Aristotle led theologians to accept sexual pleasure, but Mary made sex acceptable in prayer and devotional life. . . .

Apart from Mary, Christianity since the 1830s has become more domestic in its concerns and more open to female leadership than any religion in recorded history. This is especially true in the United States. Scholars have suggested that our feminine religion compensates for the aggressive, masculine stance of Americans in business and politics. Whatever the cause, the Pilgrim Fathers and the Founding Fathers long ago yielded their churches to Mother's Day, flowers in the sanctuary, the effeminate Jesus of nineteenth-century portraits, and "the family that prays together." Several of America's new religions were founded by women, including Christian Science (Mary Baker Eddy), Seventh-Day Adventism (Ellen Gould White), the Church of the Foursquare Gospel (Aimée Semple McPherson), and the Pillar of Fire Church (Alma White). The student bodies of divinity schools at Yale, Harvard, Union, and the University of Chicago are now almost half women.

To some degree this results from the feminist movement rather than from any internal tendency of Christianity; but then, feminism in the United States began among fervent Christians. Elizabeth Cady Stanton convened the first women's rights convention in a Methodist church. She inherited the same perfectionist spirit that led Aimée Semple McPherson to seek spiritual ecstasy and inspired Margaret Sanger to fight for birth control.

Belief in the moral leadership of women linked Catholic devotees of Mary, who have often been political reactionaries, and radicals like Margaret Sanger. The same faith joined Francis Willard, the head of the Women's Christian Temperance Union, with abolitionists like the Grimké sisters. In the terms of the Christian story, these women knew that women would conquer the serpent of Eden, that women remained with Jesus when the men fled, and that the church itself was called the bride of Christ. These visions arose from Christianity, not from Islam or Judaism or Marxism.

So it was natural that the movement to redeem sex, and then to aspire to redemption through sex, took place in Christian cultures, and that this movement came through women and the self-appointed friends of women. The priests, the doctors, the evangelists, and the visionaries all spoke on behalf of women. Whether the results have helped either women or men remains to be considered.

CONCLUSIONS:
INNOCENT ECSTASY

The crucial evidence that Christianity has given us more than repression, but also a positive sexual ethic, appears in the (largely unrecognized) American ethic of sexual pleasure itself. I have called that ethic innocent ecstasy.

"Innocence" here means both the absence of guilt and a certain healthy feeling. For some, it may imply inexperience, youth, or virginity; Americans hold many different opinions as to whether innocent sex requires marriage, heterosexuality, or anything else. What everyone approves, and even demands, is an innocent attitude. Some people see guilt as a symptom of psychological sickness; others understand guilt as a sign of something wrong with the relationship or the action in question. No one, from the Campus Crusade to Dear Abby to Masters and Johnson, recommends living with guilt.

"Ecstasy" means sensation so intense that it exceeds physical capacity, obliterating self-consciousness. The word derives from Latin elements meaning "out of" and "stand," denoting a state of being beside oneself. In sex, Americans expect orgasm to approach ecstasy. To neglect the potential for ecstasy in oneself or in a partner evokes the same universal intolerance as guilt does in the United States. The inhibited and the incompetent now suffer the cultural condemnation that once befell the licentious and the demonstrative. Among

our medical procedures, the artificial penis has supplanted the clitoridectomy.

Only a Christian culture, reacting against the sense of original sin derived from Paul and Augustine, could have developed innocent ecstasy. The ethic persistently demands that sex be *proved* innocent. When Americans speak or write about sex, whether from a conservative or a liberal standpoint, we reveal our descent from evangelicals by taking up a prophetic stance, denouncing abuses in the name of an ideal.

Perhaps we have made progress toward some ideals. The sense of progress, the sense that the modern era offers more sexual pleasure and justice and honesty than the past, is one of the charms of innocent ecstasy. Sixty years of positive advice must have led to some improvement in the skills and the sensitivities of sexual partners. Surely women, at least, more commonly enjoy sex today than they did in 1830, or 1880, or 1930. And outside the bedroom, the redemption of sex from sin has promoted cultural innocence. American men and women display a durable innocence that is not hypocrisy, but a real capacity to undergo experience and even trauma without becoming jaded, disenchanted, or sophisticated. Women maintain their self-respect and their reputations despite attitudes, fashions, and behavior that would have marked them as "fallen women" in all previous Christian cultures, and that still mark such women in most of the world.

On the other hand, we fall victim to special miseries. The effort to separate sex from sin demanded so many declarations of the sacredness of sex, especially from people like Margaret Sanger and Dr. Robert Latou Dickinson, that Americans began to approach intercourse with a seriousness more appropriate to a spiritual discipline. The quality of sex became a standard for judging our relationships and ourselves. Under such pressure, both divorce and marriage have increased in frequency, not because we revere marriage less but because we expect more. Young people must engage in premarital sex as a matter of prudence, because they need to know how well they will perform with each other before they can commit to marriage.

Because of the emphasis on women in Christian thinking on sex, the sexual desires of women have lost their associations with sin more completely than have the desires of men. Science has also paid more attention to women. This leaves women with the double task of embodying innocence and certifying sexual success (the impossible status of the Virgin Mother), while men take responsibility for satisfying women but develop little comprehension of what they themselves might want. Both sexes resent their respective burdens.

Most unfortunately and insidiously, concentrating on ecstasy has deprived American sex of sensuality. We have a good conscience about orgasm but we hate the body. Mystics have always known that in ecstasy the action of the senses is suspended; for example, during St. Bernadette's prayers with the Virgin, someone held a candle to her hand without Bernadette

noticing. In the United States, the pursuit of orgasm now approaches an ascetic practice, best performed by those whose bodies are thin, clean, and odorless (in other words hardly there). Marabel Morgan urged wives in *The Total Woman* to seduce their husbands every day for a week. But she also demonstrated the difference between sex and sensuality when she assured her readers that "sex is as clean and pure as eating cottage cheese."

Our worst sexual problems reflect what has been excluded from our ideal. For example, we would rather be violent than sensual. Our pornographic districts assault rather than entice the senses; we don't want to know how to make a pleasure garden. But the market for pornography grows, because pornography absorbs the sensuality that is banished from the majority ethic. Anorexia, aerobics, drug abuse, and sex crimes all testify to our flight from the body, into ecstasy. Confronted by the plague of AIDS, we regress into finding fault, bewildered that the association between orgasm and health could fail.

Christianity deserves some blame in all of this, as well as some praise for the liberating aspects of innocent ecstasy. But simply calling Christianity a repressive force will not do. Augustine has been dead for fifteen hundred years; and even Augustine, after all, was probably a bisexual and certainly an unwed father.

POSTSCRIPT

DOES CHRISTIANITY PROMOTE
AN ANTISEXUAL CULTURE?

The history and influence of dualistic philosophies which Bullough traces from early Greek times through Plato and Augustine cannot be ignored when we ask the question, "Why is Western culture and Christianity so uncomfortable with sexuality and sexual pleasure?" Both the distant roots and the recent past must be considered in answering the question.

Bullough does not mention the clear and strong influence of apocalyptic expectations which led many Christians to put sex on the back shelf while they prepared for the imminent Second Coming of Christ. Why indulge in pleasures that would distract one from preparing for the Second Coming? Why bring children into this world when many believed there would soon be an earth-ending battle between Christ and Satan? The belief that Armageddon was just around the corner promoted the prestige and primacy of virginity and celibacy. Pagan dualism and the antisexual theology of the Christian convert Augustine were only part of the story.

At the same time, the positive sex views endorsed by more recent Christian theologians must take into account and deal honestly with the antisexual heritage that is still with us. The essence of Christianity may, in fact, prove to be not nearly as antisexual and against sensual pleasure as it appears to be from first reading. Tracing an "authentic" Christian thought that affirms the goodness of sex back to the writings of the disciples of Christ may help some overcome the religious guilt people have been raised with, but the antisexual dualism, whether it is labeled "pagan" or is a Christian adoption, is still with us. See the bibliography for further readings on this subject.

ISSUE 18

IS THE SEXUAL REVOLUTION OVER?

YES: John Leo, from "The Revolution Is Over," *Time* magazine, April 9, 1984

NO: Lester Kirkendall, from "The Sexual Revolution Is Just Beginning," *The Humanist,* November/December 1984

ISSUE SUMMARY

YES: John Leo, a social critic and a senior writer for *Time* magazine, brings together statements from a wide variety of family life specialists, sociologists and sex counselors to defend his claim that the sexual revolution is over because it was a failed experiment in sexual freedom that was rejected, beginning around 1975.

NO: Lester A. Kirkendall, professor emeritus of family life at Oregon State University, argues that the real sexual revolution is just beginning. The changes which will produce the revolution include the separation of sexual relations from reproduction, the minimizing of male/female differences, a breakdown in the rigidities which have walled off certain sexual expressions as unacceptable, and a shift in the sources we accept for our appraisal and decisions about moral/ethical issues in sexuality.

When we speak of a revolution, we usually mean something that has been turned completely around or upside down. One seldom, if ever, finds such 180° turns in human behavior and attitudes; still, we talk of cultural revolutions. As a rule, cultures and attitudes change slowly. There are times, however, when rather radical changes can be observed in our culture, and these times have become much more frequent as the pace of our techno-logical changes has accelerated. In some ways, revolutions are like volcanic eruptions and earthquakes. Major eruptions and quakes may be signaled by a series of warning signs of ever-increasing intensity over a short or long period. Afterward, nature and cultures readjust, learning to cope with tremors of decreasing intensity until a relatively stable state is again achieved.

In terms of revolutions in the ways in which men and women relate and structure their families, several periods might qualify as so-called sexual revolutions. In prehistoric times, nomadic humans were food gatherers. In such cultures, males and females had equally productive roles because neither sex had a clear advantage in meeting the primary concern of gather-ing food. Women, because of their childbearing ability and nurturing role, may have had some social priority, but men and women were roughly on a par. When human groups shifted to hunting, males gained social superiority because of their prowess in the hunt and their ability to provide food, but women were still important in turning the raw material of the hunt into usable garments and food which they cooked with the wood they gathered.

About ten thousand years ago, some human groups in the Fertile Crescent of the Middle East gave up nomadic gathering and hunting when they made the seemingly simple discovery of planting, cultivating and harvesting food. This opened the way to a new complexity in societies. Life in the early cities of Sumer and Babylonia gave men an upper hand in the politics, economics and warfare of public life while women were increasingly relegated to the domestic hearth. A sexual revolution of sorts then occurred in relations between urban men and women and in their relative powers and roles. In the centuries that followed, little changed in human relations as a strong patriarchal culture prevailed in Western civilization.

The Industrial Revolution and the Victorian age of a hundred years ago only emphasized the sex roles and power that had become dominant in the West. There were rumblings though, in England and the United States, as women sought the power of suffrage. In the turmoil following the Civil War, women began to gain some employment options and economic status in the new careers of nurse and secretary. Diaphragms and condoms of vulcanized rubber prepared the way for the revolution in methods of contraception half a century later.

World War I brought many social changes. Shorter skirts without multiple petticoats replaced Victorian hoop skirts as part of the effort to save cloth for bandages. Contact with the more open and sexually sophisticated French and English gave American farm boys a liberating cultural shock to which they exposed their wives who had remained at home to work on the farms and in the factories. The Roaring Twenties that followed—the era of the "flapper"—might well qualify as the first significant sexual revolution of this century.

Still, the 1960s and 1970s are popularly known as the sexual revolution. The advent of the birth control pill, antibiotics to control VD, civil and gay rights movements, Vietnam protests, rock music, television, a new leisure and affluence in the middle class, a growing economy, legalized abortion, and the works of Kinsey and Masters and Johnson, all helped create a fertile atmosphere for our most recent sexual revolution.

But what was the character and outcome of this revolution?

In the selections that follow, John Leo argues that the sexual revolution of the 1960s and 1970s was a failed social experiment, while Lester Kirkendall contends that the full impact of the continuing revolution is yet to be felt.

YES   John Leo

THE SEXUAL REVOLUTION IS OVER

"It's terrible to wake up and wonder why this person's head is on the other pillow," confesses a New York City writer who slept with about two dozen women in the first months after his divorce. "It was painful for them and me too." Says a Chicago bar owner: "All the happy-go-lucky singles in my place tell me that they do not want a relationship. Then six months later they are engaged." A businessman in the Boston area, currently in mid-divorce, is swearing off the one-night stand. "I don't want it, don't need it and don't believe in it," he says. "I hope to find one person to share my life with. Who doesn't?"

After the sexual revolution, the voices of Thermidor. From cities, suburbs and small towns alike, there is growing evidence that the national obsession with sex is subsiding. Five-speed vibrators, masturbation workshops, freshly discovered erogenous zones and even the one-night stand all seem to be losing their allure. Veterans of the revolution, some wounded, some merely bored, are reinventing courtship and romance and discovering, often with astonishment, that they need not sleep together on the first or second date. Many individuals are even rediscovering the traditional values of fidelity, obligation and marriage. Or as one San Francisco sex therapist, Lonnie Barbach, puts it, "We've been going through a Me generation; now I see people wanting to get back into the We generation."

The buzz words these days are "commitment," "intimacy," and "working at relationships." There is much talk of pendulum swings, matters coming full circle and a psychic return to prerevolutionary days. "We are in a '50s period again," says Miami psychiatrist Gail Wainger. "People are looking for more lasting relationships, and they want babies." In the '70s Wainger's case load was predictably heavy with patients complaining about sexual inadequacies. "Not having an orgasm was an O.K. reason to come in for therapy. Now they come in because they are not happy with their lives, their jobs, their inability to find relationships."

Fear of herpes obviously prods the trend along but explains the new caution only in part. In 1980, when herpes was just beginning to impinge on the nation's consciousness, a *Cosmopolitan* survey found that "so many readers wrote negatively about the sexual revolution, expressing longings for vanished intimacy and the now elusive joys of romance and commitment, that we began to sense that there might be a sexual counterrevolution under way in America." *Cosmopolitan* Editor Helen Gurley Brown, never one to miss a sexual trend, says, "Sex with commitment is absolutely delicious. Sex with your date for the evening is not so marvelous—too casual, too meaningless." The tide of conservative prose, in fact, has become too much for *Playboy.* An article in the December issue grumpily complains that scribbling erotophobes are out to restore puritanism to America. *Playboy's* most recent campus poll found more sex than ever among collegians but also signs of the new traditionalist trend. Most of the sex took place in stable relationships, and a third of the students said that they had to be in love before going to bed with someone.

One problem in gauging the nation's sexual temper is that those in charge of the effort seem to know very little about what is really going on. On the subject of the sexual revolution, the specialists divide into three categories: the experts who think the revolution has ended, those who insist it is still continuing, and a small group who say it never existed at all. In the last faction is John Gagnon, a sociologist who says the idea of a sexually permissive society was basically a construct of American journalism.

Sex polls do not settle the matter. Sampling is often flawed, questions may be sloppily phrased, and results sometimes vary erratically. More important, all the pollsters have to go on is what people say. New York psychologist Mildred Newman reports that a close friend was interviewed for the Kinsey report on women. The friend, who led a robust and varied sex life, gave chaste and virginal answers because she was not willing to let anyone know how she really behaved. Nowadays many people may offer up attitudes designed to depict themselves as properly liberated. Anthropologist Lionel Tiger, while studying a kibbutz in Israel, noticed that kibbutzniks whose daily conduct was clearly liberal almost always checked off conservative attitudes, and many conservative men and women reported liberal attitudes. This led to Tiger's First Law of Polling: "Attitudes are antidotal to actual behavior."

Even so, some statistics indicate that a glacial shift toward conservatism is under way in sexual matters, and probably has been since the mid-'70s. Weddings and births are up, divorce is down, according to the National Center for Health Statistics. A record 2.5 million couples were married in 1982. It was the seventh annual rise in a row and an increase of 16% over 1975; the marriage rate, with the exception of two years in the early '70s, was the highest since 1950. The number of divorces dipped slightly, to 1.2 million, in 1982; that was the first decline in 20 years. The total number of births, as well as the birth rate, was the highest in a dozen years. Births to women in their 30s are still on the rise, one sign that doubts about motherhood are fading among females exposed to the heaviest antifamily criticism. The birth rate for women 30 to 34 stands at 73.5 per thousand, up from 60 per thousand in 1980.

In the late '60s and early '70s, marriage, motherhood and the "nuclear family" were scorned by the counterculture, feminists, and radicals. Psychiatrist David Cooper denounced the family as a "secret suicide pact" and "an ideological conditioning device in any exploitative society." Yet by the late '70s, says writer Fran Schumer, "marriage became something hip, ambitious women could do." Most of those now divorced can hardly wait to get back into the game: some 60% to 70% of younger divorcees remarry within five years. One national poll taken in 1978 found that 23% of Americans said they would welcome less emphasis on marriage. Four years later, a follow-up poll showed that only 15% wanted marriage de-emphasized. Those who wanted traditional family ties rose 3%, to 86%, while people who wanted general acceptance of sexual freedom fell by 4%.

The shift in behavior extends to the young. Premarital sex is still prevalent—youngsters are starting earlier and marrying later—but some polls are picking up signs of sexual conservatism. A July 1983 reader survey by *Psychology Today* reported considerably more conservative attitudes, particularly among the young, than a similar poll taken in 1969. Half of those under age 22 felt that sex without love is unenjoyable or unacceptable. A survey of a group of juniors and seniors, selected last year from *Who's Who Among American High School Students*, found that only 25% had experienced sexual intercourse. A similar survey in 1971 found that 40% were nonvirgins. In 1976 one-fourth of the 300 Yale students who enrolled in Philip and Lorna Sarrel's course, Topics in Human Sexuality, said they were virgins. In 1983 one-third of the 259 students in the class said they had never had sex. Says Mary Olsen, director of the health center at Wheaton College in Massachusetts: "When you reach a certain age, it's a natural thing to explore your sexuality. The difference now is that things are not so casual. The women I speak with seem to want to know their partners." At Northwestern University, the director of the student health service, Helen Wilks, says, "Students on campus today are just more serious in general."

The sexual revolution was born in the mid-'60s, the product of affluence, demographics and the Pill. Women had been pouring into the work force since World War II, and the Pill offered sexual liberation to go with growing social and economic freedom. The baby-boom generation shaped its culture around sex, drugs and defiance of traditional values. The California therapies, chiefly those derived from the ideas of Abraham Maslow and Carl Rogers, supplied much of the rationale for the sexual revolt. Fulfillment and growth came from close attention to the needs of the self. Maslow taught that the self is a hierarchy of inner needs and that culture and tradition push people toward inauthentic selves; living for others is a trap. At the pinnacle of Maslow's hierarchy stood the self-actualized person, virtually independent of culture or troublesome ties to others. Rogers too stressed the goal of self-actualization and personal growth.

Daniel Yankelovich's study *New Rules* showed how the self-fulfillment ethic, largely confined to the campuses in the late '60s, had pollinated much of America's culture by the late '70s, wafted along by a score of pop-psych books, from *How to Be Your Own Best Friend* to *Passages* and *Your Erroneous Zones*. By the late '70s, according to polls conducted by Yankelovich, Skelly & White, 72% of Americans spent a great deal of time thinking about themselves and their inner needs. "The rage for self-fulfillment," wrote Yankelovich, ". . . had now spread to virtually the entire U.S. population."

In the sexual arena, self-fulfillment converted almost every sexual itch into a sexual need. Acts that had traditionally been viewed as perversions, like sadomasochism, were now proclaimed "alternative life-styles," presumably self-fulfilling for those attracted to them. Joseph Epstein, in his book *Divorced in America*, argued that for those on a lifelong mission of self-fulfillment, the very thing that led individuals into marriage—more growth—was bound to lead them right on out; the ties and obligations of wedded life blocked the proper unfolding of the self. But, points out Carlfred Broderick of the University of Southern California's marriage and family therapy program, "total growth, total narcissism, which is supposed to fix everything, doesn't."

Yankelovich's study, published in 1981, captures the theology of the revolution at its peak. Future historians of the movement, in fact, may set the years of sexual revolt at roughly 1965 to 1975. Since the mid-'70s, according to some small surveys, the revolution has decelerated or reached a plateau. One such study shows that rates of premarital intercourse for students at the University of California at Davis rose sharply to 62% by 1977 and then increased to only 64% by 1981. Said Ann Clurman, a vice president at Yankelovich, Skelly & White: "In the latter part of the decade, we see a slowing down in support for [the sexual revolution]. People are reassessing. They're moving away from the extremes."

Polls on nonsexual attitudes trace the same trajectory during the '70s, suggesting that the softening of support for the sexual revolution owes something softening of support for liberalism in general. The National Opinion Research Center in Chicago, which has been surveying liberal and conservative attitudes since 1972, reports that the dominant social views in America are still liberal, but not so solidly as they once were. Tom W. Smith of N.O.R.C. writes that in most categories, liberal sentiments "either leveled off or slowed their rate of increase around 1973-1975. Instead of a conservative tide, the period since about 1973 can be better described as a liberal plateau."

Sociologist Seymour Martin Lipset of Stanford's Hoover Institution thinks the "destabilization of belief systems" wrought by the Viet Nam War helped propel the sexual revolution along. The end of the war and the onset of a recession, he says, brought "a movement back to more stability" and a turn away from far-out sex in the mid-'70s. British journalist Henry Fairlie, an astute observer of the American scene, thinks the tinkering with personal life-styles that characterized the '60s and early '70s inevitably bred distaste for further social change. "Endless questioning of all aspects of life from food, dress, dropping out, child rearing and commune living led to mere exhaustion," he says. "There simply was no energy left. People found it an isolating and cutoff way to live." Yankelovich too thinks the turn away from sexual adventuring is a byproduct of other change. It is, he says, "only one part of a larger phenomenon of society going through a sober, responsible phase."

An uncertain economy may also have helped quiet the sexual scene. Though no one can demonstrate a cause-and-effect relationship, sexual caution and money troubles seem to go hand and hand, in the '30s as in the '80s. A common saying among sex therapists is "sex goes up with the stock market." The free spirits of the '60s are the busy careerists of the '80s, hustling for a dollar in a competitive job market. "The students you talk to want to do well," says retired Harvard sociologist

David Riesman. "They want to do more than pass their courses, and they want more than a job. They want a career. Sex and drugs are distractions, things that are no longer new and exciting." Robert McGinley, Buena Park, Calif., head of the North American Swing Club Association, believes the economy is probably the major factor in the recent decline of swinging, a euphemism for mate swapping and group sex. Attendance at swing parties, he says, dropped 15% to 30% in early 1983, and attendance at Plato's Retreat, a Manhattan sex parlor, was down 40% in the same period.

According to sociologist William Simon, "The affluence of the '50s, '60s and '70s gave us courage to experiment with our lives. With the present economy, there is a sense of cautiousness. There is more commitment to careers and coupling because we are hedging our bets for social and economic security. We think, 'How can I financially and emotionally budget my energies?' and the career is winning out over thoughts of sex."

Another important but unwelcome accelerator of the conservative trend is herpes. Since the late '70s, when it was often misdiagnosed as psoriasis, genital herpes has emerged as a major sexually transmitted ailment. Some 10 million to 20 million Americans have genital herpes, and an estimated 200,000 to 500,000 new cases appear each year. The one-night stand is now so risky that a couple interested in casual sex must get to know each other well enough to pop the herpes question—and believe the answer. Many sexologists think herpes is the chief reason for the new conservatism. Others consider it more of a symbol or the capping of a trend that began before herpes came to full public attention. Says California sex-

ologist Harvey Caplan: "In a funny sort of way, some people are actually relieved by the threat of herpes. It's a good excuse for them to give up a life-style that had become unsatisfying." Yankelovich thinks the rise of herpes has revived feelings of guilt and the idea of disease as a form of moral punishment for promiscuity. Beneath the veneer of liberation, he says, "we have a residual guilt, and the idea that promiscuity breeds disease falls on prepared ears."

Age is another contributor to revisionism. As many of the baby-boomers begin to hit their middle years, they are following the normal course of settling down, devoting more energy to their work and in general becoming more conservative. Caroline Stewart, 34, a Philadelphia journalist, managed to juggle both the new morality and the old during the '70s. As she grew up in Pittsburgh, her father blinked the message "Stay a virgin at all costs." She headed to Washington and became a grudging conscript in the sexual revolution. After her first romance broke up, she recalls, "I was wild, for me. Many people had a great smorgasbord of relationships. You had them without giving thought to what you needed instead of what you wanted."

Like some other female veterans of the revolution, Stewart thinks she was tricked into playing the male's game of easy sex. "Men compartmentalize their feelings. They can be casual about their sex lives," she says. "For women it's more of a bonding experience. Men use intimacy to get sex. Women use sex to get intimacy." She thinks men are so cavalier that the only sensible strategy is the one her mother recommended: "Keep mysterious, play hard to get and never give in."

Some analysts think the history of the sexual revolution is the story of the everready male gaining access to a larger poof willing women. "There hasn't been a change in male sexual patterns in the 20th century," says Vern Bullough of the State University of New York at Buffalo, a historian of sexual trends. Though most analysts in the field would not go that far, studies tend to agree that changes in male premarital sexual behavior since the '30s have been rather modest. Premarital sex rates for women have more than doubled between the 1930s and 1971, and sharply rose again to a new peak in 1976.

"In sex," says Tiger, "women are the gatekeepers." At least some slowing of the sexual revolution seems traceable to the reassertion of traditional values by women. As always, women have more to lose from casual sex than men: they are left with the unwanted pregnancies, the abortions, the possible damage from contraceptives and the risk of cervical cancer associated with having multiple sex partners. To many women, random sex seems more and more a pointless diversion or a trap.

One female television personality in New York, a veteran of the sexual scene in the early '70s, later joined a loosely structured "celibacy club" of women who went out socially in groups of six or eight to avoid sexual entanglements. Says she: "It's hard enough for a women to get ahead in this business without waking up in a different bed every morning."

A University of Kansas study of college women over the past decade found a significant increase in sexual activity during the years 1973-78 but almost none in the past five years. Says Meg Gerrard, the psychology professor in charge of the survey: "I think we have reached a ceiling with 50% to 60% of college women active sexually."

Sex is alive and well on campus, but it seems to be subdued by the standards of the early '70s. Says Louis A. Pyle Jr., director of university health services at Princeton: "Although some freshmen boys arrive here asking, 'Where's the party? Where's the orgy?,' students today are more monogamous. There's not a lot of promiscuity. This is substantiated by the fact that we see very little gonorrhea and no syphilis." At Mount Holyoke, senior Jennifer Shaw observes: "The trend for women is not to sleep with men they meet at parties." The one-night stand is as potentially entangling for men as in prerevolutionary days. "The women who have one-night stands are really looking for further commitment," she says. Nancy Boltz, a nurse at the University of Southern California, says students age 20 and over want long-term relationships. Some younger students sleep around, but in these encounters the trappings of commitment are common. "They may only stay together six months," says Boltz, "but during that time they think they are in love."

Counselors describe today's students as sexually sophisticated but wary. Says Julianne Daffin, a dean of campus life at Atlanta's Emory University: "They have already been the dumpee or dumper, and they don't want that any more." Instead of floating into relationships, she says, students are more likely to go out socially in groups. "It isn't that sex as recreation has gone back into the closet," she says, "It's just that it's not considered a primary pursuit any more."

One Chicago graduate student, 37, now in her second marriage, echoes that uneasy change. Says she: "Many of us are unable to break the habit of self-absorption, unable even to live with someone else because it interferes with our own space." She still has trouble with commitment, but feels a push toward it because she wants children and does not care to have to raise them by herself. "I can still regress, but I don't want to," she says. "The only time I get really nostalgic is when I get stoned and listen to Pink Floyd and think about when everyone was everyone else's lover. But it just doesn't work." With her first husband, she experimented with open marriage. "The trouble is that emotionally you spread yourself too thin. What women who tried to break out of traditional relationships found is that it doesn't work."

Judy Meyer, a marketing executive for several Houston nightclubs, observes that "ten years ago, I would walk into a nightclub and be literally pinched by men, and guys would ask me pointblank if I wanted to get laid. Today there is a general softening in attitude. The days of the hard hustle are gone." Says Stephen Greer, 33, co-owner of three Chicago nightclubs: "If you don't work in a candy store, every piece of candy looks great. But today everybody works in a candy store—it's so easy for everybody to have sex. So people are becoming more selective: holding out for just the right candy, just the right person."

Manhattan sex therapist Shirley Zussman says that her patients these days complain about the emptiness of sex without commitment. "Being part of a meat market is appalling in terms of self-esteem," she says. "Fears, of both loneliness and intimacy, are a backlash against the 'cool sex' promoted during the sexual revolution." Psychiatrist Domeena Renshaw, director of the Sexual Dysfunction Clinic at Chicago's Loyola University, has a waiting list of 200 couples seeking help. "Many have tried group sex and the swinging scene, but for them it has been destructive and corrosive. Often the partner who suggested it first is the one who suffers most."

For sexologists these days, the new frontier is inhibited sexual desire (ISD). The problem accounts for 30% to 50% of the case load for many therapists. "We didn't look for excitement problems in the mid-'70s," says therapist Stephen Sloan in Atlanta. "It was assumed that everyone desires sex." Some therapists, accustomed to reporting 75% to 90% success rates in treating sexual difficulties, report a 10% to 30% success rate in treating ISD. Philadelphia sexologist Harold Lief has estimated that 20% of all adult Americans are afflicted with ISD. "It is clear that we are talking about enormous numbers," he says.

Most therapists believe that these sexually apathetic people are not casualties of the revolution. They are simply showing up for help now because the new freedom, besides raising expectations, has made it easier for people to admit to sexual problems. Sexologist Caplan is not so sure; he thinks that the sexual revolution has been a highly significant factor in the spread of ISD. Because of boredom, satiation, and the elimination of taboos, he says, "it is becoming increasingly clear that the excitement value of average sexual practices is diminishing." Psychologist C.A. Tripp argues that sexual excitement depends on obstacles and barriers. As barriers fall, so does pleasure. Caplan says that he knows many men who carry out sexual seduction on a purely mental level: once they have psychologically won a woman, excitement fades, and they dread having to go to bed with their conquest.

America has been through it all before. In the '20s another generation shaken by war, disillusioned with authority and fueled by easy affluence conducted its sexual revolution. The flapper symbolized a sharp break with prewar Victorian morals. In one poll of 2,200 women, taken during the

'20s, more than half said they regularly masturbated. By the end of the decade, a prominent gynecologist said, "sexual experience in some form has been known by 100%" of unmarried patients. The divorce rate soared, and according to one estimate, up to 1 million illegal abortions took place each year during the Roaring Twenties.

Rapid urbanization, the growing intellectual and economic independence of women and the dislocations of World War I had all helped loosen traditional morals. As Americans read Sigmund Freud's dark warning about the effects of suppressed desire, writes historian Geoffrey Perrett, "sexual freedom appeared to be scientific, more or less." By 1926 F. Scott Fitzgerald testily complained that "the universal preoccupation with sex had become a nuisance."

Though some researchers say the sexual spree of the '20s was confined to big cities and campuses, the famous study, *Middletown*, by Robert and Helen Lynd, found otherwise. By the middle of the decade, their typical American town (Muncie, Ind.) was in full sexual bloom. The change came with erotic fashions, literature and movies, and an unsuspected sexual aid, the automobile. A team of sociologists, reassessing Middletown from 1976 to 1978, concluded: "The Middletown studied by the Lynds during the 1920s was in the throes of a sexual revolution as far-reaching as the one we have experienced during the past two decades." There were differences, of course. Many women in the 1920s stopped short of intercourse. Those who "went all the way" often convinced themselves that they were in love, and the hasty or shotgun wedding was common.

Says Boston psychiatrist Henry Abraham: "We are now seeking a balance. We realize that revolving-door sex is not the answer to true love and commitment. The '60s kids brilliantly saw the problems facing us, but their solutions were the solutions of children. After all, a roll in the hay does not a sexual relationship make."

Sexologist Wardel Pomeroy of San Francisco, a co-author of the Kinsey studies, predicts that sexual conservatism will not last. "In another three or four years, we're going to go back again," he says. "This is inevitable. I don't think it can be bottled up." Few other analysts, however, see any sexual energies being repressed.

The new conservatism is no victory for puritans. No sexual counterrevolution is under way. The sexual revolution has not been rebuffed, merely absorbed into the culture. America is more relaxed and open about sex, but also blessedly a bit tired of the subject. A sexual revolutionary at a party, chattering on earnestly about sex as a natural function, a panacea and the cutting edge of social change, would quickly end up standing alone. Many sexual techniques and practices that were shocking a generation ago—oral sex, for instance, or living together—have been widely accepted. So has premarital sex, particularly in urban areas. Girlie magazines, which have long since gone gynecological, circulate freely, and adult access to sexually explicit novels, movies and video cassettes is rarely questioned. Attitudes toward masturbation have shifted too: it is hardly seen as the triumphant act of self-love heralded in some of the quirkier sex manuals, but fewer and fewer Americans view it as morally repugnant, much less a health hazard.

In the gray area is homosexuality, increasingly tolerated but not approved, as well as porn on television and teen-age sex. Other practices and proposals, along with their advocates in the heady days of the '60s and early '70s, have been firmly rejected: "open marriage," group sex and child sex. Though many values are still being sorted out, most Americans seem stubbornly committed to family, marriage and the traditional idea that sex is tied to affection or justified by it. "Cool sex," cut off from the emotions and the rest of life, seems empty, unacceptable or immoral. "The whole culture is on a swing back to more traditional expectations," says Dr. David Scharff, a psychoanalyst and author of *The Sexual Relationship*. "There is a return to the understanding that the main function of sex is the bodily expression of intimacy."

NO
Lester A. Kirkendall

THE SEXUAL REVOLUTION
IS JUST BEGINNING

During the 1960s and the 1970s, both my lecture agent and my academic peers frequently scheduled me to speak on "The Sexual Revolution." I accepted this as a topic, but to open discussion I would often say to an audience that, while I didn't think that there was a sexual revolution, I could tell them how to make one. At that time this was a true position, for following historical antecedents, sexual matters were narrowly defined and attention was concentrated heavily upon the genitals, upon an increasingly frequent participation in intercourse for those unmarried, and upon a greater readiness to acknowledge and enjoy sexual pleasure. These emphases have varied from culture to culture and throughout the ages, however. It was this limitation that led *Time* magazine, April 9, 1984, to feature a cover story which proclaimed, "Sex in the '80s: The Revolution is Over."

Today, however, we *are* experiencing an oncoming sexual revolution. Various social and technical features have affected many aspects of our cultures, sexual and otherwise, and they have revolutionized or are revolutionizing both individual living and couple and group relating. I refer to the impact of technological, cultural, legal, ethical, and religious changes which have in turn affected our educational procedures and research findings and also the ways in which we regard sexual matters. This has produced our upcoming sexual revolution. It is exemplified in (a) the presently emerging reproductive techniques which even now, and certainly will in the future, alter procreative procedures; (b) in liberating experiences coming through alterations in male-female life patterns; (c) in the breakdown of rigidities which have historically placed very definite limitations on acceptable sexual expressions; and (d) in a shift in the acceptable sources for determining our appraisal of moral-ethical issues.

From, "The Sexual Revolution Is Only Beginning," by Lester Kirkendall, *The Humanist*, November/December 1984. Copyright © 1984. Reprinted by permission of *The Humanist*.

We have moved from accepting religious edicts to a concern for fulfilling human needs. These are the developments that constitute the sexual revolution, both current and in the offing. For readers of *The Humanist*, it will be intriguing to ascertain the extent to which humanistic reasoning resides in the trends we will be discussing.

The first development which will have momentous effects is *the divorcing of reproductive processes from genital copulation*. There are numerous supportive features which have made this possible. Robert E. Francoeur, a sexologist with a religious background, discusses this development in his college-level sexology textbook, *Becoming a Sexual Person*. He notes among the supportive features the use of artificial insemination, sperm banks, surrogate mothering, embryo transplants, tests for eliminating potential birth defects and genetic diseases, "test tube" or *in vitro* fertilization, frozen embryos, and artificial wombs.

With certain of these we are already familiar. Artificial insemination has been around for quite some time. At first it was used mainly with domestic animals and only infrequently to promote human reproduction. Francoeur notes that the first human conceived through artificial insemination was born in 1799, although artificial insemination was then known as "ethereal copulation." It has come to be widely used with humans within this century, however, and it is thought that around one percent of the children born in the United States today are conceived through this procedure. Its use was spurred by several technological developments. One is the capacity to freeze semen and store it in sperm banks for later use. The sperm might come from a particular male who wishes later to reproduce or might simply be the deposit sperm from some other male. For married couples who use artificial insemination, there seems to be few problems when the husband is the donor, for in this case the donor is known. Problems begin to arise, however, when the donor is not known or known only according to a few physical characteristics. For both men and women, various emotional problems may arise. Males in particular may feel that they have failed in an important respect; they cannot produce a pregnancy, they are sterile. Then, too, whose child is this anyway? The mother is known, but not the father. In some cases in which some [only a few] sperm are found in the semen of a prospective father, his semen is mixed with a donor's sperm to heighten the chances that he has sired the child. Despite such perplexities, however, the future will rely even more upon artificial insemination.

A variety of social considerations has already led to the acceptance of technological developments that make it possible to separate sexual intercourse from reproduction. Blood tests can reveal whether defective genes, which may result in deformed children, exist in the germinal cells of prospective parents. If they do, what course of action will probably be followed? Few couples are likely to seek conception without doing something to prevent deformation in potential children. They may decide not to have children or to use prenatal amniocentesis to check the fetus in the womb and, if defects are indicated, resort to abortion. Or once the technology is in place, they may decide to use those germinal cells acquired from both males and females not known to them personally to begin the pregnancy they desire. They may authorize *in vitro* fertilization and have the fertilized egg implanted in a surrogate female. Another possibility is to use an artificial womb for a full-term pregnancy.

While this technique is yet to be perfected, Francoeur speculates it may come before the end of the century. Certainly the use of an artificial womb would alter the roles and legal responsibilities of those involved in thus producing an infant. Those supplying the sperm and egg may never know that their germinal cells have been used; the prospective parent may be a single person, and, if a couple, they might be female-female or male-male. If frozen sperm or ovum are used, the persons supplying germinal cells may be long since dead. Do inheritance rights follow the usual reproductive associations? If there are such rights, how long can they be sustained? Would the rights and responsibilities of the parent (or parents) of an *in vitro* conceived, artificial-womb gestated child be the same as those of the parents of a traditionally begotten child? Certainly there are vexing legal and ethical issues! Recall those raised recently in Australia when a frozen embryo was left with no one to safeguard its future after its two progenitors (should they be called parents?) were killed in an airplane crash.

Another social consideration which will promote germinal storage banks is the increasing number of males and females subjected to pollutants. Studies indicate that males who work or have worked in a polluted environment may have a decreased number of sperm in their semen. Thus they may need storage of semen in a sperm bank (this could be done at the time of puberty, hopefully before exposure to a pollutant). Or they may have to accept artificial insemination for their spouse by donor, adopt children, or remain childless.

So a possible, and I think probable, scenario is this. As a child reaches puberty, each person will be required to have his or her reproductive cells examined. If they are free from chromosomal damage, they can then be stored in a germinal bank to be used later for reproduction if desired. Once this is done, the individual could then be rendered either temporarily or permanently infertile and, so far as physiology is concerned, experience male-female intercourse freely without any threat whatsoever of an unwanted pregnancy. An individual wishing to become a parent could postpone having children until in midlife or until retirement. Whether this will become common, no one knows, but certainly the possibility is that those teenagers and newly married couples who read this article may find themselves as adults or parents dealing with infertile teenagers. Forthcoming generations of youths may well regard "sex" as an outmoded word—a word that their laggard superiors still use simply because they grew up in a different era. Instead they will speak of the value of intimacy which comes through body closeness but can be experienced in other ways as well. (In my boyhood, when someone wanted to note that a couple had experienced intercourse, they were described as having "been intimate.". . . I remember, too, that then people referred to the "reproductive organs." These later became the "sex organs"; perhaps in the future they will be the "intimacy organs.")

The second development to be explored, *the movement toward minimizing male-female differences,* is the result of both technological and social changes which are revolutionizing relations between men and women. Usually when this issue is raised, attention is directed toward the need to free women from their subordinate role in relation to men. Men have been dominant both in the work world and within their families. But males have been so preoccupied with competition and the need to become leaders that they have overlooked ways in which this role has deprived them of certain very significant life satisfactions. The issue should not be to make women equal in power with men but simply to make males and females human beings regardless of their genital anatomy, then identify them as females or males when particular circumstances demand it. . . .

These efforts toward liberation have been aided by technological, educational, and political developments. The divorcing of reproductive processes from sexual relating, the global concern about overpopulation, and the growing knowledge which has advanced family planning programs have all contributed toward smaller families. These have freed both men and women from unwanted pregnancies and have made it possible, for women in particular, to redirect their lives, quite bypassing their child childbearing anatomy. Now, too, it makes little or no difference if females are less able to exert the same physical strength as males. In other words, one of the determinations which futurists must make concerns the differences physical anatomy and hormonal secretion have on the needed or desired behavior of females and males. I suspect that by the year 2000 there will be little attention paid to male-female physiological differences beyond the fact that each will perform differently in intimate genital exchanges (using potential 2000 terminology) and that certain inequities in occupational affliations will still be in the process of being ironed out.

Females have chosen their liberation by entering the work world, by choosing occupations other than motherhood or by coordinating motherhood with another occupation. For many males, females have become coworkers, and both sexes have been freed from hard, exhausting physical labor by technological advances. One can now pull a switch, push a button, or shift a lever regardless of gender.

American women now easily enter many occupations which were formerly denied them. Space flights of both the United States and the Soviet Union have had female astronauts. Women are also entering the political field. India, England, and Israel have already had women prime ministers, and the selection of Geraldine Ferraro as the Democratic vice-presidential nominee for 1984 has brought American women one step closer to the presidency of the United States. Women are wending their way into the military. Certainly females displayed their competitive nature in the Olympics held in Los Angeles in August 1984. And the legal system has come down on the women's side. The *Christian Science Monitor* (August 3, 1984), reporting on a conference of state governors, noted that the governors

> endorsed the principle of pay equity for men and women public employees in comparable jobs. The state of Washington last year was ordered in a court ruling to pay $1 billion in back pay to its female employees. And in Minnesota, where a study found large discrepancies in pay, the state has set aside $22 million to raise the wage rates of women workers.

Liberation for men has presented more difficulties. A few men are now nurses; others teach in the lower grades of elementary schools. A few men have become interested in nutrition and food service and have graduated from schools of home economics. Generally, however, these men work out some kind of combination, such as managing a restaurant or food service in an institution. This also helps them to maintain a financial income generally accorded to males.

Technological and political developments have helped males as well. Through improved medical service, the establishment of Social Security, and state annuity funds, males have been freed of the onerous task of raising a family of five or six children in order to have three or four survivals. With lengthened life expectancy also, the number of childrearing years now takes a smaller proportion of the total life span.

A few men, too, have become *househusbands*—men who care for the household and work with their children while their wives work outside the home. An increasing number of men are leaving their nonemotions, to which my father clung so desperately, to find that emotions add to the joy of living. Some males may not regard this as liberation, but I suspect that the number who do will increase greatly in the future. Further adjustments will doubtless be required, particularly on the part of males, with the increased use of robots in producing manufactured products. The consequence will be an increasingly larger proportion of both men and women, but especially men, moving into service occupations such as education and childcare. Will this be accompanied by the emotional liberation of males? I anticipate that it will.

The two developments just discussed are clearly revolutionary in nature. In the culture of ancient China, the concept of *yang* and *yin*, the male and female elements, while maintaining sexual differentiation, attempted to find and maintain a harmonious relationship and to express the congeniality for which the Chinese were striving. So through the ages this struggle has continued. If sexual equivalence is now achieved through equality rather than diversity, these developments will surely have contributed to the current sexual revolution.

The third development producing the current sexual revolution is *the relaxation of certain rigidities which have limited acceptable sexual experiences simply to intercourse for reproduction*. The moral restrictions dictating approved sexual expression have stemmed from religious edicts. What was demanded was that sexual associations should involve only those males and females who had met certain stipulated requirements, such as marriage, and whose sexual connection was handled in such a way as to permit procreation if at all possible. The genital organs, it was said, were given to humans by a benign God with the understanding that they would be used to beget children. As religious authority declined, the sexual bans it had approved were taken over and enforced by medical authorities, as Brecker points out in his book, *The Sex Researchers*. Holding sexual associations wholly within this religious or medical concept was impossible, however, and so it was frequently violated, even though the violations were punished by disapproval, even ostracism. This restriction became even harder to enforce as the age of puberty declined, as youth had more freedom to be alone and to experiment, and as the inhabitants of one culture became aware of the variations in sexual practices which existed in other cultures. And so the movement toward approving diversity was underway.

Probably the two most obvious diversities which are now in the process of being accepted, and which will be fully accepted in the future, are same-sex relating (now called homosexual relating) and the family forms within which sexual relating is experienced. Thinking of the two preceding developments—divorcing sex from reproduction and the changing nature of male-female roles—I think it becomes immediately clear why homosexual relating is becoming more acceptable. My own expectation is that within a decade or two the categories of heterosexual and homosexual will disappear entirely. A major step toward that end was taken when the concept of bisexuality was introduced. In the future I anticipate that people will relate intimately with the ones they love without being concerned as to whether their partners are of the same sex or the other sex. (Notice, too, my choice of words; I have chosen them after careful consideration.)

In the past, approved sexual relating occurred within the nuclear family and was directed toward procreating. There were other forms in which sexual relating did occur—in communes, such as the Oneida Community. However, these communities were looked at askance; their inhabitants were hardly regarded as normal, often referred to as "hippies." Today, however, family forms are proliferating. Due to mobility, changes in occupation, freedom to travel, an increasingly long lifespan, and a growing acceptance of singleness both in single living and in parenting, one may experience a number of life-styles during one's lifetime. The old nuclear family arrangement, whereby two persons pledged themselves to be faithful to each other until "death do us part," doesn't have much meaning any more.

A number of other disapproved sexual expressions have also come to the point of being accepted. The medical authorities, who succeeded the religious authorities, referred to the male phenomenon of nocturnal seminal emission, or "wet dream," as *spermatorrhea* and warned that, "As for the termination of the disease: if left to it-self, it has a constant tendency to increase. The patient may, after years of suffering, sink into the lowest stage of weakness and die."

Masturbation, also formerly known as *onanism*, was regarded by both religious leaders and medical practitioners as a dangerous practice. Once referred to as "a secret vice," "self-abuse," or "self-pollution," it gradually emerged from this shadow to be referred to directly as masturbation. Today this rigidity has receded to the point where masturbation is frequently suggested as a procedure for releasing tension, even as "self-pleasuring."

There are other practices about which concepts are being assessed, reassessed, and reassessed again. In the past, unmarried males and females participating in sexual intercourse were automatically labeled promiscuous. Later this practice was called premarital intercourse, and recently I came across a reference to it as premarital testing. Another illustration: formerly, intercourse with other than one's spouse was an "affair" and participants were unfaithful and lacked fidelity. Today we read of open marriage, tomorrow we are almost certain to see a further relaxation— perhaps it will become the joy of intimate interchange.

I realize that the preceding three paragraphs may have a sarcastic tone to them. I do not intend them to be so; I do think that the recital and exposing of semantic labeling is a quick and accurate way of showing the nature of existing attitudes. . . .

Many times our sexual conduct becomes exploitative because we focus on genitality and penile-vaginal penetration. We seek satisfaction ourselves without communicating freely or openly with others; we satisfy ourselves, evidencing at the same time little concern for the welfare of partners. This was highlighted for me once when in a counseling session I asked a college-level male who was having intercourse with a casual acquaintance if his partner was enjoying the sexual relationship. He replied first that he didn't know and then, rather reproachfully, said, "After all, I couldn't ask her a question like that. We aren't very close friends."

This conceptual narrowness is displayed in many ways. If pornography is mentioned, the image which comes to mind centers on the nude body, the genital organs, and likely sexual coupling. An event or picturization that results in sexual arousal is labeled pornographic. However, today's feminist leaders have a different approach. They say, and I agree, that these depictions generally show women in subordinate roles, often being taken advantage of by males. The center spreads and outside covers of sexological magazines make women into sex objects. The female portrayed is always undressed, a demure young thing in her late teens or early twenties awaiting the arrival of someone who will seduce her.

This analysis has been set up in terms of women, as most analyses are. The August 15, 1984, *Oregonian* carried a column by Gloria Allred. It noted:

> Women clearly need more protection against pornography. . . . The law passed but vetoed by the mayor in Minneapolis defines pornography as "the graphic, sexually explicit subordination of women" through pictures or words and in which one or more of several scenarios are depicted. They include women presented as sexual objects who enjoy pain, humiliation, or rape; women bound, mutilated, dismembered, or tortured; women in postures of servility, submission, or display; or penetrated by objects or animals. Men, children, and transsexuals can sue if similarly treated.

. . . What is needed then is to broaden our sexual concepts, to think of sexuality in different terms. Certainly we can take pleasure in the human body, whether male or female, and enjoy sexual experiences, but at the same time we can disparage presentations which subjugate women and set men in positions of dominance simply because they are males. Let us reject statements quite apart from sexual discussions which categorize human beings because of their genital anatomy. Meg Bowman in her play, *Why We Burn: Sexism Exorcised* (excerpted in *The Humanist*, November/December 1983), has numerous quotations in which women and men are categorized because of body form. Three quotes will provide a bit of insight:

> "One hundred women are not worth a single testicle."
> —Confucious (551-479 BCE)

> "If a woman grows weary and, at last, dies from childbearing, it matters not. Let her die from bearing; she is there to do it."
> —Martin Luther (1483-1546)

> "In the year 584, in Lyons, France, forty-three Catholic bishops and twenty men representing other bishops, held a most peculiar debate: 'Are Women Human?' After many lengthy arguments, a vote was taken. The results were: thirty-two, yes; thirty-one, no. Women were declared human by *one vote!*"
> —Council of Macon

This kind of thinking will vanish only as we first see females and males as persons with a deep concern for others and for experiencing a satisfying life. We need to see them as persons first, then as females and males.

These [developments] which are even now being accepted, and which I believe will be increasingly accepted in the future, will constitute a genuine sexual revolution.

Each is providing freedom for people, whether male or female. But each calls for a more penetrating awareness of human nature and of the essential qualities which must be advanced, worldwide, if people are to experience joyous, satisfying lives. Only when our world becomes imbued with these ideals will we be able to say, "The Humanist Revolution is here—now." This is our challenge!

POSTSCRIPT

IS THE SEXUAL REVOLUTION OVER?

For John Leo, the essence of the latest sexual revolution was an unbounded sexual license, the compulsion many heeded to experience sex in as many outlets and combinations as could be conceived. But does Leo's analysis really touch on the essence of what happened in American culture in those decades?

Lester Kirdendall focuses on some deeper changes he believes form the basis for the real sexual revolution which has just begun. Indirectly, he suggests that interpretations that focus on statistical changes in how much and what kind of sex went on between whom, how many people marry or divorce, and when they become sexually active are dealing with superficialities.

By nature, revolutions do come to an end. The old order is overturned, and the new order is accepted and established in the mainstream. Leo admits this when he states that the new conservatism will be no victory for the puritans, and that, despite herpes, AIDS, the New Right and the Moral Majority, there does not seem to be a strong sexual counterrevolution with enough strength to take us back to "old fashioned traditional values."

The continuing shift away from brute strength to computers and an equality in mental abilities will help undermine the male patriarchy built on physical differences. The numerical surplus of women will give them an edge in giving character to the ongoing revolution. Old values of intimacy, communications and commitment will resurface, but with new nuances. If Kirkendall is correct, the separation of sex from reproduction will continue to grow. Male/female differences and the monogamous/heterosexual rigidities for sexual expression will continue to weaken.

Another perspective sees an ongoing sexual revolution. The recent conservatism may be seen as marking a time of consolidation during which we can adjust ourselves to the radical and deep cultural changes that began in the 1960s and 1970s. In a few years, a new human may emerge to fly in a world of which the puritans and Victorians could never conceive. Whether or not one agrees with this perspective, it certainly will be interesting to watch the future unfold. See the bibliography for further readings on this subject.

CONTRIBUTORS

EDITOR

ROBERT T. FRANCOEUR has taught human sexuality in college and high school for over 20 years. He is the author of a leading sexuality textbook, *Becoming a Sexual Person* (1982 and 1984), and such popular books as *Utopian Motherhood: New Trends in Human Reproduction* (1970), *Eve's New Rib: 20 Faces of Sex, Marriage and Family* (1972), *Hot and Cool Sex: Cultures in Conflict* (1974), and *The Future of Sexual Relations* (1974). He has contributed to over 40 handbooks and readers on human sexuality, including the *Handbook on Marriage and Family* and the *Encyclopedia of Sexology*. He has 30 some technical papers and over 70 popular articles on sexual issues to his credit. A guest lecturer on sexual topics at over 200 colleges and universities, he is also a Fellow of the Society for the Scientific Study of Sex and President-elect of the Society's Eastern Region. His current base is as professor of biological and allied health sciences at Fairleigh Dickinson University in New Jersey. He holds a doctorate in embryology, master's degrees in Catholic theology and biology, and is a charter member of the American College of Sexology.

AUTHORS

LORI B. ANDREWS is a research attorney at the American Bar Foundation in Chicago. She writes extensively for professional and popular publications on legal issues of the new reproductive technologies, and is the author of *New Conceptions: A Consumer's Guide to the Newest Infertility Treatments* (rev. ed., New York: Ballantine, 1985).

LARRY BARON, a lecturer in sociology at Yale University, was invited by Philip Nobile and Eric Nadler to join the "Shadow Commission, a group of journalists, sex therapists, feminists and civil libertarians who abhor censorship and are willing to consider erotica dispassionately and without bias."

BETTY WINSTON BAYE is a reporter for the *Courier Journal* in Louisville, Kentucky and the author of *The Africans* (Banbury Books, 1983).

SANDRA LIPSITZ BEM, a developmental psychologist, teaches at Stanford University. She has studied sex-biased job advertising and lectured widely on sex roles and the changing nature of marriage.

HARRY A. BLACKMUN is an associate justice of the United States Supreme Court.

VERN L. BULLOUGH, a noted historian of sexuality, is dean of natural and social sciences at the State University of New York at Buffalo, and a fellow of the Center for Sex Researchers, California State University, Northridge. He has authored *Sexual Variance in Society and History* (John Wiley, 1976) and *Sin, Sickness and Sanity* (New American Library, 1977), as well as coediting *Sexual Practices and the Medieval Church* (Prometheus Books, 1982).

GENA COREA received her B.A. from the University of Massachusetts. Author of *The Hidden Malpractice: How American Medicine Mistreats Women* and *The Mother Machine*, her articles have appeared in *The New York Times*, *Ms.* magazine, *Mother Jones*, *Omni*, and *Glamour.* She is the founder of the Feminist International Network on the New Reproductive Technologies.

LISA DAVIS is the pseudonym of a well-known Hollywood television and screenwriter who, for personal reasons, does not wish to be identified.

BARBARA EHRENREICH, a journalist and the author of *For Her Own Good*, was invited by Philip Nobile and Eric Nadler to join the "Shadow Commission."

PETER GARDELL, author of *Innocent Ecstasy: How Christianity Gave America an Ethic of Sexual Pleasure* (Oxford Press, 1985) is assistant professor of religion at Manhattanville College in Purchase, New York. He has also taught at Yale University, Colgate University, Indiana University and Miami University of Ohio.

DEPAUL GENSKA, a Catholic priest, belongs to the Order of Friars Minor. Since 1972, after a chance encounter with two prostitutes in New York City, he has worked with prostitutes and their families in New York, New Jersey and Chicago. He has carried his message to such national groups as the National Organization of Women and the National Council of Catholic Bishops where he lobbies for legal and financial support for prostitutes. He is currently stationed at the Catholic Theological Union in Chicago, working also at Genesis House, a house of hospitality and nurture for women involved in prostitution, which he helped found in 1984.

GEORGE GILDER is the author of *Men and Marriage* (Pelican Books), a 1986 revision of his 1973 book *Sexual Suicide*.

ROBERT GORDIS is Rappaport Professor of the Bible at the Jewish Theological Seminary in New York City. He is also the editor of *Judaism* magazine.

JEANNINE GRAMICK, a School Sister of Notre Dame, is a co-founder of New Ways Ministry, a Catholic group working with gays and lesbians within the Christian community. She recently completed a sociological study of lesbian women.

ORRIN G. HATCH, a powerful and visible member of the United States Senate, has chaired the Labor and Human Resources Committee which has oversight responsibilities for the Department of Labor, the Department of Health and Human Services, and the Department of Education. Senator Hatch has also been very active in the movement for a Human Life Amendment to the US Constitution.

SUSAN INCE, a feminist activist and freelance writer, was trained in medical genetics. She has written for *World Medical News*, and works in urban neighborhood health clinics providing information and support for women's reproductive choices.

HILARY JOHNSON is a freelance writer and contributor to *Vogue, Rolling Stone*, and *Life* magazines.

RICHARD D. KENNEY, MD is the director of Ambulatory Pediatrics and Adolescent Medicine at the Charlotte Memorial Hospital and Medical Center, Charlotte, North Carolina.

LESTER A. KIRKENDALL, internationally recognized as one of the great pioneers in family life studies, is professor emeritus of family life at Oregon State University and the author of numerous books and articles on sexuality and family life. He is a co-founder of the Sex Information and Education Council of the United States (SIECUS). Recipient of the 1985 annual award of the Society for the Scientific Study of Sex, he has lectured widely in the United States and abroad, particularly in Japan, Israel, England, and Scandanavia.

JOHN LEO, a social critic and senior writer for *Time* magazine, has authored numerous articles and satirical commentaries on issues in human sexuality and family life. In his earlier career, he was associated with the weekly commentary *Commonweal*.

BARRY LYNN, legislative counsel for the American Civil Liberties Union, was invited by Philip Nobile and Eric Nadler to join the "Shadow Commission." Lynn testified before the Attorney General's Commission on Pornography and then traveled throughout the country to monitor its activities.

LONNY MEYERS, MD, is vice president of the Midwest Association for the Study of Human Sexuality and director of medical education for the Midwest Population Center, where she leads workshops for couples and individuals. A practicing physician, she is married and has three children. Her studies in human sexuality include work at the Masters and Johnsons sexuality clinic in St. Louis, the Kinsey Institute in Bloomington, Indiana, the Institute for the Advanced Study of Human Sexuality in San Francisco, and the University of Minnesota Medical School. Her essay here is adapted from *Adultery and Other Private Matters* (Chicago: Nelson-Hall, 1975) which she co-authored with the Reverend Hunter Leggett.

JOHN MONEY is professor of medical psychology and pediatrics and director of the Psychohormonal Research Unit at the Johns Hopkins University and Hospital. An internationally acknowledged expert on paraphilias or unusual sexual orientations, Money's many publications include *Love and Love Sickness,* and *Lovemaps.* He was invited by Philip Nobile and Eric Nadler to join the "Shadow Commission."

ROBERT NUGENT, a Salvadorian priest, is co-founder of New Ways Ministry. Currently studying for a master's degree in theology at Yale Divinity School, he has lectured and written widely on the Church's pastoral ministry for gay and lesbian Catholics. His articles have appeared in *America, Ministries, Catholic Digest,* and *The Priest.*

JAMES W. PRESCOTT, a developmental neuropsycholgist and cross-cultural psychologist, has studied and published extensively on the developmental origins of violence and its relationship with antisexual attitudes. He is currently president of BioBehavioral Systems and the Institute of Humanistic Sciences, with offices in Maryland and California.

PHYLLIS RAPHAEL is a journalist, novelist, and short story writer. She is the author of a novel, *They Got What They Wanted* and has published in *Cosmopolitan, Redbook, Playgirl, The Village Voice,* and *Forum* magazine. She lives in New York City with her three children.

ROBERT H. RIMMER, the prolific novelist and apologist of alternative lifestyles, is best known for his 1967 underground bestseller *The Harrad Experiment*. His later novels, *Rebellion of Yale Marratt* (1967), *Proposition 31* (1969), and *Thursday My Love* (1972), detail his vision of new marital forms. Many of his avid readers contributed their insights on the changing forms of marriage to create collections such as *The Harrad Letters to Robert H. Rimmer* (1969), *You and I . . . Searching for Tomorrow* (1971), and *Adventures in Loving* (1973).

BRUCE RITTER was one of 11 Commissioners who served on the 1986 Pornography (Meese) Commission. A Catholic Franciscan priest, he is internationally recognized for his work with teenage runaways. Covenant House, which he established in New York's Times Square area, now has branches in several large American and Canadian cities.

HERB SAMUELS holds an M.S. degree in social work and works as a consulting sexologist in New York City.

PETER SCALES is currently the director of education for the Planned Parenthood Federation of America. He directed the first MATHTECH study of sexuality education programs for the Centers for Disease Control.

PHYLLIS SCHLAFLY is well known as the founder of the conservative newsletter *The Eagle Forum* and a staunch opponent of the Equal Rights Amendment (ERA).

RAMI SHAPIRO, a Reconstructionist Rabbi with Temple Beth Or in Maimi, Florida, earned a Master of Arts degree in religious studies from McMaster University, rabbinical ordination from the Hebrew Union College-Jewish Institute of Religion in Cincinnati and a Ph.D. in contemporary Jewish thought from Union Graduate School, also in Cincinnati. Past editor of *Humanistic Judaism Quarterly*, he has authored several books, including *A Primer for a Davenen Universe*, and *Open Hands: A Jewish Guide to Dying, Death and Bereavement*, and articles in many magazines and anthologies both here and abroad.

ELLEN McROBERTS SHORNACK is a child and family therapist at the Guilford County Mental Health Clinic in Greensboro, North Carolina.

LAWRENCE L. SHORNACK is an associate professor in the Department of Sociology and Social Services at North Carolina Agricultural and Technical State University, Greensboro, North Carolina.

PETER SINGER teaches in the department of philosophy at Monash University in Australia. He is also the director of the Monash Centre for Human Bioethics.

DONALD SINGLETARY is a freelance writer and public-relations consultant in New York City.

WILLIAM STACKHOUSE is a consultant to the United Church (Congregationalists) Board of Homeland Ministries. His professional involvement with sexuality concerns has included work in parent-child communication, adolescent sexuality and gay/lesbian issues.

ROBERT STAPLES is an internationally recognized specialist in family life and professor of sociology at the University of California, San Francisco. He was invited by Philip Nobile and Eric Nadler to join the "Shadow Commission."

MURRAY STRAUS, a professor of sociology and chairperson of the Family Research Laboratory at the University of New Hampshire, was invited by Philip Nobile and Eric Nadler to join the "Shadow Commission."

TERRY TEACHOUT is a conservative and a student of psychology at the University of Illinois in Champaign-Urbana.

CAROLE S. VANCE, an anthropologist and epidemiologist at Columbia University, is also co-director of the New York-based Institute for the Study of Sex in Society and History. As a member of FACT, the Feminist Anti-Censorship Taskforce, she has closely followed the development of feminist-designed antipornography legislation.

BYRON R. WHITE is an associate justice of the United States Supreme Court.

CHARLES WINICK is professor of sociology at the City University of New York and co-author of *The Lively Commerce: Prostitution in the United States*.

BERNARD ZILBERGELD, a clinical psychologist, headed the Men's Program and co-directed the Clinical Training in Human Sexuality at the University of California, San Francisco. More recently, he has taught sex and sex therapy at several California colleges, maintained a private practice, and authored a book on male sexuality. He was invited by Philip Nobile and Eric Nadler to join the "Shadow Commission."

APPENDIX I

A Summary of Contrasting Views on "The Silent Scream," an Antiabortion Film by Dr. Bernard Nathanson

"The Silent Scream" Claims	Medical Critics Counter
1. A 12-week fetus experiences pain.	1. At 12 weeks, most brain cells are not developed and without a cerebral cortex pain impulses cannot be received or perceived.
2. A 12-week fetus makes purposeful movements and will attempt to avoid the suction cannula that will destroy it.	2. At 12 weeks, all fetal movement is reflexive, not purposeful, much like an amoeba reacts to touch.
3. The sonogram clearly shows the open mouth of the fetus as it screams.	3. The mouth of the fetus cannot be identified in the image with certainty.
4. At 12 weeks the fetal head requires the use of "crushing instruments" for extraction.	4. No instrument other than the suction tube is needed up to 13 or 14 weeks.
5. Brain waves can be recorded as early as 6 weeks after conception.	5. Genuine brain waves do not occur until the third trimester of pregnancy.
6. The heart rate of the fetus shown being aborted in this film rises from 120 to 200, a clear fetal response to "imminent mortal danger."	6. A fetal heart rate of 200 is within the normal range for a 12-week fetus; a rate of 140 is generally noted in the later half of pregnancy.
7. Organized crime is heavily involved in and profiting from the abortion industry today.	7. There is nothing to prove or even suggest that organized crime is involved in provision of abortion services since it was legalized by the Supreme Court.
8. Planned Parenthood does not inform pregnant women about all the alternatives to abortion, nor does it obtain true informed consent for abortions.	8. Planned Parenthood takes great care to advise and counsel women and their partners of all the options for dealing with an unwanted pregnancy, including abortion.
9. This film should be shown to all women requesting abortion. If every member of Congress could see "The Silent Scream," President Reagan believes, "they would move quickly to end the tragedy of abortion."	9. To require that women view this film goes beyond the bounds of information required for informed consent, according to US Supreme Court decisions.

This chart was adapted from both antiabortion and pro-choice publications, and articles in the *New York Times*, March 11, 1985, *Newsweek*, February 25, 1985, *Ms.*, August 1985 and *Glamour*, August 1985.

APPENDIX II

Members of the 1986 Attorney General's
Commission on Pornography

HENRY HUDSON, Chairman. As the Commonwealth's attorney, Hudson closed all "adult" bookstores and theaters in Arlington County, Virginia. In 1983, President Reagan specifically commended Hudson for his efforts, including his campaign to stop rental of X-rated tapes in local video stores.

HAROLD LEZAR, the Commission's early architect and its vice-chairman, previously served as a deputy sheriff, an editorial assistant at William F. Buckley's *National Review,* a Nixon speech writer, and legal policy analyst for the Justice Department.

DR. JAMES DODSON, president of "Focus on the Family," a national organization "dedicated to the preservation of the home and the family and the traditional values growing out of the Judaeo-Christian ethics." Dodson regularly attacks pornography, the "Playboy" lifestyle, and other liberal views in his newsletters, books, and syndicated television and radio broadcasts.

FR. BRUCE RITTER, a Franciscan priest, is widely respected as the founder of Covenant House, a network of urban homes providing shelter for young runaways. A vocal opponent of explicit pornography on cable TV and the legally obscene pornography he believes flourishes in 20,000 bookstores nationwide, Father Ritter has repeatedly stated his opposition to any material which presents non-marital sexual relations in a positive light.

JUDGE EDWARD GARCIA was appointed by President Reagan as a federal district court judge in California. As a county prosecutor, he prosecuted a number of obscenity cases.

FREDERICK SCHAUER is currently a law professor at the University of Michigan. Writing in the *Georgetown Law Journal* prior to serving on the Commission, he had argued that pornography is not protected by the First Amendment because it is not an exercise in free speech or communication of ideas but rather analogous to purchasing a dildo or visiting a prostitute.

DR. PARK ELLIOT DIETZ, a psychiatrist and sociologist at the University of Virginia Law School, has maintained a major academic interest in violent crimes and sexual disorders. As a social learning theorist, he argues that violent and antisocial behaviors develop when young males masturbate to images of deviant or criminal behavior. He also believes that all pornography contains a sado-masochistic component.

DEANNE TILTON, head of the California Consortium of Child Abuse Councils, brought a special interest in child pornography to her work on the Commission.

DIANE CUSACK has been politically active, as vice-mayor and city council member in Scottsdale, Arizona, using restrictive zoning laws and regulation of "public dancing" in places where liquor is served to control "adult" businesses

DR. JUDITH BECKER, a professor at Columbia University and a nationally recognized expert on the treatment of sex offenders and their victims, is the director of the Sexual Behavior Clinic at the New York State Psychiatric Institute.

ELLEN LEVINE, editor of *Woman's Day* and mother of two teenage boys, was personally concerned about Dial-a-Porn and cable erotica.

ALAN SEARS, who served as the Executive Director for the Commission, is Chief of the Criminal Division of the United States Attorney's Office for the Western District of Kentucky where he was one of the few federal prosecutors to actively prosecute adult pornography cases.

BIBLIOGRAPHY

ISSUE 1

General Readings

Fasteau, M.F. (1975). *The male machine.* New York: Delta Books.

Jones, J. (1985). *Labor of love, labor of sorrow: Black women, work, and the family from slavery to the present.* New York: Basic Books.

Murstein, B.I. (1974). *Love, sex, and marriage through the ages* (Ch. 14-18). New York: Springer.

Sherman, A. (1973). *The rape of the A.P.E. (American Puritan Ethic): The official history of the sexual revolution.* Chicago: Playboy Press.

Staples, R. (1981). *The world of black singles: Changing patterns of male/female relations.* Westport, CT: Greenwood.

Tolson, A. (1977). *The limits of masculinity: Male identity and women's liberation.* New York: Harper & Row Colophon.

Wallace, M. (1978). *Black macho and the myth of the super-woman.* New York: Dial Press.

Readings More for Women

Brothers, J. (1981). *What every woman should know about men.* New York: Simon & Schuster.

Ehrenreich, B. (1984, May 20). A feminist view of the new man. *New York Times Magazine.*

Fleming, A.T. (1986, October 26). The American wife. *New York Times Magazine,* pp. 28-39.

Friday, N. (1977). *My mother, my self: The daughter's search for identity.* New York: Dell Books.

Frieze, I.H., et al. (1978). *Women and sex roles: A social psychological perspective.* New York: W.W. Norton.

Readings More for Men

August, E.R. (1985). *Men's studies: A selected and annotated interdisciplinary bibliography.* Littleton, CO: Libraries Unlimited.

Farrell, W. (1975). *The liberated man. Beyond masculinity: Freeing men and their relationships with women.* New York: Bantam Books.

Farrell, W. (1986). *Why men are the way they are.* New York: McGraw-Hill.

Lewis, R.A. (Ed.). (1981). *Men in difficult times: Masculinity today and tomorrow.* Englewood Cliffs, NJ: Prentice-Hall.

Pietropinto. A., & Simenauer, J. (1977). *Beyond the male myth.* New York: Signet.

Staples, R. (1982). *Black masculinity: The black male's role in American society.* San Francisco: Black Scholar Press.

Zilbergeld, B. (1978). *Male sexuality.* New York: Bantam Books.

Singer, J. (1976). *Androgyny: Toward a new theory of sexuality.* Garden City, NY: Anchor Doubleday.

Weitz, S. (1977). *Sex roles: Biological, psychological and social foundations.* New York: Oxford University Press.

ISSUE 2

Andelin, H.B. (1980). *Fascinating womanhood.* New York: Bantam Books.

Blumstein, P., & Schwartz, P. (1984, September). The new sexual balance. *Ladies' Home Journal.*

Breen, T., Breen, M., & Ehrlich, R.S. (1986, August 18). Business booms for bride brokers. *Insight (Washington Times),* pp. 38-40.

Durden-Smith, J., & Desimone, D. (1983). *Sex and the brain.* New York: Arbor House.

Gilder, G. (1973). *Sexual suicide.* New York: Quadrangle/The New York Times Book Co.

Illich, I. (1982). *Gender.* New York: Pantheon.

Money, J. (1977). Destereotyping sex roles. *Society/Transaction, 14*(5).

Money, J., & Tucker, P. (1975). *Sexual signatures: On being a man or a woman.* Boston: Little, Brown.

Morgan, M. (1975). *The total woman.* New York: Pocket Books.

Pogribin, L.C. (1980). *Growing up free: Raising your child in the 80's.* New York: Macmillan.

ISSUE 3

Altman, C. (1980, September). We are not monogamists! *Forum,* pp. 13-16.

Blumstein, P., & Schwartz, P. (1985). *American couples: Money, work, sex.* New York: Pocket Books.

Dale, S. (1981, May). Monogamy is a lie. *Forum,* pp. 40-44.

Myers, L., & Leggitt, H. (1975). *Adultery and other private matters.* Chicago: Nelson-Hall.

Neubeck, G. (Ed.). (1969). *Extramarital relations.* Englewood Cliffs, NJ: Prentice-Hall.

Paetro, M. (1986). *Manshare.* New York: Evans.

Pomeroy, W. (1980, April). Infidelity and extramarital relations—There is a difference. *Forum,* pp. 72-76.

Ramey, J. (1976). *Intimate friendships.* Englewood Cliffs, NJ: Prentice-Hall.

Ramey, J. (1975). Intimate networks. *The Futurist, 9*(4), 174-182.

Rimmer, R.H. (1973). *Adventures in loving.* New York: Signet.

Rimmer, R.H. (1980, August). Say goodbye to traditional marriage. *Forum,* pp. 28-34.

ISSUE 4

Atwater, L. (1982). *The extramarital connection: Sex, intimacy, and identity.* New York: Irvington Publishers.

Francoeur, A., & Francoeur, R.T. (1974). *Hot and cool sex: New cultures in conflict.* New York: Harcourt Brace Jovanovich.

Mace, D.R. (1970). *The Christian response to the sexual revolution.* New York: Abingdon Press.

Murstein, B.I. (Ed.). (1978). *Exploring intimate lifestyles.* New York: Springer.

Myers, L., & Leggitt, H. (1975). *Adultery and other private matters.* Chicago: Nelson-Hall.

Myers, L. (1975, December). *Open marriage: Dating after marriage. Forum,* pp. 6-12.

Neubeck, G. (Ed.). (1969). *Extramarital relations.* Englewood Cliffs, NJ: Prentice-Hall.

Pomeroy, W. (1980, April). Infidelity and extramarital relations—There is a difference. *Forum,* pp. 72-76.

Ramey, J. (1976). *Intimate friendships.* Englewood Cliffs, NJ: Prentice-Hall.

Ramey, J. (1975). Intimate networks. *The Futurist, 9*(4), 174-182.

Rimmer, R.H. (1973). *Adventures in loving.* New York: Signet.

Rimmer, R.H. (1980, August). Say goodbye to traditional marriage. *Forum,* pp. 28-34.

Taylor, R. (1982). *Having love affairs.* Buffalo: Prometheus Press.

Vannoy, R. (1980). *Sex without love: A philosophical exploration.* Buffalo: Prometheus Books.

ISSUE 5

Sociological and Historical Research

Bell, A.P., & Weinberg, M.S. (1978). *Homosexualities: A study of diversity among men and women.* New York: Simon & Schuster.

Bell, A., Weinberg, M.S., & Hammersmith, S.K. (1981). *Sexual preference: Its development in men and women.* Bloomington: The University of Indiana Press.

Blackwood, E. (Ed.). (1985). Anthropology and homosexual behavior. *Journal of Homosexuality, 11,* 3-4.

Boswell, J. (1980). *Christianity, social tolerance and homosexuality: Gay people in western Europe from the beginning of the Christian era to the fourteenth century.* Chicago: University of Chicago Press.

Bullough, V.L. (1979). *Homosexuality: A history.* New York: New American Library.

Green, R. (1987). *The sissy boy syndrome.* New Haven: Yale University Press.

Mendola, M. (1980). *The Mendola report: A new look at gay couples.* New York: Crown Publishers.

Stayton, W. (1980). A theory of sexual orientation: The universe as a turn-on. *Topics in Clinical Nursing, 1*(4), 1-7.

Social and Religious Dimensions

Batchelor, E., Jr. (Ed.). (1980). *Homosexuality and ethics.* Buffalo: Prometheus Books.

Bullough, V.L., & Bullough, B. (1977). Homosexuality, sex labelling and stigmatized behavior. In *Sin, Sickness and Sanity*. New York: New American Library.

Edwards, G.R. (1984). *Gay/lesbian liberation: A biblical perspective*. New York: Pilgrim Press.

Gramick, J. (Ed.). (1983). *Homosexuality and the Catholic church*. Chicago: Thomas Moore Press.

Gramick, J. (1983). Homophobia: A new challenge. *Social Work. 28*(2), 137-141.

Jones, C.R. (1978). *Understanding gay relatives and friends*. New York: Seabury Press.

Matt, H. (1978, Winter). Sin, crime, sickness or alternative life style: A Jewish approach to homosexuality. *Judaism, 27*(1), 13-24.

McNeill, J.J. (1976). *The church and the homosexual*. New York: Sheed Andrews & McMeel.

Nugent, R. (Ed.). (1984). *A challenge to love: Gay and lesbian Catholics in the church*. New York: Crossroad.

Scanzoni, L., & Mollenkott, V.R. (1978). *Is the homosexual my neighbor? Another Christian view*. San Francisco: Harper & Row.

ISSUE 6

Andt, B. (1985, June). Sex . . . or intimacy? He wants one, you want the other. *New Woman*.

Atwater, L. (1978). *The extramarital connection: Sex, intimacy and identity*. New York: Irvington.

Brothers, J. (1985, March). Why you should not move in with your lover. *New Woman*.

Francoeur, A.K., & Francoeur, R.T. (1974). *The future of sexual relations*. Englewood Cliffs, NJ: Prentice-Hall.

Francoeur, R.T., & Shapiro, R. (1979). Recognition of alternatives to traditional monogamy in new religious and civil rites. *Journal of Sex Education and Therapy, 1*(5), 17-20.

Lawrence, R. (1973). Guidelines for a flexible monogamy. In R.H. Rimmer (Ed.), *Adventures in loving* (pp. 57-65). New York: Signet Books. Also: The affair as a redemptive experience. *Ibid* (pp. 65-69).

Lawrence, R. (1974). Toward a more flexible monogamy. In R.T. Francoeur & A.K. Francoeur (Eds.), *The future of sexual relations* (pp. 66-74). Englewood Cliffs, NJ: Prentice-Hall.

Murstein, B.I. (1978). *Exploring intimate life styles*. New York: Springer.

Novak, W. (1983). *The great American man shortage and what you can do about it*. New York: Bantam Books.

Paetro, M. (1986). *Manshare*. New York: Evans.

Ramey, J. Intimate networks. *The Futurist, 9*(4), 174-182.

Richardson, L. (1986). *The new other woman*. New York: Free Press.

Salholz, E. (1986, June 2). Too late for Prince Charming? *Newsweek,* pp. 54-61.

Smith, J.R. & Smith, L.G. (Eds.). (1974). *Beyond monogamy: Recent studies of sexual alternatives to marriage*. Baltimore: Johns Hopkins University Press.

Westoff, C.F., & Goldman, N. (1984). Figuring the odds in the marriage market. *Money, 13*(12), 32-41.

ISSUE 7

Anchell, M. (1983). *Sex and insanity.* Portland: Halcyon House.

Annon. (1985). Teachers and public, strongly in favor of sex education in schools, differ on appropriate topics. *Family Planning Perspectives, 17*(4), 183-184.

Cleary, J.L. (1982). *Classroom sex education.* Washington, DC: Free Congress Research and Education Foundation.

Dawson, D.A. (1986). The effects of sex education on adolescent behavior. *Family Planning Perspectives, 18*(4), 162-170.

Echaniz, J. (1982). *When schools teach sex.* Washington, DC: Free Congress Research and Education Foundation.

Kirby, D., et al. (1984). Sexuality education study: Research findings explored. *Sex Education Coalition News, 6*(1), 1-5. Washington, DC.

Lentz, G. (1972). *Raping our children.* New Rochelle, NY: Arlington House.

Marsiglio, W., & Mott, F.L. (1986). The impact of sex education on sexual activity, contraceptive use and premarital pregnancy among American teenagers. *Family Planning Perspectives, 18*(4), 151-162.

Muraskin, L.D. (1986). Sex education mandates: Are they the answer? *Family Planning Perspectives, 18*(4), 171-174.

Orr, M.T. (1982). Sex education and contraceptive education in U.S. public schools. *Family Planning Perspectives, 14*(6), 304-313.

Schlafly, P. (1981, February). What's wrong with sex education? *The Phyllis Schlafly Report, 14*(7), 1-3.

Sonenstein, F.L., & Pittman, K.J. (1984). The availability of sex education in large city school districts. *Family Planning Perspectives, 16*(1), 19-25.

Zelnik, M., & Kim, Y.J. (1982). Sex education and its association with teenage sexual activity, pregnancy and contraceptive use. *Family Planning Perspectives, 14*(3), 117-126.

ISSUE 8

The Center for Population Options. (1986). *School-based clinic policy initiatives around the country: 1985.* Washington Support Center/CPO (1012 14th Street NW, Suite 1200. Washington, DC 20005).

Dryfoos, J. (1985). School-based health clinics: A new approach to preventing adolescent pregnancy? *Family Planning Perspectives, 17*(2), 70-75.

Mosbacker, B.L. (1986). Special report: Teenage pregnancy and school-based clinics. *U.S. Senate, House Select Committee on Children, Youth and Families, Minority Report.* (Available from the author, 1201 East Boulevard, Charlotte, NC 28203.)

Schlafly, P. (1986.) School-based sex clinics vs. sex respect. *The Phyllis Schlafly Report, 19*(11), 1-4.

Zabin, L.S., Hirsch, M.B., Smith, E., Streett, R., & Hardy, J.B. (1986). Evaluation of a pregnancy prevention program for urban teenagers. *Family Planning Perspectives, 18*(3), 119-125.

ISSUE 9

The Alan Guttmacher Institute. (1981). *Teenage pregnancy: The problem that hasn't gone away.* New York: Planned Parenthood Federation of America.

Avallone, F. (1985). *New Jersey women speak out!* East Brunswick, NJ: Right to Choose Education Fund (P.O. Box 343).

Catholics for a Free Choice. (1985). *Reproductive choice: What it means and where Congress stands.* Washington, DC: Catholics for a Free Choice.

Callahan, D. (1970). *Abortion: Law, choice and morality.* New York: Macmillan.

Dillon, V.V. (1977). *Nine facts to know about abortion.* Washington, DC: Catholic Bishops' Committee for Pro-Life Activities.

Jaworski, P. (1986). "Thinking about 'the silent scream' " (an audio tape). New York: Jaworski Productions.

Krebsbach, R.L. (1984). *Abortion: Have we the right?* Tulsa, OK: Right to Life Crusade, Inc.

Nathanson, B. (1979). *Aborting America.* New York: Doubleday.

Prescott, J.W. (1978, July/August). Abortion and the "right-to-life": Facts, fallacies, and fraud. I. Cross-cultural studies. *The Humanist,* pp. 18-24.

Prescott, J.W. (1976, March). Violence, pleasure and religion. *The Bulletin of the Atomic Scientists,* p. 62.

Prescott, J.W. (1975, April). Body pleasure and the origins of violence. *The Futurist,* pp. 64-74.

Prescott, J.W. (1975, March/April). Abortion or the unwanted child: A choice for a humanistic society. *The Humanist.* pp. 11-15.

Prescott, J.W., & Wallace, D. (1978, November/December). Abortion and the "right-to-life": Facts, fallacies, and fraud. II. Psychometric studies. *The Humanist,* pp. 36-42.

Tietze, C. (1981). *Induced abortion: A world view.* New York: The Population Council.

Wilke, J.C. (1984). *Abortion and slavery: History repeats.* Cincinnati: Hayes Publishing Co.

Wilke, J.C. & Wilke, Mrs. (1979). *Handbook on abortion* (rev. ed.). Cincinnati: Hayes Publishing Co.

Two Contrasting Biblical Views

Shoemaker, D.P. (1976). *Abortion, the Bible and the Christian.* Cincinnati: Hayes Publishing Co.

Simmons, P.D. (1985). *A theological response to fundamentalism on the abortion issue.* Washington, DC: Religious Coalition for Abortion Rights Educational Fund.

ISSUE 10

Andrews, L.B. (1985). *New conceptions: A consumer's guide to the newest infertility treatments* (rev. ed.). New York: Ballantine Books.

Andrews, L.B. (1984, August). The stork market: The law of the new reproductive technologies. *American Bar Association Journal, 70,* 50-56.

Arditti, R., Klein, R.D., & Minden, S. (1984). *Test-tube women: What future for motherhood?* Boston: Pandora Press.

Corea, G. (1985). *The mother machine: Reproductive technologies from artificial insemination to artificial wombs.* San Francisco: Harper & Row.

Edwards, R.G., & Steptoe, P. (1981). *A matter of life.* New York: William Morrow.

Etzioni, A. (1975). *Genetic fix.* New York: Harper & Row.

Fletcher, J. (1974). *The ethics of genetic control: Ending reproductive roulette.* Garden City: NY: Anchor Press/Doubleday.

Frncoeur, R.T. (1985). Reproductive technologies: New alternatives and new ethics. *SIECUS Report, 14*(1), 1-5.

Francoeur, R.T. (1977). *Utopian motherhood: New trends in human reproduction* (3rd ed.) Canbury, NJ: A. Barnes.

Holmes, H., Hoskins, B., & Gross, M. (Eds.). (1981). *The custom-made child.* Clifton, NJ: Humana Press.

Keane, N., & Breo, D. *The surrogate mother.* New York: Everest House.

Singer, P., & Wells, D. (1985). *Making Babies: The New Science and Ethics of Conception.* New York: Scribner.

ISSUE 11

Adelman, S. & Rosenzweig, S. (1978). Parental predetermination of the sex of offspring: II. The attitudes of young married couples with high school and with college education. *Journal of Biosocial Science, 10,* 235-247.

Corea, G. (1985). *The mother machine.* San Francisco: Harper & Row.

Etzioni, A. (1975). *Genetic fix.* New York: Harper & Row.

Etzioni, A. (1968). Sex, science and society. *Science, 161,* 1107-1112.

Fletcher, J.C. (1979). Sounding board: Ethics and amniocentesis for fetal sex identification. *New England Journal of Medicine, 301*(10), 550-553.

Francoeur, R.T. (1985). Reproductive technologies: New alternatives and new ethics. *SIECUS Report, 14*(1), 1-5.

Gordon, A.D.G. (1978, May). Bicarbonate for a boy, vinegar for a girl. *Nursing Times.*

Hanmer, J. (1981). Sex predetermination, artificial insemination and the maintenance of male-dominated culture. In H. Roberts (Ed.), *Women, Health and Reproduction.* Boston: Routledge & Kegan Paul.

Holmes, H.B., Hoskins, B.B., & Gross, M. (1981). *The custom-made child?* Clifton, NJ: Humana Press.

Hoskins, B.B. & Holmes, H.B. (1984). Technology and prenatal femicide. In R. Arditti, R.D. Klein, & S. Minden (Eds.), *Test-tube women.* Boston: Pandora Press.

Lappe, M. (1974, February). Choosing the sex of our children. *Hastings Center Report.*

Powledge, T.M. (1981). Unnatural selection: On choosing children's sex. In H. Holmes, B. Hoskins & M. Gross (Eds.), *The* custom-made child? Clifton, NJ: Humana Press.

Roggencamp, V. (1984). Abortion of a special kind: Male sex selection in India. In R. Arditti, R.D. Klein, & S. Minden (Eds.), Test-tube women. Boston: Pandora Press.

Rosenzweig, S., & Adelman, S. (1976). Parental predetermination of the sex of offspring: The attitudes of young married couples with university education. Journal of Biosocial Science, 8, 335-346.

Sangari, K. (1984). If you would be the mother of a son. In R. Arditti, R.D. Klein, & S. Minden (Eds.), Test-tube women. Boston: Pandora Press.

Steinbacher, R. (1981). Futuristic implications of sex preselection. In H. Holmes, B. Hoskins & M. Gross (Eds.), The custom-made child? Clifton, NJ: Humana Press.

ISSUE 12

Greenhouse, L. (1986, July 1). Privacy law and history: Sixty years of expansion interrupted by ruling. New York Times, pp. A1, A19.

Press, A. (1986, July 14). A government in the bedroom. Newsweek, pp. 36-38.

Taylor, S. (1986, July 1). Division is bitter: Dissents assail ruling's refusal to extend the privacy guarantee. New York Times, pp. A1, A19.

ISSUE 13

Bendet, P. (1986, August/September). Hostile eyes: A report on homophobia on American campuses. Campus Voice, 3(1), 34-39.

Buckley, W. (1983, March 18). On handling gays. National Review, 35, 14008ff.

Gay professionals are beginning to achieve success in getting "domestic-partners benefits." (1985, March 12). Wall Street Journal. 37, 4.

Gay professionals band together in workplace to help careers, battle prejudice. (1985, March 12). Wall Street Journal, 37, 4.

A Houston referendum that would protect homosexuals from discrimination. (1985, January 17). Wall Street Journal, 58, 1.

Houston voters reject city ordinance to protect homosexuals. (1985, January 21). Wall Street Journal, 46, 2.

Lubenow, G. (1982, April 5). Gays and lesbians on campus. Newsweek, 99(14), 75-77.

Smith, M.J. (1982, October). The double life of a gay [Los Angeles] Dodger. Inside Sports. pp. 57-63.

Right's reaction. (1985, February 2). The Nation, 240, 100-101.

ISSUE 14

Blakely, M.K. (1985, April). Is one woman's sexuality another woman's pornography? Ms., 13, 37-38ff.

Boycott closes store. (1985, January 30). *Christian Century, 102,* 96-97.

Charles, B. (1985, October). The pornography explosion. *Ladies' Home Journal, 102,* 104ff.

Conley, H. (1985, February 1). Protests lead to removal of pornographic magazines from more than 5,000 stores. *Christianity Today, 29,* 50.

Copp, D., & Wendell, S. (Eds.). (1983). *Pornography and censorship.* Buffalo: Prometheus Press.

Dworkin, A. (1979). *Pornography: Men possessing women.* New York: Perigee Books.

Hefner, H., & Malamuth, N., et al. Pornography and its discontents: Letters in response to symposium of November 1984. *Harper's.* pp. 4-6, 73-76.

Kocol, C., et al. (1985, July/August). Porno prone. *The Humanist. 45,* 45.

Lapham, L.H., Goldstein, A., Decter, M., Jong, E., Brownmiller, S., Elshtain, J.E., & Neier, A. (1984, November). The place of pornography. *Harper's,* pp. 31-45.

Lederer, L. (Ed.). (1980). *Take back the night: Women on pornography.* New York: William Morrow.

Minnery, T. (1985, February 15). What it takes to fight pornography. *Christianity Today, 29,* 10-11.

The war against pornography. (1985, March 18). *Newsweek, 105,* 58-62.

Pally, M. (1985, June 29). Ban sexism, not pornography. *Nation, 240,* 794-797.

Weiss, P. (1986, March). Forbidden pleasures. *Harper's, 272*(163), 68-72.

Technical Studies

Ashley, B.R., & Ashley, D. (1984). Sex as violence: The body against intimacy. *International Journal of Women's Studies, 7*(4), 352-371.

Ceniti, J. & Malamuth, N.M. (1984). Effects of repeated exposure to sexually violent or nonviolent stimuli on sexual arousal to rape and nonrape depictions. *Behavior Research and Therapy, 22*(5), 535-548.

Donnerstein, E., & Berkowitz, L. (1981). Victims' reactions in aggressive erotic films as a factor in violence against women. *Journal of Personality and Social Psychology, 41,* 710-724.

Donnerstein, E., & Linz, D. (1984, January). Sexual violence in the media: A warning. *Psychology Today,* pp. 14-15.

Donnerstein, E., & Linz, D. (1985, September 12). A paper presented at a hearing of the Attorney General's Commission on Pornography. Houston, TX.

Greenslinger, V. (1985). Authoritarianism as a predictor of response to heterosexual and homosexual erotica. *The High School Journal, 68*(3), 183-186.

Kelley, K. (1985). Sex, sex guilt, and authoritarianism: Differences in responses to explicit heterosexual and masturbatory slides. *The Journal of Sex Research, 21*(1), 68-85.

Kelley, K. (1985). Sexual attitudes as determinants of the motivational properties of exposure to erotica. *Personality and Individual Differences, 6*(3), 391-393.

Kelley, K. (1985). Sexuality and hostility of authoritarians. *The High School Journal, 68*(3), 173-176.

Malamuth, N. (1985, September 15). The mass media as an indirect cause of sexual aggression. A paper presented at a hearing of the Attorney General's Commission on Pornography. Houston, TX.

Malamuth, N., & Donnerstein, E. (Eds.). (1982). Pornography and sexual aggression. New York: Academic Press.

Stengel, R. (1986, July 21). *Sex busters: A Meese Commission and the Supreme Court echo a new moral militancy. Time,* pp. 12-22.

ISSUE 15

American Civil Liberties Union. (1986). Polluting the censorship debate: A summary and critique of the final report of the Attorney General's Commission on Pornography. Washington, DC: American Civil Liberties Union.

Bullough, V. & Bullough, B. (1977). Pornography, obscenity and personal preference. In *Sin, Sickness, and Sanity.* New York: New American Library.

Copp, D. & Wendell, S. (Eds.). (1983). Pornography and censorship. Buffalo: Prometheus Books.

Dworkin, A. (1979). *Pornography: Men possessing women.* New York: G.P. Putnam, Perigee Books.

Gordon, G.N. (1980). *Erotic communications: Studies in sex, sin and censorship.* New York: Hastings House Publishers.

Lederer, L. (Ed.). (1980). *Take back the night: Women on pornography.* New York: William Morrow.

Nobile, P., & Nadler, E. (1986). *United States of America vs. sex—How the Meese Commission lied about pornography.* New York: Minotaur Press, Ltd.

The Presidential Commission on Obscenity and Pornography. (1970). *Report of the Commission on Obscenity and Pornography.* New York: Bantam Books.

ISSUE 16

Adams, N.M. (1978, May). Why the shocking rise in prostitution? *Reader's Digest, 112,* 203-204.

Bullough, V.L., & Bullough, B. (1977). Prostitution and the pox. In *Sin, Sickness, and Sanity.* New York: New American Library.

The Center for Studies of Crime and Delinquency. (1972). *Not the law's business?* Rockville, MD: National Institute of Mental Health.

Finlayson, A. (1985, May 6). A new proposal for prostitution. *Macleans, 98,* 48.

The Great Britain Committee on Homosexual Offenses and Prostitution. (1963). *The Wolfenden Report.* New York: Stein and Day.

Hall, S., & Adelman, R. (1972). *Gentlemen of leisure: A year in the life of a pimp.* New York: Quadrangle/Times Books.

Hochstein, R. (1985, May). Prostitutes: Happy hookers or society's victims? *Glamour, 83,* 184ff.

James, J. (1976). Prostitution: Arguments for change. In S. Gordon & R.W. Libby (Eds.), *Sexuality today and tomorrow.* North Scituate, MA: Duxbury.

Murtagh, Justice J., & Harris, S. (1957). *Cast the first stone.* New York: McGraw-Hill.

ISSUE 17

Bullough, V.L. (1976). *Sexual variance in society and history*. New York: John Wiley & Sons.

Bullough, V.L., & Bullough, B. (1977). Sex need not be a sin: Some alternative views, China, India, Islam. In *Sin, Sickness, and Sanity*. New York: New American Library.

Gardella, P. (1985). *Innocent ecstasy: How Christianity gave America an ethic of sexual pleasure*. New York: Oxford University Press.

Money, J. (1986). *The destroying angel*. Buffalo: Prometheus Books.

Nelson, J.B. (1978). *Embodiment: An approach to sexuality and Christian theology*. Minneapolis: Augsburg Publishing House.

Noonan, J.T., Jr. (1986). *Contraception: A history of its treatment by Catholic theologians and canonists* (rev. ed.). Cambridge: Harvard University Press.

Phipps, W.E. (1975). *Recovering biblical sensuousness*. Philadelphia: Westminster Press.

ISSUE 18

Francoeur, R.T. (1982). Becoming a sexual person. *American Sexual Customs*. New York: Macmillan.

Gravatt, A.E., & Kirkendall, L.A. (1984). *Marriage and the family in the year 2000*. Buffalo: Prometheus Books.

Leonard, G. (1982, December). Sex is dead. *Esquire*, pp. 70-80.

Smith, B. (1978). *The American way of sex*. New York: Gemini/Two Continents.

INDEX

abortion, 192, 295; and fetal pain issue, 154; and government, 142; historical view of, 142; legal status of, 142, 144, 146-147, 152; and school-based health clinics, 130, 131; see also, Silent Scream, The
Abraham, Henry, 303
adolescence, 111; health care of, 126-132; and sex education, 108, 109; sexual behavior of, 131; see also, tennage pregnancy
adoption, and surrogate motherhood, 176-177
adultery, 95-96; and convenant tradition, 90; laws regarding, 265; in Jewish tradition, 277
Adultery and Other Private Matters, 56, 58-61, 90
Advocate, The, 229
Agbasegbe, Bamidele Ade, 96
Agnes of God, 287
Agnes of Sorrento, 287
AIDS, 292; and legislative discrimination, 215, 220, 221; and prostitution, 265; and sex education, 123, 135, 138, 139; and sexual exclusivity, 57, 97, 98; and sexual revolution, 313
Akron v. Akron Center for Reproductive Health, 151
Albert the Great, Saint, 286
alcoholism, and homosexuality, compared, 82
Allred, Gloria, 311
Alorese society, 72
Amadeus of Lausanne, Saint, 290
American Association of Sex Educators, Counselors and Therapists, 121, 136
American Civil Liberties Union, 93, 215
American Psychiatric Association, 214
American Psychological Association, and homosexuality, 84, 214
American Red Cross, and sex education, 136
American School Health Association, 106, 114
amniocentesis, and sex

determination, 185, 186, 192, 194-195; and surrogate motherhood, 169, 181
Andelin, Helen, 43
Andrews, David, 134
Andrews, Lori B., 162, 174-182
androgyny, 38-42, 43; see also, sex differences
androsperm, 184, 185
antiabortion movement, 142-154, 156-160; see also, Silent Scream, The
Aquinas, Saint Thomas, 75, 285, 286, 290
artificial insemination, 31, 162-163, 176, 306
assertiveness, measurement of, 40; and sex roles, 41
Assyrians, 72
Astor, Bart, 40
Augustine, Saint, 282, 283, 284, 290, 292, 293
Availability Index, 94
Awful Disclosures of the Hotel Dieu Nunnery, 287

Baker, Gwendolyn, 125
Barbach, Lonnie, 296
Baron, Larry, 246
Bart, Pauline, 237, 240
battered women, and pornography, 239-240
Bauman, Robert E., 215
Baye, Betty Einston, 16, 17, 24-26, 27
Beach, Frank A., 74, 88
Becker, Judith, 250, 256, 261
Becoming a Sexual Person, 306
Beethoven, Ludwig von, 148
behavior, feminine, 40, 41; masculine, 40, 41; sexual, 202-213
Ben, Sandra Lipsitz, 28, 38-42, 43
Bem Sex Role Inventory (BSRI), 39
Bennett, Michael, 154
Bennett, William J., 125, 133
Bernadette, Saint, 292
Bernardino of Siena, Saint, 290
Bernard of Clairvaux, Saint, 290
Bhimani, Nisa, 182
Bible, and abortion, 145-146, 149,

due April 11 (Tuesday)

Only Yvonne - Wed. night 8:00
(> Helms theatre   3 pg. summary
Sympathies
    due April 11 (Tuesday)

50 working class ⎱
25 middle class ⎰ # Families
                     interviewed

TRIPP
971-1104
Chaz Home: 751-2017